THE APOLOGY THE UNITED STATES OWES THE VIETNAM VETERANS

THEIR SOULS WERE LEFT IN THE JUNGLES OF VIETNAM

RAYMOND C. CHRISTIAN

authorHOUSE®

AuthorHouse™
1663 Liberty Drive
Bloomington, IN 47403
www.authorhouse.com
Phone: 1 (800) 839-8640

Published by AuthorHouse 11/21/2019

ISBN: 978-1-7283-1928-5 (sc)
ISBN: 978-1-7283-1927-8 (hc)
ISBN: 978-1-7283-1931-5 (e)

Print information available on the last page.

Any people depicted in stock imagery provided by Getty Images are models,
and such images are being used for illustrative purposes only.
Certain stock imagery © Getty Images.

This book is printed on acid-free paper.

CONTENTS

SPECIAL PREVIEW OF THE LATER CHAPTERS IN THE BOOK

———

I am disclosing an important part of the book now in order to enhance your interest just a little. My intentions are to make you more inquisitive and to tempt your palettes concerning the life and death of the United States of America's Vietnam Veterans.

In battle there is only one winner. There is only one person left standing. The one who has the victory is the one who will get the chance to go home, after taking another person's life in order to sustain their own. This is about war, it's about the Vietnam Veterans and how they were returned to us, to America. They did not return home in the same condition they left. Some would say damaged goods just throw out the whole bunch they are all spoiled and bruised. Do you think one bad apple spoils the entire barrel? For those in America who stayed back and were not called to war had a different viewpoint on how they saw the Vietnam Veterans after they returned home. American citizens could see the soldiers were captivated when they looked into the Vietnam Veterans eyes, it was like walking into a room with no light. The soldiers had no feelings, no signs of emotion, they were empty of life, a whole of darkness void and detached, they were lifeless of existence. These young men had seen so much death that their very souls had been left in the jungles of Vietnam, far away in a distant place. In a place of darkness hidden in a land of dead and dry bones. Only these bones were not going to reattach themselves together and come back to life this was man's war not God's. Their souls were left in a faraway land and would remain in search of its physical body to never be rejoined again. For the Vietnam Veterans that made it out of the jungles of Vietnam in a place where death was present with every breath they took, and life was counted by the seconds. Vietnam was not a place for eighteen or nineteen-year-old boys. It was a man's war not some video gaming war, and it was real. If you lived past sixteen minutes which was the life expectancy of a soldier in Vietnam, then you were doing good. If these young soldiers lived past the first sixteen minutes, they had to figure out how to take those sixteen minutes and turn them into hours, days or months. If you were in for the long haul, then you had to learn how to stay alive for a year in the jungles of Vietnam. Believe me when I say this was how the Vietnam

Veterans were able to make it back home by living second by second. They had to keep their mind on the battlefield every second, every minute and every hour. There wasn't any peace in his heart until his plane landed back in the United States of America. Thinking too far ahead or getting too relaxed could actually cost another soldier their life. Simply because they took their mind off war for a brief second. They survived the jungles of Vietnam leaving the battlefield headed for the United States returning to home where another battle began. It was a battle of acceptance getting acclimated back into society.

The Vietnam Veterans no longer had to worry about the estimated sixteen minutes to live rule. Their battle had now become internal. There was a chemical inside of them and the worst of its kind, TCDD a (dioxin) mixed with other chemicals to produce what was called "Agent Orange." Along with having to deal with the negative activity of co-workers if they were able to get their job back. There was an even bigger battle brewing inside of them. The toxic herbicide chemical "Agent Orange" would become the enemy the soldiers would fight for a lifetime after they figured out what they were battling. You might even want to say the battle with "Agent Orange" was just as bad as the Vietnam War. It became the worse nightmare in the history of war because "Agent Orange" would end up taking more lives than the 58,220 lives lost in the Vietnam War. It is now 2019 going into the new year of 2020 and there are approximately 850,000 Vietnam Veterans estimated to be alive today. The Vietnam Veterans have been filing claims since their return home due to what "Agent Orange" was doing to their health, their physical and mental state of mind. Since many of the Vietnam Veterans health had depleted because of "Agent Orange," so had their life expectancy. Due to denial by non-governmental agencies researching "Agent Orange" and not admitting the facts of its relationship to the soldiers. The lack of adequate research through the years extended the suffering of the Vietnam Veterans for over forty years. The Vietnam Veterans by the time this book is published in 2019 going into the new year 2020 they are estimated to live another 6.4 years before they have all died off. I will go into these stats of how I came up with 6.4 years a little later in the book as it relates to the Vietnam Veterans and the number of lives being lost closer to the end of the book. Including what "Agent Orange" has done to the Vietnam Veterans. But for now, here are the stats and they are quite shocking. The Vietnam Veterans are said to be dying at a rate of 390 a day. Which means there are 2730 dying a week, 10,920 dying a month and 131,040 dying a year. According to my research there is only 850,000 Vietnam Veterans alive today. This is how I came up with the 6.4 years. I am certain not one of those soldiers signed up for this.

Therefore, in my efforts to seek an apology from the United States of America's government and the citizens of America. There should also be more research done concerning "Agent Orange." Please keep in mind this is not just a Democrat or Republican issue. This is about our soldiers who went to war in defense of the United States of America. There wasn't any blue states or red states showing a division in their cause of serving their country or a reason for them to raise their right hand. They all bled the same red blood on the battlefield. We must respect the men and women who gave their life for you. They signed up not to give up but to protect this nation against all enemies, foreign and domestic. And I will close by saying to you, "**America Don't Forget**."

For their Valor and Servitude
To the Vietnam Veterans the Men and Women who Served

A real soldier knows for those who have been in a real war and was able to live to tell about it is a feeling that will never leave his consciousness. The wiping away of his blood-stained tears in the wee hours of the night is something that occurred with even the strongest of those who served. Even their strength, their strong minds and willful efforts are not able to suppress the wetness that falls from their face, their teardrops. The soul of a man can be contained in many aspects of life. Most of the time it all depends on what his forte is and how the nature of its development comes about. The men and women who swore to protect this country during the Vietnam War will never be the same again. Their lifeless spirits are all that was left of them when they returned home. Seeking, searching, looking in mirrors with no reflection of who they once were. Trying to smile through their fear of unawareness with their eyes that continuously searched through the night even as they stood and spoke. You would think they were there talking to you. You heard the laughter and the saw the grin on their faces. But their hearts and minds remained thousands of miles away searching for the little innocent boy who left his soul on a battlefield of death. Many were able to return home to see the names of their fellow comrades who died on the battlefield preserving the rights of all Americans. As they look at the "Wall of Names" wondering to themselves, saying "Lord why did I make it back home." This is what was left of our brothers who returned home from the Vietnam War. A soldier in a physical body still in search for his soul. If you could close your eyes and see inside of the soldier's mind for at least one minute. Just to see what all he had to do in order to survive. The pain would be so excruciating that you would never want to revisit it again. But just keep in mind that was only one minute of a visit you were privileged to have. But the soldier, the Vietnam Veteran closes his eyes every night and begins to see the same things over and over and over again every day of his life.

You can remove the dagger from their heart America, while there is still time. Listen to the cries of the soldiers, listen to the sleepless nights in the jungles of Vietnam…Is that you Charlie?

The Apology the United States Owes the Vietnam Veterans

Dedicated to my Father in Heaven, the one true God:

In respect of his Glory and the knowledge he has vested in me I must refer to Romans 1: 20-25. I am using this scripture to let you know who has given me the authority to write a book such as this. My Father in heaven has anointed my mind, my eyes, my health and brain to bring the suffering of the Vietnam Veterans to your understanding. And to reveal how mankind today claims the glory of God. I pray you will read these scriptures and understand by not acknowledging God in all thing's mankind has brought damnation upon their self.

Romans 1: 20-25

(20) For the visible things of him from the creation of the world are clearly seen, being understood by the things that are made, even his eternal power and Godhead; so that they are without excuse:

(21) Because that, when they knew God, they glorified him not as God, neither were thankful; but became vain in their imaginations, and their foolish heart was darkened.

(22) Professing themselves to be wise, they became fools,

(23) And changed the glory of the uncorruptible God into an image made like to corruptible man, and to birds, and four-footed beasts, and creeping things.

(24) Wherefore God also gave them up to uncleanness through the lusts of their own hearts, to dishonor their own bodies between themselves:

(25) Who changed the truth of God into a lie and worshipped and served the creature more than the Creator, who is blessed forever Amen.

A SPECIAL DEDICATION

———

To the woman in my life, my darling wife Araceli. She continues to be my companion in many ways. In times when I feel alone, she's my friend when I want to sit and talk, my eyes for things I cannot see. My support in my times of doubt. She believed in the reasons why I wrote this book about the Vietnam Veterans. My wife continues to inspire me every day with her love and devotion. Although she has an attentive ear it is refreshing to see the love in her eyes when she comes into my study to check on me. I look forward to eating the bowl of fresh fruits prepared by her loving hands in order to keep my nourishment up. She knows that many times I would work without taking a break. Other times she would check on me and give me a hug or kiss. She never once complained about me spending too much time researching or writing. My wife is a very big part of my success concerning the completion of my 7th book. Moral support is important. She showed lots of concern throughout this project. It was fun sharing my new findings of information with her as the book was being written, we would get excited together. She never disturbed me when I was working, she would only say, "Babe dinner is almost ready." It's a blessing to have you as my wife, Araceli and God's gift to me as bone of my bone and flesh of my flesh. When others tried to discourage me, I can still hear her saying, "Write the book Babe." Thank you, Mi Amor, Mi Vida.

My two Precious Gifts from God

Kenli Christian, it is with extreme joy in my heart that I let you know (mi hija) how proud I am of you and your accomplishments. You have proven yourself to be more than exceptionally intelligent and talented. Winning the beauty contest and still graduating as the valedictorian of your class. You scored thirteenth in the country on the PSE. Once again, your hard work put you at a level of education where you became the first and only student in the history of the Cayo, District to accomplish this task. You continue to be a positive impact on others around you through the many leadership positions you hold. Mom and I are very proud of you and your accomplishments, keep striving to be the best. Thank you for being supportive… I love you, more, Dad

Elaine Christian, I am speechless (mi hija) and only with words of pride when I think about your modest and untiring efforts as you strive to reach your goals. I was so proud to be with you at your Confirmation and then to later find out you were going to graduate as the valedictorian of your class. Your continued success makes looking at your subtle approach in life and education quite noticeable. Your hard work has paid off as you continue to meet your educational accomplishments. Your personality has made you impactful in others' lives. You continue to move forward towards your future goals. My heart is filled with joy knowing that your drive and understanding in education is continual. Mom and I are very proud of you. Thank you for being supportive…I love you, more, Dad

My Special Thank You

Robert Christian, **my father, your constitution and dedication to your work through the years was significant to embrace as you looked toward a better future and life. Your hard work and diligence paid off. I want to say thank you for the foundation you instilled in me of wanting to be a better son, a better man and a better father.**

Christine A. Jones, **my mother, I want to say thank you for sitting with me on the porch and teaching me and exchanging ideas about what we thought about scriptures in the bible. And of course, for being the best Bible School Teacher for over twenty-five years of dedication to:**

Faith Temple Church of God in Christ

James M. Jones; **my uncle, your patience and understanding earmarked who you are when it comes to being an ideal uncle. Thank you for always giving your last and for forever being there to listen. Although you have departed from this world, I know your presence has been well received in heaven…You are truly missed.**

Maximiliano Garcia… **you are quit the role model to follow which exemplifies your loyalty to Mamita, family, friends and the community. Being known and loved by those who have drawn close to you through your hard work as a Superintendent of schools in the Cayo, District. You also hold the knowledge of creating your own organic honey where people come from many miles to gather what you have extracted from your beehives. Since I have personally used your organic honey it is known to revitalize and restore energy and strength the immune system. People have traveled as far as San Pedro, Guatemala, from the entire country of Belize, Mexico and the United States to receive the benefits of your homemade organic honey.**

Freddie Ervin…**has been a big brother to me for many years. He is what I would call one of God's silent humanitarians. Simply because he goes about his day helping as many people as he can to be able to get back and forth to work. Along with being a big brother his accomplishments go beyond the call of Christianity of being a good Samaritan. Freddie is** the perfect example of what God would have us to do when our brothers and sisters are in need. If you open your bible to the book of Psalms what you will find is this particular scripture describes Freddie Ervin perfectly, Psalm 37:25, "I have been young and now I am old, yet I have not seen the righteous forsaken, nor his seed begging bread."

Edward Pott… You have been gifted with a rare talent of freelance drawing and have blessed this book with your natural raw talents. The American Eagle you have drawn will be symbolic for everyone to look at as it pertains to the Vietnam War. Yes, Edward you are right "Agent Orange" kills. Thank you for your freelance sketch of the American Eagle and your support for the Vietnam Veterans.

Elder Ivory Martin, your loyalty to God your teaching and your patients has been one of quality bestowed upon a Saint. You have exhibited an even greater show of restraint when it comes to your dedication and loyalty to the church of God and respecting the temple of which God has given you. Your leadership in the Church of God in Christ has surpassed any and all expectations of what a man of God and Assistant Pastor of Faith Temple should uphold. Thank you for reaching beyond the boundaries of the pulpit in your extension and love for Christ Jesus to not only the Church of God in Christ but wherever you walked, telling people about Jesus.

Elder David Blakely, through the years you have expressed your love for Christ Jesus, and you have exhibited your faith in an admirable way. Through preaching, praying and teaching the word of God. Because of your untiring faith you have been able to overcome enormous hurdles in keeping the grounds of the church safe. Your dedication and service to the United States Armed forces allowed me to give a ceremony in reflection of the men and women of the Armed Forces. I thank you for your service and for being in support of the Vietnam Veterans and the Armed Forces of the United States of America.

Valarie T. Gardner, LCSW, I will never forget the deep concern you have shown all soldiers. It is truly a pleasure to honor you in this book about the Vietnam Veterans your dedication and loyalty to the men and women of the United States Armed Forces is truly unforgettable. Your professionalism earmarks the high standard of military service and emits the proficiency required of military personnel. Thank you for your service and your support of the Vietnam Veterans.

Veronica L. McFadden-Jones, "Freedom is not free." Freedom is something that is achieved through merits of sacrifice. Which is the giving of one's self something many of you are not willing to do. The Vietnam Veterans brought back with them the cost of freedom and it still waves freely over this great nation, the flag of the United States of America. Because of their sacrifices the Vietnam Veterans have had to deal with the effects of war they returned with. They should be honored and not made to feel like the loyalty they showed by fighting in the Vietnam War is non-existent.

Mr. Mitchell, I thank you for your support concerning the struggles of the Vietnam Veterans and for wanting to be a part of this historical book. It is important to know the Vietnam Veterans have not been forgotten.

Checkered Flag Imports, INC.

After servicing foreign and domestic cars for forty-four years I know from experience that bringing my vehicle to Checkered Flag Imports, INC. is a place where I cannot go wrong. Their professional service and willingness to go the extra mile lets you know that Checkered Flag Imports, INC. stands behind their work 100 percent. Their business is highly recommended for all customers in search for loyal, dedicated and qualified mechanics to service their foreign or domestic vehicle. You will be able to leave with a smile knowing Checkered Flag Imports serviced your vehicle. If there is a problem with your vehicle, they will find it and fix it. Their loyalty and honesty to this day remains impeccable. Thank you, Rich Hassan, Jim Beddome and Gregg Dees for your support of the Vietnam Veterans and the Armed Forces of the United States of America.

Coachman Antique Mall

We thank David Nadolski and Brent Lemaich for your support of the Vietnam Veterans and the Armed Forces of the United States of America. Coachman Antique Mall when you are out looking for quality antiques Coachman has it all.

Honorary Men, Women & Businesses the Vietnam Veterans & I render a hand SALUTE and say, Thank You;

Dr. Albert Lee Powell Sr., my mentor I will remember the golden bowl when it breaks. I pray that I will have good God-fearing people around me in my old age who will do the right thing. You have taught me that doctrines concerning this nation are not going to change but if I abide within the laws that have been set, the laws that govern this nation there is hope for change. I should never give up on understanding who I am on the inside that is something that is not displayed unless I display it. You have served as a foot soldier in the war and I am more than honored to say thank you for your service to the United States Armed Forces of America.

Dr. Eddie LaShay, thank you for the many blessings of helping me to understand what being a man of many talents and blessings entailed. You would always say, "One day you will not have time to wash your car, cut the grass and do the things that take up so much of your precious time." I appreciate the time God kept you hear on this earth Doctor LaShay, you have been a lamp during my dark days.

Judge Donald Davis, your knowledge and intellect remains within the realms of the law. And your loyalty has been exemplified with an honor of having fifty years of honor to the State of Oklahoma Bar in June of 2019. Although the Arc of the Moral Universe Bends towards justice. It is only through time and change that those who control the gavel will be able to sway how it falls. Thank you for your patients Sir, I am honored. What remains to be unseen does not mean that others are not aware of the wrongs that have taken place. Time has brought about change where your position has made a notable difference for people of all walks of life to be allowed such a privilege of being accepted into the ranks of judge. Being the Christian man, you are, although the judgment of others was ruled upon there were so many others who were left out because it was not their turn. E pluribus unum, it was God Almighty who chose to bless you. Your service in the United States Air Force and honorable discharge gives you the profound right to be a proud American. I appreciate you assisting me with legal matters concerning this book. And I thank you for wanting to be a part of this historical book about the world's finest, the United States Vietnam Veterans.

Lt. Colonel Terry May, **founded the ROTC Program at the University of Central Oklahoma. Lt. Col May was instrumental in getting me into the ROTC Program. He instructed me on what I needed to do to become a military officer. Lt. Col May was not only an asset to the ROTC Program, but he was an asset to the University where he served his later years in the administrative department. I will always keep his sound advice before me and his noted three taps on the shoulder.**

Lt. Colonel Randy Roll, **what a leader and inspiration to all soldiers. It is not everyday someone can see the good in others. This is what made Lt. Col Roll so unique in his abilities to see who officers were and what made them tick. To one of the greatest officers to ever put on a uniform. A man, an officer and a gentleman, someone I wouldn't have to second guess going to war with. I render my hand salute to one top notch officer who not only made a difference in my life but in so many others. Thank you for your service to the Armed Forces of America and for supporting the Vietnam Veterans.**

Major Tom Roll, **United States Air Force (retired). We like to send out a special thanks to Maj Roll for his service to the United States during the Vietnam War. Maj Tom Roll was a navigator who flew into Cam Rhan Bay on the C-124 and also the C-130 aircraft. After his tour in Vietnam he became an instructor at the USAF Academy in Colorado, Springs. There is so much more to tell about Maj Tom Roll and his dedicated service to his country. The Armed Forces of the United States of America is proud of the honorable service you have shown the United States of America. Your son LTC Randy Roll says, thanks for being the best (Father) ever. Thank you for being in support of the Vietnam Veterans and the men and women who serve.**

Danny Butler (BKA) Dangerous Dan, **a special salute to you my friend here's to our tour in the 2nd Combat Eng. 2nd Mar Div, Marine Corps made us become more like brothers and of course it was nice to know I had a big brother to look out for me. I will always cherish our years of training as Combat Eng. and making history on Camp Lejeune by being the first African American surveying team. And the first all Marine Corps surveying class that consisted of 17 Marines to graduate from Fort Belvoir, Virginia in the history of the Marine Corps. All 17 Marines graduated in honor blues. Take care old friend.**

The Honorable Senator Dick Durbin, **for your loyalty and untiring dedication to the men and women who served in past wars and are now serving in the Armed Forces of the United States of America. The integrity you have exhibited to not only the citizens of Illinois but throughout the United States makes me proud to say, thank you for your selfless support and for fighting to make things better for all veterans, the dedication you exhibit is admirable.**

The Honorable Congressman Lane Evans, **your loyalty and dedication to the men and women who served in the Armed Forces of the United States of America must never be forgotten. Although you are deceased the groundwork you set forth to getting things going for many soldiers who needed help will always be at the forefront and forever remember. RIP, the torch is still being passed.**

The Honorable Secretary of State Jesse White, **it is with great pleasure that I personally say thank you for the dedicated service you have shown the United States Armed Forces. Your respect is well received in the state of Illinois. Your public service reflects the dignity of which you have governed your office through the years. As a military officer of the United States Army I say thank you for all you have done for the men and women who put on the uniform to serve.**

The Honorable Congressman Bobby Rush, **in honor of the Vietnam Veterans I am proud to say thank you for your response in recognition of my request for your assistance in relations to the Vietnam Veterans. I am acknowledging the fact that you felt this matter was noteworthy enough to take into consideration the proper protocol to follow in respect to the Vietnam Veterans. Thank you for responding.**

The Honorable General Colin Powell, **as one infantry graduate of Fort Benning, GA to another. I salute you Sir, for your dedication to making the United States Armed Forces a better place for all. I am very proud to know you are a Vietnam Veteran who survived in the Vietnam war and I am prayerful you will understand my reasons for writing this book. I thank you for your support of the Vietnam Veterans Sir, and may you continue to be a positive impact in the future in making others aware of how the Vietnam Veterans have suffered through the years. I thank you** for inspiring me in becoming an Infantry officer and for your dedicated service to the Armed Forces of the United States of America. Thank you for being an example for all.

The Honorable Senator Tammy Duckworth, your willingness to continue to give of yourself by serving in the United States Armed Forces exemplifies who you are. You have shown both men and women of the military that your dedication to servicing the United States of America does not stop when the war ends. Your service to the U.S. military and later becoming an elected U. S. Senator is boundless.

The Honorable Senator John McCain, I am honored to say you were a true advocate when it came to helping those in Congress and the Senate who had not served in the military or been in a real war understand the needs of not just the Vietnam Veterans but all soldiers in past and current wars. As a Vietnam Veterans we were all inspired by your war stories and your dedication to the people of America. Being a Prisoner of War says it all and should not leave any questionable doubt of your service to not only in the military but also as a Senator elected to public office. Thank you for your service.

Jan Scruggs, you had a vision and brought it to life. I thank you for building the Vietnam Veterans Memorial. I understand you are the founder of the Vietnam Veterans Memorial. Mr. Scruggs says, "Building the wall was of remembering those who had fallen protecting the United States of America. It was also a way of helping him to cope with what he went through during the Vietnam War." All I can say to that is thank you Mr. Scruggs for your dedicated service and for filling empty spots on a Wall for the Vietnam Veterans that will never be forgotten.

Dr. Margaret Burroughs, you have always been inspirational during the time I had the opportunity to get to know you. It was shocking to see that someone of your caliber, someone who had created the first African American Museum (The DuSable Museum) in the history of America located in Chicago, IL on Cottage Grove could be so kind and modest. I will never forget how you took the time out to read my first book and some of my poetry as you inspired me to keep writing. Everyone should be reading Dr. Burroughs book

"Life with Margaret"

There is always a quiet before the storm. Just when you think everything is almost over and everyone has settled down for the night. What is all so surprising to me as I researched and wrote the book based on factual evidence as it related to the Vietnam War, I noticed there was an unmentionable lack of preparation concerning the return home of the Vietnam Veterans. What appeared to be a quiet storm has now turned into a tsunami. And the aftereffects will be more devasting than a 9.5 earthquake. As we as a nation face the aftereffects of what "Agent Orange" will have on the children, grandchildren and possible great grandchildren of the Vietnam Veterans. Will this nation continue to turn its head as though nothing is wrong?

I would also like for you to not forget another unbelievable inhumane act that is taking place. If you have the time please read my sixth book titled "The Cocoa Plantations America's Chocolate Secret, Forced Child Labor, Rape, Sodomy, Abuse of Children, Child Sec Trafficking, Child Organ Trafficking, Child Sex Slaves." I do not want you to forget the children who are suffering on the Ivory Coast of Africa and Ghana. Little boys and girls only five years old working 100 hours a week to get the cocoa bean to America for the Chocolate Industries. The Cocoa Plantations is noted as the worst form of child slavery in this history of the world. I beseech you to please read this book and pass the information along. I will continue to bring awareness as I begin preparation in book 2 of the "Cocoa Plantations" second edition.

I most also mention the abuse of Hispanic boys and girls who work for the Tobacco Plantations in the United States. These are seven-year-old child, boys and girls work 15 hours a day. Due to their immune systems not being strong enough to fight off the bacteria from the tobacco plants these 7-year-old Hispanic boys and girls are dying from terminal cancer. They have no medical insurance, no protective clothing and are receiving very little wages. These children are also being raped and sodomized. This true story is also an addition to my sixth book, The Cocoa Plantations…

In order to bring change, we must all find the humanity and trust we lost during the Vietnam War and assassination of our great American leaders. We must go back to work for America!

ACORN FENCE & CONSTRUCTION, INC

The professional way to have your fence put up today. The name is Acorn, they have 26 years of experience behind their name. Every hole they dig in preparation of erecting your fence is dug with precision and every post is set to perfection. All links are connected. Whether it is an open fence, partial privacy fence or privacy fence, Acorn will get the job done. Acorn Fence & Construction, Inc is built of a team of men and women who are willing to work around the clock to get the job done and make sure their customers are satisfied. There isn't a long waiting period to complete a job, once the materials have been measured and proper procedures have been followed, Acorns team is ready to go to work. Which is usually in a matter of days, I can vouch for Acorn, my fence has not buckled. The new PVC is a durable material the fence is made of which makes it able to endure the test of time and caring for the fence is minimal. Acorn Fence & Construction are made of professionals and are able to customize the fence you desire to fit what you need.

The United States Armed Forces in respect for the Vietnam Veterans want to say thank you Acorn for your contribution. We appreciate your support of the Vietnam Veterans & the men and women who served and are now serving in the Armed Forces of the United States of America. If you would like to have a fence put up contact:

Acorn Fence & Construction, Inc by calling 800-293-4472

PEPE'S MEXICAN RESTAURANT

———

Pepe's is the place to be when you have a taste for the best authentic Mexican food in town. My family and I make it a habit to dine at Pepe's. Its captivating serene ambiance and unique decorative walls with Mexican culture gives you the relaxed feeling of being across the border right at home. Pepe's Mexican Restaurant a place for family, friends and even business associates to meet and enjoy one another's ideals where the meals are reasonably priced. There is a bar to serve drinks and if you feel like singing karaoke that is only a mic away. Pepe's Mexican Restaurant also offers special services to the public. Depending on your tastes of recreation Pepe's has a party room and space for other events which is not limited to 1st Communion parties, Confirmation parties, Birthday parties and that's not all. Come to Pepe's, we aim to satisfy your family and business needs. Pepe's Mexican Restaurant is a great place to dine and your wait is never long. The hostess will assure your satisfaction before you leave, while the managerial team awaits your beckoning call to make sure you feel like a part of Pepe's family. You will not be able to find great authentic food anywhere else in town, here's a list of

Pepe's Mexican Restaurant locations:

63rd & Kedzie	773-778-6670
6336 W. 111th St	773- 425-3060
131 E. 79th St.	773-994-1525
1999 W. 75th St.	630-910-3333
6230 S. Western	773-737-1628
222 E. Ridge Road	219-923-6293
8313 S. Cottage Grove	773-488-5576

The Armed Forces of the United States of America gives a special tribute salute to Pepe's Mexican Restaurant for being in support of The Vietnam Veterans and all military soldiers past and present who honorably served The United States of America.

A SPECIAL THANK YOU

Cahal Pech Resort, San Ignacio
Cayo District, Belize

In Honor of Mr. Daniel Silva
Thank you for your support of the Vietnam Veterans
A Five Star Resort for your Comfort

Cahal Pech is a fun resort to bring your family to, its breath taking and quite eloquent. It's a fun place where tour guides can be set up at the resort. You will be able to visit sites throughout the Cayo District of Belize. I personally enjoyed the "Underground Caves" where I had the opportunity to see where the Mayan Indians actually lived, you will be able to see skeletons, skulls, pots and artifacts left behind. A memory you can enjoy with your family and after completion have a great meal waiting.

Cahal Pech is an exhilarating resort to vacation. It is a place where the owner is personally involved with a professional staff to assure your complete happiness. There are chefs on call to take your order whether it is by the pool or personal room service; they will bring it to you. A tasty breakfast buffet prepared by the chefs is set out each morning where you are able to serve yourself. Or if you like, make a personal order. There are exquisite views to partake of and beautiful sites overlooking the city of San Ignacio. You just might want to have dinner on your veranda of the resort its just breath taking. Or take in the cool summer breeze from your Cabana overlooking the city.

Cahal Pech is an exciting resort with pools to swim in and baby pools for your children's safety. There are places to sunbathe or just relax. You also have pool service from their attentive waiters and waitresses to assure your enjoyment throughout your visit.

I highly recommend you stop and chat with their untiring staff. You will have an opportunity to get to meet some of the staff; Tonya (upper management), Rhondine in hospitality, there is Oscar and Walter who supervise the poolside bar. The staff at **Cahal Pech** Resort are well trained professionals. They will assure your everyday needs are met. They are sincere and dedicated to making your stay at **Cahal Pech Resort** a memorable vacation.

Cahal Pech Resort in San Ignacio is the place to be if you want to experience the beauty of Central America in Belize.

I personally want to say thank you to Mr. Silva and staff for showing me such a magnificent time. Two Thumbs Up!!! I can hardly wait to return.

ADMA'S FREELANCE PHOTOGRAPHY

―――――

Adma Robinson is the most sought-after freelance photographer in Belize. Adma started working on her photography business in 2011. At the young age of thirteen she already had her hands on the camera while being trained in the dynamics of photography in the Cayo, District. When you think about professionalism and getting the perfect shot of you and your loved ones Adma's Freelance Photography is who you want to call. If you are in Belize and you are looking to have memorable moments captured by the best freelance photographer around do what we did call Adma's Freelance Photography for special events or any occasion. Adma will work the crowd for you and bring out shots of family, friends, and loved ones that you would have never captured. Adma's passion and spontaneity will give you different and unique looks for your photo album. Her creativity and talents will astound you. Adma's Freelance Photography covers Birthdays, Anniversaries, Family Reunions, Baptisms, Confirmations, Social and Church events, and are not limited to other events that may require a photographer.

Contact Info: Adma's Freelance Photography 0115016502424

LDW PLUMBING

LDW Plumbing is a very reputable and professional business. Plumbing with service you can trust. Lee is a man of dignity who stands by his work and guarantees your satisfaction. Mr. Lee has over 30 years of loyal service and is on call 24/7. He can be reached at (708) 310-8889. Mr. Lee, the United States Armed Forces says, thank you for being in support of the Vietnam Veterans and the men and women who have served and are now serving the United States of America. Call LDW Plumbing for all your Plumbing needs.

Tony, a special acknowledgement to the best jeweler ever. Tony is professionally skilled and able to satisfy all your needs and requested creations. Anything your heart desire Tony will make your dreams a reality. Thank you Tony for being in support of the Vietnam Veterans

McDonalds, I want to say thank you for responding to my letter in support of the Vietnam Veterans.

Speedway LLC, I want to say thank you for responding to my letter in support of the Vietnam Veterans

LARRY WAIGHT

"The Ultimate Belize Bucket List"

Larry Waight is a native-born Belizean. He has released his first book on a place you need to visit. A place that is becoming one of the most traveled countries in Central America, Belize. Larry's book titled "The Ultimate Belize Bucket List" is 366 pages of culture unraveled right before you. It will not only leave you astonished about the numerous places and things to do while in Belize. You will also have the opportunity to observe and learn a new culture. While enjoying the lavishing resorts where the hospitality will have you booking reservations to come back for next year's events. There are so many exciting things to do like horseback riding, and visiting the Underground Caves, where you can see where the Mayan Indians actually lived along with some of the ancient pottery they left behind, you will be within inches of it. You will have the opportunity to visit the Mayan Temples where kings walked, and human sacrifices were made. Larry's book "The Ultimate Belize Bucket List" covers areas of enlightenment, enough to keep you entertained for a lifetime of enjoyment. The Howling Monkeys are a nice hike up the trail. The Monkeys are not captured they are in the wild and you will see them as you walk. They will even stop and howl at you. I can't say enough about Belize. But whatever you do, don't forget to taste their fried red snapper with rice and beans, their ceviche and escabeche are meals you will most certainly want to bring back to the states when you leave. The flora and fauna on the countryside will amaze you, the rivers and beautiful beachfronts will astound you. Yes, Belize has become one of the most requested vacation areas from people all over the world. Larry Waight's book, "The Ultimate Belize Bucket List" will open your mind to fabulous new beginnings as you learn the Belizean way. Enjoy vacationing in Belize.

THE ULTIMATE
BELIZE
BUCKET LIST

101 Insider Tips on What to See and Do

From the Nation's Top Travel Marketer
LARRY WAIGHT

"If you're going to visit Belize, this book is well worth reading first."   Lord Michael Ashcroft

What's unfortunate is that I cannot list every Congressman and Senator I have written to. Neither can I list every organization in support of the Vietnam Veterans or soldiers in past wars or those who are currently serving. As I walked around and spoke with different men and women about the Vietnam War. I gathered a small list of names from people who wanted to be in this book. I stopped wherever I would see a Vietnam Veteran just for a moment and talked to them. I would tell them about the project I was working on to let them know they have not been forgotten.

"America Don't Forget".

If by chance you are reading this book and you served in the Vietnam War and your name is not listed below because I did not have contact with you. Please feel free to add your name here _____. It is your God given right for having served as a United States Vietnam Veteran

Below you will find a list of names of men and women I was able to speak with who served in different branch of the military mostly Vietnam Veterans. Some of the people listed their relative or friend who served. The organization listed are those who continue their fight for the rights of the Vietnam Veterans and are still trying to make it better for Veterans throughout the United States of America.

This section is Dedicated to men and women who gave their names to be in this book. Some gave the names of family and friends. Some were family of deceased Vietnam Veterans who wanted their relatives commemorated in this historical book. Their names were added without reservation. They served their country and stood in defense of, The United States of America.

Here are the few names and a few organizations I came across:

Christobal Espinosa...	Vietnam Veterans
Christopher Jarrett...	remember by his grandson in honor of his service in the Vietnam War
George M. DeYoung Sr.	served during the Vietnam War

Elijah Baldwin…	in honor of your service in the United States Army during the Vietnam War. Your daughter Malinda Baldwin commemorates your life and service to your country, the United States of America
Frank Pfister…	thank you for your service during the Vietnam War
Lieutenant Bob Pollock…	served in Vietnam in 1966 U.S. Navy
Joe Barnes…	served with the 11th Calvary
Raymond Ellers…	served in Pearl Harbor
George Clay Dow…	In honor of your sacrifice to the United States of America. Serving in the United States Navy 1959-79. And being deployed to Danang, Vietnam 1968-69. your son Buddy Dow memorializes you for your hard work and dedicated service to the United States of America. A well deserved "Thank you for your service"
Reginald Havey…	served in U.S. Navy 1972-1975
Leon Jefferson…	served U.S. Army, Vietnam 1967-1968
Dennis Rynn…	served U.S. Navy instructor, Vietnam 1964-1968
Monroe Haynes III…	served 1st17 Air Mobil, Vietnam 1967-69
Steve Danielzuk…	served
Hank Deshane…	served
John Kelleger…	served
Max Szalbierz Jr.	served in U.S. Army during the Vietnam War. Because of your dedicated service To your country the U.S. of A. your loving family at Arrenellos Pizza wants you to know they love you very much and miss you (RIP)
Dennis Pennington…	served 243rd Aviation

Doug Bathin...	served during the Vietnam War 1967-68
Dennis P. Jeppson...	served during the Vietnam War 1968-69 2 purple hearts honorable discharge
Michael Ross...	served in the United States Army during the Vietnam War. In commemoration of your service your sister Jayne Ross sends you a personal thank you for your service to the United States of America
Leo Gonzales...	in honor of your service in the Vietnam War 1967-72 your grandson Zachery Wants you to know you are appreciated
Chris Demas...	served 7-17-1954 – 7-10-56
Jim Beddome...	deceased, served in the United States Air Force. He will be greatly missed at Checkered Flag, Imports, INC. RIP

DAV National Headquarters
3725 Alexandria Pike
Cold Spring, KY 4106

Thank you for your service to all the disabled veterans and the untiring support you have shown through the years.

Cook County Veterans Affairs
c/o Bureau of Administration
118 N. Clark, Room 801
Chicago, IL 60602

Thank you for the support you give the soldiers who return home and are not aware of some of the benefits they have earned for their service to the United States of America. The Silver Star Banner Ceremony is a well-deserved presentation that earmarks a new beginning for soldiers who have been wounded during their time of service. To Toni Preckwinkle, President of Cook County Board of Commissioners and Bill Browne, Director of Cook County Veteran Affairs, and Martha Martinez, Chief Administrative Officer, in support of the United States Armed Services I say thank you. Contact information to find out if you qualify: 312-603-6423

V. F. W. Post 802
5820 Hohman Avenue
Hammond, Indiana 46320
Contact Information 219-933-9660

A personal thank you for all the great work I hear is being done in support of getting the Veterans claims and other busy taken care. It is nice to heard about good people and good things taking place to bring positive changes into our soldier's lives. Thank you for the unconditional and untiring work you do.

National Headquarters
Army Emergency Relief
2530 Crystal Drive, 13th Floor, Room 13161
Arlington, Virginia 22202
Contact: 703-601-2768

As a unified group of men and women we have an obligation to have funding available for all soldiers who serve. It is important to show our concerns by continuing to invest in the future of our up and coming soldiers. As soldiers we know that Emergency Relief funding is not only needed but necessary since we are aware that emergencies in the military happen daily. Funding must be there to ensure our brothers and sisters are able to make it home on time whenever an emergency arrives. We must continue to support the Army Emergency Relief. I personally want to thank the Army Emergency Relief for making sure when a tragedy occurs while the soldier is away. That the solider is able to make it home in a timely manner which exemplifies our concerns as a Force of One.

Warrior Transition Unit(s) (WTU)

I want to personally thank everyone on base at Fort Benning, Georgia (Home of the Infantry) for all your dedicated service to helping to assist soldiers to getting back on track as they returned home from war. The (WTU's) are much needed facilities and should be accessible throughout the country. I am thanking everyone at Fort Benning, Georgia who were instrumental in my life. Thank you to all staff and personnel for showing great concern for all soldiers. The base housing staff, the hospital staff, transportation staff and to those who worked on special assignments cognitive reasoning, communicative skills, brain trauma units, mobility skills, personal case managers who went the extra mile to make sure the soldiers treatment programs were working. Last but not least, I want to thank the Vietnam Veterans who wrote to Washington, DC about what was needed to help and assist the soldiers returning home from war and helped to create what is today the Warrior Transition Units.

MY INSPIRATION FOR WRITING

THE APOLOGY THE UNITED STATES OWES THE VIETNAM VETERANS

I have a personal spiritual obligation to my Father in heaven when it comes to writing about controversial issues concerning the world today. I write to open the conscious mind and try to delve just a little by taking you into an uncomfortable place into your very own subconscious thoughts, to implant thoughts and questions of either why something happened? Or could that something that happened been done a different way? Because we, the common everyday folk are only able to scratch the surface of our governmental intellects. Many times blocked and not able to reach the hierarchy of the super wealthy or the filthy rich. I am expressing what I feel our Vietnam Veterans did not get the opportunity to express. For those who suffered brain damage, cocaine addictions, heroine addictions and internal wounds of the body, and mind. The Vietnam Veterans who remain captive today in a system and American citizens who have not stepped up to the plate in their behalf like they have stepped up to show an act of a greater love and gave their life for you, the government they served and the American people they loved. If you know any of these top ten billionaires personally let me know. I would like to know how I can reach them. Not to just get the assistance I need to get 800,000 homeless veterans off of the streets of America into some form of government funded hotel or apartment building. Or to feed the 450,000 thousand veterans who are hungry each day. There is a need far beyond my reach of why these men have been left out on the streets when the greatest nation on the face of this earth (The United States of America) has the capability as well as resources to help them. This book which will be my seventh book is about The Vietnam Veterans. My second reason is also to keep you informed about my sixth and how something should be done to help these children who are sold and living in slavery today on farms on the Ivory Coast of Africa and Ghana. The title of my sixth book is, "**The Cocoa Plantations**

American's Chocolate Secret, Forced Child Labor, Rape, Sodomy, Abuse of Children, Child Sex Trafficking, Child Organ Trafficking, Child Sex Slaves" It's about five-year-old boys and girls being raped and sodomized. Working one hundred hours a week every week to get the cocoa bean to America in order for you to have chocolate. If you are able to contact anyone on this list of the top 10 Black Billionaires, please tell them I need their help. Here are their names: 1. Aliko Dangote 2. Mohammed Al-Amoudi 3. Mike Adenuga 4. Isabel Dos Santos 5. Oprah Winfrey 6. Robert Smith 7. Patrice Motsepe 8. Folorunsho Alakija 9. Michael Jordon 10. Mohammed Ibrahim. I am hoping this book being written about the Vietnam Veterans will make you aware that problems just do not go away by being ignored there is a level of commonality that we all have to meet in life. Last but not least to let you know in the eyes of God you have been blessed with the finances for a cause a servitude of purpose and it is only due to his will that we all will meet on common ground in a holy place. The Vietnam Veterans need your help this book is about them. The children need your help and I will continue to bring their issues up as I have through the years.

Proverbs 15:3 King James Version (KJV)
"The eyes of the Lord are in every place, beholding the evil and the good."

Whereby those who are corruptly involved in such heinous actions in society knowing they are wrong has now been revealed to the world. Enjoying Gods gifts, and talents is a blessing in life linked with an obligation to do the will of God of which we all will be held accountable for. Our blessings from him and how we so chose to use them. For some of you it takes a lifetime to understand the blessings because you are zealous enough to think you are doing it all yourself, (man plans, and God laughs). Your ability to step in and stop the pain and suffering of others is not something many of the wealthy will do. You must have the love of God in you to want to change someone's life just because you can. Not realizing everything you have been blessed with by God was already prepared for you prior to your existence here on this earth and your blessing to be able to give to others.

1 Corinthians 2:9 King James Version (KJV)
"But as it is written, Eye hath not seen, nor ear heard, neither have entered into the heart of man, the things which God hath prepared for them that love him."

I am prayerful that you are willing to do the will and work of our father in heaven.

Joshua 24:15 King James Version (KJV)
[15] "**And if it seem evil unto you to serve the Lord, choose you this day whom ye will serve; whether the gods which your fathers served that were on the other side of the flood, or the gods of the Amorites, in whose land ye dwell: but as for me and my house, we will serve the Lord.**"

Unfortunately, you enjoy the afflictions, the pain and hatred of this world and the father of this world is who you chose to serve. I am writing for the love of humanity, for the goodness of all in hopes that those of you in the decision-making positions will be able to make the necessary changes, giving credence to all human life. This book is not a finger pointing book. Although, at times it may appear to be calling people out. You will have to read this book from cover to cover to get an understanding of where I am trying to take you mentally, spiritually and emotionally. This book is based on the pain and suffering of the Vietnam Veterans. What happened to them? What "Agent Orange" has done to them and why they deserve the respect they earned protecting of the United States of America? Therefore, I write.

PREFACE

As I sat in the comfort of my home looking at the American flags in my office that has been certified, they read, "**This American Flag was flown in the face of the enemy.**" I began to do some deep soul searching before deciding to write this book.

I thought back to when I was a little boy and used to dream about wanting to be a military soldier. Little did I know I would one day not only be a soldier in the military but a military officer who would one day go to war in defense of the Constitution of the United States of America. I thought back to a time when I was an innocent child with no worries in the world. Life was fun; you know no worries, no bills, concerns, problems, jealousy, envy and hatred etc. Life had not begun to unveil its many sides to me as it had been revealed to others. It's sad to say but many people experience the ugly side of life early. Many times, our dreams of how life should be are altered and the life we planned gets disrupted due to situations out of our control. I was fortunate my dreams, desires and goals had not been tampered with at least not yet. When I was a child, I use to wonder what it was like to be in the military. I won't take you to my (G-I Joe) toy soldiers, yes, we had to create an imagination back in the day. Unlike kids today everything is electronic, and their toys talk back. I could not wait to join the service so I could be running through the jungle with my M-16, sleep in my sleeping bag in the forest at night, getting wet in the rain and all the other fun things my imagination told me military soldiers did. It looked like fun, but I would find out different later. After I swore in and put on my military uniform for the first time, I realized the dream I had as a little boy of being a soldier was not as fun as it appeared to be. It was a job. A job that men during that time had signed up to give their life for. Putting their John Hancock on the dotted line is what made them men. They would become soldiers later and that would be only if they made it out of bootcamp. The military schools of course would come later, but only if you graduated. I remember the drill instructors telling us "The fastest way out of Marine Corps boot camp is to graduate."

I am being a bit factious, but my so-called fun lasted for 28 years. I started off as a private first class, enlisted Marine Corps. My military career was completed as a Major in the United States Army. I went through Marine Corps boot camp, Leadership Training School, ROTC, Infantry Officer Basic

Course, Advanced Captain Career Course, Commandant Training etc. I put my body through some very intense training while asking in prayer that God strengthens my body so I can stay on my mission to make something out of my life. I was able to service my country during four wars Beirut, Dessert Storm, Iraq, and Afghanistan. With Afghanistan being my last tour of service for my country. When I returned home from Afghanistan, I remember civilians saying to me and other soldiers as we walked through the airport "Thank you for your service." I thought to myself that is really nice to be acknowledged for protecting the "Free World." But my mind often wrestled with what went wrong with the Vietnam Veterans. Why did they receive such a horrific homecoming? The Vietnam Veterans were more deserving than any soldier who put on a uniform to receive such an honor from the citizens they went to war to protect. We should really be thanking the Vietnam Veterans; they paved the way by sending in reports on their experience in war so the soldiers in today's wars would be able to make their transition back into society.

This book will hopefully make you aware of some of the important information you were not made aware of during the time of the Vietnam War. This book will take you to a place that will help you to be able to see the need to say to the Vietnam Veterans words they have been longing to hear for over forty years now "**Thank you for your service**." Those words were put in place for the Vietnam Veterans; they are more deserving than any soldier who has served on the battlefield in the armed forces to hear those word "Thank You." When I began writing this book, I tried to interview many Vietnam Veterans but many of them did not want to talk about the pain they were in or how they felt being rejected in their own country by their government and the citizens they defended. It's over forty years later and many Vietnam Veterans are still hurting today, but they are soldiers trained by the best military force in the world, the armed forces of the United States of America. They were trained to do a mission and complete the mission no matter what and they did. These soldiers were trained to hold up their head and drive on through all adversity. After reading this book I am prayerful you will understand why I said the Vietnam Veterans deserves to hear the words "**Thank you for your service**", and welcome home, it has been an extremely rocky road for them. As a Major in the United States Army I render the American soldiers who served in the Vietnam War a proper hand salute.

God bless the Vietnam Veterans for all they did to protect the shores of the United States of America.

INTRODUCTION

———

Vietnam and its many interesting stories concerning our American Veterans put me in a different kind of understanding as to what actually happened to our Vietnam hero's. One of the big questions that remains in the skeletal closets of our government's history is what really took place in Vietnam? Not just with the war but with our soldiers, our American soldiers who went to war to fight and protect the United States of America? Not being an active part of the war because I was a young boy maybe three when it all started. Although I was young, I can recall so much. I was a United States citizen and I wanted to know why these soldiers were being treated so disgracefully? As a young boy I remember talking to my mother and asking her what did the soldiers do? You see, I was raised to have the utmost respect for men and women in the military. Men and women who were willing to give their life for what they believed in, for the protection of this great nation. And to highly respect families who had lost loved ones who had given their life defending the "Free World."

The home welcoming the Vietnam Veterans received was horrifying. It was something no one should have participated in with all of the name calling they had to endure as they walked through the airports coming home. It was something even I as a young child knew was wrong, how do you spit on someone who defended your honor, someone who didn't even know you? Although I was too young to serve at that time, I was embarrassed for the Vietnam Veterans who returned home expecting a hero's parade. In fact, it was quite shocking and quite tragic for them. The Vietnam War remains an ugly blemish against the soldiers who were able to return home. They should have been celebrated. By the time you finish this book you will see that I am not exaggerating when I say they are owed an open apology from our government and the people of the United States of America.

Some of the graphic details I will convey in this book maybe shocking to the reader and quite disturbing to some. I suggest if you are under the age of eighteen you should be supervised if allowed to read this book. There is a high probability if you are not older than eighteen years of age you may not be able to handle some of the graphic information I will be talking about. I will ask that you stop reading at this time and seek guidance from your parents. I feel the book will be sensitively graphic to some and please let your conscious be your guide. But the truth must be told in order that you are able to grasp why the Vietnam Veterans are so deserving of an apology. I am hoping you the reader will be able to decipher the use of common sense based on survival skills built up in the mind of young American soldiers who only had two weeks of training. Taken by helicopter and dropped in the midst of Vietnam's jungle, a land away from home. Vietnam is to this day considered to be the hottest war zone in the history of America. A war played out in a jungle where the young soldiers who were sent did not have a sense of a day of peace or a piece of mind until their tour ended. For those of you who do not know the terminology of what a tour is it is usually for a year no less than six months in a war zone, without a break. During the Vietnam War our Vietnam Veterans were not given any breaks from the war to come home. They served their entire time in the jungles of Vietnam unless their tour ended, or they were carried out on a stretcher. Some soldiers did more than one tour in Vietnam, the question that should arise here is; should the soldier been allowed to go back to "Nam" once their tour in the war zone was completed. What we are finding out in relations to today's wars is that the soldiers mind needs a rest from war and should not be allowed to turn around and go right back into the war zone due to the trauma his mind and body has already endured.

Today's soldiers are given leave time from the war zone in order to get a break from the stressors of war. This break from war is attributed to the Vietnam Veterans writing about their experiences in the Vietnam war to those in government and telling them the importance of having a break from war. It was not until 1980 that the Vietnam Veterans were officially allowed to be diagnosed and classified with Post Traumatic Stress Disorder (PTSD), almost twenty years after the war. What many American citizens are not aware of is the Vietnam Veteran did not get much relief they served their entire tour in the war zone without a break. Just how much pressure were these young soldiers at the age of eighteen years old supposed to take? And what exactly had they learned when it came to jungle warfare? With only two weeks of bootcamp when it came to trying to survive in such a vicious and monstrous jungle? It was a war where shadows became people and trees came to life. The statistics I read says the life expectancy of a soldier in Vietnam was sixteen minutes. The longest I heard was one week. Take your pick as it relates to your life. Please tell me your preference would you want to live sixteen minutes or one week? If you are smart, I am one hundred percent certain that you said neither, I want to be able to go home in one piece. Unfortunately, in war you don't have the luxury of just packing up and leaving. The funny thing about war is bullets don't have names and they do not have time slots listed on them once they are fired it becomes random as to what target they will hit. What became noticeable to the American people was the number of bodies (American soldiers) that were returned to the United States in body bags.

I am prayerful this book will enlighten you and help to ease your mind as to why the Vietnam Veterans and their wives should be looked at differently and honored as men and women who served the United States of America. They were young men who became soldiers and women who became wives of soldiers. Their wives due to having to move when the soldiers received new orders to go to another state or country in support of their husbands earned the same respect as if they were on the battlefield themselves. Our American soldiers, the Vietnam Veterans were sent to the hottest war zone the United States was ever in and told they were protecting the shores of the "Free World."

Throughout the course of this book I will try to give you subject matter that appears to have not been considered as important during the time the Vietnam Veterans were returning home from "Nam." For a better choice of words, the lack of information in keeping the public, our citizens informed from what I have learned through my research has turned out to be what has inflicted institutional damages to the Vietnam Veterans. When I say (institutional damages) what I am referring to is the bad press they continually received as well as the lack of proper paperwork being implemented to back up what the Vietnam Veterans were saying. Partial truths were given with no explanation as to why a statement bearing negative content would be released. This caused a lot of soldiers to retaliate in a way that would not be considered honorable or acceptable to the American people. We can go as far back as 1968 and take a look at the May Tai Massacre of 1968. What remains in question concerning the moral aspect of war is the big question, is there ever considered to be a normal side to war even though war is attributed many times to positive change. A disagreement amongst powerful men in different countries who challenge each other with retaliation by sending soldiers to what we call war. Through so much blood shed and loss of lives no one is able to say we won, or they lost. Since the reason the war started in the first place is all based on a disagreement. Someone in another country wanted something the other country was not willing to give up. In the process of their disagreement governments get involved and decided to battle it out by attempting to take what they wanted by sending men into battle until the other person would be willing to concede. Unfortunately, everyone pretended they did not know what the war in Vietnam was about. As a military officer the one thing I have found out is that America is the most powerful country on the face of this earth. And we feel we are being politically correct when we ask a favor of another country out of respect. With the fire power we have on land and off shoreline positions on the ocean fronts. In all actuality the United States is honestly being diplomatic. Believe it when I say, "we do not have to ask anyone for anything" our resources are unlimited, and our armed forces are powerful enough to infiltrate any enemy line. But we are not a tyrant nation we are a nation of civilized people who work alongside of our allies to maintain peace. War is always a last alternative. It is not something the moral side of our government embraces but the formality of war cannot be a preparation period. We are a country who prepares for the worst and our defense funding stipulates the position we take when it comes to either keeping peace or a show of force. As a trained infantry officer in the United States Army we are trained to never say never and there isn't any mission to tuff for us to complete. Through my many years of service and dedication to my country I have been trained to understand power and what power is. Power is not something that is given it is something that is taken. Any sign of weakness is not acceptable in the ranks of a military officer or the soldier under his command. Leaders in the military must not show any signs of weakness. Leaders must be decisive and quick in their actions in order to protect the sanctity of our Constitution and our American way of life. Strength and power are what our nation was built on. It's honorable to say those who are selected to be in leadership positions will have control, will maintain control, and by any and all means necessary will do what it takes to make sure the mission is completed. It is very important to the leader of the United States that other nations realize that America remains tolerable to the mistakes they have made and accepts their faults without apology.

For me to be able to write a book about the Vietnam Veterans is a concern of mine always in good taste. Due to my service to my country I felt that after over forty-years of suffering the Vietnam Veterans deserve to have an apology and some form of relief for what has been done to them. I want the reader to understand although this book may leave you with some skepticism it is not being written to point fingers. What I would like to convey through this reading material and research is the eleven chemical companies is that stepping in to help and assist does not admit fault. IIt does mean there is some responsibility you feel on your part to at least try to help correct what has taken place with the Vietnam Veterans. Now that Agent Orange has spread into their children, grandchildren DNA will it continue into the bloodstream of the great-grandchildren DNA. The truth is you can never admit to 100% fault because it makes you liable. The solution to the problem would be to donate as much money for proper research of the Vietnam Veterans causes and effects of "Agent Orange." In order that the funding will become a continual sustained account for research and funding needed for medical treatment and hospitalization in the future. With proper research and funding, we will be able to find out just how long the life expectancy of TCDD (dioxin)= Agent Orange will remain in our Vietnam Veterans body, their children, grandchildren and their great-grandchildren. Agent Orange is a problem that is not going away anytime soon. The American people want the truth and it is about time they receive it. I must question the statement of the truth and make it a fashionable statement for you the reader I am going to get a little dramatic here and try to laugh through the pain. But in the movie a "Few Good Men" Jack Nicolson played the part of a general excellently when he was on the witness stand and said exactly what I am going to ask out government and the citizens of America, "Can you handle the truth?"

Being caught up in a windfall of negativity the Vietnam Veteran are still our brothers who had to learn how to survive on a battlefield that was also fought in tunnels underground. Tunnels that the Vietnamese had dug in the sticks (forest areas) of Vietnam. American soldiers were already suffering a great loss of life in the jungles of "Nam." And the underground tunnels the Viet Cong dug were also efficient in taking American soldiers' lives. Leaving our Vietnam Veterans with even more training needed to survive not just in jungles of Vietnam. The battle was also being fought in man-made tunnels underground tunnels dug in the midst of the forest. This would later be called guerrilla warfare. Guerrilla warfare is defined as, "a form of irregular warfare in which a small group of combatants, such as paramilitary personnel, armed civilians, or irregulars use military tactics including ambushes, sabotage, raids, pretty warfare, hit-and-run tactics, and mobility, to fight a larger and less-mobile traditional military."

Some of the stats are hard to believe so I am going to repeat once again. The life expectancy in Vietnam for our American soldiers was anywhere from 16 minutes to a week, you will hear that again later in the chapters of this book. Can you honestly say what you would do in a war zone as hot as Vietnam if you have never been in a war zone before? Given your estimated chance of survival to be anywhere from 16 minutes to a week what would you do to assure your return home to your family? Does normalcy play a part on the battlefields of war?

It is unfortunate you have pointed a guilty finger at the Vietnam Veterans and called them baby killers, murderers and animals. You even threw animal feces on them and spit on them. What is very rarely spoken of is how the Vietnamese women in the villages were also used by the Viet Cong. These women would lower our American soldiers in their huts leading the soldier into having sex with her. She would have razors inside of her uterus to inflict serious damage on the soldiers this was done intentionally. This was validated by one of the Vietnam Veterans I met. He stated this is what happened to his friend although he did not die, he is barely functional today. For this reason, we must remain openminded when it comes to guerilla warfare and the Vietnamese women as stated were used for that purpose. Keep in mind guerilla warfare is also a process of using civilians in nearby villages to immobilize American soldiers.

By not being given all the critical information to make a valid point who actually displayed the animalistic behavior by name calling and spitting on the Vietnam Veterans when they returned home and had not served one day in any war? Yet you call yourselves American and live in the most civilized country on the face of this earth. A country where the American soldiers were once praised for defending the Constitution of the United States of America. They are now being crucified by the same people who sent them into the war zone. Pointing the shame finger at the Vietnam Veterans and blaming them for what the American people only heard put the soldiers in a very bad position after they returned home. Where were the Vietnam Veterans going to go to live when they returned home as outcast in their own country? As you can see there are lots of questions needed to be answered in relations to the actions taken in a war zone by the Vietnam Veterans. When do we as a nation bend the moral arc of justice toward our brothers who fought in our defense? I would like for you the reader to categorize, "what is considered to be going overboard in a war zone" in the heat of a moment where you only have a split second to think? Where your life literally flashes before your face while in the same split second you have to make the decision of taking someone else's life or letting them take yours. The moral value of life is to preserve your life at all cost whether in peace or in conflict. I am certain being dropped in Vietnam the hottest landing zone in the history of any war would have put the subtlest of minds on survival mode. Let me take you to the word of God, let's go to scripture and bring in what thus said the Lord. John 8:7, "So when they continued asking him, he lifted up himself, and said unto them, "He that is without sin among you let him cast a stone at her." It is unfortunate there are people in this world today who feel they are sinless. I would have to ask you to search yourself and see is there anything worth salvaging inside of you? If you are the Christian believers you say you are than you should go back and review 1 John 1:8, "If we say that we have no sin, we deceive ourselves, and the truth is not in us."

When I think of the bitter hatred mankind has in doing the opposite of what God would have him to do. It becomes evident he (mankind) remains defiant to Gods will of man to be submissive unto him. In having an unforgiving nature, you must ask yourself this question how long do I dangle the mischief in question over my brother's head? Jesus made it plain when Peter was asking him a question in Matthew 18:21 "Then came Peter to him; and said, Lord how oft shall my brother sin against me, and I forgive him? Till seven times? Jesus saith unto him, I say not unto thee, until seven times: but, until seventy times seven." It is unfortunate that mankind does not have enough compassion and lack the obedience in the word of God to be submissive to his creator. For if we judge not then we are not judged, Matthew 7:1-3 "Judge not, that ye be not judged. (2) For with what judgement ye judge, ye shall be judged; and with what measure ye mete, it shall be measured to you again. (3) And why beholdest thou the mote that is in thy brother's eye, but considerest not the beam that is in thine own eye." In our understanding as Christian's we are not to judge. The world provides its judgment and condemns its own without any revocation of its own condemnation in realizing the inability for the unaccused to have the authority to condemn. We the people of this nation prejudged the Vietnam Veterans before they had a chance to defend themselves. These disrespected soldiers did nothing more than to defend the Constitution of the United States of America. To this day we the American people are beholden to the Vietnam Veterans for the good they had done. For those of you who have never put on a uniform or served one day in a war zone you did not have the right to point fingers at the young warriors who served in the Vietnam War. Unless you have stood side by side with the Vietnam Veterans on the battlefield in the midst of an ambush or firefight on patrol, I ask that you read this book from cover to cover and see if your opinion about these soldiers will change? Or maybe you have had the unfortunate experience of being able to view some of the film or sit and talk with some of the Vietnam Veterans about what really took place in Vietnam and the reason behind why things happened? Or maybe you witnessed the actual slaughtering of our young soldiers who were captured while out on patrol, tortured and butchered, and left to suffer where not even medical attention would be able to bring them to a successful recover once their bodies were found. Many of these soldiers had to be taken out of their misery by friendly. What I am saying to make it very plain as graphic as it may sound if a soldier is found in a situation where he is suffering after being tortured a decision has to be made by the officer in charge do you let the soldier suffer or pull the trigger to take him out of his misery? What would you do if it was your child, your friend, your mother, father etc.? I do understand a lot of what is being said is hard for you to swallow. So, I am going to ask you another question, what would you do if you saw your best friend or a close comrade with his guts in his hands and there was nothing medically able to help him? He is begging you to take him out of his misery or if he is able to pull the trigger himself, he is asking you to give him a loaded weapon, so he can do it himself? What would you do? This is how some of our Vietnam Veterans were being found after they were captured and tortured by the Viet Cong.

When I think about how the American flag still waves freely over this nation. American citizens have begun to take for granted what freedom in America stands for? Yet the American soldiers who fought in the Vietnam War and the soldiers fighting in today's wars continue to fight for the freedoms of the America people in order to protect the "Free World" as we know it, in hopes that it remains free and uncompromised for our children and our children's children. This great nation the United States of America, has stood on its moral values of, "In God We Trust." When placed in a position of vulnerability Americans become subject to conditions of the enemy. An enemy is someone or thing which opposes a threat to our American democracy whether it be foreign or domestic. Due to an occurrence of a foreign or domestic entity which attempts to stretch outside of the circumference of the norms of our society and there is a possibility that it may cause bodily harm to innocent people a decision has to be made on how do we stop it? I can even bring up characteristics of the death penalty. But I will not get involved in a discussion about the death penalty at this time although the scenario at most part is very close in nature.

Putting a man in prison on death row who has been found to be legally guilty of the crime he has committed according to the law in some states makes it legal for some states to put him to death by lethal injection. I must say at this point a chicken is a chicken and murder is murder. I am not saying that I agree or disagree with the death penalty. What I am saying is under the laws of the democracy of which we serve due to a threat being presented against the law or moral values under which we as Americans live it is legal by a rule of judgment to protect our values to murder a murderer synonymously under the same reasoning of the murderer who wanted something they could not have. So, we subject ourselves as Americans in a court of law to take the same life of someone who is on trial for what our democracy has just said is wrong. As you continue reading this book base on the Vietnam Veterans and the treatment, they have received for over forty years now. What you will find is truths in what is being said here and the terminology being use as it relates to the legal system is "Business that Affects Public Interest." You expect the court system to carry out the punishment by putting that person to death or by stopping what is considered to be an action that has wronged someone. In this case it would be the Vietnam Veterans and their bout with Agent Orange. Well the same scenario applies to the soldier in the war zone. He is trained to defend the United States to the best of his ability. There is a battle taking place and there is an enemy before them. The status of the mission is to eliminate the enemy and clear the path. Meaning he is trained in combat to do one thing in a war zone and that is to cause the enemy to submit and if that fails to kill the enemy if necessary. This is synonymous with the legal system when there is a threat and possibly no correcting the threat the only other alternative is to eliminate the threat. Keeping in mind it is your taxpayer's dollars that paid for the soldiers training making this soldiers position in the war zone without question even more reputable of which there isn't any question or dispute of what the soldier is going to have to do in the midst of war. In case you did not know or seem to have a blockage in your moral thinking, the objective is to destroy the enemy. The soldier took an oath to defend the Constitution of the United States of America and of which its citizens abide and that's just what they did during the Vietnam War. So how can you after being a part of all that took place condemn what you were in support of. The soldiers went to Vietnam to defend the United States and to kill anyone who got in the way of the peace, freedom and moral values of the American way of life. Trusting in God and that this great nation would uphold its beliefs and stand by those who volunteered to not only serve this country. What we have is a nation in agreement of both men and women who were willing to give their life in defense of the Constitution of the United States of America.

Pointing fingers seems like such an arbitrary gesture of one's personal incite of an unattested whimsical thought of what war may appear to be to someone sitting at home playing with television channels. The Vietnam Veterans could not just turn on and off war, pain or hunger when they got tired of being in a war zone. You see war is not as casual as you would think? It's not as easy as pointing the remote control and changing channels because you did not like the movie. War is not something that is just switched around until you find a channel that is favorable to your liking. If that was the case, we could remove the finger pointing because there would not be a need for war since the majority in favor of democracy would find something suitable for their viewing. Unfortunately, we will always have the finger pointing and those who will contest what takes place during war that they will never be able to grasp the concept of such. This is probably how most soldiers feel when they are sent to war, "It's not like that, I really don't hate you or have anything personal against you, it just that we are in a war zone and it is your life or mines. It's real and the Vietnam Veterans lived it, those who made it back home and those who gave their life. Not one person sitting at home watching television, not even those in government involved in the Vietnam controversy could say what they would have done because they were not there and more than likely would not have sacrificed their freedoms for such a cause. This is why I am asking you to think about the soldiers who were able to return home, think about the Vietnam Veterans who came back with one arm, no hands, or legs, blinded, parts and pieces of their body missing, one eye in body bags, mentally ill, etc. There are also those who lost their families, their wives and children due to their inability to readjust to society, unable to "Turn It Off," once they returned to the United States. The Vietnam Veterans who are still alive today over forty years later are still suffering from with the chemical "Agent Orange." A chemical which will remain in their blood stream for life. (I will be discussing Agent Orange later in the chapters to come). Those whose parents may have passed away while they were trying to complete their tour of duty in Vietnam these are just some of the things many of you have not taken into consideration, it's called sacrifice. What I am trying to tell you is these eighteen-year-old (boys) men, they are soldiers not animals, they are human beings with feelings. I am certain by now you are saying but look at what they did in Vietnam. And I am saying to you I am looking at what they did, they did their jobs and what it took for them to make it back home. Before you become judgmental please list the number of wars you have served in and the sacrifices you made to make this country safe. In case you have not grasped what, I am saying here, let me make it plain for you. Unless you have served in a war, an actual war were bullets, bombs and dead bodies are lying all around you please think about what you have done to the Vietnam Veterans for over forty years. Refusing them their benefits, denying them the right of being called heroes and belittling them in front of the world. There is no other country I can think of that has done this to their soldiers other than America. It makes those of you who have not shown compassion for men who joined or were drafted to go to Vietnam. Not knowing what they were fighting for insensitive to your thoughts of fairness and evasive in relations to your own insecurities which says to me you did not want to be the ones to go to war? The Vietnam Veterans are heroes within their rights of not just returning home safely but the burden of being ostracized in their own country for over forty years now. Could you have endured such a show of nonacceptance? If you said yes, I would have to say you are not being frugal with your thoughts. The year is now 2019 going into 2020, you, the American public have held these men who serviced you mentally hostage in a country they have been rejected in. You have stagnated their progress in a country they loved and defended to the best of their ability. The problem is you just don't get it or understand their positions as soldiers in war. The Vietnam Veterans should have been given a hero's welcome when they returned home from a war that not even the American government could explain. Although the loss is real the families who are still crying or in search for their loved one is real unless your son's name is on "The Wall." You should have very little to say unless you have a child or relative listed as KIA (Killed in Action). Here is the numbers to help you rethink what you have done to the 58, 220 who died for you during the Vietnam. From August 5, 1964 through March 28, 1973 (2,709,918) American soldiers served in Vietnam. There were 47,434 killed in action and 10,786 died of other causes (These statistics come from the Vietnam Historical Statistics-US War Dog Association. These records were transferred into the custody of the National Archives and Records

Administration in 2008. In case you were wondering about the opposition the Vietnamese had an estimated loss of between 200,000 and 250,000. Did anyone really win the Vietnam War? The point I am making here is that you did not hear the Vietnamese disowning their soldiers for torturing and mutilating the American Vietnam Veterans? No! they praised their troops when they returned home. But the American people were caught throwing feces on the Vietnam Veterans when they returned, spitting on them or calling them murderers. The Vietnamese soldiers were given a hero's welcome when they returned home from the Vietnam war. For killing, murdering and mutilating our American soldiers; their country received them with honor. What the American public seems to have forgotten about is the fact there is a strong possibility there are still American Prisoners of War (POW's) serving in concentration camps in remote areas of Vietnam today. I am pleading with you to keep in mind the only American soldiers who were release through negotiations in Washington from the concentration camps were the concentration camps the United States where aware of. We still have American Vietnam Veterans alive today and because of this we must be cognizant in our understanding as American citizens that since all (POW's) were not released there must be some still alive and still being tortured and abused. The biggest part of abuse a soldier will suffer is the thought of never returning home again. Although a soldiers training teaches him not to hold on to things and how to adapt given any condition. We should never give up looking for our soldiers because they never gave up on us. Keep in mind the American POW's and MIA's are always prayerful and hopeful that we have not given up looking for them. They are still out there, and we must make the effort of a continued search, so their hope is not in vain. And the families who have not received the body of their loved one are remaining hopeful of at least a chance for them to possibly see their loved one again. If you look at the stats being presented closely what you will see is the soldier who was taken out of boot camp in 1964 at the age of 18 and was captured as a POW. Someone's family member our American soldier is only estimated to be only 72 years of age today. The probability of these POW's still being alive is not something we can overlook. What is the price you are willing to pay when it comes to being able to see someone you love again, when all you have is someone's word and all you have to hold onto is hope? The Vietnam Veterans are men who served, they gave all they had, and we must continue to give to them whatever support we are able to. We must also make sure the families they left behind are comfortable in knowing the United States of America has not given up.

During battle in a war zone when we are trying to expose the enemy so we can see their whereabouts we release a star bust in the air which illuminates the entire area so we can see anything moving. It is not a one hundred percent detectable device, but it helps to get the job done in exposing the enemy whereabouts. What I am alluding to here is although we have done our searches and probing is it possible, we could have miss something? Are there still American POW's left in remote concentration camps we do not know about? Toss the coin in the air if you like but if it was you would you want the United States to continue searching for you? Our soldiers have the mind set even at the age of 72 by any means necessary he is still trying to figure out when he is going to be found or released to be returned to the United States of America.

Survival for the soldier in a war zone was not like being at home and trying to figure out what's for breakfast or even if you wanted to eat breakfast. It was not questionable if dinner would be served at home or at Pizza Hut, McDonald's, Wendy's, Burger King, or Red Lobster? The soldier was not concerned about having it his way he just wanted something to eat. Life in "Nam" was no walk in the park it was a second by second life experiencing situation. Every second counted in the sticks in (the jungles of Vietnam). I don't have time to pick on the government because this book is about what you did not know concerning why you should have forgiven the Vietnam Veteran many years ago. In fact, they should have never been blamed for anything. I will say this much, why don't you first stop the finger pointing because it was pointing at the wrong people the whole time. You know the old saying better you than me? Well the Vietnam Veterans got the blame you know stuff always rolls downhill and of course the Vietnam Veterans were the lowest on the totem pole. By the time you finish reading this book I am hoping the President, Congress and Senators can rewrite history for the most deserving soldiers who ever put on a uniform. Those in question did not serve one day the Vietnam Veterans have served their entire life. Traveling back and forth to Washington, DC to try to make things right for those who could still possibly be missing. They deserve to wear the badges of hero's and the respect of the United States of America. Those of you who did not serve one day in "Nam" you truly do not have the right to say these men who survived the Vietnam War and those who served and gave their life did not deserve a hero's welcome? With so much controversy taking place with the Vietnam Veteran and all of the negativity attached to the war itself the American people forgot to say, "Thank you." Not just for defending and representing the United States of America but "Thank you" my brother for not abandoning the American people during their time of need. Thank you for not embarrassing this country by running away and not showing up for duty. Thank you because you did the ultimate of sacrifices you followed your military orders and Christian beliefs and completed the mission you were told to complete, John 15:13 "Greater love hath no man than this, that a man lay down his life for his friends." With so many issues at hand like questioning the reason for the war in Vietnam that many Americans fled to Canada so they would not have to go and fight? They avoided the draft and refused to go into a war that had no objective. We questioned why American soldiers were being sent to Vietnam. There was protest after protest even I can remember the (Peace Signs) people had on t-shits and the sign was the split to fingers held high. The American people did not like how these young soldiers were being sent to Vietnam by the thousands and returning home in body bags by the thousands. For the soldiers who went to war and did not flee the United States to find a natural country like Canada to hide. When the Vietnam Veterans returned home, they were treated worse than those who deserted the United States. People were frantic when it came to sending their sons into a war they felt hadn't an objective worthy of sending their son to his death. Many turned their heads and sent their sons to other countries Canada was one of the neutral countries. They felt it was easier for them to go to Canada and make a life than to come home in a body bag. The feeling of disgrace only fell on those who were drafted and did not fore fill their obligation to the United States of America. Those who fled the country could care less. Yet there were many who stayed and gave their life. They turned out to be the real Vietnam Veterans. They are the real soldiers who neglected family, friends, and loved ones to stand up to the demands of the letter they received in the mail from the President of the United States saying their service to their country is needed. You live in America and willingly forgive those who deserted this country in its time of need. Yet you do not want to forgive the soldiers who left everything to make sure the security of this country was preserved. The Vietnam Veterans were the men and women who remained obligated to the oath they had taken and swore or affirmed to uphold it even if it cost them their life.

In relations to the book I am going to give you a little more information that has not been written about in defense of the Vietnam Veterans who stayed and fought and the many who gave their life to protect the future of this nation. Men who lived up to their obligation to protect the shores of the United States of America against all enemies foreign and domestic which cost them more than their life. It cost them the country they grew to love, cherish and respect. I asked this question earlier, and I am going to ask it again. Given the situation of war what would you have done to survive? Given the nature of the Vietnam War and how big it had gotten, it involved a certain level of trust. The young soldiers trusted the government enough to swear in and be flown to a country they never been in and to fight a war they did not create. I enjoy asking you, "What would you have done? Because it so easy to judge someone and say, "I would not have done that" Yet you not only spit on the returning Vietnam Veteran, you rejected them. The men who went to war in your defense to retain your dignity and honor, but you stripped him of his in his defense of the "Free World." By disrespecting the Vietnam Veterans who returned home you also disrespected those killed in action and never made it back home. You disrespected the dead on the battlefield of Vietnam. Those who were shipped home in body bags. You totally forgot about those who gave their life in honor of the Constitution of the United States of America. I am hoping this book can help you to reflect and see the unfair treatment the Vietnam Veterans received. You will also be reading other complications you did not consider because of war the Vietnam Veterans were already going through before they returned home. In respect to not understanding the worst war a teenager could have been dropped in, they were there to not only to protect the U.S. but also to protect the one life they had. The American people need to rethink who they are obligated to and give thanks to our unsung American hero's, the United States of America Vietnam Veterans.

CHAPTER I

THE GENEVA CONVENTION

WHEN WE AS A civilized nation of American people look at the position concerning the Vietnam War in hindsight with respect to the Vietnam Veterans, the trials, tribulations and rejection the soldiers had to go through. The only information we had as they returned home was what was fed to the media and newspapers. Our American soldiers were painted in a sense of being disgraceful before they ever got off the plane. They were brought back to America to return to their homes and families they had left behind. Were the Vietnam Veterans ever given a fair chance to explain themselves? Or was just their return home too much for the government and American citizens who sent them to "Nam" turn out to be too great of a cost to repay. Big mistakes were made we all must admit during the war and after the war, we can agree on that. Unfortunately, it has been the Vietnam Veterans who have suffered the most due to misinformed American citizens and media. Isolated incidents where a few soldiers may have gotten out of hand should not have cost the entire return of the Vietnam Veterans to go unnoticed, and unappreciated by the American government or its citizens. I am going to continue to add the American citizens because the fault of the Vietnam Veterans does not just fall on the government, tax paying U.S. citizens also had a voice in this war. In order to get to the truth, you first have to want to search for the truth then you have to set aside personal differences and be open about what went wrong. Ask yourself were these your eighteen-year-old boys who were trained to be men in two weeks of bootcamp training aware of the rules of engagement in a war zone. If you want to go a little more in depth even the young lieutenants who were responsible for these young men were not certain on all the rules of engagement. Everyone was not given a rule book of the Geneva Convention laws and regulations to study. Our troops were sent out on a mission and the mission was to complete the mission given. War is exactly what it is war and the only rules during a war are the ones made up as they go, at least this is what many of the soldiers thought. You cannot find fault if there were rules to war the Vietnam Veterans did not know about. Although the moral conduct as a military soldier hold within itself ethics of respect for the uniform and the country it represents. Fortunately, this was the case during the Vietnam War because I am certain it could have been a lot worse if some of the allegations you may have heard could have questionably happened. The Geneva Convention came into play, which conveyed rules and regulations soldiers in combat were now obligated to follow. The definition of the Geneva Convention: "One of a series of agreements concerning the treatment of prisoners of war and of the sick, wounded and dead in battle first made at Geneva Switzerland in 1864 and subsequently accepted in later revisions by most nations." The Geneva Convention covered the treatment of civilian, prisoners of war (POW's) and soldiers who are otherwise rendered hois de combat (French, literally "outside the fight), or incapable of fighting. The convention produced a treaty designed to protect wounded and sick soldiers during wartime."

Soldiers who were put on the high end of knowing what the correct procedure is to follow of course were the higher-ranking officers in charge. Some more aware than others of the rules of war agreed upon by other nations in reference to the Geneva Convention. It was also understood there was not a 100% agreement with all nations under which the Geneva Convention would apply. Or other nations would have to abide to in reflection to them not being in agreement with the Geneva Convention rules of war alien nations would not be sworn to uphold. Many people who are not aware of government policies which introduce the rules of war, think war is exactly just that war. What rules are there to follow in war? That is not the case as I have already stated, regulations had already been agreed upon concerning war, the Geneva Convention goes as far back as 1864. There are rules to war so do not be confused on the part of the American soldiers that were tortured and mutilated by the Vietnamese on the battlefield of Vietnam. Some Vietnam Veterans even received advances from the Vietnamese women who were armed in the private areas with razors. Some with infectious diseases. Unfortunately, the some of the consequences the Vietnam Veterans had to experience were mediocrely exposed to the American citizens and media. As I stated earlier in the introduction, I have tried to get many Vietnam Veterans to talk about what they remembered, and many did not want to say what they saw or had to do to sustain their life. The torturing and murdering of our American soldiers who were captured was real on the battlefield of Vietnam, but the butchering of the American soldiers' comrades would not go unanswered. The Geneva Convention was being violated; American soldiers were complaining to higher command about how their comrades were being found. It became obvious that someone was not following the rules of the Geneva Convention. The American soldiers who went through boot camp together, trained together, showered together, ate breakfast lunch and dinner together, and got to know each other as brothers, grew to understand their fellow soldiers. Understanding the ways of the other soldier, they even shared family pictures and talked about their wife or girlfriend. This is not speculation these are facts because this is what I have also done prior to going into the war zone. Although it is somewhat personal it is important to let your war buddies know how you feel about family and other issues in the civilian side. Someone close to you must know what kind of person you are. Some of these soldiers after getting to know one another are even asked to be the other soldier's best man at their wedding that is just how close these soldiers get, if they live to make it back home. The Vietnam Veterans were true soldiers who knew the probability was high as to whether they would be able to make it home alive. I am trying to share with you the comradery these men had for one another they were retrained and re-raised in boot camp as brothers to cover for one another. The love and respect they had for one another was not going to change, not even in Vietnam, the hottest war zone any soldier had ever seen in America, they had each other's back to the end. There was nothing that could separate the way these men respected one another. When a soldier was missing search parties were sent out and many times these soldiers would find their friends bodies tortured, mutilated and some decapitated. It did not help the issues of responsibilities concerning the Vietnamese obligation to the rules of war as to what they could do to American P.O.W.'s. The soldiers who found their friends bodies dismantled and mutilated had to bear the burden of remembering how their friends' dead body looked. This picture would be logged in the back of their subconscious mind for life. Soldiers bodies found that had been tortured, some beyond recognition. As you continue reading this book, I will continue to bring to your conscious mind the question of "What Would You Have Done?" Had this been your friend you found tortured beyond recognition and still having an understanding this was not to take place within the agreement of the

Geneva Convention. You must have questions at some point concerning the rules of engagement who would be able to say what really took place on the battlefield of Vietnam. The reality of it all is something any of us cannot overlook that there were over 47,000 American soldiers who were killed in action. Whether they were killed on the battlefield, caught and tortured before being murdered is something the American public did not get a list of, all you know is the soldiers were (KIA). The history books will not reveal what actually happened to the soldiers. And it is best for the families to not know what really happened, it's easier for everyone.

There is so much that needs to be taken into consideration concerning the Vietnam War, it's over forty years later, and the American Vietnam Veteran is still suffering. I have spoken personally with Vietnam Veterans and I have watched the tears began to trickle down their face or sometimes just watch their eyes tear up. Because they feel they have been forgotten, tossed aside in an old dark room where a person hides things they want to forget. The Vietnam Veterans are our brothers, war heroes who deserve a big pardon from the government and the American people. If you would ask me, I would say the apologies would start with the President of the United States, the Congress, the Senate and last but not least the American people. The Vietnam Veterans are hurting because the media exploited the stories being given to them and the American people believed the stories that were being printed. This gave the Vietnam Veterans a strong sense of insecurity and made them feel as though they were strangers in the same country, they were sent to Vietnam to defend.

This is a true story of my personal conversation with a Vietnam Veteran. The location was at Office Max in Columbus Georgia. I decided I would print a prose I had written and design it in a way that the President, government officials, the base Commander, Senators and Congressmen would be happy to receive and hopefully display it in their office. I was very happy to be able to get a copy of the prose to Congressman Lane Evans. If I am not mistaken the prose is in Congressman Lane Evans memorabilia room in Washington, DC. While I was getting the copies printed, I noticed the clerk was laying the prose face up where it was readable, and the gentleman next to me begin to read my work. I did not say anything because it was my work and I already owned the copyrights. As I paid for my copies and begin to leave the store the gentleman reading the prose was a Vietnam Veteran who came out of the store behind me. He stopped me and wanted to talk for a second. He asked if he could read the rest of the prose? He apologized for trying to read it in the store and said he just could not read it all. He asked me if I would read it to him, I said, "yes." I begin to read him the prose in the parking lot of Office Max as tears began to run down the sides of his face. He was a bit emotional. The title of the prose is; **America Don't Forget.**

American Don't Forget

Do not forget the soldiers who died;
The ones who gave their life for the freedom ride;
Those who volunteered to serve and did not hide;
American Please Don't Forget
Wave our blood-stained flag and wave it real high;
Yes! It is my brothers and sisters who have given their life;
For justice all over the world they did not compromise;
The soldiers who served to protect our lives;
America Do Not Forget
Do not forget those who are wounded and scarred for life;
They will carry it around when they return
home, the memories of war;
Rejected, traumatized, disfigured, badgered but not beaten;
Fighting a cause they were willing to die for, freedom;
America Do Not Forget Them, Don't Forget
Arlington's cemetery is filled with soldier's good deeds;
Those who lost their life defending our Constitutional needs;
Searching for weapons of mass destruction we never did find;
Look at Vietnam over fifty-eight thousand did not make roll call;
It is still a tragedy that haunts us all;
America We Cannot Forget Our Soldiers
"America the Beautiful" soldiers sing with pride;
Some will salute while others raise their hand;
While "Mother Liberty" rings freedom throughout this great land;
America Don't Forget the Soldiers Who Fought For You
The flag still waves its colors of red, white and blue;
For those unable to serve we sent a round down range for you;
In a country built on these precious words "In God We Trust";
Don't Forget the Soldiers America, Don't Forget
Body bags are sent home with soldiers both young and old;
They cry out from Vietnam, Iraq, Afghanistan let their stories be told;
Our National Anthem says, "Let freedom
ring from every mountainside";
Let it ring for every soldier, male and female,
and when it rings remember;
The soldiers who took an oath to protect America against all foreign,

**And domestic enemies with the last drop of blood in their body;
On the battlefield of justice protecting the shores of this great land;
My God, My Country, My America Don't Forget**

After I read the prose the expression on the Vietnam Veterans face was one, I would never forget. As I watched a tear fall from his eyes he said, "I thought you all had forgotten about us." I said no you have not been forgotten; the Vietnam Veterans will never be forgotten." He thanked me for reading "America Don't Forget" and asked if he could have a copy. I thought who would be more deserving, my first copy being put into the hands of someone who actually served in the Vietnam War a Vietnam Veteran. I remember telling him, "It was the Vietnam Veterans who lead the way for every soldier going into a war zone today. The following statement is one I would employ you to pay close attention to, it was the Vietnam Veteran who gave those who served in Beirut, Desert Storm, Iraq and Afghanistan the opportunity to have a chance at some form of recovery once they returned home." It was because of them writing about their experiences and the love they have for the soldiers who were coming up behind them. For them to write about solutions and what could have been done differently during the war and after the war for the soldiers to be able to recover from the war zone and be acclimated back into society. As the tears fell from the face of the Vietnam Veteran, I was talking to I could see the pain in the eyes of (my brother). All I could think to myself was, "Oh my God, the American people are not aware of how our Veterans of the Vietnam war are really hurting inside. I was more than honored to see, this Vietnam Veteran, this soldier, this man who sacrificed his life for his country, my brother in green comforted from the words inside the prose I had written… "**America Don't Forget**". Don't forget the Vietnam Veterans, the men and women today who gave more than their life for the freedoms you enjoy each and every day. If you read the prose **"America Don't Forget"** I am prayerful the words enclosed will give you a sense of understanding what you have done to the men who answered with their life above and beyond the call of duty. What remains fortunate and in favor of the Vietnam Veterans is they are not at fault for what took place behind closed doors in Washington, DC whether it was in the chambers of the White House a political decision was made to send eighteen year old boys to war, into the jungles of "Vietnam." There isn't a line of defense for America sending eighteen-year-old boys who trained for approximately two weeks into the hottest war zone in the history of America. You made them the animals they had become. It was you who did not train them properly. You knew nothing or very little about guerilla warfare. So, these young soldiers were not only at a disadvantage going to war, but real life set in as they watched their friends killed on the battlefield. They went to Vietnam unprepared. And it was you, the citizens of America who paid your tax dollars to put the weapons in their hands to defend you. Another question arises, I must ask you, the American public who jumped so quickly into judgment and pointed fingers at the young boys (men) eighteen and nineteen years old that your tax dollars sent to war. If you take a moment to look at things just a little closer, you have to keep in mind this was not some trivia game where you get to play again if you lost the first time. These boys where being sent into a war zone where there were real guns and bullets. Oh, by the way in case you forgot they only had one life, you do not get a do over. I am frantically waiting to hear your response, "just what would you have done?" Would you have turned and ran like so many others did? Would you have intentionally flunked the military test, the eye test or just played crazy? What would you have done to get out of having to go to Vietnam? And just how did you expect a young boy (man) eighteen years of age to respond to seeing his friend, his best buddy, found dead and castrated with his testicles shoved in his mouth? I keep saying exactly what did you expect the Vietnam Veterans to do? The even bigger question is what would you have done? Excuse my ignorance I forgot you were not there. There has to be some consideration given to every soldier sent to Vietnam as young boys (young men if you would have it) as a military soldier and officer I just cannot see eighteen-year-old being called men. They are the same boys who sit around the house on the weekend and ask their father if they could use his car. There is a process into becoming an adult and the time it takes to get there is not the age of eighteen. These boys were trained at the age of eighteen to defend your rights as citizen in the "Free World." Let me recant for one second and say in the process of giving them some consideration under the circumstance involved they had already earned your respect. But the respect they should have been given was not brought into fruition because it was you who chose to believe everything you did not see and all that you heard on television the media was putting out. They were son's, husbands and fathers who went to war for your defense and many were never heard from again. I am trying very hard to get you to see it is not just the Vietnam Veterans who are still suffering from their battle wounds today, but it is also their families and loved ones who suffered along with them. Because of the of information you were given about the Vietnam Veterans by media and government officials who did not serve one day in the jungles of "Nam." The bigger question here is how do we fix it? Can it be fixed? I believe it can be fixed and it can start with stopping the finger pointing. The shame of what took place in Vietnam falls on you as a nation. You all bear the burden whether you like it or not. Its truths are so intermingled with hearsay, "I heard the Vietnam Veterans did this, or I heard the Vietnam Veterans did that." The young boys eighteen and nineteen years of age are the ones who held up their right hand in honor of your protection and because of their volunteering this country remains free today. There are so many stories that have not been told. Stories of our American soldiers, our Vietnam Veterans hidden secrets of how they survived, the pain and fear they have held inside for so many years the inwardly hidden little boy who had no one to cry out to for help. The child that remained secluded in a shale that did not have any relief as he walked through the jungles of Vietnam. What they had to do in order to survive to make it home again not knowing the most damaging part of the war that would hold them hostage was not going to be the travesty of the Vietnam War. It was our own government and American citizens who would judge them and keep a dark cloud over their heads for life. For those who still sit in dark rooms, those who isolate themselves from society, those who remain heavily medicated to cope not only with their war injuries but with a country which has made them feel over the past forty years like they do not belong. These men who were able to return home did not return whole. The physical damage you can see is permanent. What you do not realize is the internal damage you cannot see. It is also permanent and deeply rooted in the nightmares you do not see them having at night, their ability to cope with the so-called norms of society. But what is so real is that when you look at the soldier, you do not see a wounded soldier you see a whole man.

Only because you are blinded by the outer layers of skin that only appears to be undamaged. Untouched by the swamps, the dirt, the filth and the blood these men had lost on the battlefield in defense of what they were told to believe in. They were given a mission to complete and they completed it.

The one thing you do not realize is the man you are looking at although he did not lose a limb, or some other part of his body. The internal damages in many cases are much worse than the physical damages. And this is where you the American people have failed the Vietnam Veteran and every soldier who has served his country. Looking at the soldier thinking he or she is okay. Judging them because they are able to walk without showing a limp. Hold a conversation without letting you know their migraine headache is so bad they can barely think. Or standing for a long period of time trying to appear normal even though the arthritis in their back, knees and arms hurt so bad that they stand any way to try to appear normal. In the meantime, soldiers already know the war has taken its toll. There is such a thing called soft tissue damage, traumatic brain injuries, degenerative bone disease, intestinal infections from eating contaminated foods in a foreign land. There are so many stories of what the Vietnam Veterans had to eat to survive. Soldiers also have arthritis from having to sleep on the cold hard ground in sleeping bags etc. These are just a few of the debilitating issues not only the Vietnam Veterans but all soldiers have to deal with once they are released from the military. Yet there are the personal feelings of soldiers that you do not get to know or see. How the soldier decides to cope with the personal injuries and issues of their involvement in the Vietnam War is a choice of what the man inside of him that says he would rather conceal it keep it hidden. What they saw on the battlefield, and what triggered their mind to be able to accept what they could not change on the battlefield of the soldiers they saw killed will be forever engraved in their mind. Can I ask you a question? Have you ever had to figure out what your functioning capability is when you are looking at your best friend and his guts is just been blown all over the foxhole? Or have you had to sit in that same foxhole with a dead soldier and eat and sleep until either the body was taken out of the foxhole or you have been given the command to move? Either way the soldier is going to suffer with that vision for life, each time he closes his eyes at night or tries to talk about it with someone. This is why I understood so many Vietnam Veterans could not talk about their personal stories for this book. Some were able to talk about it, but many declined and just said thanks for writing the book. The thought of the soldier watching his buddy being carried out of the foxhole or the memory of leaving his buddy's body being flown home in a body bag is a big part of the Vietnam Veterans battle wounds. What's considered to be normal for the soldier is surely surreal to the civilian at home. You see the soldier has been trained to keep moving even after their buddy has been shot. It's a part of his training but that still does not negate the feelings he had to disregard in order for his survival in Vietnam. It does not numb the soldier since he still has the emotions of feeling the pain, he just witnessed of another soldier being shot. Only on the battlefield there isn't any time to cry nor the place to do it. The soldier must immediately detach himself from any thoughts of retreat; he must be able to nullify himself and keep himself separated from any personal attachment. He must keep moving as expected. There appears to be some kind of mutual thinking many civilians have that a soldier does not have any feelings. Well now you know that's not true. We are taught not to show our emotions openly because we have to think on our feet and move quickly and swiftly; that's what keeps us alive in a war zone. The soldier does not have time to grieve like a civilian does. Back home in the state's civilians have family, friends and relatives to comfort them but not in the jungles of Vietnam. The veterans must keep moving and pray that his friend will be found by the medics who are pulling up the rear, this is what we have been trained to do, keep moving. From my personal experience I can remember going on a twenty-five-mile road march with a full eighty-five-pound backpack strapped to our backs. My best friend had cramped up so bad he could not move. I stepped out of the formation to help him and my drill instructor told me to get back in line and continue marching with the rest of the soldiers. He told me what is taking place at the moment was a situation of not losing one soldier but possible two. If we would have been on the battlefield it could have been a matter of life and death for me, and if this happens again do not step out of formation, just keep moving. The reality of keeping it moving was part of our military training if your comrade is shot on the battlefield. The question given in the same situation is what would you do? When you are on the battlefield and your comrade is shot and goes down? The soldier is calling your name for help and to please not leave him alone, what would you do? I can create many situations which would question your integrity and loyalty to your fellow comrades. But I am trying to awaken your mind to the emergency on the battlefield where everything is happening in matters of seconds. Can you say you would have stayed with your friend knowing the next round coming down in the area your friend got shot would probably be an enemy mortar?

Therefore, I am presenting situations to you in order to get you to think. If your friend is captured by the Vietnamese and you find his body the next day and he has been decapitated with his eyes gouged out what would you do? Knowing in accordance to the Geneva Convention prisoners of war are not supposed to be tortured. These scenarios are being presented to make you think what could possibly be taking place in the mind of an eighteen or nineteen-year-old child whose friend was tortured to death? Now that you have a weapon to kill do you react vengefully after seeing what is left of your friend? What do you do?

When looking at the normalcy of life everyone looks for acceptance in some form or manner and no one wants to be ostracized by their own countrymen. Could you imagine being in a war, dropped off in a jungle and literally told to make it the best way you can? Was the Geneva Convention in affect during the Vietnam war? Yes, it was. The question that arises is did American soldiers ever violate or intentionally violate the Geneva Convention regulations? And were they fully aware of the dos and don'ts of war just as the Vietnamese were also obligated to the rules of war within the Geneva Convention? This is where it gets a little touchy. Who violated the rules of war? What caused soldiers on both sides to violate or should I say disregard the rules of war and to be pushed to the brink of what took place on the battlefield of Vietnam? American Vietnam Veterans, soldiers on their return home would be unaccepted and disrespected by the American people and would be called murderers, baby killers, and mocked. What pushed these eighteen and nineteen-year-old boys (trained to be men in two weeks) past the point of normalcy?

What the Geneva Convention was supposed to do was to create some form of sanity in a war built on hate. The Geneva Convention in its creation was supposed to distribute diplomacy to mean an international agreement, or treaty. Due to the revisions of this agreement there was a specified focus on soldiers wounded in war, those who had gotten sick in Armed forces in the field (first adapted in 1864, revised in 1906, 1929 and finally in 1949). If you want the truth as to whether or not the Vietnamese were obligated to the Geneva Convention like the American soldiers? The answer is yes, they were. The Vietnamese were just as obligated as the American soldiers to the Geneva Convention.

In attempts to clear up issues in Asia the Geneva Convention posed problems not only with the Vietnamese but the United States as well. Within the heart of the war already taking place in Asia and the French suffering their greatest loss. Representation from the world powers met in Geneva. The confession was a turning point which the United States would now get involved in Vietnam. In July of 1954 the Geneva Agreement was signed by both world powers Vietnam and the United States which obligated both to the rules of war agreed upon.

CHAPTER II

THE PURPOSE OF WAR

WHEN YOU LOOK AT war and what it entails you must question the morality thereof? No matter what conditioning process an individual may go through or what training a person may have to complete. The process of war itself is an incomplete/completed task, meaning with all of the training being given there is no fool proof soldier. There isn't a perfected book to prepare any man to take another man's life. Even with all the self-denial training the military soldier has to endure during his time of separation within himself. With him trying to become the new person they must become in order to survive in a war zone. The stress of just the training by itself will put the soldier in a state of mind of what the soldier is being trained to feel. The soldier is being put into a place of almost immortality. Soldiers are made to feel like they can go into a war zone and not be changed. Even though they are physically and emotionally touched they don't understand they are being affected just through the conditioning process but in their heart, they feel they are not venerable to anyone or anything. Keep in mind they are put into a place with a group of men with the same attitude they are trained to have, believing there is nothing that can stop them. Once the soldier is dropped into the war zone, he and everyone in that LZ (landing zone) becomes a group of individuals. Meaning they work as a group, but they still have to look out for number one and that is the nature of the beast (self-preservation). The mission these soldiers will be journeying together to compete is the same and they have eyes, ears and a dedication that is indescribable as far as their loyalty is concerned to one another. With the objective being to complete the mission at all cost. In one's instinct of survival, the goal is to complete the mission but given human sentiment of the soldiers it was also important for them to make it back home no matter what. There is true unity which also displays sincere cohesiveness training during the formative weeks of training in boot camp. It is not something that drops off when boot camp is completed; it stays with these men for life especially when they need one another the most in a war zone. They will carry that love and respect for one another for the rest of their life. If you allow me to explains the military life is not like graduating college, of pledging in a fraternity it's much deeper than that and the soldier's appreciation for each other is for life. Look at it this way, we trained together, we fought together, and we died together. We were all trained to look out for the weakest link, and no one does it better than through the training of the most elite of men and women today. That is, through the Department of Defense, the Armed Forces of the United States of America. The training is exclusive to all soldiers no one is better than the other. If he or she is the better soldier they better not brag and show off it is the nature of a unit to watch out for the weak link, no one wants to embarrass the other. Soldiers are trained in a sense of brotherhood and sisterhood, if they cooperate with the training everyone will make it through. Although I must say that is not true in every case. There are many who fall by the wayside not everyone is qualified to be a part of the elite force of men and women, so they give up, but the military does not give up on them. The slogan, "The few the proud the brave the Marine" means exactly that not everyone is qualified to say, "I am a Marine." Or even more so qualified to be an Infantry Officer, that's another branch of the military those who know about the training do not want to mess with. It's six months of growling pain. I am proud to say I was blessed by God to be able to survive the Marine Corps and Army Infantry Officer School not bragging but the experience is noted. I once was asked what branch is the hardest, I love them both and I will not make a choice on either. When I went through the Marine Corps, I was younger and had all of the energy in the world. Fired up to go through the training necessary to meet the goals I wanted to reach as a Marine. I have no regrets. When I graduated from the Infantry Officer Basic Course, I was wiser and more conditioned. Since I respect both branches, I will not say which was harder although IOBC was six months of beating the bush and no joke in relations to an individual's stamina. Just remember once a Marine always a Marine. But my officers braid cuts even deeper. So, who is the best, the Officer Corps or enlisted? Marine Corps or Army that's a privileged question and I retain the right to not answer it. Both training facilities were difficult given the time they had taken place in my life. My training began as a young man at MCRD San Diego, California this is where I trained as a young enlisted soldier to become a Marine. It was difficult because this was my first time being away from home and was restricted from leaving until I graduated bootcamp or was either sent home with a stamp on my record saying I was not qualified to be a Marine. I later wanted to be an officer. Yes, I must say the military was in my blood and I was enjoying finding out who I was as a man. The military instilled in me even higher morals and integrity, giving me a sense of not only belonging to the greatest nation on the face of this earth but also the privilege to defend it. After graduating from ROTC I attended Fort Benning, Georgia as a young Second Lieutenant to complete the Infantry Officers Basic Course which was challenging. The training was very demanding because there were many obligations set before myself and my comrades. The training was mandatory and had to be completed. IOBC was six long months of pressured training. I will not go into the training itself, but it was either pass your requirements or be sent home. And yes, the military does uphold that obligation. Only I and maybe a few others alive today have went through both branches of service, meaning from enlisted to officer. Usually when a person completes one bootcamp especially Marine Corps bootcamp they have had enough. I couldn't tell you, which is harder if any, but you will never get a direct answer. In making that statement let me finish by saying my officers commission meant the world to me and I have no regrets in respect to my transfer of service. I did what I had to do to make my career work as a young man in the military.

Just remember the comradery shown during training in the military embellishes the title of family. Blood, sweat and tears is the military moto. Meaning we train until we can see the blood in our veins. We sweat every day on and off duty, there is no slacking, and every day is hard work to make ourselves better and better at what we were trained as soldiers in defense of this great nation to do. Last but not least the pain of getting up every day and giving our all to say you are a part of the team makes us who we are. Brothers and sisters of a different mother, different blood but the same beliefs. No matter how much pain a soldier is in he will show up for duty ready to give his all every day all day until the mission is complete this is the motto we live by, it's called no pain, no gain, feel it, do it and believe you did your best. We are only as strong as our weakest link.

If you want to look at it in a biblical since let's look at scripture Romans 15:1, "We then are strong ought to bear the infirmities of the weak, and not to please ourselves." Although America, the "Free World" for which it is known does not live by this scripture but appears to be more based on Charles Darwin theory "survival of the fittest" which better fits the civilian world. This type of thinking of survival of the fittest is not fitting to a soldier trying to find his way back into a society that has very little structure. Its sad that people on the civilian side of the spectrum can stand by and watch a person struggling or literally lose everything they have even their life and do nothing to prevent it. This is not the mindset of the armed forces military soldier we are trained to help a new recruit find his way. We have to make sure everything is filed for him or her and they are properly checked in. That is part of the cohesiveness needed to assure everyone's survival. Unlike Caine in the bible, "We are our brother's keeper." I am referencing scripture simply because I want to bring you to a place and time that relates back to the Vietnam Veterans and the reasoning behind the messages that was given to the American people prior to the Vietnam Veterans returning home. This explains the same feelings as demonstrated when family feels their loved ones have been threatened or wronged in some kind of way. Military soldiers are trained from day one to look out for the weakest link. Being mindful of weak soldiers is evidence of a strong group working together to complete the mission. This takes good military training and it is to be understood that if we all don't make it in together than no one will. This kind of comradery is not the attitude displayed in the part of American society outside of the military. This is why you will often hear a military soldier say when he checks out of the military he is going back to the "Civilian side of the fence." It's a different world with different viewpoints of how things are depicted in life.

CHAPTER III

A RECONDITIONING PROCESS

WHAT'S UNFORTUNATE IS THE soldier who served in the armed forces past and present, especially in the Vietnam War did not have a reconditioning process to help them to get acclimated back into society once the soldier decides he or she will not be reenlisting. I am fully aware of the ACAP Program and the process for checking out of the military but there is a training school to reprocess and evaluate the condition of the soldier once the soldier makes the decision to get out of the military. This reconditioning process to prepare the soldier for returning back to the civilian side of the fence, it's a program I feel the military is going to have to start looking at now. It is needed in order to save the soldiers who are transitioning back into society it will help to keep them out of the criminal justice system and out of the jails and prisons waiting with empty cells waiting for them. Without a formal out-processing transitioning program set up to help recondition their thinking soldiers will continue to be misunderstood in society which normally leads to incarceration. With the Veterans catching the butt end of everyone's problems for not being understood, because their conditioning is structured. So when they enter back into society they are usually ignored. Not realizing there are other problems that could possibly be attributed to their reasoning process and inability to reacclimate properly. What is so sad is that when I as an officer look at being reacclimated or transitioning back into society when I think about the Vietnam Veterans they never had a chance. We at least now have the Warrior Transition Units which helps a lot but there is even more needed in relations to today's soldiers.

Everyone I have spoken with concerning this book I am working on about the Vietnam Veterans say many things should have been done differently prior to them being released from active duty. And one of the main things the older veterans talk about is how the Vietnam Veterans should have been forgiven many years ago. Their much-needed apology has been dragged out way past the time frame of it being a slap on the wrist or someone put in prison for something they did not do. This is not the case for the Vietnam Veterans most of it was a buildup of unrealistic preconceived propaganda American citizens were fed through the media and some citizens discontentment with having to work side by side with so-called murderers. On the other flipside of the soldier transitioning, the American public were just not prepared for their return home. People on death row have been pardoned and given another trial for a crime they may or may not have committed. For some reason the Vietnam Veterans remain hostage to the Constitution they fought to defend. No one wants to take a little time to look at the bigger picture in relations to what the soldier's needs are then bring into consideration what they had to go through and what they were up against in the jungles of Vietnam. If you ever have the opportunity, take a minute out of your busy schedule and watch a movie called the "Tunnel Rats." I am certain I will mention the movie again later in the book. In case you decided to go rent it I am 100% certain it will help you understand what these young eighteen-year-old boys in Vietnam who were trying to be men and fight in a war of which they had no idea what they were up against. Keep in mind you were only told part of the story you were not told what took place with the American soldiers. You were just told all of the disgusting things they were said to have done only referencing what you were told by the government, the media and some of the things the Vietnam Veterans conveyed openly to the public during the war and after their return. This country owes them so much, therefore I am trying to help you to understand how writing this book is to inform you of how you have continued to let these soldiers suffer and their suffering is truly unjustified. I am prayerful there will be more books after this one to show what has been done to the minds of these men who served you. Have you ever been rejected? And if you have been rejected as the Vietnam Veterans were then you already know there is an emptiness that remains void inside of the soldier sometimes for life. I am certain that you did not know the Vietnam Veterans were not given a break during the war. By given a break I am saying to you they did not have the opportunity to go home on leave the war zone once they were dropped off. These eighteen-year-old boys were left to fin for themselves until their tour was up. There was one body after another being sent to Vietnam to relieve the soldiers who were going home and also those who died on the battlefield. It is very hard for anyone especially an eighteen-year-old boy who has been told since he graduated bootcamp that he is now a man. It is hard for him to perceive living in fear and being placed in the hottest war zone in the history of any war the United States has been involved in without a break from the madness for an entire six months to a year. Do you think that would change you and your concept of life? Then to be released from active duty coming home without any medical treatment or any help finding jobs or dealing with the issues which today would be considered to be combat related injuries. Our American soldiers our Vietnam Veterans were never diagnosed for the mental illnesses they acquired, traumatic brain injuries acquired, nightmares they were suffering from etc. There is so much I am putting before you but there is no finger pointing in this book remember. It is about accepting guilt although no fault has been established so we can come to a mutual agreement on how to correct the problems the veterans are suffering from since the Vietnam War. I just want everyone to realize a lot of misrepresentation took place mainly against our soldiers in Vietnam. What occurred in Vietnam was the abuse of our military soldiers. What's so wrong about it is that it continues to go unaddressed as if there hasn't been any wrong done to our veterans at all. What happened to our America soldiers in Vietnam? During the Vietnam War the entire situation must be looked at on a different level a different format. What happened to these young eighteen-year-old boys (men if you will have it) is kind of like creating a template with only enough supplies to go around once. You know the old saying before you cut you measure twice. This did not happen with the Vietnam soldiers they were the templates of the Vietnam War. Not artificial fake men but real live bodies with life still in them. A young mind that hadn't any experience in war and was not prepared. Young boys who had not seen chaos or a war or war zone as tragic as this but had to grasp an understanding quickly that it was their position to kill or be killed. Young boys put in a jungle and left like wild animals having no choice other than to kill in order to survive. Unless you have been to war please understand there is no satisfaction in having to kill anyone. The Vietnam Veterans were not diagnosed properly prior to returning home. One of the questions we are seeking an answer to today is were the Vietnam Veterans ever diagnosed as being stable and able to function in society? Were they given a complete medical exam, psychiatric exam where they could be treated before they were released? Did they have any trauma or was there any mental illness involved? These are all of the things that were missed in relations to the Vietnam Veterans. I hope this is helping you to understand where we are as a country when we cannot admit there are a lot of things that should have been done differently when it came to the care and concern of our own American soldiers. The actual Vietnam War was over by 1974. But the war on the Vietnam Veterans continues to this day due to a lack of understanding on the part of American citizens protesting in a negative way against the Vietnam Veterans when they returned home from Vietnam. What fault can you find in these young boys made into what is supposed to be soldiers in two weeks? Young boys trained for two weeks and dropped into a hot LZ and made to kill in order to survive? The Vietnam Veterans received more negative press than any war in the history of this country.

One of the biggest problems the United States government had failed on is they did not find a way to treat the Vietnam Veterans for their Post-Traumatic Stress Disorder or mental illness before they were released back into society. Once again, I will go back to the making of (template) metaphorically speaking about the soldier being created, made into the killing machine he had to become. You will find sometimes you have to do things over again in order to get them to function the way you would like for them to function. When we look back at war itself the situation concerning the soldier was time. Times is what created his short boot camp training. They needed bodies in Vietnam to replace bodies unfortunately this was a situation that was never going to be right no matter how many young boys were sent. The Vietnam War is not something we can redo and if we could I do not think we would do it again due to over 58,220 lives lost, someone's son in Vietnam gave his life for a greater cause. So, what template do we use to fix the problem? There is none that I know of but there are doctors, medical teams, therapist, psychiatrist and medicine to help with the needs of the soldiers. When I talk about the Vietnam Veterans being released back into society without the proper help, they needed our government to step in and this statement is more than transparent. The evidence speaks for itself considering the help they needed and did not know what to ask for. The return home from war for the Vietnam Veterans was an unprepared journey for everyone. The situation would in the future become more than disastrous especially when you include "Agent Orange." Our government did not know what to expect and neither did the Vietnam Veterans. The one thing we all can agree on is that war changes things. The Vietnam War humbled this nation in a sense of not being able to understand the lives that were being wasted and the value of someone's son's life. There is not enough money you can give the family who lost their son to war to replace him. And there is no template to measure hurt, pain, most of all love. How do you say, "oh well" the value of your hurt is only worth fifty thousand and thank you for your son's service? Our government was not prepared to suffer the consequences of a war they did not have a grasp on the loss of life that occurred it was too great and the damage that continues to spew out is crystal clear. No one was wanting to admit fault and negated the fact that several problems had already presented itself to the United States government. But where was the template that formatted every life we had in our hands? Where is the book we used before when we had such a vast number of young boys returning home in body bags, there was none? No script, no file, no video, no documents in Washington, DC to open up to read to find the mistakes being made and then say this is how we are going to handle this problem. This is how we are going to fix it. But to this day there is no global apology for the Vietnam Veterans how sad.

I do feel much of the embarrassment came from not understanding "Agent Orange" and all the future problems that would come with this horrific chemical herbicide. Our government did not know how to accept the fact they subconsciously made a mistake a big mistake. It was a wrong that was done but it was allowed to be swept under the rug and it stayed there for many years until the health problems of the Vietnam Veterans began to escalate. It only escalated the pain of the soldiers who were suffering because they were suffering and knew why. Only the government they served knew they were not forthcoming with the Vietnam Veterans and the information being withheld was intentional. Remember these are not templates but human lives we are talking about, American soldiers. Secrets kept in closed chambers and behind locked doors would only cost the government more time and more research to come up with uncertainties of what "Agent Orange" was actually doing to the Vietnam Veterans. Although the government was aware of having sprayed the chemical Agent Orange in the war zone and on its own American soldiers. What had not been said is that our government was never aware that TCDD a highly toxic (dioxin) was being used in the chemical "Agent Orange" which was different from the other five chemicals used, I will be talking about that later in the book. The scale was set to not receive the Vietnam Veteran back home as the hero's they were but tarnish them by calling them baby killers and murderers etc. I have to question the discouragement of the soldiers return home and say was all this to cover up the mistakes that were made concerning the use of the herbicide chemical "Agent Orange." Keep in mind these young boys trained to be men were trained in the United States of America. On their return home they were allowed to be called murderers and spit on. American citizens forgot they were our soldiers, young boys who had to cope with death, killing and learning survival skills in the jungles of Vietnam. These soldiers were taken to Vietnam to win a war, to defend the Constitution of the United States of America and to kill any and all Vietnamese that got in their way. Going into a war zone is not a meeting for a social event or a gathering of celebrities for the red carpet to be interviewed for the Oscars. It is a place and time where men and women today are trained to service their country even with the possibility of it costing them their life. The probability of a soldier today with all the modern technology involving training to come out of the military without any issues and be the same person he or she was prior to joining I would say the probability is zero. This book is going to be published in 2019. I must say the Vietnam Veterans that served in a war that began in 1963 did not stand a chance of avoiding both mental and physical traumatization. Not only to their physical appearance but many of them had internal injuries that were damaged beyond repair. I am not just talking about the damage Agent Orange caused of which I will discuss a little later in the book. But I also want to talk about the Vietnam Veteran physiological abilities to function within the norms of society would also become a big factor in their life. Just think of yourself being in a pitch-black forest with trees and bushes that moved. I wonder if you would be capable of functioning normally after experiencing all of that in a war zone when you returned home? This is why so many of those guys minds just completely left them and they could not let go and regain their sense of normalcy again. In the blackness of the night even at home they still see "Charlie." Their minds stayed in the game in the sticks of Vietnam where how to survive became real for them. Yet the help they need and the hero's welcome home they deserved was being overlooked because of what the media put out and what the public chose to believe. In the jungles of Vietnam, the soldier's body nor his mind really got a chance to rest the entire time they were honorably serving their tour of duty in the jungles, in the war zone, in Vietnam.

The Vietnam Veterans ability to adapt would later be challenged in his return home. He would now have to defuse himself, recondition his thinking of survival skills. What he had to become in order to survive in the jungles of Vietnam was not something society could use. The question everyone should have been asking is how do you get a young eighteen or nineteen-year-old boy to turn off the conditions under which he had to teach himself in the jungles on how to survive overnight? How long does something like that take to realize you do not have to sleep with your knife in one hand and your rifle in the other? It is human nature to survive under any given situation. So, these young boys eighteen, nineteen, twenty year olds, each one individually had to turn on a survival instinct within their self in order to assure them they would see their family again. While many of you sat at home and enjoyed watching your children grow up and spending time with your family. The Vietnam Veterans were laying in the sticks in the jungles of Vietnam. They had to walk through swamp water, many times they did not have food to eat so they ate whatever bug that was in front of them, it's called nourishment. They did not have the everyday necessities you take for granted at home. They did not have a change of clothing or underwear, no gas or electric stoves to heat their meals, no heater or air conditioner to comfort their never-ending days and nights while they tried to stay alive in the jungles of Vietnam. They spent their nights patrolling the jungles in order to survive. How do you evaluate your day at work? You see, you get the opportunity to go home and receive some relief from your day of stress and some free time for yourself to turn off all of the negative stuff that went wrong at work. You are able to bring some kind of peace into you mind after a hard day's work in the officer because the Vietnam Veterans were in the war zone fighting to maintain the peace in America. You have options to make; you can go to your bedroom and relax, go to your study if you have one or maybe you and your wife can just go walking or go out for ice cream that always works. Unfortunately, the soldier is not able to turn off the wars zone. He does not have those options. Although it would be nice, the American soldier does not have the luxury of turning off the war no soldier does. The unsung heroes, the Vietnam Veterans are so deserving of the hero's welcome they never received. These men did not have a wind down period where they could get away for a moment of peace. They could not afford to get comfortable. Their mind had to stay alert in order for them to stay alive. Their mind stayed on alert for any unexpected noise or movement in the bush. They were living on the edge the entire time they were in Vietnam. I can honestly say this to be true because the entire time I served in Afghanistan I stayed on edge as well. The funny thing about this and I am I am not overreaching when I say you never get a chance to relax. Your body never shuts down completely. It's not just outside the wire but the entire time you are in the war zone even in your own camp. And Vietnam was 100 times worse than Iraq, Afghanistan or any war Americans has ever been involved in. Your entire body, mind, soul stays on complete alert never really knowing when to shut down, every second of the day is vital when you are outside the wire. It is life threatening to stay alert because the second you relax too much it can most certainly be costly not only to yourself but also for those who are relying on the soldier to be on watch for their life as well. The American soldiers in Vietnam did not have the privilege of turning the station to another channel. I was a life or death situation consistently and like anyone else who wants to go home alive, you do what you have to do to make it happen. In a war zone we all breathed the same air as individuals, but we moved like one machine, one organism, one mass because we all had to think alike and everyone in the war zone at that time had to be one fused body of eyes and ears. No room for mistakes. In Afghanistan we had to train to find IED's and booby-traps, be made aware of areas where there could possibly be a potential missile attack on us. We had to pay close attention to possible suicide bombers cars that could be driven at us to intentionally explode on contact. I am still talking about the Vietnam War but I wanted you to have a taste of a little of my Afghanistan War experience so you could compare the two. And when your attempting to compare "Nam" with any war Americans have been in you will always hear someone bring up their horrifying experience in Vietnam, there really isn't a comparison. In Vietnam they had to be prepared for everything, including what was underground. This is where the Vietnamese were coming up from out of the ground and earned the name "Tunnel Rats." The Vietnam War was much different than any war our American soldiers have ever been involved in. Looking back at Afghanistan and its many intricate parts soldiers had to feel somewhat safe after their daily missions were over. **Let me deviate briefly from the Vietnam Veterans for another short true story. I think about the safety zone inside Kabul. There were check points set up of which soldiers and vehicles had to pass through in order to be allowed on the base. The first check point at Kabul, Afghanistan is where I met the real "Rambo." Yes, Rambo really does exist at least this one in Afghanistan does. I will be talking about the real Rambo in my next book. Very briefly, the Rambo in Afghanistan literally pulled a suicide bomber out of the car at the first checkpoint station. He (Rambo) saved a lot of soldier's lives that**

day. So, look forward to seeing pictures and hearing my interview with the real (Rambo).

Although there was never a time, we were without our weapons I mean literally unless we were taking a shower, we were armed at all times. It was important at all times for a soldier to be reminded he or she was in a real war and that anything could jump off at any time. The Vietnam Veterans did not have the luxury vehicle checks coming close to their camp site, or dogs to sniff out bombs in the area. They had to stay focused on staying alive, that was part of their daily mission. Yes, staying alive would be their daily mission from dusk to dawn, from the second they woke up from their dismal sleep. There wasn't any peace of mind to be found at any hour, minute or second of the day. No one could afford to slip up while in Vietnam. There was no room for mistakes and too little time to correct them. There was so much these young Vietnam Veterans had to be cognizant of when it came down to making it home alive. Believe when I tell you from my personal experience of being in a war zone the Vietnam Veterans remained on edge the second their boots touched the ground and they could not turn it off. You really don't want to turn it off. It was good to be on edge. Their nerves could not be defused what I mean by defused is they did not have the luxury of relaxing. It was critical for them to remain on edge the entire time they were in the war zone especially outside the wire. Even when the body was so called resting or I should say appeared to be sleep the soldiers mind was never turned off. I would say sleep but alert. I can remember explaining my feelings of the war when I returned home from Afghanistan to a friend of mine. This is how I explained the tension of going outside the safety wire, this is what really takes place. When we load up in the Humvee to set out for our daily mission the second that Humvee is outside the wire this is what takes place. First of all, your head and your eyes are continually in rotation of a 180-degree circular motion. You are constantly reporting to the others around you what you see while you are visually scanning the area for what would or would not appear to be safe or not safe. Keeping everyone informed is the name of the game because there are three other soldiers in the Humvee with you that must be kept informed. It's a feeling like walking through a dark alley not knowing if someone was going to jump out and scare you. It's hard to imagine a person's adrenalin staying at such a high peak level for an entire year. Well! Unbeknownst to many of you this form of rush of adrenalin for the Vietnam Veterans remained constant. I know it would be hard for you to imagine what living in fear of losing your life would be like. To have that kind of an adrenalin rush in your body is not something that would be considered to be normal given the conditions the Vietnam Veterans had to survive in. This is the kind of edge the soldiers in Vietnam stayed on and I am certain it was even worse than I have described it. I will say that during my tour in Afghanistan and during my preparation as a young Marine preparing to go to Beirut that maintaining that edginess is an edge you cannot turn off and you do not want to. Being on edge is what keeps you alive in a war zone. I can remember being the commander of the Humvee I was in and there was a young soldier sitting behind me to my left. When I turned around to do a safety check on everyone instead of the young soldier having his weapon pointing straight up and down. He had it in his lap loaded and pointing at my back. If that weapon would have accidentally went off and shot me in the back I more than likely would not be writing this book today. Just figure the average person who is scared gets an adrenalin rush for a few seconds. The soldiers who were in the war zone with me in Afghanistan had a chance to relax just a little when we were inside the wire of Kabul. But the Vietnam Veterans in the war zone did not get the opportunity to turn it off at all they knew "Charlie" was everywhere. In any given situation in a war zone you never know who is going to commit suicide or snap (go off the deep edge). While serving in Afghanistan I can remember an incident where one of the soldiers had some mental issues and was getting ready to walk outside of the wire without any protection other than his machine gun, but he was stopped before he was able to get to check point 3. He had his weapon loaded and was ready to go. The fortunate part about this incident is that once the soldier was stopped from going outside the wire, he did not lose it and began shooting at the soldiers who were trying to help him.

When war is in question and the United States of America needs bodies for war it's country first. The one thing that involves the normalcy of war is to keep in mind that just because the soldier has completed boot camp does not mean he is sound and stable. The soldier just like some people walking around in society who have completed college does not mean just because they have graduated, they have a sound mind with morals and standards on how they want to be respected in society. This is something that you must ingest please try to grasp and understand what I am about to say here. The war zone is a different kind of animal to face. And if you ever get the opportunity to ask a soldier what a war zone is like what you will find him telling you is there isn't any normalcy in war. Especially if you are a Christian you must realize war is just the opposite of what we are taught, do not kill. But what is also written in the bible is "there is a time to kill." Soldiers in a war zone see things differently and they have the ability to have what is considered to be not normal behavior at times. Can mental illness occur with a soldier during war? The answer to that question is yes. The meaning behind that behavior is due to an insurmountable amount of pressure inherent to the soldier at any given time. I can recall at least three suicides when I was in Afghanistan. I will not discuss the reasons why, but this is what war and leaving home sometimes will cause some soldiers to do. Although the break down may have occurred on the battlefield it did not present itself openly, it was not exposed so it could not be taken as an immediate problem. As a need for a mental illness diagnosis until the soldier returns home, sometimes the illness is caught on the other hand many times it is not. There are many reasons as to why the diagnosis of mental illness is missed. Sometimes the soldier does not want to admit to having difficulties adjusting to society. Other times the soldier just does not want to appear to be letting down fellow soldiers so they will not report changes in themselves they have become aware of. If there is an obvious detection of the soldier having some form of abnormal behavior will the soldier be evaluated carefully by a trained clinical physician or mental illness therapist? Not if the soldiers does not request it or states there is nothing wrong on the questionnaire they have to sign. The signed questionnaire with all of the (no blocks) checked releases the military of all its responsibilities to the soldier. As far as medical insurance is concerned once the soldier says there is nothing wrong with him the military has no further obligation to the soldier in respect to that particular health issue. The health report is an official document whereby the soldier cannot come back later and say his illness is related to something caused by the military. This is one of the reasons why during the time the soldier is processing out of the military and wanting to go home usually they will check no and will be released from active duty. This is how the soldier's illness goes undetected. I would suggest that a physiological evaluation be made mandatory for all soldiers returning home from war. Also, for every soldier who decides to get out of the military. With this document stating there is nothing wrong with the soldier on file it will make it very difficult for the soldier to receive any form of care from the military once they are released from active duty. The process of what the soldier will go through prior to their release from active duty is first the soldier will receive a check out sheet. This is a check list of things the soldier must complete in order to be released to go home. This list in order for the soldier to go home must receive checks in the (go) section of the list which means the soldier is ready to move on to the next level of requirements so the soldier can be released. There are many things the soldier will not report because the soldier is in fear of being held on base longer and will not be able to go home. The reporting of any illness of the soldier at this time jeopardizes the soldiers release so the answer to critical questions on the checkout list is usually "No." What the young soldier do not know is that because they answered "No" illnesses, no sickness and no change in his or her behavior that has been noted by the soldier. The soldier cannot come back to the military doctor's years later and say they now have mental problems and blame the military for it. What the young soldier is not aware of is the documents being signed are legal documents and the legal documents release the military of all liabilities. The soldier doesn't realize the importance of these documents he is signing And if they are signed off showing nothing is wrong with the soldier that document will later come back to haunt the soldier in a negative way. Simply because he doesn't realize he will probably need some assistance in the future and by signing the medical documents stating there isn't anything wrong with him, what he is doing is releasing the military of all liabilities and any future claims he may need to make concerning related military issues. Later in life the soldier may feel the military is responsible for their illness or health problems taking place in their life in reference to them not being able to cope with certain stressors in life. The soldier may need some psychological counseling, or therapy sessions and the military will not pay for them due to him signing "No" on the medical reports that he or she does not have any health or medical problems at the time of discharge. This is one of the biggest draw backs for the soldier which involves military documents that will be in the soldiers file for life involving his military release records. The military falls short concerning the soldier and his return back into society because many are released and do not know what they are signing. They are anxious to return home, so they end up going home back into the civilian sector of life without a thorough medical evaluation or medical insurance. The problem which remains persistent is the soldier is expected to function like a normal everyday person when they are released from military duty, but they are not. There are many issues concerning the soldier's life that needs to be looked at on an individual basis. When there are a bunch of soldiers waiting to be released to go home and are crammed into a room and told if they check yes to any question on the medical checkout list, they are more than likely going to be held over after everyone else is released to go home. It is unfortunate these are young soldiers who do not know any better and checking "NO" is going to hurt them in the near future. But for right now the soldier just wants to go home to his family. And if I can put it bluntly, he wants to get back home so he can make love to his wife or if he is not married his girlfriend. This is one of the biggest reasons every soldier is trying to get back home to hold his wife's soft body once again and make love until the break of dawn. There isn't anything like being gone for a while and returning home to make love to the woman you love. If you are staying focused to what I am saying right now remember the soldier just came home from a war and has not had physical contact with his wife or girlfriend for the past six months to a year. Of which clearly explains why there are so many ex-soldiers (veterans) convicted of crimes that could have possibly been prevented if they had been diagnosed properly. Their issues could have been medically treated prior to them being released from the military and also given a continuance program of care after returning home. If there was a mental issue there could have been medication issued to control the mental issue. If there had been a physical issue that would have been diagnosed prior to getting out of the military it would have been under control and not only would the military had known about the illness but the civilian hospitals would have also known about it after finding the soldier the proper doctor or a doctor of his choice. With this problem being exposed the solider would have more than likely been treated differently by officials and of course the courts would have been made aware of the soldier's illnesses and would have been able to be a little more lenient with the soldier. There is always a strong possibility that the medication the soldier was taking could have been in need of an adjustment or there could have been some form of behavioral program the soldier could have been placed in to be observed and then re-evaluated instead of being put in a prison. The soldier is actually being judged for a conduct the soldier was not in control of due to the mental issues the soldier was diagnosed with. The mental problem was not able to be controlled by the soldier due to the lack of proper diagnosis. Due to the damages the soldier has suffered the soldier has stepped in to defend your rights as American citizens. This is what American has done to the soldier who has allowed you the American citizen to reach your goals and grasp the American dream of, God, Family and Success. The soldiers who have fought in past wars, the Vietnam Veterans and soldiers of today who have fought in the Afghanistan and Iraq War has given every American citizen the opportunity to strive for, opportunity. To make their dreams a reality. While he or she volunteered to give their life for the betterment of the United States of America and protect the rights of its citizens. When you talk about loving God and being able to go to church on Sundays and worship and pray the way you chose to pray. There is a big difference than being born in a communist country where dictatorship prevails. A place where you cannot do as you desire to do, a place where even your education is selective by the government. You forgot the soldiers who gave their life in America to make all the freedoms possible for you. There is a big difference between what the soldier is able to do verses how you perceive family as a civilian when you are able to sit down and have dinner with family and celebrate your birthdays and holidays with your loved ones. There is a difference in the opportunities you have in reference to giving of yourself a ride to college verses a helicopter dropping you off in the hottest landing zone (LZ) the military has ever been in, the Vietnam War. Can you imagine what it sounds like when a civilian's son or daughter is leaving home in the morning to go off to school. "Hey mom and dad loves you; we will see you when schools is out." For a soldier who has graduated boot camp this is what he hears from his drill instructor, "Private your orders say you are going straight to Vietnam you are not going to a training school, you are going straight to "Nam" so get packed your bus leaves at 0400 in the morning, from there you will catch a flight to Vietnam with the rest of the soldiers. The next thing you will see will be a battlefield where you will have to fight every day you are there in defense of the Constitution you swore in your oath to defend." There is a big difference of how the perception of what those who had to go to the war zone in Nam verses those of you who missed the draft and was able to go to school to have a better life. It's unfortunate because the Vietnam Veterans are still suffering and there is not many left. What is even sadder is that I had to write a book about the Vietnam Veterans because you stopped taking the time to acknowledge what has been taking place with these veterans and Agent Orange. You have forgotten about the men who died on the battlefield so you could enjoy your life, the Vietnam Veterans.

CHAPTER IV

TURNING IT OFF

AFTER THEIR RETURN HOME the Vietnam Veterans discovered they could not just turn off the war. It was in their blood; it was in their mind and it could not just be turned off like someone who was switching on and off a water faucet. There were some mental issues that needed to be addressed before the soldiers returned home and they were not. Which put the Vietnam Veterans at a greater risk in a country that was not prepared to handle this kind of problem. There were many Vietnam Veterans who just could not turn it off. The ultimate question I must ask is, could you?

Can you turn it off? Do you think the young boys eighteen; nineteen years old who were told they were now men would be able to return home and snap back to society and just turn off everything they had been through, everything they had seen? Many of you think they should have been able to turn if off after they returned home. That being home again would be the medicine the cure they needed to snap back to who they use to be. Unfortunately, that person they use to be was now gone. It's should be an complete embarrassment to our government and the citizens of the United States because of how they have allowed our own soldiers, the Vietnam Veterans to suffer such a hardship. For the lack having a better understanding and knowing the Vietnam War was a war where many would say, a war without a cause. What our American soldiers had to watch concerning their follow soldiers being shot down like dogs and the bodies found were sometimes mutilated beyond recognition. The Vietnam War is still the most controversial war the United States of America has ever been in. The United States had never been in the jungles of Vietnam. It was a war where so many men had given their life on the battlefield. Americans did not know how to accept what they were hearing in reference to the American soldiers and how they were fighting in Vietnam. When you talk about turning it off there isn't any rationalization there for a soldier to stop remembering, seeing his best friend blow up, or his legs cut off or decapitated on the battlefield and expected to not do anything about it once he encountered the enemy. Where is the rationalization there? How were they supposed to turn it off? Was there a way to turn it off? When I say turn it off, I am talking about the dreams the nightmares. The anguish, the hurt, the pain of having to leave a friend, a comrade on the battlefield. Having a continual adrenalin rush not for killing but being able to stay alive and remembering you had to stay alive to make it home again? How do you turn it off when there is no de-conditioning process set up? Since there was nothing to reference in relations to the Vietnam War. Everything appeared to be on a trial bases, you know, "let's see if this will work." The trial basis is one of the reasons why there was six different chemical herbicide "Agents" used and why so many soldiers were coming home in body bags. It was all new to the political figures in Washington, DC and the American people. The Vietnam War being the worst war the United States had ever encountered as a nation? If you look at the actions of the soldiers you can look at it in a way of being given a conditioned stimulus and the stimulus they were given was kill or be killed. That is not much of a choice to see if one is able to be conditioned to survive that is an automatic human instinct. Ivan Pavlov one of the great physiologists which many of us studied during our time in college used dogs as a stimulus to a condition the dogs were to respond, and the condition was for food. Our American soldiers were given a stimulus to survive. Congress and the American citizens, the taxpayers gave them the necessary equipment to survive and it was the tax payers who paid for the weapons and ammo that was placed in the soldiers hands. To go on the battlefield and do their jobs to do what soldiers do in a war. To go in and take what Congress and the American taxpayers paid them to do. Maybe I should be saying the United States of America paid them to do, because the Vietnam Veterans were there defending the President of the United States and all entitled to be a part of the United States of America. It is unfortunate in war there are things so-called civilized people who never served one day in the military let alone a war zone do not want to hear about and that is what took place during war time. Once again, I have to present this question to you, "what would you have done" if you were the one trying to survive in the jungles of Vietnam? It's like putting yourself in a life-threatening situation where you had to save your son or daughter and you had one of your children in each hand and you could only save one. You had to let one go to grab the other child with both hands, but you could only save one, "what would you do?" During the Vietnam war the soldiers had two choices life or death. If you chose to live you had to become part of the jungle you were learning to survive in, the animal instinct. These young boys (men) went to war due to the signing of Congress to go to war the American taxpayers' dollars that endorsed it. And these young boys who you sent to war had to find a way to survive so they had to become like the animal they were hunting in the jungles of Vietnam. They had to learn fast. These soldiers stayed on edge the entire time they were in "Nam". Do you think it's normal to have a continual shock of adrenalin to your system consistently for an entire year? Do you think that kind of intensity that constant adrenalin rush is something the human body was designed to put out continuously? Speaking from my personal experience after returning home my normal functioning capabilities were not up to being able to cope with many things as far as being able to deal with everyday life. But I understood myself; I knew myself and other things I had already accomplished that's what kept me going. I had to do an overview of myself to find out my levels of coping. My personal experience after returning back to the states would be to deal with my lack of vitamin B12, my eye sensitivity, and the internal pain my body had been through for so many years. The vitamin B12 was a part of my not getting enough vitamins while in the war zone of Afghanistan. According to the doctor when I returned home, I was almost depleted of many vitamins but my B12 was his biggest concern. I was told my B12 was so low that I should have not been able even hold a decent conversation of disagreement because my nerves were on edge. I immediately began to receive B12 injection. Due to my B12 being so low my doctor told me I did not have to worry they caught the deficiency in time. But anyone who suffered the same lost that had not been checked through blood work would have been like touching a positive and negative wire together, yes I would have been, one big explosion. I later found out what B12 does, it helps to build up the human body ability to think issues out logically, it also helps to energize the body in many areas. I was grateful it was caught in time. This was a small part of my personal issues, but I made it back home from the Afghanistan War, visually and physically whole. If you compare the difference in years and changes in modern technology. The Vietnam Veterans did not have the special treatment many of us received on our return home from war. The medical training was not as accurate and the facility availability the Warrior Transition Units, WTU to hold the soldiers over was just not there. So, when you look at today's veterans returning home from the war zone the situation concerning the time in the actual war zone is not the same. This is why the Vietnam

Veterans deserve the right to receive a formal "Hero's Welcome Home." The Vietnam Veterans truly need a "We Are the World" announcement timed by all the radios in the United States at the same time. That would be one of the biggest gifts you could give the Vietnam Veterans, have every radio play "Taps" as a tribute to the Vietnam Veterans that died, the POW's who are still alive, the MIA's that are still alive and last but not least every Vietnam Veteran who made it back home and felt the bitter hatred of rejection. This can happen and it can be timed to happen the same way we all joined in to sing "We Are the World." I am asking you to please make this happen for the Vietnam Veterans. And due to the suffering of our soldiers there should also be a **Vietnam Day** to help to celebrate the United States forgiveness to the Vietnam Veterans and to show a force of unity within this great nation. I don't know if it will ever happen, but I do know there is a God. Just think the Vietnam Veterans had it much worse than any of us who served during our war time. Not counting the swamps, they had to travel through with no change of clothing or dry boots and socks, the bugs and spiders and other insects they had to eat for nourishment. There is so much that has not been considered concerning the conditions the Vietnam Veterans had to live under. I would have to say their situation would be considered to be indescribable. There wasn't any bacon and eggs and orange juice at their breakfast table. If they were looking at anything they were probably looking at their friend lying in the trenches next to them dead, or either bleeding to death. Given these abnormal circumstances my question must raise its logical face once more so I will ask the question, "What would you do?" What is your normal everyday life like? I guarantee those of you who did not go off to war can tell me about all the pleasant things that took place in your life. Like making love to your wife, putting your children to bed at night or even being able to make it to a Chicago Cubs baseball game, Chicago Bears football game or a Chicago Bulls basketball game and if you life hockey the Chicago Black Hawks hockey game. The Vietnam Veterans did not have these luxuries, death was at their breakfast foxhole because there wasn't any breakfast table, to eat from. What was considered to be a normal day with family and friends would be no more. And what was left of their innocence was taken away on the battlefield as they watched the blood and guts of their comrades splattered all over the place on the battlefield in the jungles of Vietnam.

There was nothing left to hold onto other than "**They had a job to do and they did their job to the best of their ability simply because they**

wanted to make it back home. But they would not come back as whole men they came back as men who only appeared to be whole and in the appearance of still being a man." These soldiers would in their return back to America would have appeared to be bigger than life, bigger than any movie star actor or actress. Because of what they had survived but their glory was taken from them. Due to a lack of knowledge of the American people not understanding war. The Vietnam Veterans should have been received properly they were already larger than life and more of a man than any man who had not put on the uniform in defense of the United States of America at this point. They were real men of valor and they deserved the title as well as the recognition. They were the men and women who were able to fight to the bitter end until the bugle was blown to cease fire and return home. Even those who were able to return home in one piece did not realize although they made it back their life would never be the same again. The normalcy of life the Vietnam Veterans once enjoyed was now lost from the very grasps that had driven them to want to return home in one piece. The soldiers would not be able to regain that kind of peace ever again. You know the innocence of doing the simple things in life, like hanging out with family, walking with your children in the park and holding hands with his wife or the woman that he loves, going shopping or just hanging out with old friends. The American people were just not prepared or educated enough to be able to understand the Vietnam Veterans mind set. In his eyes he is trying to visualize the joy everyone around him is having but in his mind, he is still looking at the battlefield of being in "Nam." His PTSD is something that is internal you cannot see what is on the soldier's mind but he can be brought back to reality just by talking to him for a while to calm him down. His thinking is different, and it shocks the mind of what the Vietnam Veterans visually sees in his mind due to the fact that he saw so much death on the battlefield, so much blood, suffering and his brothers he went to war with crying out for help. So he is looking at what is taking place around him from a totally different perspective. Sometimes it is through guilt and how he is trying to cope with the fact that out of all of the blood and guts he saw spilled on the battlefield he was able to make it back home. I can remember my return home from Afghanistan and trying to deal with the dead bodies I had seen in Kabul as well as standing on the battle ground where six Italian soldiers were killed from a missile attack. They were killed in the same spot I was standing on three days prior to our humanitarian drop on the same site to help the

Afghans who were in need of food and clothing. The soldiers mind drifts back into the war zone from time to time it's sad to say some never regain their normalcy back without the aid of medication and talking it through with their wonderful wives who decide to stay with them out of love. Knowing the same young man that left is not the same one who use to laugh and find new things to do all the time many of the Vietnam Veterans were never diagnosed for a mental illness. When I made it back to the states as much as I loved celebrating Christmas, I would not celebrate Christmas my first three years back in the states. This was my sacrifice, I did it in honor of the thirty-seven soldiers who did not make it back from Afghanistan alive when I served. These were young men who would never see their families again, but they did it all for you America. I am asking that you please give them some peace and appreciate the sacrifice of them giving their life for this country. I knew it was out of respect, but I thought it was just a little trivial with people walking up to me saying thank you for your service and they did not have a clue of what war was like. I had to ask myself what are they thanking me for they were clueless of what I found out about the war zone and the things I had to do to survive in it. They hadn't any idea of what it was like to miss your loved ones during the holidays, to miss your wife and children, to miss the simple things in life like getting up to have breakfast or how about missing your favorite uncle's funeral. This not only happened to me but many other soldiers who loved ones passed and they could not make it back to the states for the funeral. Most of the time there is no one with us when we return home to go out to the cemetery to say our special goodbyes to those who passed while we were in the war zone. Yes, well I was in a war zone and I am certain the military did their part on getting the emergency telegram to me unfortunately I arrived home a day late when I arrived home my uncle James was already buried. That is another emotional pain indescribable a hurt and emptiness that never leaves. What society seems to forget is that we are still human beings with feelings. When you think about just going to breakfast or having breakfast in bed, those are fun moments everyone enjoys eating a good breakfast. But the Vietnam Veterans have two sets of thinking about fun times and how they would like to reflect on what breakfast is for them now verses out in the jungle of "NAM." The first is with his family and friends and how it use to be. The second is when his mind begins to reflect back to when he was on patrol in the midst of the jungle and breakfast was whatever insect he could catch for some form of nourishment. A spider, a bug, a snake from what I remembered one of the Veterans was telling me they would pull the legs off the spiders kill them and eat them. Sounds discussing doesn't it but once again I present the question of "what would you do?" Survival is something else when it comes to saving your life in your hands. Yes! The reality check was real they were not back in the states at McDonalds or Burger King having it their way. They were in the jungles of Vietnam and as far as nourishment was concerned, they could not make fires to cook their food. It was eaten raw, let's just say out of a sense of humor they created their own delicacies. Have you ever asked yourself what goes through the mind of a soldier returning home from war? It has to be something that has remained in question for many years and the relevance the Vietnam Veterans sought to be accepted back into a society that rejected them because of the job they had to do as soldiers. This was not acceptable in a society that now began to frown on the number of body bags that were coming home filled with their loved ones both young and old soldiers. Now Americans could no longer find a place of acceptance in a society that did not want their hands dirtied with what was being rumored about the Vietnam Veterans. But keep in mind this is the same society of people whose tax dollars sent them to war. These young boys (men) joined for a reason and that was to protect the Constitution of the United States of America and that's what they did. Young boys eighteen, and nineteen years of age trained to be men in two weeks of training, are you kidding me? It does not make sense. Take a good look at your eighteen or nineteen-year-old son and if you can honestly tell me he is a man ready to go to war to kill another man than there is something wrong with you. But because the young soldiers completed two weeks of military conditioning some complete their full training they were made to feel like men and ready for combat. These young boys were taken to the hottest war zone this country has ever been in and were led to believe they had the skills and mental capability to survive with just two weeks of boot camp training and that was all it took. I must grant the fact that they were proud to be young soldiers and they graduated bootcamp, but they needed much more training then what they had. These young men went in believing in you America. Believing they were doing something great for the United States of America because they were told our country was being threatened. It may be reaching a bit far to say even with all of the mistreatment the Vietnam Veterans have taken for over forty years these soldiers who took the oath and swore to defend this country even with their life would more than likely do it all over again. I find this statement to be factual because I actually spoke with one of the Vietnam Veterans. He told me one of the questions soldiers often bring up is, if they had to do it all over again would they, his response was yes. He informed me that every Vietnam Veteran he had spoken to would not have a problem with doing it all over again. They were led to believe something that was not true, and many paid the price with their life. Other Vietnam Veterans returned home to walk around in disbelief because they were having to endure the bitterness of being rejected by the American people and the United States government the same ones who sent them to war. They went in as good men, good soldiers, doing what they were trained to do.

CHAPTER V

FAMILIAR WITH THE COMBAT ZONE

LET ME HELP YOU familiarize yourself with the Combat Zone. I want you to stay focused because you will not and should not put the book down until you have found out what a war zone incorporates. I mentioned earlier about being on edge and having the ability to push yourself beyond your limits of exhaustion. This is what every soldier does in a war zone. He pushes himself or herself beyond their normal mental capacity of what they can endure. I know it is not normal, but this is consistent with their bootcamp training. So, what would seem abnormal to you was actually instilled in them as young recruits. Officers of course are trained at a higher level of mental testing and training. Some will call it going above and beyond the call of duty. You will only find out the truth from reading this book that the Vietnam Veterans character of what they were trying to do went beyond the measure of loyalty, trust and honor. It even went beyond the actual obligation taken to defend the United States of America against all enemies both foreign and domestic. Being on edge for the Vietnam Veterans is putting it lightly because they were never able to turn off the adrenalin rush. They stayed wired up the entire time they were on tour. And of course, there were the speakers from the Vietnamese constantly telling the Vietnam soldiers how they had been deserted by their countrymen and how he should join the Vietnamese. I must say some of this is easy to talk about because while being stationed at Kabul, Afghanistan I along with every soldier in camp experienced the same brain washing attempts by the enemy. The speakers continuously telling us our American government had betrayed us, how we were forgotten, and this is why we should join them. This went on continuously unfortunately for the Vietnam Veterans it was not just a mental exhaustion but a physical exhaustion they suffered as well. For the Vietnam Veterans many missed issues concerning their health and mental alertness went undetected and they were released from duty after their tour and went home with not just mental issues but also a nutrition deficiency. With the depletion of nutrients in their bodies there would be circumstances behind their lack of vitamins in their bodies, but studies had not been researched as they are today. To not only detect a vitamin deficiency but to also be able to tell what problems this lack of nutrients would cause in the body if the vitamins in the body were not replaced. There would be complications that would definitely take them out of character, and they would not know why. Taking them out of character is what lead many of them to a strange behavior and caused them to respond to things out of character. Sometimes leading to violent behavior or even attempts of suicide. There were also those who ended up in jail or even prison for certain outburst of violence. No one really took the time to understand the Vietnam Veterans. Congress and the American citizens thought their behavior was affected because of the Vietnam War. That was part of it but much of it was due to the lack of medical and physiological assistance needed. This war was bigger than what the nation expected and neither the government nor the military prepared itself for what was coming due to Agent Orange. With Vietnam being the worst of all wars there was not really a war that could set precedent over the many afflictions the Vietnam Veterans suffered from due to the multiple herbicides used. The Vietnam Veterans outbreaks were outrageous, and the American people just did not know how to handle them. They did not know what triggered their rage, their anger, their sense of withdrawal from a society they no longer felt a part of. How do you fault soldiers who just did not know? How do you fault our government our country that in all actuality went into a war without preparation of thought of what to do once the war ended? The Vietnam War was going to end one day, and it did. Now it's, Oh boy! the war has ended and what are we going to do with all of the soldiers who are going to be returning home? What is the plan to aid and assist them with the things we currently now know but they did not have or do for the Vietnam Veterans when they came home? The soldiers would be suffering but there was no plan prepared for the treatment they needed, and no buildings set up to house all the soldiers who needed immediate treatment? We are talking about soldiers who also came home strung out on drugs they used while they were on the battlefield. I won't go to far into the drug problem because I know that is an entirely different book I would have to write. There are several illnesses I can relate to but their bodies had depleted necessary vitamins to help them function that were not replenished. Vietnam Veterans were released and sent home. I really hate to say it this way but many of them returned home like ticking time bombs waiting to explode. Their resistance was low and along with the drugs and mental illness that had not been treated the Vietnam Veterans were left to find their own way. They were not as Informed as soldiers are today on how to seek the help they might need and even today the assistance needed for soldiers can be more forthcoming. It's tragic and undisclosed as to what each soldier returning home was going through many of them would end up in the prison system, devoiced from their wife, homeless and hungry or in a facility for the mentally ill. The suicide rate for the Vietnam Veterans was also high. The Vietnam War was the worst blood bath in the history of the United States. Because of the mental pain of trying to recall all that took place it is obvious the Vietnam Veterans harbor a lot of personal pain. The Vietnam Veterans still carry those memories and wounds today and many refuse to talk about what they went through or what they had to do to make it home alive. There is not an apology big enough that this country could give these men and women who gave their life for the love of this great nation. They are waiting America, yes, they are waiting on an apology and their proper place in the history books as heroes in America. They do not want to be noted as baby killers, murderers, or rapist or having the blame of shame placed on them for their involvement in the Vietnam War. Remember we are talking about the worst blood bath American soldiers have ever been in and their place in the history of the United States, the Vietnam War. A war that was beyond any award or citation that could be given to these soldiers who returned home. Those who died on the battlefield, Missing in Action or could very possibly today in 2019 going into 2020 still be Prisoners of War in some concentration camp. The Vietnam War was just not any war, it was even beyond the conference call of the United Nations above the ranks of any general, even the Chief of Staff. What these brave men did for this country surpasses any meeting table and beyond any apology that could be given but an apology is needed. These brave men were just tossed in a war as numbers to be filled. Their bodies where retuning home in body bags as fast as they landed in the jungles of "Nam."

With the Vietnam Veterans returning home and for a lack of better words and being thrown back into a society that was not ready to receive them was very damaging to the civilian streets they roamed in and to the Vietnam Veterans now homeless nature. A society that did not know what to do with the veterans or how to assist them in their search of being able to find who they are again. That's on the short end of it the other part of it was the disassociation with everyday people and how it was difficult for them to cope with everyday life without some form of support from their wife, family or friends. In life we sometimes say it is good to suffer a little humiliation because it teaches the individual how to endure pain and overcome. Only in such a situation concerning the Vietnam War and the Vietnam Veterans who fought in it humiliation is something that remains continual since their return. It is unfortunate as you can see throughout the book I will continue to use the word (unfortunate) that our government and the citizens of American appear to be subliminally in another world. Or either walking in a place of denial concerning the apology the United States is going to one day have to give to the Vietnam Veterans for what not only "Agent Orange" did to them but for what they have allowed the system to do to them. These men who returned home should have been better taken care of. And they should have been given a better life and hand then what they have been dealt in America. How do you give these men back their dignity, their respect, their honor and their life which is what they gave in sacrifice for the love of the United States of America? This is not counting how they have suffered and how they are still suffering today if not only for the lack of the word respect. How about just first starting off with what is long, long overdue and that is a well-deserved apology for the Vietnam Veterans? No one is above the law and it would not take much more than what I had (ASKED) for earlier. To have all the radio stations play taps all at the same time across the nation. An apology on national television from all living Presidents to show respect for John F. Kennedy, Lyndon B. Johnson even Richard Nixon who gave the order to stop dropping the chemical herbicides. What this tells our Vietnam Veterans and soldiers today is our past Presidents had nothing to do with what the chemicals companies who knowingly added the TCDD (dioxin) which was highly toxic in their creation of "Agent Orange." Our government had nothing to do with the creation of Agent Orange. While you are reading this book based on facts of experience please try to take some time out of your busy schedule and think on how you would have wanted to be treated once you returned home from the Vietnam War. Even though we look at things in the present tense I am asking you to give some consideration at this point and let's reverse the scenario of the war for a brief second. Let's look at it this way for a brief second and say the war was on American soil and the Vietnamese were fighting in the United States. Given what they had done to our American soldiers just what do you think they would have done to our American women? I know this is a hypothetical analogy but if you will allow me to expand your thinking on the normalcy of war. This is already a given concerning the Vietnamese women of which during the seventies were treaty less than fourth class citizens. As I look at this with as much logic as I possibly can what chance or opportunity do you think the American women would have had once their homes were invaded? What do you think the Vietnamese would have done to our American wives, mothers and daughters? Are you naïve enough to think they would have just let them go? This is just a little food for thought. Now that I said that please let me take the followers of Christ and believers in God to the word of God. Please read and evaluate the scriptures I am about to give you with an open heart and understanding that even the most prudent of believers can see the thorough and swift judgement of God.

Exodus 32:26-28 King James Version (KJV)
[26] Then Moses stood in the gate of the camp, and said, who is on the Lord's side? Let him come unto me. And all the sons of Levi gathered themselves together unto him.

[27] And he said unto them, Thus saith the Lord God of Israel, Put every man his sword by his side, and go in and out from gate to gate throughout the camp, and slay every man his brother, and every man his companion, and every man his neighbor.

[28] And the children of Levi did according to the word of Moses: and there fell of the people that day about three thousand men."

This is the word of God this was one of many slayings taking place on Gods command. Please don't become pious and say well it was God who was ordering the slayings of men, women and children. So, it's okay for Joshua and his armies to go out and murder people to start the takeover of the land promised to the Israelites. Even then God made specific orders to not take the spoils of the land during some of the raids. And to take the spoils of the lands during other raids. In some cases, the order was given to kill all the seed, which includes all men, all women, all children and all animals. Once again, I am asking you to look at this openly do you think the Vietnamese would have treated our American women or soldiers any differently than the American soldiers treated them? You can't answer that one right, yes, I know hypothetical situations can sometimes be a big brain buster when you stop for a while and think back. I am not saying our

American soldiers did anything wrong I am just asking you to think about the war if the situation was reversed and the Vietnamese had invaded the United States of America. That of course is a matter that would never be resolved but it is something you can most certainly ponder on and still not weigh any credence of a vote of pro or con. Food for thought is good and helps the digestive system to disperse what it needs to get out whether in discussions or actions. Those of us who have been in war we know what war is like. But for the young boys who went to Vietnam that was an entirely different animal their eyes were being awaken to a new birth.

I often wondered as a little child how the soldiers were going to survive in a country that looked down on them? Everyone keeps talking about the insanity the Vietnam Veterans displayed once they returned home. Well if you did not get the memo this is when the "Liberty Bell" should have been ranging. And just maybe Lady Liberty herself could have come off its base and said take a good look at these men who have fought for your freedoms. With all of the humility and death they have witnessed and what they have been through you civilians have not lost anything, where is your compassion? You have not been in a war; you were only listeners of what had taken place from a distance. How can you stand in judgment and say to yourself what a horrific scene these military soldiers are coming home with Vietnamese body parts as souvenirs? Oh, excuse me if I stand to be corrected but how many of your friends were found in Vietnam with their ears cut off, their heads cut off, fingers cut off or maybe even their private parts cut off? Yes! It all sounds detestable, but you did not have to live that life in the sticks or play in the devil's playground. That's a question, you can go ahead and answer it now, "what would you have done." I can remember the one picture I saw as a child with a Vietnam Veteran returning home with Vietnamese ears hanging on his dog tags. At what point America did you say these are our soldiers who went to war for us. But on the other end of it you forgot to remember they were young eighteen and nineteen-year-old boys you sent into combat and they did the best they could. They may have been in a war, but they were still developing into men. Going to war does not make you a man it makes you understand the value and the importance of life. Did you ever say, Wow! Thank God our soldiers made it back home safely and recognize the issues you were seeing. And acknowledge the fact that their behavior was not normal and realize the Vietnam Veterans were going to need some special assistance like medical and psychiatric counseling? After all these are the same young boys you threw into the jungles of Vietnam. You expected them to fight your battle like men so you could go to college, stay home, work your 9 to 5 job and come home to your family. What about your sons who later became police officers, firemen, doctors and lawyers etc.? I am quite sure you are proud of them, but they were able to do it off the backs of the Vietnam Veterans and those who served in the wars before "Nam." It's sad that you cannot have enough forgiveness in your heart for young boys who were eighteen and nineteen years old that did a job to the best of their ability given the fact many of them only had two weeks of training and off to war. I do not know if you know this or not but that minimal level of training is unheard of in reference to a soldier being given adequate training for a war zone. There is so much refresher training needed after graduation it takes many more months of training. And then there are those who are given refresher training in their specialty fields. This is a fact because this is what we go through prior to being sent to the war zone, refresher training. From learning all over again how to set claymores, throwing live hand grenades, how to properly search for IED's, how to spot an IED, how to zero a weapon, how to inject yourself in case of chemical poisoning, how to set a bomb, the list goes on. But the Vietnam Veterans went straight from bootcamp to the war zone. It was impossible for this extra training to take place given the fact they were shipped out in two weeks. Of which would not even be considered today in sending a soldier into a war zone. What the Vietnam War was for America without anyone realizing what was taking place with our young soldiers was nothing more than trial and error we did not know what was or was not going to work. It is sad to see how things actually turned out, but we had to come up with a "show of force" no matter what the cost. The unfortunate part of it is the chess pieces happened to be the real sons and daughters of American citizens of which over forty thousand would never be seen alive again. The travesty behind this trial and error is there could possibly still be some soldiers who are alive and in the jungles of Vietnam as PRISONERS of WAR (POW's). I strongly believe there is. There were so many mistakes made, so much finger pointing, and no one could find the compassion in their heart to say the biggest mistake America made was sending boys into a war they were not qualified to fight. Let's just start with, hey fellow Vietnam Veterans we APOLOGIZE. We did not mean to ignore the suffering you all were going through when you returned home. As a nation we did not know how to accept you, how to deal with all of what you as soldiers had went through, so we ignored the facts before us and now we have several situations not only with the Vietnam Veterans but also the chemical herbicide Agent Orange. But we are now looking at the year 2019 going into 2020 and it is only getting worse. What we relied on to assist us with the Vietnam Veterans was not thorough or sufficient enough. We as a nation of people are still not prepared for what is now taking place with the children, the grandchildren and possibly the great grandchildren of the Vietnam Veterans who now have the chemical herbicide "Agent Orange" in their DNA.

CHAPTER VI

MISTAKES WERE MADE

FIRST OF ALL, LET me explain what, (call for fire) exemplifies. When soldiers are under attack and find they may or may not be overtaken by the enemy. (Call for fire) is usually a request made by the Officer In Charge (OIC) to higher command because they have come under attack and are under heavy fire. The (OIC) will call in the grid coordinates of the enemy to have the Air Force bombers for an air attack. Another call for fire is when there is a strong possibility of being overtaken by the enemy and there is no other alternative the OIC will have the Air Force bombers zero in on the camp site while already in the process of moving the troops back. With friendly soldiers in the area, (friendly) is what we call our own American soldiers because they are ours, they are fighting on our side. The grid coordinates on (call for fire) of which usually consist of anywhere from eight to ten digits it gives the location of where the missiles are going to be fired at the enemy within ten to fifty feet. In the process of the grid coordinates being called in wrong there are missiles already being dropped right were the grid was called on the original grid given. If that grid is called in wrong and adjustments need to be made. Unless an early adjustment is made American soldiers could possibly be either wounded or killed by friendly fire. This is one of the courses that is mandatory for passing in the Infantry Officer Basic Course (IOBC) as a young lieutenant. In the process of the wrong grid being given missiles are being fired on American soldiers. Once this is discovered that a wrong grid coordinates was given another call has to go back to command to stop the bombing on the first site. This is when an (adjust fire) is called in and the correct gird coordinate is given. By then many American soldiers have already been killed by (friendly fire). When you hear the term "killed by friendly fire" that means the American soldier was kill by Americans. I must say our American and foreign officers are trained by the best at Fort Benning, Georgia, "Home of the Infantry" but the scenario was to let you the reader know what happens when a bad grid coordinate in (Call for Fire) goes out, it does not happen often, but the possibilities are always there.

Although this is not a finger pointing book it is a book of truth. At some point in time fault is something that does not have to be admitted to, but if all of the evidence is pointing to you then what is the obvious thing to think? Is it necessary? I would have to say no, not at this point in time! Is an apology needed? I would have to adamantly say yes, it is needed and long overdue! Mistakes were made in many ways and that is the purpose for me writing this book to take everyone back to the conference room where the finger pointing can stop, and the healing can begin. In case you did not get the memo earlier I believe I did state the Vietnam Veterans had been suffering for over forty years now. So many soldiers were killed in Vietnam and so many were contaminated by the herbicide chemical "Agent Orange." Due to the mix up of where Agent Orange was dropped once again friendly soldiers were in the area and those who were ordered to spray Agent Orange did not know it was being sprayed on top of our own soldiers who were in the area. Congress (our government), finally admits decades later that yes; Agent Orange was sprayed but they did not know American soldiers were in the area. It was not intentionally sprayed on American soldiers but the consequences involving the chemical "Agent Orange" would not only leave a lasting negative affect on our government officials but it would also leave a negative effect on the Vietnam Veterans lives for the rest of their life. Vietnam turned out to not be a cake walk in the park. It was a lingering war of which you could smell death in the air and its hunger never left. After many years of research and a history of Vietnam Veteran talking about health problems they had trying to cope with the chemical "Agent Orange." The Vietnam Veterans were not aware the herbicide chemical was going to lay dormant in their bodies. And from what I have found out through research our government was not aware of the damage Agent Orange was going to cause many years later. It was attacking the Vietnam Veterans blood stream and for over forty years now would cause health problems both physical and mental. This was the long term after effect of the chemical "Agent Orange" it would prove to be devastatingly uncontrollable. The war in Vietnam in accordance to my research notes was started in the early years of the 1960's. Only today in 2019 going into 2020 as I do my research for the book, I am writing I am finding out that not only is this devastating chemical going to kill off the Vietnam Veterans. It is also going to kill off their children, grandchildren and possibly their great grandchildren as well. Please keep in mind this chemical "Agent Orange" is in the blood stream of their DNA which will continue to be genetically passed on from generation to generation. I am not even certain if the chemical companies of which there are eleven involved that created the chemical herbicide Agent Orange even know how long the TCDD (dioxin) will be passed in through their DNA? Will it be passed on from generation to generation throughout the lives of not only the soldiers who fought in the Vietnam War where they came in contact with the deadly herbicide chemical Agent Orange. But we are now finding out the children and grandchildren are being affected. We are finding out the herbicide chemical Agent Orange is now in the blood stream of the soldiers and early death is definitely a given as it is being transferred through the DNA of which will make it generational. How long it is going to stay in the DNA of future generations we just don't know neither do we have any disclosed research at this time to prove its life expectancy. It was just a matter of time as to how the chemical was going to react within the body of the soldier, each case would be different. The end result will unfortunately be the same as the herbicide chemical disease attacks the body and continues to destroy the body. Death is inevitable. It is already estimated that 390 Vietnam Veterans will die a week. I will talk about that later in the chapters to come. I know we look at soldiers and the pain they have had to endure after the Vietnam War differently. What we as a nation of American citizens are not aware of is the suffering the family of the soldier who's also suffering with the soldier as his body continues to deteriorate from "Agent Orange." It's the immediate family who has to deal with the Vietnam Veterans lack of proper medical attention and lack of proper medical diagnosis. When I think about the medical diagnosis it is not just Agent Orange. It also covers the mental issues which are triggered through the effects of war and aftereffects of war added in with "Agent Orange." As I continue to gather my research, I find it to be tragic that not only are the Vietnam Veterans facing extinction. Those who fathered children with the herbicide chemical "Agent Orange" in their blood stream was now transferring the herbicide chemical genetically into their children's DNA.

Are the Wives Affected

Since the wife is the recipient of the sperm what would be the effect of Agent Orange inside of her body? It is very important to make you aware of what the soldiers are still going through today because of "Agent Orange." During some of my interviews with Vietnam Veterans and wives of Vietnam Veterans some of the stories were just horrific. Here is one of the stories of how Agent Orange began to take over her husbands' life.

She said, "they had decided to get away and go on vacation. She told me everything was okay with her husband when they left. After they arrived at their destination, she said the sickness just hit him all at once and he could not get out of bed. She said from that day on he began to deteriorate quickly. She began to tell me how Agent Orange began to affect his heart, liver and kidneys. She called it a very slow death." Basically, many of the soldiers I spoke with said close to the same things at different interviews and places. A silent killer, it just creeps upon you and changes the life you use to have forever. These were brief statements on how they felt individually. I must say a little compassion goes a long way but when we look into the silent screams of the lives Agent Orange has destroyed there isn't a big roar in Washington, DC to find a cure for it because it is still spreading. It's just something the Vietnam Veterans have to deal with on a one on one bases. Are they owed an apology? The answer without thought is yes! They are owed one from the government who created the war, Congress who decided to go to war and the people of the United States of America who supplied their tax paying dollars to finance the Vietnam War in order for them to be protected by the soldiers who went to war.

The Dim Light of Justice

Life is not fair. Although I live in the greatest country on earth,
justice served is sometimes a justice that is long, long overdue.
I believe in this country and what the justice system stands for.

A very important quote to remember is, the race is not given to the
swift or the strong but to the one who holds out to endure to the end.

In the light of my reality I search the deepest darkest rooms
looking for those special scales in quest for truth and justice,
watching just watching for the flicker of a flame.

I know they are there truth and justice, so my search is not
in vain. As I seek, I shall find, when I ask it shall be given,
when I knock, it shall be open unto me. These things are in
my grasp (seeking, asking and knocking) so, I see the flicker
of the flame, burning dim but still so encouraging.

My heart opened up and poured out its blood into swollen belly of a slowly burning Constitution. A Constitution that conveyed a promise of all men being created equal, a promise of all men and women having a fair chance at justice, gave me hope to believe in my dying land.

Many say America is a land that can no longer produce, the tides are beginning to change, and the NAFTA Bill is bringing this country down to its knees. Some say this great land called America has filled its melting pot to the rim.

Now that this land, this great land is in despair it has begun to reject its own native born. But oh, let me tell you, I will never lose faith, as long as I can see just a flicker of the flame. That is in my mind, my heart and soul.

The flame I speak of is not always a visual one. It is a deep burning desire to embrace the joy of what I stand for and believe in (Justice), but where do I fit in your due process of law. If the forefathers who called this great land America, the home of the free were here today. I would have to ask this question; which part is free? To this day there are still city areas and places of which some people are accepted, and others are not.

The Declaration of Independence for which it stands clearly states freedom as an inalienable right. A right endowed to all men and women.

The amendments are noticeable changes to a more positive future.

God bless America and her thoughtful deeds.

Although freedom, equality and justice are supposed to have been distributed equally there are still biases involved.

What appears to be written compared to what is overtly being acted upon leaves those of us who honestly want to believe in what this country stands for in dismay.

A scale that has been given a precision calibration will always balance its equal. A pound is only a pound; a dollar is only worth its face value regardless of the spender or the receiver. All things of the same should be conducive to the same be it man, woman or child. So, I see the flicker of the flame.

Although the scales of justice are still in need of a fine tuning, as long as there is hope I will continue to see the flick of the flame.

If I told you of my dream could you see my vision? If have given all that you have asked of me, will you now assist me in my time of need by any and all means necessary. So, the flame continues to flicker.

As I stare out over this great land called America, as long as there is a chance for freedom, equality and justice to prevail unconditionally, I will always see the flicker of the flame.

Written by: Author/Hall of Fame Poet
Raymond C. Christian

CHAPTER VII

VIETNAM WAR "HERO'S"
DENIED THEIR RESPECT

AFTER RETURNING HOME FROM war the Vietnam Veterans were denied their hero's welcome. There was no parade for them just a lot of embarrassing comments made about them and the so-called actions they were involved in during war time. The American citizens were only being fed information in parts and pieces by the media. The rest of the story was not being told as to what the Viet Cong (Charlie) was doing to our American soldiers to make them want to retaliate in an unjust manner. But all the hearsay leaked was not proven facts it was just that hearsay? That remains in question with the American people to this date but there is no apology across the United States to vindicate the Vietnam Veterans in their defense of the United States of America. There was no great Macy's parade, Bud Billycan Parade, Christmas, or New Year's parade to mark the honor the Vietnam Veterans should have been given. Considering the fact that every civilian in America had the opportunity to either watch on television or go with their families to the actual parade. Our Vietnam Veterans received mockery and whispers of disgust. It was a trail of blood that put them in a place of being ostracized by their own people. Little did the Vietnam Veterans know their suffering would be even more intense after their return home. It would be over forty years later these men who put their life on the line to protect this country against all foreign attacks would still not be forgive and it is now 2019 going into 2020. The correct information is slowly being released after careful review by the Veterans Administration which explains a lot of the soldiers from Vietnam reactions to certain situations and new information received years later. The American people are now able to see the wrong that has been done to these war heroes that served in the Vietnam War. Since the Veterans Administration has begun to admit some of the fault involved with releasing the Vietnam Veterans back into society without going through any mental evaluation or reconditioning procedures. There has been some progress made as far as the Vietnam

Veterans receiving their benefits from claims filed. Some mistakes by the government over forty years later have now been accepted as their fault regarding treatment the Vietnam Veterans should have gotten but did not. We can go as far back as 1983 when Congress finally admitted that they made mistakes especially with not treating the soldiers of the Vietnam War for mental illness with the number one reason being post-traumatic stress disorder (PTSD) before they were discharged from the military. Soldiers were already having nightmares and having difficulties coping. They were just thrown back on the streets the same way they were thrown into the jungles of Vietnam and expected to function as normal citizens. You should also question just how were they going to survive when they returned home after serving in the Vietnam War. During their time in service the jobs they had left behind did not have to rehire them and give them their positions back. Or even give them a job to sustain themselves. Many of these men were drafted into the military and others volunteered to go to the defense of this nation. It is unfortunate what they did not know is they would never be able to see the bright side of life ever again due to the suffering they had to endure during the war. Even if they did not have families, they needed their jobs back once they returned home in order to sustain their own life. During that time there weren't any laws established to make the employers give the Vietnam Veterans their jobs back. That became another struggle. Many companies and factories did not want the soldier at their facility working. There was an imaginary line of blood that seems to have been following the Vietnam Veterans, and no one wanted them around. Many companies did not want to help the Vietnam Veterans with gainful employment. And they were the same man who went to war to defend their rights to have businesses and factories to work side by side so-called descent everyday good old American people. The heads of companies and factories were afraid of the Vietnam Veterans simply because they did not know how to receive them back into the work force. They did not know what the Veterans would do at work, would they cause some kind of a commotion, would there be problems with other employees. Once again, the same men who returned home from the Vietnam War, these same men who gave more than their life for the betterment of this country for the good of all humanity were no longer welcomed in America. Please tell me where were they supposed to go? I thought the purpose of returning home was to be able to work and forget about the war? With so much denial in the past the evidence now speaks for itself. With so many of the Vietnam Veterans dying due to their unintentional interaction with the highly toxic chemical Agent Orange it is now over forty years later. Congress (our government) finally begins to admit the Vietnam Veterans did in fact come into contact with "Agent Orange." The Vietnam Veterans are being compensated by receiving proper medical care to help ease the blood contamination of "Agent Orange." The soldiers have had to suffer with physical illnesses since the chemical Agent Orange was sprayed in the jungles of "Nam" on the Vietnam Veterans. It is unfortunate the Vietnam Veterans children and grandchildren are all going to possibly die with the chemical Agent Orange in their DNA. Someone other than me should be drafting up a new bill to give the Vietnam Veterans their heroes welcome. The Vietnam Veterans are the men the soldiers who returned home badgered but not beaten. They are the men who could have been killed in action, they could have become prisoners of war, and they could have been (MIA). These are the men who returned home not just missing parts and pieces of their body, but a big part of their soul was left behind in the jungles of "Nam." For those who made it out and for the soldiers who do not want to revisit what they had to ingest in their mind many chose not to talk about it their experience. These are the men you spit on and denied their rights to freedom and justice in their own country. When you should have held them in the highest regard with a special Vietnam Veterans Day, a big parade for their service to the United States of America. You still can do it, give them their well-deserved parade. The faces of the men I have seen, and the wives of the Vietnam Veterans have spoken openly about the hurt they had to endure while watching a misled nation of people curse them for over forty years now. When does it stop? Now that you are aware these men where not adequately trained for war; they were just bodies needed to substantiate the numbers needed for a war. Which appeared to be based on numbers of bodies needed to fight in the jungles of Vietnam? And as these young men died on the battlefield another body was being sent in to replace the one already in the body bag tagged for home. I am an American soldier and officer who was in grief due to the lack of understanding the American people had concerning the Vietnam War. We can all agree now it was a war that should have never happened. What was its purpose? I don't know. What was its cause? I don't know. Until you have served one day in a war zone as critical as the Vietnam War how can you judge anyone and please keep that nasty spit in your mouth and the finger pointing to yourself. If you must, please go back and read my chapter when I was asking you the question, "What Would You have Done?" What morality can one peacefully distribute in a war zone? What values that you have created make you so unblemished that you can stand in judgment of those who served in the Vietnam War? Although you did not sacrifice anything your success is based on the lives of men and women who fought and died for peace. Unless you have tasted that side of life and I am certain you are saying right now you have no intention whatsoever on serving in the Armed Forces and that is my point. Unless you are willing to get in there to figure out exactly what we as soldiers' men and women on the battlefield do today to protect this nation. A nation many of you so proudly and freely are able to still move around in. It is with your own better moral judgment to continue on with what you have to do so you can do something to contribute to the betterment of the United States of America by not condemning the Vietnam Veterans for maintaining the peace. Most of you are only interested in making as much money as you can to achieve a position in America that will give you some kind of social status. Soldiers do not go into the military for the purpose of getting rich. They go in for the moral intent of being able to say I did something for my country, and I am proud to have served in the greatest branch of the Armed Forces of the United States of America. I do feel that John F. Kennedy's famous quote fits perfectly after the statement I just made, "Ask not what your country can do for you but what you can do for your country." An honest day's work for an honest day's pay is not a statement many people look for today. Even with that vision almost lost you must be cognizant that it is only because of the men and women who have served this country and represented them in this cause. It is only because they served this country that you are able to walk around freely and aim for the goals you have set for yourself no matter what they maybe. It has been past wars, the Vietnam war and our current wars that has put you in a place of being able to be competitive and has allowed the citizens of America to act upon the dreams you are reaching for in the "Free World." These soldiers who are inside of the war zone may have a split second to think before they react. Given this kind of a time frame rest assured mistakes are made and many cannot be corrected. This is why it is important to inform you the Vietnam Veterans may I remind you did not have the training or technology that we have today. How can you expect a young boy to be a man in a war zone as intensified as Vietnam or a girl to be a woman who is able to give birth? You can't. There are many stipulations put on the stigma of what makes a boy a man and what makes a girl a woman? In a war zone would you consider a soldier who is able to take the life of an enemy soldier a man. It only requires split second thinking, "kill the enemy" this is the ultimate when it comes to taking the life of another human being. This is what you put these young boys in Vietnam to do and they will never be the same neither will their families ever be the same again. You should be able to understand just by what you have read so far that life for them ceased when they returned home and so did the families that were torn apart due to the Vietnam War. The suffering of the men, father's and son's who came back to the United States for the same peace they created but found none. It seems like when the Vietnam Veterans returned home everyone wanted to play God. If you consider yourself a follower of Christ or even if you are not a follower, you need to read the scriptures I am giving you for your enlightenment. I do feel the word of God helps to bring those who are lost to a better level of understanding. Matthew 5:25 "That ye may be the children of your Father which is in heaven: for he his maketh sun to rise on the evil and on the good, and sendeth rain on the just and on the unjust." With this being stated Jesus said in John 8:7 "So when they continued asking, he lifted up himself, and said unto them, He that is without sin among you let him cast a stone at her." We are also taught as a nation of Christian believers in Matthew 7:1" Judge not that ye be not judged." There is scripture after scripture if you are believers as most Americans feel that America was founded on the blessings of God Almighty. It is because of their belief in God that the necessity of war does fall into play. There is always a need for a military force it represents a show of power in case of an emergency such as America coming under attack. Americans have used the military for peace keeping missions and they have instilled in the hearts of other nations that our military is there to help. In representation of Congress who passes the laws to go to war the Americans tax paying dollars are used to fund the war. So, our soldiers are not sent to war in representation of themselves they are sent to war to protect our government and the United States citizens. It is unfortunate that the need of such young boys came at a time of war in the jungles of Vietnam. This is a critical area of finger pointing and that is something I do not want you to get from reading this book. Because the blame game is a loss epic within itself. If you would look at the matter concerning the Vietnam Veterans strategically. What you would find out is these American soldiers who fought in the Vietnam War was dropped off in the hottest LZ in the history of all wars. Please note that a lot of the soldiers were privates taken fresh out of bootcamp and dropped into the heart of Vietnam. Finding these men who served in the Vietnam War to be so young to be eighteen or nineteen years old and to have the mental thinking of wanting to serve their country is an honorable challenge that they had signed on the dotted line without any reservation to protect the citizens of the United States of America. Those that went to "Nam" remained loyal and many gave their life for the betterment of all mankind. Even with the minimal training they had received they wanted to believe in their hearts they were going to be able to survive in an area they did not have gorilla warfare training or tunnel training. While fighting in Vietnam American soldiers found the Vietnamese were fighting the war underground in tunnels in the jungles of Vietnam. When I talk about formal combat training I am talking about preparation training to teach the soldiers how to spot booby traps, how to set claymore mines, how to detonate bombs, what to do when a mine field is in question, how to enter a building when enemy presence is anticipated, how to prep a bomb, how to work with C4, all this is special training let alone how to clean your weapon correctly of which there was a lot of complaints by the soldiers about the M-16 jamming. What to do when a weapon jams, how to set your front and rear sites, learning about wind elevation when shooting from a distance. There was so much to do concerning the training of these Vietnam Veterans that we know now about that many soldiers were not able to get. Soldier's bodies were needed in Vietnam and that's what our government and taxpayers sent bodies with numbers attached whether they were ready to go to war or not. It was trial and era then and all we knew to do was to drop the young eighteen and nineteen-year-old boys in the jungles of Vietnam and tell them to fight. From formal training we must also look at specialty training. The point I am making here to the American public as well as our government is these young men did had a few rushed hours of specialty training and the little they had was not enough. Two weeks of boot camp and no guerrilla warfare training equals disaster. Two weeks of boot camp is just what it was basic training and it just, basic. The rushed training was not enough for these young boys to get through Vietnam or the war without natural survival instinct which is why so many were killed in action. Meaning they did what they had to do in order to survive. Don't forget these young boys did not have any combat experience. I believe everyone was under the assumption these soldiers were going to be dropped off in this war zone and where going to survive off of natural instinct and every combat veterans knows training is not negotiable. You must train in order to not make mistakes, it cuts down on safety issues and lives lost, training is essential. The extremely short process of getting them ready for war was not fair to them. Then to fly them over onto foreign soil and leave them in an environment, a jungle they knew nothing about. It was a catastrophe and the only outcome was to fight or die. This was a jungle environment that would alter their lives forever. Our soldiers did what they had to do in Vietnam in order to survive. And for those of you who have not served in a war zone there is no but ifs or maybes. And I do not want to appear to be too blunt so let me make it plain, pull the trigger and keep it moving. That is the only way the Vietnam Veterans or any soldier in a war zone was going to be able to come back home alive and see their families again. Forgiveness for the Vietnam Veterans is way beyond the normal realm of patience and understanding you had to be there, and you were not. It is certainly unbelievable that these young boys would have the capabilities or combat awareness to survive one day in the jungles of "Nam." I believe I mentioned earlier in the book the survival ratio for a soldier in "Nam" to be sixteen minutes after being dropped off in "Nam." With that being said how were they expected to survive six months to a year in Vietnam with no relief from duty until their tour of duty was up? If you will allow me to go a little deeper on what was not revealed to the America public in relation to the Vietnam Veterans going to an military official school (MOS), school training I will talk about that a little longer. Please let me explain. When a soldier graduates from bootcamp they are given orders from the President of the United States of America/Congress because that is who the soldier works for. The soldier receives orders to report to his (MOS) that is his/her Military Official School. This means the soldier is sent to a military training school. A school mainly conducted by military personal who are professionals and certified to teach in the area of study they are teaching. Men and women who are the best at what they do and are credentialed by military professionals to hold those positions. These soldiers are taught inside of a classroom no different than a college student being taught by a college professor in college. We can all agree here that a college professor is not skilled on how to arm or disarm a claymore mine as the military staff would be trained to do. But after retiring from the military many military officers and soldiers do teach college courses at a college or university. It was evident they both are professionally trained and educated but a soldier's skills are not limited. These soldiers are taught their skills inside of a classroom. They are tested and are given grades on their test just like a college student would be tested by his professors. For example, if you are going to school to be a doctor then you are trained in the particular field of study, be it oncology, pediatrics, brain surgeon, heart surgeon etc. If you are going to be a teacher, you have to have a specification of what area you want to teach. You have to select whether you are you going to teach elementary school, grade school, or high school? Then you have to determine whether you are going to be an English, Mathematics, Science, and Language Arts, Biology or Physical Education teacher. These are variables that have to be determined in order for the proper training to be given so the students can be trained in the area of which the professor's received knowledge of understanding on how to teach in relations to their degree. Let's also look at lawyers. They are trained in law school as future attorneys. These attorneys are trained in the field of prosecuting attorneys, defense attorneys, child rights attorneys, family attorneys, civil rights attorneys etc. They also have variables to what classification they are going to pursue. It is unfortunate that we must admit that mistakes happen. It could become quite devastating for someone in the aforementioned professions to not be trained adequately and it does happen. Doctors, schoolteachers and lawyers are insured when they make mistakes. But who goes back to ensure the lives that were lost in the Vietnam War? How do we go back and tell a mother or father their child will not be returning home because the child is missing in action or was found dead on the battlefield? Or maybe the child was blown to bits and the body parts was not able to be recovered. And if the body parts are recovered the bits and pieces are gathered and placed in a bag labeled remains. Do you think the parents will want to see that? You see there is no error of correction for the dead bodies to say a mistake was made. The soldier is insured in the war zone, and please pay attention if you have children and you are reading this please tell me what amount of money is going to be enough for you to replace the child you lost on the battlefield? The answer to that question is there isn't an amount of money to cover the pain the mother, father or brother and sister will feel for the rest to their life. And it goes even further concerning the soldier's death don't forget the grandparents, aunts, uncles and cousins, friends. Everyone is affected. These scenarios I just gave you concerning the Doctors, Lawyers, School Teachers and Surgeons training could be somewhat life threatening given certain circumstances. The scenarios were given to afford you the opportunity to help you reflect back to what was not considered during and after the Vietnam War. The young men (boys) I might add were not given the opportunity to assesses the entire situation they had gotten into, some volunteered but remember many were drafted. Either way their lives were taken from them and they never stood a chance. I find that many of the soldiers had to make peace within themselves to carry on with their life after they returned home. The odds of them making it back home again were phenomenal it's just hard to believe they were able to survive. Being a combat veteran, you just don't understand what I see and know that did not take place for the real war heroes the Vietnam Veterans. Were they supposed to be able to come back home? When you review the scenario, I just gave you, you will see it was a life-threatening situation put before them before they every left bootcamp. They were never properly trained in tunnel warfare let alone guerilla warfare. The tunnel training (tunnel rats) came later during the Vietnam War after the soldiers were reporting to higher command how the Vietnamese were coming out of tunnels in the ground in the jungles of Vietnam. After the war the Vietnam Veterans were returned to a society that was not properly prepared to receive them due to the physical, mental and emotional problems they were suffering from when they arrived back in the states. The truth of the matter is the Vietnam Veterans return home would turn out to be total chaos for them. This would be considered to be highly detrimental to a soldier dropped in the hottest LZ in the history of America. They were not only inexperienced and inadequately trained considering no combat training or guerilla warfare training, jungle training etc. It was so much the Vietnam Veterans were just not trained in to prepare them for the Vietnam War. What you were looking at was eighteen and nineteen-year-old boys who wanted to fight for their country but were undertrained with no combat experience. They were not trained in what should have been considered to be a critical MOS of someone who specialized in guerilla warfare in the jungles of Vietnam. These young boys as what you consider them to be men at eighteen and nineteen years old would be considered in today's military training as being inadequately trained even during their training time. Putting a weapon in a young boys' hands and telling him the power it has and allowing him to shot and qualify on the rifle range does not make him qualified to go to war. I am certain every mother and father in this country today would be writing to congress and making sure that something was done to protect their children? This did not take place during the Vietnam War; you were either drafted or you enlisted. Now we have a broader view of what should not have happened and in order that the same mistakes that were made in America as well as Vietnam with the over 47,000 soldiers who lost their life on the battlefield during the Vietnam war would not happen again more incentives today are placed on training and the safety of the soldiers. This is where the admission part comes in for this country to admit that mistakes were made and these men and women who fought in the Vietnam War need to be given some relief. The United States of America can start with an apology to the Vietnam Veterans they deserve an apology to start with. These young boys were not trained in a critical or special profession, but they were dropped in a war zone and told to figure it out for themselves. How important is your life to you? What would you do at an instance notice when life or death presents itself to you? The American soldiers in Vietnam were dropped in the hottest war zone this nation had ever been in and expected to survive under the most adverse conditions any human being could possibly think of. Under trained in both combat and explosives devices. What I am trying to do here is get your mind ready, prepare it for what I am about to say. These young boys where dropped in a hot LZ with minimal training to sustain them. Now I want you to go back to what I said about the schoolteachers, doctors, lawyers and surgeons etc. I am asking you this question which only requires a yes or no response? Would you take your child to a doctor who has not been professionally trained and certified? Yes or no? Would you go to a brain surgeon still in training to operate on your child? I am prayerful that you have answered each of the questions I have presented to you with a definite "No". So, my next question is why would these young men who decided to stay and fight and not desert the United States of America as so many others did be treated with so much disrespect as I have witnessed through the years? My final question in relations to the aforementioned questions I have just asked you is why were our boys eighteen and nineteen years old forced (drafted) to go into the God forsaken jungles of Vietnam unprepared? Why was this allowed to happen? What sense did it make? I am asking you to look at this in a civil manner with only some of the mistakes made and we are only into one-third of the book. There are still many questions that have not been resolved in relations to the Vietnam Veterans and so many voices that went unheard, remember it was over 47,000 that did not make it back. We put up a "Wall of Names" in Washington, DC in remembrance of those who died. While those who are alive and barely holding on due to Agent Orange and other injuries are still waiting to be accepted by our government and the America people. They have fought in a war zone and returned home to fight another war. And that is a war of battling for their right to be recognized as other soldiers before them and after them. The hero's welcome for their contribution for protecting the citizens of the United States of America after being put in a war zone sweltering with such a catastrophic loss of life of men, (brothers) they had trained with who had given their life on a battlefield covered with dead bodies. It is beyond ones understanding as to what their level of being able to survive was. No one can compute the level of endurance or pain. No one can comprehend what it would take to be able to survive in a situation that required split second thinking as to whether they would live or die. Every given second of life was precious for the Vietnam Veteran and nothing was considered beyond that. I am certain his thinking is either I will live to see another day or die in his attempt to sustain his life and stay alive. Jumping to judgment was prompted by a lot of political enhancement when the media began to openly discuss what they felt was taking place in Vietnam was wrong. I am certain it was very easy to write about when it came to sitting behind a typewriter and taking notes. But the journalist did not actually serve in the thickets of the jungles for days and live like the animal the Vietnam Veterans had to become. Some of the journalist went to "Nam" but not into the really hot zones where death was prevalent. It's always easy to point fingers and say what someone would or would not do. But when you actually live the life not for one day in the midst of death for six months to a year not protected by checkpoints or able to shower and shave when you get ready. The media did not have to eat bugs and crawl through swamps and live in tunnels and around dead bodies as the Vietnam soldiers did. Yet they found the time to print what they did about men who defended the United States of America with their life. The truth was hidden from the American people about what the Vietnam Veterans had to deal with in a war far, far away from home. If history had to repeat itself, I do believe in my heart the soldiers would sign up to go fight because they felt the cause was just in the defense of their family, friends and loved ones. On the other hand, I do not feel that Congress would sign the war bill to send these young boys eighteen and nineteen years old into a slaughterhouse, where the jungles of Vietnam would become a death trap a coffin for so many soldiers. Unfortunately, we cannot turn back the hands of time on the Vietnam War and tell the men who died on the battlefield that they would be held as heroes. But the Vietnam Veterans who returned home battered, wounded and mentally disturbed would have to suffer for the rest of their life for defending the country they served with no one standing up to defend them once they returned home. What's so sad is the American people keep forgetting they were the ones who helped to make the decision to send these eighteen and nineteen-year-old boys off to war. These young boys through a conditioning process were made to believe they were now men with some of the soldiers being taken out of bootcamp with only two weeks of basic training? Our boys were dropped in the hottest war zone in the history of the United States of America. What was literally said to them was (Do what you must do to make it back home). Kill the enemy and teach yourself how to survive. Become the animal you need to become in order to have the privilege of seeing your family, friends and loved ones again. What show of compassion has this country, the United States of America displayed in respect to these young boys who have given their life to what many would consider to be a frivolous cause? There are American citizens in this country today who would still say they did not know what justification America had with getting involved with the Vietnam War. If the Congress and Senate do not know and the American citizens do not know I say this as a military officer that served my country faithfully. Both in the enlisted ranks and officer that I can assure you the soldiers who were there fighting in the Vietnam War did not know the reason they were there. They were given their orders and told to go fight. Why they enlisted or why they were drafted to fight for the United States of America that is one unanswered statement that remains in question to this day? Why? And why Vietnam? What was the Vietnam War all about? Mistakes were made and I do mean major mistakes. My question to those who remember and never did get the true picture of the war is why do you blame the Vietnam Veterans who had nothing to do with the administration part of the war? Why are you blaming the soldiers for something they hadn't the slightest idea as to what took place or why the Vietnam War happened? They received orders from the President of the United States to defend this country and fulfilled their obligation. All the soldiers wanted to do was to be able to return home again once the war was over. No one really knows how brutal war can be until you have boots on the ground. And believe it or not America you have denied the Vietnam Veterans the right to return home. What I am saying is the Vietnam Veterans returned home but they were never made to feel at home. This is why so many claims of Agent Orange concerning the soldiers are still being filed today. They never received the peace or support they deserved to have once they touched American soil. You are at fault whether you know it or not for keeping the mind of the Vietnam Veterans in question as to why they ever came back to America. Yes, America was home but the soldiers who returned never received the thank you they should have gotten. They were caught up in an era that will be no more, these are the true American hero's, the Vietnam Veterans, they fought until a cease fire was called. As long as you continue to deny them their true position in the history books of America as fighting a war in defense of America and the American citizens who dwell therein. The message of concern here would be to retreat waving your white flag in peace. Not to an admission of guilt but to an understanding of saying you did not know all of the players in this ruthless game of war called Vietnam. You, America are crucifying good men who only went were they were told to go. They only fought because they were told to fight, and they fought out of the love in their hearts for you. Can't you see these were young boys eighteen and nineteen years of age who did not know anything about the political involvement concerning the Vietnam War. As a soldier, a man who has worked his way up through the ranks of enlisted noncommissioned ranks to the position of officer in the Armed Forces of the United States of America, I am telling you the way the Vietnam Veterans were received in America and how they are treated to this day is wrong. These men who fought in the Vietnam War have suffered past their time of forgiveness. Their internal suffering is something you cannot see, were their mind takes them on a day's end or how they were not equipped to handle the grueling visions they saw in the aftermath of war is quite somethings else. Something you only see on television, but they lived through the screams and yells at night of their friends, their comrades being tortured in the jungles of Vietnam. Their minds could not digest the horrific decapitations, death, and visions of their friends left behind, blown to pieces or found tortured to death. This is why your forgiveness is so important to them because of what you cannot see that is taking place inside of them. I have lived through several wars and just dealing with the situation of combat itself is enough but to return home and be dealt a bad hand because of what was said would be too much to bear. The history of surviving war is tragic enough. But to ask the Vietnam Veterans to relive it over and over again bypasses the physical sense of torture in testing how much a man can endure. We will never know the whole story behind the Vietnam Veterans and what they had to do in order to be able to return home from a bloody battlefield of death that I call the devils den. Unless you have been in a war especially one as brutal as Vietnam you do not know the stipulations of what it actually took for some of the soldiers to be able to make it home again. Criticizing the Vietnam War, I do not have a problem with that because as I stated earlier no one truly knew what the war was for or about. But to not allow the Vietnam Veterans who were seeking refuge once they returned home is not right and only made matters worse for them as well as the rest of the country. All they did was what they were told to do by their superiors and that was to fight the war that was in defense of the United States of America, for your rights, and your freedoms. For the ones who were able to return home they have given all but their physical life. Their inner life, their soul was taken from them and left to roam in the jungles of Vietnam. And their souls still roam searching for a place of peace because you America did not allow the soldiers to come home, you left them empty and void with no light of hope and you gave them nothing but a place of darkness to reside in. For the ones who were not shot while the bullets were flying, or did not step on a land mine, or get blown up by a grenade. For the ones who did not get ambushed while they were sent out on patrol; did not get captured by the enemy and become a prisoner of war. They stood and fought for what they believed in and it's not that they let you down, but this country has given the Vietnam Veterans the bitter end of the stick a sour lemon. The Vietnam Veterans were unable to make lemonade because of what happened to them in the Vietnam War, but they trudge along daily, I see them. I will not stop there, the shock to the Vietnam Veterans did not just come from the war. Their return home and encounter with the citizens of the United States of American was just as traumatizing. You cannot imagine what it is like to go into a war zone and return home and have to find the help you need to try to get you through what you experienced in the war experiences embodied in the traumas of war, the shock one receives to the body and mind each day you are in the sticks (the jungle) in the war zone. These young boys who returned home had to find people who were willing to give them a chance. Since citizens in the companies who once worked with the Vietnam Veterans where in so much fear of working with these young men who returned home many did not get their jobs back. The Vietnam Veterans were now being seen as anything other than war heroes. But they were put in a war to defend the citizens of America and their Constitutional rights. It just keeps getting ugly and uglier when you look at the bigger picture the Vietnam Veterans were not the hypocrites the government and the citizens, they protected turned out to be. In fact, they came home with their dignity; they did what they were trained to do. On the other hand, America did not. You sent these young boys into a war zone at a very impressionable age of eighteen and nineteen years old. Just what did you expect these boys to do? You see this is the part I do not get. Our American government/citizens sent these boys in a war zone to fight your battle for you and then looked upon them when they returned home as though you were looking inside of a sewage system. Did something back up or did the stench of what they had to become overwhelm you so much that it just slipped your mind. That you, yes it was you America my beloved American government and citizens that sent these boys into battle. Yes, it was you who armed them in support of the military through your hard-earned taxpaying dollars. Along with the congressman or congresswoman you elected to speak for you on the green carpet and declare a war. I might add they spoke in behalf of you in your favor of sending these boys to war in the jungles of Vietnam. If you notice I continue to say young boys because they are only eighteen and nineteen years old. This is what your congressional order passed to put these young boys in the midst of war and forget there was a war going on that no one could make sense of to this day. And because you were not prepared for their return home a plan two was not developed until much later. Oh! But don't let me forget just how many years it took before congress could admit they made a big mistake with the Vietnam Veterans. Somewhere in the pages of this book I will stop calling them boys and call them young men. Although I must admit they earned the title of being called a man when they signed their signature on the dotted line and said, "I swear I will protect and defend the Constitution of the United States of America. These were boys who did not know how to be men and of course they did not have a role model to teach them while they were growing up on how to kill another man and be thoughtless about it. They did not learn that in bootcamp either, they only go through simulated exercises. You know the five-death point, hand to hand combat with a bayonet etc. For those who were accepted into Special Forces, the Berets and the Seals, training was totally different. This is something that you don't have to discover on the battlefield of war, it's kill or be killed. I am only putting a few things before you good citizens who have never sat foot onto the battlefields of any war. This is just some of the things America, I am asking you to reconsider. Can I present this question to you, "What is it like to kill another man?" What is it like to have the sights of your weapon pointed down range at another man's head who will never see the bullet coming or even hear the sound? Because he is called your enemy and just because of the word war you have a right to take this man's life to kill this man without recourse. What is it like to pull that trigger and watch another man fall dead at 500 hundred meters not knowing whether this man had a family, a wife and children he also wanted to go home to? Do you think you could do it? This is where the little boys you gave two weeks of training in bootcamp did not have time to debate. This is now real war, it was not hide-and-seek, it was not peak-a-boo. This was not a game of the boogie man being in your closet where you could jump out of bed and hide in the closet. Or scream for your mother or father to come get you, it was a real war with real bullets that killed. There was no returning home for the man you just shot and killed at 500 hundred meters. There was no getting up saying, "the war games are over, and we can all go home now." There was a cancelation of someone's life permanently taken away there is no recovery or rewind button to play it over again. This enemy soldier's wife, son and daughter, his mother and father and siblings will never see him again. At least not in this lifetime I am certain with the wild animals in the forest on the prowl he will be food for someone. Shooting a target in bootcamp to attain your marksmanship is a great accomplishment. Training hand to hand combat with battlesticks is also an added advantage. Only there aren't any dead bodies or puddles of blood left behind to visualize or assess the damage that has been done once training is over, everyone goes home. Simulation training is good for experience but to see a man's life leave his body is an experience you will never forget. After training the soldier will go back to the barracks and be ready for training at 5:30am until he graduates from bootcamp. There are injuries to some soldiers during boot camp, but they are usually able to recover. Although a soldier can die during training also from time to time there are life sustaining injuries in bootcamp. This is not the scenario in the war zone, it's an exchange of bullets for a life, someone is not going to be able to go home. These are the split decisions a soldier in a war zone is left with and just like you enjoy being with your family the Vietnam Veterans enjoy being with their families again as well. Nothing is beneath the normalcy of war, but everyone has a place and position they have to be willing to uphold in order for peace to exists. And everyone plays a part in the war game it's just that they see themselves differently because they did not actively participate in pulling the trigger but remember when a soldier goes to war the entire country goes with him, it's not just the soldier pulling the trigger but everyone that sent him. I keep reminding you good American citizens it was your tax dollars that supplied the bullets, the machine guns, the grenades etc. This is why I referred to it as a blood bath because everyone's hands are bloody not just the soldier. It was you America, who sent these young men into the war zone of Vietnam. Not realizing all the ramifications of what would take place inside the war itself like "Agent Orange" and PTSD, soldiers on drugs and mental issues. All this would occur and more to these young men who went to war to fight for your freedoms. Little did we know the person they use to be would be lost inside of himself and his payment in search for who he used to be would be lost forever. Unable to recover from his participation in the Vietnam War once it was over. The Vietnam Veteran the soldier you saw that leave home will never be the same person again. There is not enough money, or assistance you can give to the Vietnam Veterans for the suffering they had to endure. They are still fighting to this day to receive the benefits they deserve it's not so much the Veterans Administration fault but please continue reading and you will find out there are other entities involved called the Health and Medicine Division (HMD). The past name that was used for researching veteran's illness as well as "Agent Orange" was the Institute of Medicine (IOM). I will be discussing the (HMD) and Agent Orange in the later chapters of this book. Today is October 23, 2019 soon to be 2020 the Vietnam Veterans suffering remains consistent with their struggle to maintain who they are while "Agent Orange" continues to take the rest of what is left inside of them. It's just not their dignity and pride they suffer with but also personal ailments and injuries that occurred during battle. These young soldiers in Vietnam did not have a clue as to what they were going to have to deal with until they arrived in "Nam." What was expected of them? They signed the contract with the government unaware this country had never been in a war of this caliber before and that it would take a certain kind of soldier to make it home again. They became the animal within, with Vietnamese coming out of tunnels in the ground our American soldiers had to become what they were seeing. They became their environment, animals, trees, rocks to sustain their life and predators in order to survive.

He Gave Us Light in Darkness

What light can one man see when there is only darkness present?
Darkness that encompasses his heart infused within his soul;
Is there a release an outlet for him to bring joy back into his life?
So many seek after him to disprove what he has done.
He has done the work of his father and brought truth into the world.

Can justice prevail in its blindness in a courtroom of open travail?
Red Oak wood and marble floors await the ruling gavel of the judge,
What say ye; guilty or not guilty? Does this question require a response?
How many jurors does it take to convict an innocent man?

(Romans 14:16-17)
"Let not then your good be evil spoken of, For the kingdom of God is not;
Meat and drink but righteousness and peace and joy in the Holy Ghost."

Although justice is sought after in the chambers of the law;
The books remain unbalanced yet justifiable and equally charged;
The scales balance in accordance to which book is being used;
There isn't a tilt in the scale of law to show a calibration is needed;
Could it be the moral arc of the universe is only permissible in time?

Time has no time or clock to monitor its change so how long do we wait;
How much of our preconceived thoughts do we
relinquish to bring change in time?
We are not in a capsule that requires an expiration date of time;
But we are quantified by the moral ethics instilled in us individually.

"The True Crust of the Earth Shall Rise Again" in number and praise;
Bringing the perfected scales of life and love into calibration;
Living in the light of Gods beauty uncloaked from darkness;
The light became sin, so no one could hide; there would be no excuse;
You can no longer hide behind your warranted lies of injustice.
Although corruption exists time conceals and reveals what is in time.

Written by: Author/ Hall of Fame Poet
Raymond C. Christian

This prose was written to allow one's mind to take a break from what is considered to be the norm when it comes to justice throughout the world not just America. The expression of thought gives a person time to go into their private place. Whether it's in a closed room or in the privacy of their own mind. You will find it is not just an opinion, you search for the factual truth that only God can give. Remember there is your side, their side and of course God's side which without question the truth. Your privacy exposes deeply rooted emotions and unveils the idiosyncrasies of how they personally relate to justice, fairness, equality. Leaving no misconception of what is or is not equally balanced in this "Free World" we call America.

If you would go back and read the prose, "He Gave Us Light in Darkness" what you will find within yourself is a struggle for understanding the truth not as others see it and not just the way the law was perceived to be in the way in which it was written. The example I want to give here is a statement relating to what justice is: "Why would a man commit a crime knowing it is a crime as it relates to the law of the land and he is going to be punished for it?" If you take this a little deeper as it relates to the Vietnam War if you look at it in the moral sense of thinking you will have the understanding of, "What is truth?" The young men who went to fight for the citizens of America were sent to war by their fellow countrymen and women. Now go back and read the prose "He Gave Us Light in Darkness" and if you can honestly admit that what took place is Vietnam is an act of war that was created by men and women in America who sent the young men there to fight to the death if possible. Logic is not beyond reproach here, you may have a mental block when it comes to an admission of guilt but the truth is if you, America, had not sent the eighteen and nineteen year old boys to Vietnam there would have never been a need for "Agent Orange" to be created or do you think "Agent Orange was also inevitable? What is not talked about much is the fact the United States of America did not have a plan in place to help the soldiers heal properly when they returned home. Unlike the Warrior Transition Units (WTU) we have in place today to give some assistance in rebuilding the soldier's self-esteem and helping him to find as much of himself as he can prior to being released to go home. There was nothing put in place to assist the Vietnam Veterans in becoming whole again. The damage they had suffered physically, mentally and emotionally was looked upon as alien to the American citizens who ran from the soldiers instead of embracing them and trying to remedy a problem they had created. They was no brain trauma units, they was no (WTU) to assist the Vietnam Veterans with getting checked in and given a plan to follow in accordance to his needs to help him transition back into society. I am not asking the American citizens to admit fault. And Congress does not have to admit they were wrong for declaring war and sending soldiers to their death. I am hoping this book will guide you to a common ground of peace and understanding. These men who fought in the Vietnam War deserve to have peace in America and only the American people and Congress can give them their peace. The soldiers have done their part; they did what they were told. They did what you America told them to do. I am asking you to please understand their hurt for over forty years. You must make peace with the men and women who served as they continue to standby with new findings of "Agent Orange" which is still being discovered. The Vietnam Veterans are dying from Agent Orange, their children are dying from Agent Orange now it is discovered that since Agent Orange has been transferred genetically into the DNA of these soldiers it has passed on to their grandchildren. What more will we find out about "Agent Orange?" How many generations will be affected by this blood born disease? I will discuss Agent Orange later in the book. The findings will make you really just sit up and shake your head. I will be covering "Agent Orange" and just how toxic this TCDD (dioxin) herbicide chemical is to all who come into contact with it.

CHAPTER VIII

VIETNAM VETERANS RETURN HOME

WHEN I THINK ABOUT the many things that did not take place for the Vietnam Veterans concerning their future after the Vietnam War verses the treatment they received when they returned home. I and many others feel more should have been done in favor of the Vietnam Veterans to help them with whatever problem or illness they were having. Only out of fear of how Americans thought the Vietnam Veterans were going act out discouraged the Vietnam Veterans from placing any trust in the the citizens of America. American citizens were afraid of them due to what the media was printing and some of the graphic pictures that had been shown but no one questioned as to whether what was being said about the Vietnam Veterans was true or not. It is very important that I expound on what is considered to be fair treatment versus what the soldier never received. It is emphatically clear that the soldiers are without question owed a reputable amount of retribution concerning their suffering and having to deal with the problems of war. As well as the Vietnam Veterans who are suffering from Agent Orange and the problems it has caused many Vietnam Veterans through the years due to them being contaminated by Agent Orange which is now a part of their DNA. Meaning the chemical is in their DNA forever due to TCDD being the most toxic chemical and most dangerous, it's sporadic. This is what the Vietnam Veterans have suffered and died with through the years. I know that I have mentioned it before but let me mention it again that Agent Orange will also affect their children and grandchildren the question is will it affect the great grandchildren? That has already been discovered. What has not been discovered is just how many generations will Agent Orange affect before it filters out of the Vietnam Veterans offspring DNA. We are looking at three generation already contaminated. There are many reasons why the United States of America has suffered since declaring war in Vietnam. The United States subjected itself to chemical companies that had no value in concerns to human life. The chemical company's main objective is to test chemicals to see how they are going to work, on plants, in soda, on grass, food and on people. And it is true that they haven't any value for human life. The way the Vietnam Veterans are dying it is understandable to say they were sick before their return home after being in contact with Agent Orange which was created by the chemical company's during the Vietnam War. The biggest question I am certain the Vietnam Veterans, the good citizens of the United States as well as myself would like to know is, are there any continual studies taking place today, and ongoing research concerning the dangers of TCDD (dioxin)= Agent Orange? TCDD is highly toxic and sporadically uncontrollable. And if there is research taking place what are the findings moving forward to find a cure? I must admit the Vietnam Veterans have been very patient in their relationship with time concerning any research findings, but their life is depleting daily. I have already given you the estimation of the Vietnam Veterans life which is stated at least 390 a week are estimated to be dying. The pain the Vietnam Veterans had to endure through the years in dealing with Agent Orange should have triggered a reaction across the United States a long time ago. Getting behind the Vietnam Veterans would have been the best thing the people in the United States could have done. But they did not they let the issue involving Agent Orange and the chemical companies linger. Did the people think the Vietnam Veterans were lying and their health problems were something they dreamed up and would soon go away? This is what I am talking about when I disgusted earlier about being misinformed through the media when the Vietnam Veterans returned home. A lot more could have been done to save their life through medicine and continual research, but it was being intentionally overlooked. Now in today's communities when we look at Willowbrook, Illinois and Waukegan, Illinois Sterigenics is polluting the air out there and people are coming down with cancer due to the use of (Ethylene Oxide). Cancer is noted as being caused from too much of the (Ethylene Oxide) in the air. Nothing was being done for the Vietnam Veterans everyone was saying Agent Orange had nothing to do with the health problems of the soldiers, they were lying. After over forty years the script was finally flip open were everyone could read about the damages Agent Orange had caused in the Vietnam Veterans life. Those who were already aligned in the political positions were too proud to admit they made a mistake and would not hold themselves at fault for what had taken place over the years concerning the Vietnam Veterans. Even with all of the lives lost during the war Agent Orange would become a big contributor to the irrational behavior the soldier exhibited once they returned home from "Nam." It took a filtering out process of changes in Congress and continual meetings of the men in green uniforms who cared about their brothers that were already suffering from Agent Orange and could not speak up for themselves.

Wives, Women and Friends of the Vietnam Veteran's

Another thing that is not being mentioned is the women who were affected by the soldiers who returned home from the Vietnam War with the herbicide chemical Agent Orange in their system. I feel this question is within its realms of open discussion due to Agent Orange being in the DNA of the soldier. This also meant that every time the soldier made love to his wife; she was receiving contaminated sperm inside of her uterus. Whether there was a baby born or not the wife was subjected to the chemical from the blood his sperm contained. I can openly say this from experience during my service and the injections we were ordered to take before going to Afghanistan and after arriving from the war zone back at Fort Benning. I could remember just as if it were yesterday when we were told we had to be injected with the virus anthrax in 2007. Because if we were put in an environment already contaminated with anthrax we would not be affected because we were being injected with the anthrax antidote which did contain some form of anthrax. We were told while we were going home on leave to not have sex with our wife or girlfriend. Not to have intercourse for the next thirty days with our wife or girlfriend because she would most definitely contract a form of the virus, because her body would not be immune to the anthrax like ours. The reason why I am stating these facts in relations to the Vietnam War because we were told the woman would contract the anthrax virus, she would be considered to be contaminated and it would be our fault because we were warned. While at Fort Riley we had to sign a document stating we were given a class concerning the anthrax injection we had to take, we did not have an option. I am referencing this inoculation I had to take concerning the Vietnam War because the Vietnam Veterans returned home with the Agent Orange virus in their DNA. Which also means every time the soldier who was already contaminated slept with his wife and ejaculated inside of her she was receiving a form of the Agent Orange virus? Point taken if the soldier was contaminated his wife or girlfriend was also contaminated. In case you were not aware of what is consistent in sperm it is created from the males DNA his blood and is now traveling inside of his wife. In case you are not understanding what the acronym DNA stands here is the definition (**Deoxyribonucleic Acid**) it is defined as, "a self-replicating material present in nearly all living organisms as the main constituent of chromosomes. It is the carrier of genetic information." So, when we talk about the soldier's wife, I want you to be cognizant and clear that because she loved the Vietnam Veteran so she was willing to go through everything the Vietnam Veteran went through and she did not leave him. When it came time to take the Vietnam Veteran to the doctor she was there with or without the help of the VA. But it is with the help of the VA through the years the wives of Vietnam Veterans have become the backbone the (caregiver) of the man she loved and stayed in the marriage or relationship with him. Simply because she believed in what the Vietnam Veteran was doing in serving his country and decided that she wanted to be a part of it. There is so much we have to give consideration to as it relates to the wives of soldiers and the women who decided they wanted to play a bigger part and actually joined the military to serve as their counterparts did. When it is all said and done military wives and women who served deserve these same words, "Thank You for Your Service" just as every man who has put on a uniform receives recognition. Of course, he would have to be an honorably discharged veteran from a qualified branch of the United States Armed Forces who deserves to receive that honor. When you look closer at Agent Orange and the wife or girlfriend who was being a (caregiver) to her husband or spouse dying with Agent she could have very easily said she did not want any parts of it and just walked away. But she stayed and that makes all the difference in the world. One day the Vietnam Veteran's wife has children, she brings joy into the soldier's life by giving him a wholesome family. Not knowing the genetic transfer of TCDD from the Vietnam Veterans DNA from his sperm into her body that the dangers of her being infected with "Agent Orange" would be passed on to their children and grandchildren who would be born with birth defects because of Agent Orange. Her position as a military wife was to keep that soldier happy and give him the family he always wanted. The ones who stayed in the marriage I render an honorable salute. These were the wives "ride or die" who were with the Vietnam Veterans along with the wives of soldiers from all the other wars at all cost so the soldier could complete his mission by serving his country to the fullness of his capacity. In the process of making a family unit by having children the veteran's wives also subjected themselves to different noncommunicable diseases the soldier acquired while serving his country because the stressors are the same. Remember the wife is there maintaining everything the soldier and children need while he is out in the filed or out of the country, the wife is also under a great deal of stress. There is not enough I can say about the soldier's wives who have stuck with them during wartime and after their return home from war what society does not yet comprehend is the wives are serving too. I hold the Vietnam Veteran's wives in the highest of honor for understanding what it means to be in support of the Vietnam Veteran, he needs her positive feedback. She is aware that the Vietnam Veteran situation is unique in its own way because soldiers in other wars did not have a highly toxic chemical dumped on them. The wives of the Vietnam Veterans suffered right alongside of her husband. When the nightmares came, she had to get up with the soldier to make sure he was not only harmful to himself. But to bring him back to a reality of letting him know his family was not the enemy and he was not in a war zone. This is what PTSD takes some of us through and it takes a loyal and strong woman to see the pain the veteran is having to deal with. She lets him know he is home with family that loves him. These are the stories the public does not hear about which is unfortunate because society does need to know what happens to the soldier once he returns home from war. Now since times have changed, I must say not only wives, but women are now serving, and they are a big part of the military family. So, let me say that once she returns home from war the military wife is exactly what she is married to the military just like her husband is obligated to the contract. His wife and family are obligated to move when the soldier has to move and be ready and prepared for unexpected changes to occur in the soldier's life and duty stations. No one can count the sleepless nights the military wife has had trying to keep her husband from drinking to ease the pain or taking too much medication to forget the things he saw in Vietnam. Trying the talk to him and calm him down in order that he would be able to deal with whatever pain he was in at the time in a responsible manner. Many times, the soldier was given medication to relax and deal with his pain. His wife was there to discourage him from taking too much of the medication and just talk. With Agent Orange now a factor in both of their lives and with the wife having more contact with the soldiers many times she was able to help him to refrain from doing anything to himself due to the nightmares and bad memories the soldier had bottled up inside of himself from being in the jungles of Vietnam. The Vietnam Veteran wives have been the ones to keep them going. Their wives were there helping them to get to their appointments on time or to the emergency room if a problem occurred. They became the caregivers of the soldiers and did not leave the soldier in his time of need. Keeping in mind the military has the highest divorce rate and the highest suicide rate in the United States of America. The Vietnam Veteran's wife also had to endure the verbal abuse her husband was receiving in the airport and malls as he returned home from Vietnam. These are the things people do not think about, but the Vietnam Veterans wife received just as much abuse as he did while they walked together through the airports, bus stations, boats and within their own communities. Although the name calling was not directed to her, she diffidently felt the impact of what her husband was receiving. But she stayed with him knowing what was done to her husband the Vietnam Veteran was not right. It was all wrong and the one who loved him the most could see the change in him. She could see the difference in his behavior, and she could also see the changes taking place in his body as "Agent Orange" was slowly taking him apart. Since the soldier's blood was now contaminated and there was no way of getting rid of Agent Orange, it was also being deposited inside of his wife's body every time they made love. In case you are not aware of some of the long-term side effects of Agent Orange upon human contact, a toxic chemical that would later turn out to be quite devastating. Its long-term effects include cancer, liver damage, heart and long disorders, skin aliments and nervous system diseases. Scientific studies continue to update their statistical research although it's not fast enough the researchers receive their results from the laboratory in search for new effects from the chemical. It is very easy to study field rats and guinea pigs as we search for new and better ways to understand certain aliments and come up with a better diagnosis. To come up with some kind of a solution as to what would take place with the soldier once contact has been made with the chemical Agent Orange. Scientists will state the facts in their findings as to what they were able to find out from their research. They should be able to formulate on the behavioral changes in these experimental rats and guinea pigs and the effects of Agent Orange on the field rats and mice being used in the labs for testing. Most of the research would be considered to be scientific testing due to the chemists attempting to find out more about "Agent Orange." By injecting them with Agent Orange and watching the deterioration of the animals' bodies, they will be able to determine at some point what will happen to a human being who has been exposed to a certain amount of the toxic chemical. I must say these are factual statements and bear truth to the deterioration of the bodies of the animals being researched. As logical as it must appear to be determinates of the animals studied could not have been finalized. What becomes in error of what the studies of these animals pertain to are limited attributes concerning their position as scientist and their scientific research on animals. After the research is done, they must conclude if the research done on the animals correlate to the cause and effect on the human body; particularly the Vietnam Veterans. The questions I am presenting are not scientist's questions and their limited research of Agent Orange due to the use of rats, field mice and guinea pigs. But they are being designed to enhance the thinking of one's capabilities concerning research projects and say, "was their research enough." These are areas of questionable doubt of which opens an area of grey matter. Which also conceptualizes "Agent Orange" has a broader view of error of more than 40% that has not been tested resulting in the Vietnam Veteran not being able to receive the adequate attention needed through scientific, medical and or clinical research. Based on my analytical presumption it should not be questionable to say that although millions of dollars have been spent on scientific research as its findings are stated involving "Agent Orange" the findings are not enough to conclude that the side effects listed are conclusive to the point that there are no other symptoms the Vietnam Veteran could have or that science may have missed. I state the current finding to be true but still inconclusive. The probability of other damage done to the Vietnam Veterans due to Agent Orange has yet to be determined which makes the current findings inconclusive as well as indecisive. Children of the Vietnam Veteran and grandchildren of the Vietnam Veteran are still coming up with Agent Orange in their DNA. Agent Orange is being genetically transferred in their blood and the length of the damage done has not been determined. There is so much more that was not exposed through research studies due to limited federal funding's. I am always putting myself out for my fellow veterans and here is the perfect example to question if there are still Vietnam Veterans (Missing in Action) (MIA). Why were the search parties stopped when there are still soldiers who are missing in action during the Vietnam War? Their captivity still remains in question today. Are all of the soldiers home safe and are there still soldiers in concentration camps being tortured believing they are going to be found and brought back to the United States.? The one thing all soldiers are taught is to not give up hope and to never forget that we will always search for all of our soldiers until the last one is found and brought home. I personally cannot be more conclusive when I say science research is inconclusive in its findings as it relates to "Agent Orange." If you would allow me a moment, I can give you areas of study that have not been covered during the research of Agent Orange.

Let me walk you through what the soldiers everyday functioning abilities entail. Enhanced with almost 20 years later we have to go all the way back to 1983 when the Vietnam Veteran was first acknowledged as having Post Traumatic Stress Disorder (PTSD). Along with the late diagnosis don't forget the Vietnam Veterans inability to function in a systematical society that has done very little to make him comfortable. What I am saying here is the Vietnam Veteran was not given a thorough enough medical examination prior to him being acclimated back into a society that did not want him there. The Vietnam Veterans were released by the military as sheep are put out for slaughter. They did not have a safe house to return to or the friends and family to be there for them to understand what they had been through. Vietnam was an area of blood and guts, death lurked with every step they took in the jungles of Vietnam. Their minds were plagued with the horrific memories of what they wanted to leave behind in Vietnam. They had to put up with being called out of their names because of what the media was portraying them as dehumanized animals. These men were returned to a country that was not prepared to receive them even if all of the obscenities had not been a part of their unaccepted welcome home acceptance. The medicine as well as the drugs and alcohol the Vietnam Veterans had gotten involved in was their cry out for help. Glad to be out of the jungles of Nam and be home. Wanting to receive the hero's welcome they rightfully deserved to have but the citizens they defend in war pushed them away. The soldiers alienated themselves from the rest of society, a society that no longer considered the Vietnam Veterans their own.

CHAPTER IX

UNEXPECTED ILLNESSES,
VETERANS WIVES QUESTION

THE INTERNAL DAMAGE WAS not visible. The soldiers who returned home with missing limbs was a visible medical situation that went unquestioned. The wives of the soldiers knew they had to deal with that situation in order to help rebuild the soldier emotionally and mentally, to get him back to where he was before he went to war. There was no questionable doubt of what needed to be done for the soldier when looking at the soldier physically because this is what I call visible damage. The wives of the Vietnam Veterans had a much harder job to do than you could imagine yet their stories remain untold. I am going to try to give you some situations to help you think about who this soldier was before the soldier became what the United States Armed Forces made him. He was a man his family, friends, his loved ones and his wife was looking for when he returned home from war but that particular person they were looking for, the old laughter and the personality he once had was gone. The man they were looking for to return home would never show up again. The Vietnam War had taken so much out of him that it was only a shell of a man they were looking at. This is what the Vietnam Veterans wife had to deal with inside of their home, the shell of the man she was slowly trying to put back together. A man who use to go to the park, tell jokes and keep everyone laughing, talk and play. A man who use to be able to see a future ahead of him of a nice home, a job, children and a chance at a better future for himself. This man was dismantled, taken apart and all that was left was the soul he had inside of him that said I want to live. I want to be able to go home again. Well he was a rare one because those who could not coupe came back home and committed suicide, got involved in drugs and alcohol. This soldier's wife had to deal with the nightmares and the visons the soldier saw. Many times, not wanting to go out in public because he was afraid, he would see something that reminded him of war and literally snap. This is what the Vietnam Veteran's wife had to go through not knowing if she would not wake up some morning because the Veteran had an episode and killed her in her sleep. I know it all sounds bizarre, but things happen, this is why many wives left and divorced their husband. The love of a woman for the man she cares about is universal when you have a "ride or die" wife with you and will not let go no matter what. For the wives who stuck with the Vietnam Veterans they can relate to what I am talking about. It is very difficult to watch someone you love taken apart and not know how to put them back together again. That is what the Vietnam War did to the Vietnam Veterans the war dismantled them and many just were not able to put the pieces back together again. These were the ones we lost to the prison system, drugs overdose and suicides because they could not cope. While the Vietnam Veterans were dealing with Agent Orange the surprises they would receive in their body were not gifts, meaning the illnesses and sickness that began to take over the soldiers body sometimes came over night and it was just as surprising to the soldiers wife. One day the soldier was up laughing and talking and the next time the soldier was seen he would be headed to the hospital. This is just how unpredictable the herbicide chemical "Agent Orange" is and has been consistent throughout the longevity of its existence. Many wives have had to witness the outbreaks of the soldier, their cries in the dark, along with the fear in their eyes. A fear of many endless nights they thought would never come to an end in the jungles of Vietnam. A fear that would only be conveyed to the soldier in his past as he relates to a new world, he no longer knew so-called civilized people in the United States of America. A civilized nation of people that was not ready to receive the kind of damaged goods that were returning home, the Vietnam Veterans. This is why the prose "America Don't Forget" was written as a reminder to the citizens of the United States they could not just put the Vietnam War Veterans on an island and forget about them. These are our brothers and sisters who suffered for the freedoms of this country and they deserve to be honored for their service. The trauma their wives went through is priceless and worthy of praise. For those of us who are married and treasure the words until death do us part means there wasn't an option to leave. This is what makes marriage so sacred keeping in mind the soldiers wife suffered a great loss of what once was. The Vietnam Veteran that returned home will never be the same. In her loving nature of being a nurturer of life many of the wives stayed to help the soldier find himself again if that was possible. They stayed with the soldier to give some comfort to the soldier because all of the innocence he once had was no longer there for him, to be able to dream, it all had been taken away. The reality of what the Vietnam Veterans life had become was now all a fight for what not only the United States government was willing to deal with but the citizens as well. Was it fair to the soldiers to put them off for so long and say this never happened and twenty years later for Congress to say, Oh we made a mistake Agent Orange did cause some of the defects in these men and (Congress) was the reciprocators of the problem. But the wives stayed and watched these men fall apart piece by piece. Their dignity and their pride slowly taken away from them day after day. As things begin to go wrong and the Vietnam Veterans body began to fall apart no one could ever imagine the pain they were in. No one could ever imagine how many times their devoted wives went into the empty rooms of their homes and just cried but the soldier never saw it. This is such an emotional situation but not as complicated as it has been made to be. The biggest part of the entire dilemma was accepting fault for what had happened to the soldiers unfortunately it is still happening today in 2019 going into 2020 over forty years later. Although many years has passed since the Vietnam War has been over there is still offset repercussions of what has taken place after the war. If you cannot get the concept of what I am saying here, then let me make it very plain. To all who are still trying to understand the problems we as a nation of people still have to deal with and others who are still trying to make sense of the war. The Vietnam Veterans are still dying from the aftermath of what the war and Agent Orange is doing to them. Once again what we are finding out is that it is not just the Vietnam Veterans, it is their children and their grandchildren who are affected as well. I almost certain that I should be adding in the great grandchildren. This is something that has not been taken into consideration when we look at what is owed to the Vietnam Veterans for their contributions to this great nation. We are looking at gratuity owed but it would be impossible to even attempt to pay any Vietnam Veteran for all the damages caused by the war and Agent Orange. Which leave us still standing in the midst of allowing this tragic dilemma to continue without manning up to claim what we already know to be true. And that is where we as a nation of people messed up and we are at fault for every medical problem the Vietnam Veterans, their spouses and children are suffering with today. Can we fix it? Yes, we can fix the situation. It is no different than it would be for those soldiers to have to suffer any longer than what they have had to for over forty years. Being denied the right to medical treatment and denial of Congress not knowing that Agent Orange was a herbicide that was and is extremely toxic which affected the Vietnam Veterans lives. Agent Orange is not going away but is being genetically transferred to their children and their children's children DNA. It is painful when you really think about it. And we as a nation of people would have to come to some form of reassurance that the men who swore to fight and protect the rights of a nation of people, we call American citizens. We're at odds with what had taken place in Vietnam because of what is called a lack of understanding, a lack of research and knowledge about the herbicide chemical Agent Orange. Not know the length of its infestations would affect the Vietnam Veterans and literally destroy their life. Not to mention the wives or fiancés of the soldiers. I suppose you feel that because of the Vietnam Veterans life did not mean anything to you that their children and grandchildren should also suffer and die the same way? I want you to bare down and understand these men who returned home after protecting your rights as citizens never did have a chance at having a normal life again. The things we as citizens in the greatest country on the face of this earth take for granted are the things we freely do and live for every day, our freedom. Things like going to the stores with our family, going to the mall, going to our children's baseball games, soccer games, football games, basketball games, hockey games etc., Oh! Please don't let me leave out family outings. What about watching our children grow up, go to the park, take their first step, say their first word, grow their first tooth, potty train etc. These are just some of the things the soldiers who protected your life did not get a chance to experience, because they were in the jungles of Vietnam fighting for your freedoms. Can you imagine never being able to see your newborn child? How about not being able to attend your child's first birthday party? What about proms, graduations and talent shows they may have gotten involved in during their school years. Oh, and last but not least walking your daughter down the aisle. But how do you walk her down the aisle with no legs because they were blown off in the jungles of Vietnam on the battlefield fighting for citizens you don't know, the American people. Everyone need to step back for a second and take a good look at what we all have allowed to happen to the Vietnam Veterans. How about the soldier who returned home from Vietnam and wanted to have children with his wife, but he could not because the herbicide found in Agent Orange affected his ability to produce children? It is even worse for the Vietnam Veterans who haven't any excuse their limitations did not consist of having to go to a meeting or the car did not have gas, or I simply forgot. They did not have to make up an excuse; they were out of the country in a war zone fighting so all of you could reap the benefits of their sacrifices. You, America have called these men all kinds of names through the years murderers etc., Only what remains to not be in question is the fact that the very same men who you are calling murderers, and were spit on by you were the very same men who defended you in the ugliest war this country had ever been in. They are damage for life not because of their negligence but because of your negligence. Now their children and their children's children are going to be going through the same suffering as the soldier's in "Nam" because of Agent Orange being transferred genetically in their DNA. Moving forward we can look at two things to help ease the minds of those who are trying to be understanding. We can look at the men who went to war for this country and fought in "Nam" and help them due to the mistakes a lack of research has caused this nation. Or we can look at the lives of innocent children who were infected with the herbicide chemical Agent Orange and try to make them as comfortable as possible due the infectious herbicide chemical that already resides in their bodies. By watching the children of these soldiers whose DNA carries the herbicide Agent Orange in their system and setting up federal funding to assist those with the proper medical coverage needed to give them a comfortable life. Given the situation of war it is with all the variables needed that everyone should and need to consider the suffering of their fellow human being and that no one should be left without the proper medical and dental health insurance coverage to be allowed to make it in this world after serving your country. I can say beyond a reasonable doubt what has taken place with the Vietnam Veterans is unheard of, they gave their life for you. And what has been allowed to take placed with the soldiers who served in the Afghanistan War, and Iraq War would not be considered to be fair to the soldiers in the sense of saying; before the armed forces purchased the flak jackets Boeing had already tested the protective jackets and revealed to the parties involved that the weight of the flak jackets which consisted of iron plates inside the seams of the flak jackets which gave weight to the flak jackets of 55lbs. Due to the study of the iron plates and the weight of the flak jackets it was reported that the weight of the flak jacket being 55lbs alone in weight. Not consisting of all the other equipment, the soldier had to carry like the Kevlar, the rounds, magazines, the belt, the rifle, boots, and uniform. The flak jacket was already researched, and the findings were that due to the weight of the flak jacket and its consistent use by the soldier there would be permanent damage to the exoskeleton and the endoskeleton of soldier. I am putting this information in with the Vietnam Veterans because at least I know and researched documents have already revealed why damage is done to the clavicle, the shoulder and backs of soldiers who served in Afghanistan and Iraq War. It is documented that these findings were known about before the war even began. If I am recalling this correctly the dates of the researcher's findings were around 2002. Before the flak jackets were ever issued but the government still issued them, and soldiers had no other choice but to wear them. Unlike the damage done by Agent Orange, soldiers who served in Afghanistan and Iraq would still be able to function once they returned home but under very limited physical conditions. Whereas the Vietnam Veterans were victims of toxic chemicals and there would not be a full recovery. The damages done to Vietnam Veterans and soldiers of today's wars are considered to be permanent. The herbicide was in their blood to stay. On the other hand, the damage that would be done to the Afghanistan and Iraq soldiers would be permanent. True story, "I remember waiting in the lobby of the hospital waiting to see the doctor. While I waited the doctor came out in the hallway with a female soldier and she was asking him about her ability to get pregnant and carry a baby full term. I remember the doctor telling her she would be able to get pregnant but the second she found out she was pregnant that she would have to go on complete bed reset. If she did not go on complete bed rest, she would either lose the babe or not be able to carry her baby full term. This was due to the damage she had already suffered in her back from the weight of the flak jacket." These are instances that those of you in society do not consider and many of you do not know about because you did not volunteer to serve. And this is why I continue to tell you when you look at a soldier and see him out remember he is not whole but he or she wants to blend in with the rest of the world and appear to be okay. Stop looking at them and prejudging them as though they do not have any hidden pains, they do but you cannot see them. Even with that being said many Vietnam Veterans were affected with Agent Orange including the wives and fiancés of the Vietnam Veterans. The wives and fiancé's who were the recipients of their husbands or boyfriend's sperm were susceptible to Agent Orange because it is an herbicide that is blood born and sperm does have blood in it. By the Vietnam Veterans returning home from Vietnam with Agent Orange in their system it was now being transferred from the Veteran to the wife to the children. This is how the children of the Vietnam Veterans and their grandchildren have become recipients of Agent Orange and will most likely die from the chemical herbicide being genetically transferred to their DNA. What's even more mind boggling are the facts that have already been discovered by the VA concerning Agent Orange and the years it takes for the veterans claims to be worked on knowing the Vietnam Veterans are dying at 390 soldiers a day. I recall talking to a Vietnam Veterans wife whose husband had died from Agent Orange and she told me "Each day there is something different to deal with." Another Veteran's wife said her husband cannot do the things he use to do because of Agent Orange, She said before he went to "Nam" he was super active but know he cannot even tie his own shoes." Most of the factual causes of Agent Orange is researched in documents the Veterans Administration has to have time to review the document to come to a formal agreement and see if the diagnosis is fit for some kind of recovery to be able to attend to the need of the Vietnam Veterans and their family. The researched findings on Agent Orange remains inconclusive but the damages and deaths of the Vietnam Veterans are not inconclusive due to the toxic herbicide chemical Agent Orange and the health problems it continues to cause. What is also significant concerning the veterans who have served this country is the continual findings concerning Agent Orange which should be vital in setting up federal funding for the Veterans future health, medical and dental care.

CHAPTER X

THE DEVASTATING IMPACT
OF AGENT ORANGE

N O ONE REALLY KNEW the full impact of what "Agent Orange" would have on the Vietnam Veterans wife and children. They also did not know the impact "Agent Orange" would have on the United States of America. I can go a little further and even say what was also not contemplated was the impact the highly toxic chemical "Agent Orange" would have on Vietnam and the Vietnamese people who live there. By "Agent Orange" being a highly toxic chemical herbicide defoliant used in Vietnam the boundaries of damage it would produce would be almost considered to be unlimited. Due to the lack of research and testing needed during that time and the purpose of its use which was to destroy foliage in the jungles of Vietnam. American soldiers contact with the chemical was not in question of the damage to the soldiers if there was any human contact with the chemical. What remains questionable to date is why was Agent Orange sprayed in the area the soldiers were in? The argument would be the chemical Agent Orange was sprayed in an area of heavy foliage to be cleared for soldiers to walk through and have a line of sight. Making visibility and transportation easier as well as troops being able to maneuver through the jungles of Vietnam. This statement made it even more understandable that although it took the United States of America's government a little close to twenty-three years to respond to the cry of the soldiers who had become sick from the chemical Agent Orange. It still leaves a blind door open as to what took place with the soldiers to make them feel they had been abandoned by their own countrymen. What I can remember as a child is that the United States government did not want to accept responsibility for what they had done to the soldiers? I do not know if it was because what it was going to cost to treat all of the soldiers who had contact with Agent Orange. Or was it because the United States government did not want to be responsible for all of the deaths that would occur in the future concerning the chemical herbicide Agent Orange? The sad thing about the entire situation is that no one knew all of the side effects, the health and medical problems that would occur. The chemical herbicide and other chemicals used in Vietnam would appear to be something that was just stated. Because the chemical agents were available the military wanted to try it out to see what was going to benefit the soldiers, so they said, "let's try this." Agent Orange and the other chemicals used during the Vietnam War turned out to be a costly naive gesture to save the soldiers not knowing the long- or short-term repercussions behind the decisions made. It remains to be more than just unfortunate for the Vietnam Veterans. The Vietnam Veterans entire life is based on not just the war itself but their return home to be denied the right to be treated by the VA because Congress never okayed the acceptance of fault for Agent Orange as I stated earlier until many years later. Nor did they obligate the government to make payment to such a ridiculous theory that a chemical with such a high toxicity level as Agent Orange would cause so much damage to the human body. Not knowing the use of such a chemical would affect the men who had the herbicide in their system, and it would slowly begin to deteriorate their body like that of a plant which had been sprayed to only kill certain foliage but actually kills everything inside of it as well as in sight. Oh boy!!! What a mistake the only difference is plants can be regrown with seeds. All of the unexpected did happen to the Vietnam Veterans and their health to date is still deteriorating. You cannot replace a son, or daughter or granddaughter just by saying I am sorry or by saying, "we are trying." That statement is not going to bring back their loved ones. The same action the soldiers took when they had to go to "Nam" without question to fight for "the Cause." The same respect should be rendered to the soldiers as new test and findings are discovered about the herbicide Agent Orange. And please keep in mind this book is not being written to point fingers. But someone need to make people aware of what is not being done for the Vietnam Veterans. It's over forty years after the war and they are still suffering from Agent Orange. The Vietnam Veterans did not have a chance and they most certainly did not get a fair shake. Through years of research we are able to look at the Vietnam War holistically. There are documents from past wars and current wars to review and say to ourselves were the young eighteen-year-old boys we sent into the war zone with only two weeks of bootcamp training ready for such a task? Were they honestly prepared at the age of eighteen years old mentally ready to defend a country for the betterment of all mankind? Only to return home rejected and emasculated of their right to be called hero's due to politically unanswered questions concerning our position as Americans in the Vietnam War. The one thing we can say for sure is that the soldiers who fought and died in the Vietnam War is not something we have to question. They gave their life fighting for you and it is senseless to say their conduct was unbecoming of a soldier on the battlefield after they returned home. Due to the circumstances involved and the fact they were never given a chance in the jungles of Nam or if you will allow me to say the war zone back home in the United States of America. This is because of another battle the Vietnam Veterans had to fight. I understand that I am focusing on the Vietnam War but please keep in that soldiers who fought in the Iraq, and Afghanistan War are still fighting for their benefits as well. I am focusing on the Vietnam Veterans because they have been mistreated the worst and denied the most. These men are dying with pancreatic cancer, cancer of all kind, kidney, heart and live failure. And there is no recovery because even if they received a new heart, kidney, liver, or pancreas. You must keep in mind Agent Orange is in their DNA and because the blood is filtered through all parts of the body Agent Orange being in the soldier's DNA will affect each soldier differently and at different times in different ways. With organs being replaced they will eventually end up shutting down because Agent Orange is circulating throughout the Vietnam Veterans body. Although each soldier's body is different, the herbicide is going to react differently to each soldier's body mass. As I stated earlier that the Vietnam Veterans deserve the most attention even with all of the wars, the United States has been involved in. Because of the lack of respect, they have been shown. They still remain to be treated the worst.

I do not what to get to far off track, but I was asked while I was working on my 6th book titled "**The Cocoa Planation's America's Chocolate Secret... Force Child Slavery, Forced Child Labor**. Why did I choose the Ivory Coast of Africa and Ghana to write about? My explanation to that question: Was because it was noted as being the worst form of child slavery, child sodomy and child murder in the history of the world. The children working on the Cocoa Plantations and the Tobacco Plantations need help as we speak. Of course, there are other countries involved with abusing children to get the cocoa bean for the Chocolate Industries. Unfortunately, the Ivory Coast of Africa and Ghana has five-year-old children working 100 hours a week, every week. These children are being raped and sodomized while the United States just stands by and does nothing. The United States only fear is the Chocolate Industries may be boycotted and go out of business. This is the reason why they allow the cocoa plantations to function. I also found through research the Chocolate Industry is not only a trillion-dollar Industry. The Chocolate Industries give very healthy donation to government officials which would appear to be a very good reason why nothing is being done to stop the rape and sodomy of the children. I believe the donation the Chocolate Industry gives our government is somewhere around 700,000 a year. It saddens me that anyone could put their own greed before the safety of innocent children.

This is one of the reasons why I am speaking out so much about the Vietnam War. Because our Vietnam Veterans have been treated the worse in comparison to soldiers who have returned home after wars in the history of the United States. So, in my comparison to my 6th book of being the worst treated this is why I chose to bring awareness to the Vietnam War Veterans. It is also an ongoing situation that needs the attention of the American people. Since they are also the worst treated as well as overlooked. The truth about "Agent Orange" is the herbicide and what little research known was hidden from the American people for over 30 years. It was not until 1991 that Agent Orange was first admitted by Congress as being the fault of the American Government. When I think of these young soldiers' bodies and minds being contaminated with unknown chemicals that were sprayed in the jungles of Vietnam to kill the foliage but also entered into the body of the veterans giving them cancer and so many other problems for over forty years. The highly toxic chemical was in the body and blood of the young soldiers returning home not only affecting them physically, but mentally and emotionally while they were trying to adjust to the norms of an American society they had left behind. They had to learn how to live like animals in the jungles of Vietnam in order to survive. "Nam" was now their real world. In a sense of trying to survive and figure out how the enemy thought or what their next move would be was stressful enough. I can relate to this because of the missions I went out on while severing in Afghanistan. The preparation time it takes in getting a soldier ready to go to war would stun the average human being. I have been told many times by my friends "I don't know how you did it?" War becomes a way of life a way of seeing the animalistic nature of what an individual would do in order to survive. While we were all on a peace keeping mission in support of the United States of America soldiers also had to maintain the peace and integrity amongst themselves. The Humanitarian Drops and the Medical Drops we went outside the wire, the safety check points was not a joke. We were all standing in the midst of Afghan's not knowing if we would all be killed or if they knew we were there to help them by giving them food, clothes, shoes and some form of hope that things were going to get better. Even though it was part of our peace keeping missing we still had to set perimeters and make sure they knew through their province leaders we were not there to disrespect them or cause any problems. The soldiers in Vietnam did not have that luxury, it was kill or be killed. And their level of awareness was more than likely worn down to nothing simply because they had to be on a level of alert, I would say was not humanly normal. How does an individual's nerve stay on a peek level for months, how about a year? This is what was taking place with the soldiers in the war zones especially in Vietnam. Where was the down time for the soldiers who served in Vietnam? When were the Vietnam Veterans able to relax? That is a question I cannot relate to. Although I did get a chance to sleep some nights while serving in Afghanistan, I do not believe my mind was able to shut off the fact that death would be possible at any time. As I laid in my bunk to go to sleep, sleep was something that had to find me. I could not just lay down and say I am going to sleep and sleep peacefully. There was a continual radio voice intercom by the Afghans telling us how we were fighting a senseless war and how our American government hated us. We went to sleep listening to this and woke up listening to this brain taunting garbage 24 hours a day seven days a week, it seemed like it never shut off. They were trying to infect our minds and make us think the United States had abandoned us, but I knew that was not the case. It was even worse for the Vietnam Veterans, the continually loud radio messages from "Charlie." The Vietnam Veterans were not on a peace keeping mission. They were in an all-out war trying to keep their sanity. And still trying to figure out what was behind every tree, every bush that moved, and any other movement while they were out in the midst of the jungle, they knew very little about. A jungle so dark and dense with heavy vegetation and foliage that was very hard for the soldiers to maneuver in. In the darkness of the night in a jungle dense with vegetation and foliage it only takes a second while on night patrol or recon to lose a squad member who was not paying attention. This is how fast things were taking place in the jungles. "I can remember doing my jungle training we had been up for three days straight. We were taught during our training session that when we lay down to set up perimeters to interlock our boots one on top of the other. That would be one soldiers boot would overlap another soldiers boot. Because we all were so tired the soldier lying next to you just might fall asleep and hopefully if he feels your boot move, he will wake up and not miss the squad's movement. Our training paid off as we set our perimeters there were soldiers who did in fact fall asleep and did not feel my boots move when it was time to move. I took the extra split second to get the soldier up and moving. Everything was so precise involving night movement. I can remember it being so black and dark that it was important to keep your sights on the soldier in front of you in order to not get lost. Even the split second I had taken to shake the other soldier turning my head away to get the soldier up could have cost us to lose our recon patrol. Usually on recon the best four who are able to travel together at night are usually put on the mission. That one distraction could have caused us to lose sight of the rest of the squad in the pitch-black night of the jungle, where not even your hand before your face is visible." This was training which meant that at the end of the day we would be going back to headquarters to report what went wrong. For the Vietnam Veterans it was real, two weeks of training was not even close to what they needed for jungle warfare training. I have scratched my head many times just wondering how the Vietnam Veterans survived in the jungles of Vietnam. As heart wrenching as it may sound the Vietnam Veterans, yes, the eighteen and nineteen-year-old boys who received two weeks of training. And were dropped in the hottest war zone the United States had ever been in were not properly prepared, not even for their time era for a mission, a war that had so many sides to it. Our soldiers were not only looking at a war in the jungle. They were looking at guerilla warfare, tunnel warfare underground in the jungle etc. I know it all sounds horrific and of course you are going to say they signed the contract with the Armed Forces of the United States of America that part is true. But they did not sign up to be slaughtered. They signed up believing they were being prepared to take on any defense needed when it came down to defending the United States. If you notice I continue saying they were defending the United States of America because it was your taxpaying dollars that sent them there through your states Congressional vote. Now since years have passed through postwar problems the Vietnam Veterans are still the ones who are suffering and need a special kind of forgiveness from the United States of America. Just say "I Apologize" and show your love to them by expressing it with some of the ideas I have mentioned in the early chapters of the book. You read about the special awards, a special federal holiday, taps on all radio stations across the United Sates. Dinner with the President and getting their files closed so they can receive their monies owed to them. Then get the non-governmental research out and put some government researchers in to find the co-relations to Agent Orange the Vietnam Veterans had been talking about for over fifty year now, that's a start.

CHAPTER XI

VIETNAM VETERANS (BOYS) WHO BECAME (MEN) OVERNIGHT

IT IS OH SO important that America sees the other side of this story. The Vietnam Veterans have been given a bad rap in reference to the Vietnam War. They did what they had to do to make it back home. Many of you would not understand because you have not lived under the pressures of a war zone. Unless you consider being at home arguing with your spouse a war zone and some of you would consider that to be a comparison to Vietnam. You should be laughing about now because I am being just a little facetious. And if you are comparing your arguments with "Nam" you might want to seek some serious "marital counseling." lol. These young soldiers were taken out of bootcamp and dropped in the hottest war zone in American history. The disadvantages awaiting them where far beyond your wildest thinking, unless you where there? Before I continue on about the young Vietnam soldiers and before I get into Agent Orange, I want you to do some deep conscious thinking. I am including a prose from my fifth book "My Book of Poems for the World" to help you understand where you are in time and space, please read it carefully:

My Shoes, My Bed, My Table

Have you walked in my shoes?
As I pulled out my old holey run-down shoes
I thought about the many miles I had walked in them,
And the condition my feet were now in.
The places they had carried me and how well they were holding up.
I had not gotten to the cardboard I would insert in my shoe soles
So, I could keep the bottom of my feet from scraping the ground;
It was hard for me to imagine the many situations, the denial
and the neglect, that so many people are not willing to accept
after they see me but not just my situation there are many others
just like mine and they are all true; You know the help because
of their condition, we feel really does not concern us.
These very shoes would lead me to different walks and travels in life,
Although I have visited many places, I was
dedicated to staying on course;
I continue on my journey each day listening to doors close behind me;
Walking into laughter of which I had become the joke; you know
Those jokes people tell (man he smells had ha, ha, ha), did you get it;
Walking into places I thought would help, only to be left out in the cold
once again, looking in from the outside viewing what I was refused.
I am putting forth this question can you walk in my shoes
and endure the pain, the headache and mistreatment I had to deal with
on a daily basis; Yes, I am understanding of longsuffering and heartache,
it's all part of life. My shoes have carried me into a more
than reasonable slice of tribulations; Walking in my shoes put
me in a place where I had to suffer long sleepless nights,
nights where I had nowhere to rest my feet from my long journey,
Walking in the frigid cold with cardboard being used to seal the holes
in my shoes I looked for heat I found none, nor did I find compassion
and no one was there to give me a shoulder
to cry on, I realized I had no help;
You have not experienced the tireless walks and misled information;
people have given me in order to get rid of me, have you?
Even though I would be in the right place they
would tell me, no it is not here,

I know of someone up the road who can help
you and the person they would
Send me to hadn't any idea what the individual
who sent me was taking about,
Do not let me forget the empty buildings I was led to that did not exist,
Remember this infamous line I am sorry we have no openings;
Because I had any money of which was obvious, they would laugh
And tell me you cannot afford the rent here; you cannot get into the
Ivey league College because of your hygiene and lack of many things
As well as income you have none. In all of my walking in these shoes
I promise to never get weary. I will not faint or get empathetic concerning
the condition under which I have to be portrayed. My swollen
and blistered feet have taken me into places
as far as I am concerned my value of life is not any more meaningless
than the other person who only appears to
have everything. I will continue
to stay positive and keep my faith until a
breakthrough comes into my life.
I will never get tired of walking in these
busted up and holey shoes because
they have been placed on my feet for a reason. My feet ache and hurt so
bad that no one will ever be able to understand
the reason as to why I keep
walking in them. If a woman where wearing
these shoes she would say the
reason she is walking in these shoes is because she has little ones to feed,
she has a mother and father to take care of or it is just that the goals she
has set in her life have not been able to be resolved at this time.
A man will say I have mouths to feed, I have
an image to uphold concerning
my children and how they see me as a father.
Yes, I am tired but my love and hope
to give them something better than what I had is not a question of should
I keep going; this is not a decision that would
take even a second to ponder
On I have to. I cannot lose my taste of life and love because my shoes have
carried me down a different road. I have not
seen anyone wash my feet, no

one has pulled off my socks to count the numerous holes in them, no one has tried to replace the worn cardboard soles on my shoes or tender me another pair. I will work for food and a decent place to eat and sleep. I remember I was told that if I stay on my journey and complete my course that I would receive a crown of victory that will suffice all that I am going through now. You see, my walk is much different, my pain is much different, my journey is much different than yours. May I ask you this question what path did you choose? And if you so which to answer this question are your shoes fit for walking, did anyone help you to lace them up concerning your walk? I just wanted to take you through a few places I had been and give you just a little taste of the journey I have been on. Although it is not over yet and there is still so much more to do. Go ahead and try them out just lace them up for a day, see if you can walk in My Shoes.

My Bed

As my day came to an end and I had gotten a little weary my shoes brought me to a place where I would be able to rest for the night. After ending my long day's journey, I reached underneath the edge of the porch and pulled out my bed. It was a cardboard box with all my night, accessories (did you laugh yet) one hole in the top to crawl in with the bottom taped together to keep my feet warm. Yes, this was my bed at least for now it had no heat or air conditioning. As powerless and as worthless in accordance to society's norms I had to look at the bright side of my current situation. Of which I hadn't any bills to pay, for rent I was sleeping on taxpayer's property free of charge and I could not afford the rent even if I had to pay, I was destitute. Please answer this question, do you think you could sleep in my bed and have the healthy body you have with the ground as your box spring and mattress. Brush your decayed teeth without any tooth paste as I do, wash in cold water of course I haven't any soap and walk around in the same dirty clothes each day after you get up in the morning as I do? I pray instead of having a good day I would just like to be able to go back to the house that I have my cardboard boxes hidden and find them there so I can have some protection from the weather tonight. Yes, it is all hard to imagine but it's not a dream it's a reality of life and I do not get the pleasure of returning home for dinner every night like you. Nothing is guaranteed in this world that much I do know. I understand the son of God hadn't any place to lay his head. He said that his journey here was only temporal it is stated in the Holy Bible "the foxes have holes to sleep and the birds have nest to sleep but the son of God has so much to do he hasn't any place to lay his head. He did not have time to build a home here on earth. If you would take the time out and visit me in my home, you would understand even more why I am the way I am. How do you see me? The looking glass self is merely a spectacle concerning my case. You see I am not a drug abuser or user; I am not an alcoholic, I am not some weirdo out hiding from anyone. I am someone who had a life at one time and hard times have fallen upon me. Life's journeys has its twist and turns and those who love Christ Jesus will suffer persecution for his name's sake. I know you are curious about walking in my shoes I. The see you do not understand why I had myself from you. Underneath the overpass where I sleep, under the bridges and inside the manholes at night. The sewer holes, this is where I have to sleep for shelter because I haven't a home or a place to stay with all of the world necessitates of comfort. You know the electricity, gas, a bed, and hot water, a refrigerator to store my food or a stove to cook hot meals on like you. I do not have any of these things of comfort. It is nice to know I have survived another day. I can come out as one of society's so-called rejects and try to watch the children play in parks, see people moving about on the streets. Didn't you know that life is so beautiful just the mere existence of being able to do things for yourself is truly a blessing? Just maybe some stranger will have mercy on my soul one day and assist me in getting some decent clothing so I can feel like I am a part of the normal social society; I would like to be a part of once again. I forgot to mention the public parks I have been thrown out of daily because I cannot be seen sleeping in them. I am so sorry, but this is the only place I am able to rest where there is some warmth in the daytime. You know when night falls the midst and dew will wet the ground. My clothes will be soiled and musty. I do not have a change of clothing or under clothes, but I do the best I can not be a public nuisance. My skin is brisk and murky like dirty water because I sleep in my clothes and I am limited being able to wash. My hair is not combed because I do not want it to be but because I have been living in the streets for so long that I have forgotten how to groom myself. The things that are normal to society is not to me any longer because of the way I have been made to live. My lifestyle and what I have had to accept in my life is hard for many to understand. I went back to get my cardboard box and it was gone. Which alley shall I sleep in tonight, which hole shall I crawl in tonight, which bridge shall I sleep under tonight while you lay in your nice warm bed? Thinking of nothing other than what you will eat in the morning and what will take place at your place of employment. How about this, lets switch for one night? Do you think you can enjoy the plate I have been served as well as I can enjoy the one you have been served? The prose that follows this one is called "My Table." Will you dine with me? I only want you to try my bed for one night, please. I don't want to scar your reputation or have grass and dirt growing out of the sides of your face from sleeping on the ground like I have. Let me make it plain to you so you can have a better understanding. I sleep wherever I can sleep. I try to rest and find peace whenever I can because my time and space is limited wherever I go and whatever I do I am watched very close. I was just wondering since you were so quick to judge me could you just for one night…. Sleep in my Bed.

My Table
Have you Dined at my Table?

At my dinner table I never sat alone. My table is nothing more than a cardboard box. I have a wood stump for a chair and for company I do not have to invite anyone my friends come by uninvited for a visit. My dinner quest consists of ants, roaches, sand fleas, mosquito's and rats. Welcome to dinner everyone. Do you still wish to dine with me? Because I am so needy, I wonder each and every day where my meals are going to come from. Is there a possibility that someone, some stranger will be kind enough to come by and see the disgusting meals I have put together just to be able to eat today? I made my favorite stops before any other homeless person got there, alley 12, alley 24, and alley 89. Those are all the rich areas and they usually throw away a lot of food, so I got to their garbage cans first. Do you still want to dine with me? Maybe I will be blessed and receive from a stranger a hot meal, one I did not get out of the garbage. Is there an angel close by who will give from the heart and show the love of God in them and have mercy on me? I see you are embarrassed for me but please don't be I am certain the ending of this prose will shock you. Not because you do not know who I am but because, believe it or not I just might be you someday. Are you still smiling? Welcome to my table and please enjoy your meal. You will be fed quite well before you leave this book, enjoy. The funny thing about my table is I really do not have a table or chairs for you to sit and dine. I have to eat wherever I can and whenever food is available. Haven't you got the joke yet please laugh a little louder, so I can hear you. Would you really mind dining with me are you certain my table will not disgust you? I will try and make sure the bugs and flies do not bother you while you eat. I must warn you I can only afford a one course meal, stop laughing. The is the treat of the day we at least I will have something in my stomach to help me sleep tonight. You know what I mean when I say a one course meal? It's actually one course, straight to the trash cans that are situated behind the fast food stores and restaurants, that's my one course. All this equates to whatever I can get my hands on to eat. I usually have at my table some of the food left at the trash cans during the day, thrown away food, overcooked food or food that was just not good enough for the customers to eat. It's all still garbage. It's all mixed in with the one thing no one else wants something out of the trash. I have come to rely on my combo cans for survival you know the cans I am speaking about if you do not know then I will fill you in quickly. There is the Burger King trash can, McDonalds trash can, Wendy's trash can, White Castles trash can, there is also Red Lobster's and Olive Garden trash cans. It used to be plentiful at the end of the night, but people started getting carry outs, and doggie bags etc. it only made matters worse for the homeless. Everyone taking food home know. I enjoy tasty delicacies as well; the gourmet food just like the upper social class of life my only problem is that I cannot afford to set at the table inside the restaurants. I must wait on the trash to be taken out. While I am going through the trash, I just might find a treat or two. Someone will forget their carryout, or someone will leave something delicious on their place that does not look gross with I get to it in the trash can. I rumble through trash for food to help to sustain my life on a day to day basis, it's better than stealing and going to jail. Believe me a man has to learn to survive and the body has to be nourished daily. So many have come through this path once loved by the public but ended up paying the price by trying to keep to with the Jones. It is funny how the grass always seems greener on the other side. This is why important decisions must be made to sustain life. That is not the embarrassing part just think, with all the money I once had, all the important places I was able to get in, all the people who sought after me and all of the important friends I supposedly have made in my life. I can only say that anyone will ever understand how I ended up the way I have until you have Walked in my Shoes, Slept in my Bed and Dined at my Table.

After reading the prose titled, My Shoes, My Bed, My Table I am prayerful that you were able to understand where I am coming from as a man a father and military officer. It is very hard for anyone to say what they would have done during the war in "Nam" because they were not there in the midst of the actual war. If in fact if you just happened to be born during the Vietnam era, then you may have a better understanding as to what actually took place concerning these young men who fought. It is unfortunate that we cannot deal with war like we deal with cartoons on television. Or maybe even your video games I don't play them because time is so precious, and I just don't have time to waste. War is real, I mean people do not pop back to life because you pushed a button to restart the game. Once that trigger is pulled and that bullet makes impact death becomes the ultimate and death unlike a video game is real, there is no recovery. War is real, and people are killed in defense of their beliefs. This is why soldiers signed up because of their beliefs of possibly making a difference in America, a better place for all. We've had all kinds of wars in America. Some were not even called or recorded as wars like in the 60's, right in the midst of America racial wars were breaking out all over. African Americans were tired of the way they were being treated and were demanding in nonviolent marches, justice. When African Americans were being led by Dr. Martin Luther King Jr. concerning their civil rights marches caused a lot of African Americans to be shot down in the streets unarmed. Raciest Whites had high powered fire hydrant water hoses turned on African American men, women and children during peace marches. Police enforcement was based on African Americans not having any rights other than doing what they were told to do. There is so much to look at when you talk about consideration of others. These are real situations that took place in the United States. The only other reason they are not able to talk about their situation is because they are not real but when you talk about death and the real reason death takes a toll on so many it is because they are not able to separate themselves from the truth. Everyone can say what they would or would not have done given the scenario of war. But to actually live it is different and should be looked at in the sense of the Vietnam Veterans not being able to relate to the way they have been treated since they returned home. What I am trying to say here is that it is all about the rights of Veterans. Their suffering is not something that can just be overlooked it is not something that is going to go away anytime soon. Some of the men who fought in Vietnam did up to five tours. When one tour would appear to have been more than enough. Many wanted to return to Nam to fight alongside their comrades. The Vietnam Veterans have been suffering in this country for over forty years. And the distasteful nonsupport they were paid by the American people after they returned from Vietnam is mind shattering. It's enough to make you wonder just what gives the American people the right to look down their noses or call them out of their name. It seems to me what the civilians had forgotten was it was them, good American people who sent those young boys off to war. Of course, the decision to go to war was voted on by a majority rule by the United States Congress to send troops to Vietnam. We declared war on Vietnam against the Vietnamese for reasons which remains unknown, quietly kept and quite controversial to this day. When you see or talk to a United States Vietnam Veteran you should be honored and proud to know you are talking to a man who survived the odds of over 47, 000 other soldiers who did not make it back. These young men who made it back to be called Vietnam Veterans are a very big part of American history. When this great nation looks back at the history of wars fought on foreign soil. We cannot continue to disrespect our own Vietnam Veterans. Young men ages eighteen and nineteen years old were taken out of bootcamp and dropped in the hottest LZ in American history. When we as a people look at the stakes of survival for the Vietnam Veterans you just might want to question, what is the value of life? What would you be willing to do to sustain life if it were you who were having to survive the jungles of Vietnam? I have to present this question to you: What is expected of a person to know of something if they have not been taught about the value of it? How precious is your life to you and what extent are you willing to go to sustain your life? Would you take a life? Please don't get to religious on me and say "Oh, I am a Christian and it is against the word of God to kill." Let me remind you God killed the first animal to use its skin to clothe Adam and Eve. Now please let me take you even further to grasp an understanding that it is okay to kill during a time a war it is considered the normalcy of war. This makes war normal; it is expected to change things. I will give you scripture to let you know it is formidable to kill when necessary. Go with me to Ecclesiastes 3:3 KJV "A time to kill, and a time to heal; a time to break down, and a time to build up." Soldiers going through bootcamp go through a reconditioning process. They go through what is called mortification of self, they are emasculated put to a certain degree of humiliation before they earn the right to be called soldiers, trained to defend the United States of America. They are first stripped of their dignity and pride, then rebuilt and encouraged in a manner in which they have never been encouraged before. Trained beyond their imaginable beliefs and made to believe they are their brother's keeper and physically unstoppable. They are the keepers of the gait; they are the ones who guard the shores of the United States of America and no one has been prepared better than the American soldier to defend it. In the meantime, these young soldiers are being prepared for different levels of military training. Advanced levels of training such a Rangers, Navy Seals, Special Forces, Snipers etc. There are different levels of training and each soldier is trained according to his specialty. I don't feel a need to mention some of the challenges these young men face while training they face possible permanent injuries and death. In all actuality, you think war is war and that every soldier who goes into war will kill someone. This is exactly what I am talking about, the prior statement is not true. You can be in combat and never leave headquarters depending on what your specialty requires. Every soldier does not go outside the wire. I personally am a prior Marine and Infantry Army Officer. Trained and conditioned to be the best of the mean green fighting machine in order that I might be able to come home from war in one piece and see my family again.

Every soldiers MOS skills will not take them outside the wire in a war zone. This is what the public does not understand. They think all soldier are the same not true. Some of them are trained in administration, some of them are trained jagg officers (lawyers), some in supply, cooks, the armory etc. These are normally soldier's who will not be directly involved in combat although they are a part of the war. Some soldier's specialty will never allow them to go outside of the safety wire into the war zone. Especially if the MOS is a critical MOS and required special training. When a soldier says they went outside the wire, this means they moved forward into enemy territory. Here's another question, how would you feel if your son had been dropped off in a jungle where his life expectancy was just sixteen minutes? How do you survive when those kinds of odds are against you? What would you do to maintain your existence? What would you do under such challenging conditions to stay alive? If you will allow me, let's take a look at the theory many of you have come to believe in, "Survival of the Fittest." Given the human chances of survival being at least sixteen minutes in "Nam". In order to sustain one's life in order to return to the normal life you once lived what would you do to have make it happen? Since you are now in the jungle and nothing is going to change for the next six months to a year meaning every second of the day you are there your chances of coming back home becomes slimmer each day. Human nature says survival is by any and all means necessary unless you just plan on dying without defending yourself. Soldiers are taught to fight, trained to kill if necessary, this is what your tax dollars pays for them to learn and do in the military, they are trained to defend the United States of America at all costs. Soldiers are trained to protect you so you can continue to live in the United States of America without fear of being wrongfully accosted by anyone. Let's face it Americans are spoiled, and they enjoy being able to move about freely, not just in the United States but throughout the rest of the world. Is it fair that life for others is not so great? Well that is something you have to workout within your own moral thoughts for the meantime. Soldiers are trained for a purpose and that purpose is to defend this country at all cost. At the cost of war, you would even have to ask yourself is the conditioning process of the soldier's fair. That is if you really want to be truthful about the entire situation as it relates to the Vietnam Veterans and what they had to do to survive, or any soldier who has been to war. Do you want to question the government now on the tactics they use to train the soldiers all this would be a part of why some soldiers do what they do and how they become what they become in the midst of war in order to survive? I can entice you just a little and say since we know there is a conditioning process to kill and destroy the enemy and America accepts the training. Why hasn't there been a question as to why there isn't a deconditioning process for the soldiers once they return home from active duty or from a war zone? Or maybe even bootcamp to see if they would be able to live a decent life as quote unquote normal American citizen? Don't get offended when I say the streets in America is just as bad as some of the wars we fight today. There were more people killed in the streets of America when I was returning home from Afghanistan than there were soldiers killed in the war zone. That's exactly right, WOW! Somewhere in the process of their return home soldiers are lost in the system, living under overpasses and bridges because they are not able to relate to the trauma that is taking place with their life. Ousted after their return home and forgotten about because the system has failed them, soldiers have nowhere to go. I have watched many soldiers stand in the barracks and or sit on their bunks and cry because their mother or father told them to stay in the military and not to come home. This is one kind of hurt to not be able to go home and at least let your parents, friends and loved ones see the change you have made within yourself. You are not the little boy that left home to join the military. You are the man who returned home from a war zone to find a new place in life. People do not realize that you look at life a lot different now and the friends you use to have are out partying, smoking and drinking. They see that you are home but what they don't understand is your mind is thousands of miles away. You are different now, your vision of life has been changed for the better and the only one who can see it is the man inside of himself, you. To this day there's no reconditioning program or process the soldiers have to attend in order to recycle what has been skillfully taken out of their innocent thoughts, out of their mind. No one knows what is considered to be normal you don't even realize your loved ones are now looking at you through rose colored shades. They want to know what makes you tick but they are afraid to ask a question they cannot handle. They ease around you hoping to find something they can grasp onto, but you have been remade you are a brand-new man now, welcome home soldier. The ACAP program is a program soldiers who are getting ready to get out of the military go through before they say goodbye to their army greens. But the ACAP Program is most certainly overdue for changes.

In the process of the soldiers getting out and returning to their civilian life again, it is not the same. Given the nature of the soldier from the wars he or she has been in to the training and military schools he or she has attended the soldier many times is just not able to relate. Even with the benefits set aside for the soldier to attend school on many occasions he or she will not be able to condition himself or herself to the school settings as it relates to classroom time and requirements. His or her focus is just not there its still in survival instinct. In many cases of which soldiers who were involved in the Vietnam after their return home they were not able to focus in a college classroom setting, the brain trauma is just too great for most. I will be discussing the higher curriculum of education as it relates to soldiers who have been to war. Or soldiers who have some form of brain trauma and how things can be looked at as they attempt to use the educational bills given to them for higher learning, this explanation will be coming later in this book or another book in the near future.

As I reflect back to the prose of My Shoes, My Bed, My Table I only want all of those who prejudged the American soldiers who went to war and their return home after. I feel it is needed information to consider when someone asks a question of what would you had done if it were you in the war? But you have judged and crucified not just the Vietnam Veterans you stuck a knife in the backs of the soldiers of war who have given their life for you, the POW's and those Kill in Action. The soldiers whose names are on the Wall.

The American people should not have jumped to such a hasty conclusion and called the Vietnam Veterans murderers and babe killers. If the theory of "Survival of the Fittest" is believed to be acceptable by men and women in America and abroad. I would have to say it should also be recognized in the most visual place of which it would not have any repercussion and that would be inside of a war zone. What code of survival would one have to follow? In war we know it is kill or be killed. Based on a code of human instinct for survival or have a manual drawn up for the mere purpose of trying to be civilized? Is there any honor in a war or any code of training providing the proper way to kill your enemy and have a clear conscious? Is there any civility involved in relations to the manner in which the Vietnam Veterans have been interrogated by the American people? I am not being judgmental at this point, but even though I knew I was just a child when the Vietnam War started up until it was over. While I listened to men talk about the war at home and watching the news on television it was heart wrenching to me at the age of four to see these men dishonored as they returned home to America. Even then I had enough compassion in my heart to understand what many people who had served wanted when they returned home and all they wanted was to be given opportunity to get their life back on track. To stand and ask the question why? My mother once told me after I mistakenly thought I had started reading the bible at the age of 10. She corrected me and told me "No you started reading the bible at the age of seven, reading and understanding it." My mother was not shocked that even at the age of four I had an understanding of what the American people were doing to the Vietnam Veterans was wrong. How can you force these young men to be in a war they did not want to be in and then turn around after you have forced them to join and call them killers, and disrespect them? Once again these were eighteen and nineteen-year-old boys, these are not men. And remember this book is not about finger pointing so I am not going to do that. I am not even going to say you were wrong for what you did to the Vietnam Veterans when they returned home. Because if you have a conscious and I know you do it will do it for you in your quiet time of thought. But I will continue to ask you the question of what did you expect these young boys you want to call men to do in a war that failed them? This is where I have to say it should not be the Vietnam Veterans seeking your forgiveness it should be you America seeking their forgiveness. The comradery these young men were sworn to during bootcamp training is a bond that will never be broken. A bonding process instilled in their heart, mind and soul to be brothers on and off the battlefields of war until death. This is how we made it through bootcamp training although it is rigorous, and many days appear to be endless and dark.

The Bonds of Brotherhood

Through the most difficult of tasks and the fiercest of times until we all can reach our bonds of brotherhood would carry us through the darkest of nights. For the rest of our lives we will draw blood together on the battlefield. We will not run because fear is not in us. We will not stop until our mission is complete and the laurel leaves of victory grace the brow of our foreheads. Let every blow be delivered with a force that will crush the skull of a mule. Let our last breath if all possible be that of men who stood their ground in battle.

These are the soldiers, the Vietnam Veterans, the men you do not get a chance to see or the conditioning process many of you unless you are affiliated with the military will never understand. There is a mission and a goal that has to be accomplished by the military as to bind the soldiers together during difficult times. Through training the military is able to accomplish this part of the mental change by putting the soldiers through challenges. One of the true stories I will share with you is my experience of going through Marine Corps bootcamp. "I remember my drill instructors SSGT Muhammad, SGT Martin was from Indiana and a young Corporal Clark from Alabama. Of course! There was interaction with all of the drill instructors but the for some reason Sgt. Clark would not let me rest he would pick on me for no reason at all. Even when there was nothing wrong, he would have me and only me doing pushups and squats and knee bends until my body was pass the point of exhaustion. This was one young Corporal who I felt wanted me to drop out of the bootcamp, but I continued to stay focused on my goals and dreams which helped to keep me balanced. I was there to become a Marine and I would not let anyone stop that. I wanted to go to college, I wanted to make something out of my life, but I had to stay focused and not lose it like I saw others in my platoon crack. Drop out because the training was too rigorous and go on medical hold. My plan was to be a part of the elite Marine force, but Sgt. Clarke continued to pick on my and push me every chance he got. To make my training more difficult than any soldier training. I found that some things in life are painful, but my desires were even greater regardless of the pain. I needed to make my father and mother proud of me more importantly I had to remember no one forced me to join the Marines I wanted to join because I needed the challenge. This is what good parenting does to a young man. I knew my father and mother loved me because they instilled a lot of good inside of me as I grew up and of course don't let me leave out one of my biggest inspiration my uncle James Jones who spent time with me, teaching me how to write and understand the meaning of writing and the importance of documenting what I was writing about and why I wrote it. So, everyone who would be reading this book and hopefully enjoying what I am talking about you can accredit a lot of my work to my uncle James. Although he is deceased now, I can still hear him saying, go back and write this again and add a little extra, you can do it Ray. That is one voice that still remains audible when I look up in the heavens quite often finding myself thanking God for the gift and thanking my uncle James for taking the time out to teach me what he knew, how to write. My other mentor Dr. Albert Lee Powell Sr. who always inspired me to write the book about the Postal Service and Dr. Eddie LaShay who was always optimistic about how things would turn out for me in my life. He would always say, one day you are not going to have time to wash your car and cut the grass. I am not saying you are better than that it just that you are not going to have the time.

Getting back to Sgt. Clarke I felt for some reason he just hated me and did not want me to make it through boot camp. One day we were on the range for rifle qualifications and Sgt. Clarke came up to me and pulled me away from the rest of the platoon. He told me the guys in the platoon had been bragging on me about how fast I could run and that he had betted on me against the other platoon. He never told me what he had betted but he assured me he did not want to lose. He went on to say that if I won the race, he was never going to bother me again. This guy they was supposed to have been the fastest at his previous college was about 6'2 and looked like Carl Lewis. I always said to myself at any track meet that it is the training and the conditioning that counts not the persons height, he was tall and that was all. As my uncle would always say no matter how tall or how big they are when you hit a man pain is the same, make him feel it. Rest assured it was not going to be an easy race because I am certain the other platoon wanted their runner to win. They marked off 100 meters and the rest is history. I took off like a jack rabbit when the whistle blew and never looked back. When I got to the other end and won the race Sgt. Clarke was the first to jump about five feet off the ground and the rest of the platoon gathered around and congratulated me. Sgt. Clarke never went back on his word which told me a lot about people they are not all the same. I learned that day that a man's word is his bond. Sgt. Clarke never did bother me again. This was now a bonding experience for the entire platoon and they respected me even more than what I could imagine. Military comradery is an experience you will never forget because it does not just go away after bootcamp. It's not like graduating high school or college. Military soldiers' bond as brothers for life. Having served the United States of America is a privilege. It is an honor that no one else can bestow upon you. When a person talks about blood, sweat and tears. Soldiers see it all together and they never back down from the challenges that are put before them. When one is challenged, we all come. The same way we are trained to fight on the battlefield because they are my BROTHERS.

I know it is funny sometimes how life has a way of giving us a field of lemons, but God always sends the rain to dilute the taste. What I am saying here is I do not feel anyone else is going to write a book concerning the truth about the struggles of the Vietnam Veterans and Agent Orange. And I for one will never understand how the Vietnam Veterans endured suffering for so long? But God Almighty has put it on my heart to write about their mistreatment and how they are the true heroes of the Vietnam War. They are the Men who served, the Men who died, the Men who are Missing in Action, the Men who are Prisoners of War. We all went through the same training and we are all hurting, physically, mentally and emotionally and we will all always and forever be BROTHERS.

CHAPTER XII

MILITARY COMRADERY THE OATH

NOW LET ME LEAD you to the beginning of the military soldiers bonding process. Every soldier had to go to the Military Entrance Processing Station (MEPS). At MEPS we go through in processing. You know, getting blood drawn, getting examinations and checkups, drug tested, HIV tested and HTLV tested etc. I did not know that during the time of my enlistment into the United States Marine Corps everyone gets tested for HIV. Which meant that I had been getting tested for HIV as far back as 1980. It is now 2019 and my test still runs negative. It was not until twenty-eight years later when I began to review my old Marine Corps military records where I discovered all of the times the military had tested me for HIV/HTLV in both branches of which I served Marine Corps and Army. I was not aware as a young man that myself and other soldiers were being tested for HIV by the military. Of course, all of my tests results came back negative. I do remember a lot of guys being sent home and told they were not going to be able to complete the rest of the physical examination at MEPS after blood was drawn. Some soldiers were sent home due to drugs in their system. While others may have tested positive for HIV. Some of the soldiers who were asthmatic were sent home. Others had issues that would prevent them from completing the training. Issues such as heart problems, pacers, pins in their knees and feet etc. It was heart breaking for some of the guys to find out their dream of becoming a Marine or becoming a military officer was not going to come true for them. Some guys cried and others just sat down and shook their heads as if the military was their last chance. This examination was the first part of the elimination process of those who had a chance of being Marines versus those who would be eliminated. As painful as it sounds when the slogan "The few the proud the brave the Marines" was first aired on commercial television, I must say the commercial said it all. Staying on the righteous road I believe helped to get others as well as myself off to a great start by allowing us to become a part of the greatest fraternal group of men in the world. To become a part of the Armed Forces of the United States of America, we had to take an oath. The oath we took as veterans, young men swearing in young enlisted soldiers and also the oath of office for officers began the bonding process. It separated soldiers even today both male and female from the rest of the world. We were now joining an elite organization within the federal government of the United States of America. In case you didn't know taking the oath gives the soldiers a euphoric feeling of belonging to an elite force, the Armed Forces of the United States of America. If you did not have a father or family growing up, you now had a family which became every man and woman who put on the uniform. No matter where you went in the United States and abroad there was someone there to look out for you and get you started on the right track. If you did not have a father in the home growing up, after saying I do at you swearing in ceremony it gave you an even bigger sense of comradery. You now had a father and a big family. A father we respected, one who made sure all of his children had three hot meals and a cot to sleep on. The father who looked out for us became known as "Uncle Sam." Uncle Sam was also going to make sure you had money in your pocket, three square meals a day, a place to sleep and a formal education. The military became a new start for every young man or woman who wanted something different in life other than a basic everyday (JOB). These are the men and women of the United States of America who would excel into becoming the future leaders of the United States. Young men and women who believed in taking chances and aspiring to do something positive and create new heights for others while inspiring young boys and girls who wanted to someday put on a military uniform that their dreams of becoming a soldier one day could come true. Which is where many children early in life begin to grasp a major understanding through mentoring and help aid programs focusing on the importance of having an education and being able to excel once again through learning. I always say, "It is okay to be a nerd, and there is nothing wrong with wanting to learn to get "A's" and to want to go to college." To want something positive out of life for yourself while in return you will be able to help and inspire others." The education part comes from your tests scores of which the military will let you know if your scores on the Army Services Vocational Aptitude Battery (ASVAB) test will qualify you in the field of study you selected to be trained in while in the military. Since you were now considered to be close to becoming a part of "this man's army" you will also inherit a lot of brothers. Since changes have taken place within the armed forces you will also inherit lots of sisters, women are now a big part of the armed forces and we are proud they are choosing to serve. Everyone trains together and are always prepared to help a soldier who might be lagging just a little. I am prayerful the American people will get the message I am attempting to convey within the pages of this book concerning the Vietnam Veterans.

As a child I observed what was taking place with the Vietnam War. I was able to see at a very young age how the Vietnam Veterans returning home from war were suffering. I would like for you to stay focused on the comradery of the soldiers and try to grasp an understanding that when one soldier is suffering, they all suffer but not from the lack of the word togetherness. The comradery in training as well as competition will astonish you. I have a lot of stories to tell you in relations to this book based on the apology the United States owes the Vietnam Veterans and soldiers who have honorably served in the United States today. It is with great concern that I make my attempt to walk you step by step from the beginning to end as to what a soldier goes through concerning their length of stay in the military. I am putting inside this book the entire oath for enlisted soldiers and the oath for officers. I am asking you to listen to the words these soldiers are swearing or affirming to uphold carefully. Keep in mind many are young boys and girls leaving home for the first time, trying to become a man like their dad and girls trying to become a woman like their mother. They also have other goals in mind like government benefits that are set up for those who are able to endure the military life as well as having a family someday, goals of going to college and goals of owning a beautiful home of which the government will give them a G-I Bill for valued at 250,000 that is one quarter of a million dollars loan on your home just for serving honorably. These are young adults, teenage children vowing to protect what's in their heart in defense of our nation and the freedoms afforded to every citizen who lives within the Constitution of the United States of America. These young people who have taken the oath are reaching for something within themselves something they will be able share and hold onto for the rest of their life. By belonging to the greatest elite force in this nation and believe me when I tell you they don't mind dying on the battlefield as proof as to who they represent the United States of America. Mission, Country and Family this is the order in which their priorities fall with God watching above all. Their loved ones are left behind as their signature which is signed on the bottom-line stating, "I am an American soldier". These are the same soldiers who also have parents, a mother and a father whom of course would like to see again, if God is willing everyone wants to return home. Only returning home is not the finalization of it. They all want to be able to return home and be accepted not just by family but also but the American people. It is not to the point of being hailed as someone special but to be looked upon as someone who made a sacrifice for those they did not know. Some of the soldiers had a wife, some had children, a girlfriend or someone back in the states who they just wanted to see again. This is what the Vietnam Veterans and every soldier who leaves home has to let go of in order to survive. For the Vietnam Veterans the response to recondition was ten times as worse because they did not have a break in war time to come home on vacation. Out of all the many challenges confronting these young men and officers, the oath of office of enlisted soldiers and of officers ended with a signed contract these men and women were obligated to complete. What I am sharing with you right now is just how the vow to protect the United States of America was deeply rooted in the soldier's life, the tyranny of it all was they did not matter even if it costs them their life. The soldier's position in life is mainly to protect the Constitution of the United States of America from all foreign and domestic enemies. The facts of being going to war is always heavy on the soldier's mind and if you were a Vietnam Veteran it was even heavier, remembering that the life of a soldier in Vietnam was sixteen minutes. The Vietnam Veterans and soldiers of recent wars biggest concern at the time of leaving the United States was will he be able to return home from the war zone alive and in one piece. I believe this last statement to be true in all soldiers' minds, making it home safely and being able to resume the life they were living before they enlisted or were drafted into the Vietnam War. Everyone wanted to be able to return home whether they were in a war zone or just traveling abroad. The return home to the United States of America is an experience you must have at least once in your life. If you never left the U.S. and went to foreign country, you never would appreciate the freedoms Americans are born into. And it will help you to understand why those freedoms are protected at such a high cost. Therefore, you will see why the Armed Forces of the United States of America must be funded and the shores of our great country must be protected at all cost. This is what you asked of the Vietnam Veterans to do to protect you but America you did not protect them. You left them out in the open on the battlefield on American soil without any cover or protection and very few resources to get their lives back in order. As a soldier returning home from war the Vietnam Veterans were glad to see the homeland again. It's precious for every soldier to be able to breathe American air once again. Every soldier who has not only been in war but abroad appreciates the return home. It does not make a difference whether they are male or female, their return home is the ultimate euphoria of war. This is why it is so hard for me to grasp an understanding of the bitter hatred the United States citizens had against the Vietnam Veterans once they returned home. Everyone should have been able to see they needed help. To this date of 2019 the United States of America has not given a formal apology to the Vietnam Veterans in relations to the way they were treated when they returned home from Vietnam. I am not talking about a small parade or a chicken dinner, but these men truly deserve some form of a special medal one only the Vietnam Veterans can receive, a once in a lifetime medal. One that will never be recreated ever again in the history of America. They should receive it from the President of the United States of America from his hands to theirs. This is something that has been long overdue, and we don't have much time because there are not many Vietnam Veterans left. They are estimated to be dying at a rate of 390 a week. Before I go any further how can anyone give an estimation of time concerning one's life unless they have an understanding of the illness the individual(s)? These soldiers have not been given a formal apology for living up to the oath they had taken. The Vietnam Veterans have been condemned in a sense of what I call supported hearsay, or if you would have it a bunch of propaganda. What about the men who never deserted their post, the ones who stayed for the fight? Whenever the Vietnam War comes up for discussion there is always a finger being pointed at Congress and the Veterans Administration or the Vietnam Veterans. I am asking everyone to put down their hands and stop looking at the mistakes made during an era of war no one understood, and this country's government cannot or will not explain. Right now, we are moving forward, we are not looking for an explanation of why it happened. We are looking for a solution as to what is going to be done in the future to assist the Vietnam Veterans without anyone pointing the finger at Congress for taking so long to do something. We cannot go backward, but we can move forward in a sense of urgency of which we all can come to a better understanding as to why the Vietnam Veterans and soldiers of today who served in current wars Afghanistan and Iraq need our support even more so today than ever before. How do we as a nation correct a problem that has been lingering for over forty years? I have already given a few solutions. How do we defuse the bomb, the eruption that took place within the minds and hearts of our men and women in the armed forces and everyone wanted to say it was the others fault? Even at the swearing in ceremony at MEPS, in case you did not know what had taken place there is soldiers stopped racially classifying one another and they became one. A unit moving together as an intricate part of the United States of America's military, they had become "the mean green fighting machine." Green, Green, Green, color no longer had a place for men and women who put on the military uniform in defense of the Constitution of America. Men in the past vowed to give their lives in defense of the Constitution. Since times have changed and women are now allowed to join the military, women are now taking the oath to fight alongside of their male counterparts in defense of what they believe in, the American way of life. Women have already died defending the United States Constitution. There is no greater love than the giving of your life for all mankind. I continue to say it is not a Democrat or a Republican problem. It is a humanitarian issue that has not been resolved concerning the Vietnam Veterans. They gave their lives for the betterment of the United States and are deserving of an apology along with the benefits they have been denied as a show of respect and compassion for what they have been through for over forty years now. There are many problems contributory to the Vietnam Veterans concerning "Agent Orange." Their suffering continues to haunt this nation due to the lack of research of the herbicide "Agent Orange." Their acknowledgment at this time and date says a lot about the history of this country because these are men who have taken the same oath, I took many years ago and the promise of the brotherhood within the words of the oath makes me cringe when I think about the rejection our Vietnam Veterans have had to live with. These are men who have taken the same oath, bled on the battlefield and died for the words that still touch my heart when I held up my hand twenty-eight years ago. I am going to give you both of the oaths. I ask now as I asked you earlier to please pay attention to the words in the oath itself. Keep in mind also that this is the first time these young men and women have taken something so sincere and dear to their heart. The first oath is the enlisted oath:

Oath of Enlistment

**"I _____, do solemnly swear (or affirm) that I will support
and defend the Constitution of the United State against all
enemies, foreign and domestic; that I will bear true faith
and allegiance to the same; and that I will obey the orders
of the President of the United States and the orders of the
officers appointed over me, according to regulations and the
Uniform Code of Military Justice. So, help me God."**

If it is within your reasoning to understand why these men would stand in the midst of danger with bullets, bombs and booby traps and minefields set in their paths to defend a country they love and the people they want to come home to after the war is over. It is evident they were not looking for and easy road in life. But felt a greater need to want to preserve the "Free World." Therefore, they took the oath to protect this country and the citizens of America and for the very same reason it is also why they are in search for acceptance from you. Look at it this way even a child who has taken his first step wants a hug from mom and dad. The Vietnam Veterans returned home to chaos, human spit and feces being thrown on them and condemned for taking their first step to protect all of America, and the citizens that dwell therein. I will not say they are in search of forgiveness because truly it is the American citizens tax paying dollars that sent them to the Vietnam War to begin with. So, if anyone should be asking for forgiveness it is the American people and our government who helped to fund the war. If you can find a place in your heart whenever you see a Vietnam Veteran do as I do and tell them what you tell me when you see me wearing my military regalia, "thanks for your service." I am most certain they will appreciate it. What you will see next is the officer's oath of office in its entirety:

Oath of Officers

**"I,_____ (SSAN), having been appointed an officer in the Army
of the United States, as indicated above in the grade of_____
do solemnly swear (or affirm) that I will support and defend the
Constitution of the United States against all enemies foreign and
domestic, that I will bear true faith and allegiance to the same; that I
take this obligation freely, without any mental reservation or purpose**

of evasion; and that I will well and faithfully discharge the duties of the office upon which I am about to enter; So help me God."

These are not just words, but they are words which penetrated the heart of each man and woman who took the oath as future combat soldiers. There wasn't a secret code or hidden agenda. These are men and women who felt they were being given a fair chance to make it and they knew that only through hard work and dedication to training and the United States government, who was going to put them through it, that they would be able to do it. To uphold their end of the bargain by a ceremonial oath that now binds them to the United States government under which they were now obligated to serve contractually. Whether they signed up for two, four, six or eight years of their life, their obligation was now based on two things: one being the oath they had taken and the other being their signature of which they without any mental reservation signed on the dotted line to defend the Constitution of the United States of America. A contract they were now sworn and obligated to fulfill. I asked you to read the words to the oaths for yourself so you the reader would have a better understanding of what is taking place, not only in the words of the oaths but in the heart of the soldier. He or she is changing even then and do not realize the metamorphosis that is already taking place. They who proudly held his or her right hand up freely and repeated the words of the proper oath given and became a part of the Armed Forces of the United States of America. If you can grasp the many chances given by our government to join the Armed Forces of the military and be able to change the pattern in your life, the swearing in ceremony was it, "Welcome my brother, Welcome my sister." A pattern has been set which you may not have liked the way something was going or how it was looking for you in a future sense of foresight or the way things may have turned out for you. Our government gave you the opportunity to change your life around. Then you would be able to see the difference the military would make in bringing about a positive change and giving you a choice and more hope for living a respectable life in America. They did this also for the Vietnam Veterans, but America did not reciprocate the kind gesture once the soldiers returned. When I look at it from an environmental standpoint the military is the beginning of the change of what you could have become. They make you believe in yourself and this is what you have become now. A part of an elite family of men and women who call each other soldier. Since most of us are victims of our environment in search for a better life the military became my change. It became embedded in my acceptance of wanting to do something better with my life and in service of my country, the United States of America and in return I would be awarded certain benefits and privileges due to my honorable service to my country.

On the other hand, many of the Vietnam Veterans were not give the privilege of enlisting in the military to become a soldier. Many were forced in by the draft of which not only did their entire concept of life had to change but they also had to relinquish thoughts of becoming doctors, lawyers, husbands, a family man, college professions etc. Their lives were just snatched away, and this is the repayment they receive. Oh, excuse me I forgot the old cliché "You get what you get and don't pitch a fit." That is the attitude this country has taken for over forty years now. What is unfortunate is that most of you in society think military soldiers do not have an education and that military soldiers do not have higher morals or standards of living and they do not seek the higher grounds of the social ladder through higher education. Which is an unfortunate way of thinking because many of the past presidents of the United States were once former military soldiers. When I think about the Vietnam Veterans, I must ask you in a sense of honesty, loyalty and integrity, on behalf of the Vietnam Veterans, "Do you think they were given the chance to do something with their lives?" My second question, "How much does this country really owes the Vietnam Veterans?" I don't want to overwhelm you with too much thought processing so I will make this my final question for now, "Do you think more research is needed concerning Agent Orange to make a determination as to how long the herbicide is going to remain in the DNA of the Vietnam Veterans' children and now through research we are finding out the grandchildren of the Vietnam Veterans also have the herbicide, Agent Orange in their DNA?" So, let's keep in mind now that we are all partially cognizant of the truth in the words, I have given you concerning the oaths taken, be it enlisted or officer, must have had some impact on the young men who took the same oath during the Vietnam War. These men wanted to prove their love to you not only by the oath they had taken but, on the battlefield, where many were gunned down and died. What is unfortunate is that for those who did not die on the battlefield are still dying right here in America and have been for the past forty years because of their battle with the toxic herbicide chemical Agent Orange. A problem everyone thought was going away but it's over forty years now and the Vietnam Veterans are still being eaten up with cancer and other life-threatening health problems. I want you to remain focused on the fact that the Vietnam War was considered to be over in the early 70's. We are now in 2019 and Vietnam Veterans, their children and their grandchildren are still dying from the herbicide "Agent Orange." Once again do you think it is fair? Let me see, I did say I would not ask any more questions to not overload your thoughts but this one should be a **"NO BRAINER."** It should be evident about now that I will soon be discussing Agent Orange soon within the chapters of this book. Trust me Agent Orange will be a very big topic inside the pages of this book.

For now, l want to finish talking about the (swearing in ceremony) the oaths these young soldiers who were drafted or joined did believe in and decided to fight in defense of America in the worst war this country has ever been in. They fought because they valued the respect and dignity the United States of America had already earned as being a country in leadership for the Free World. The men who went to "NAM" were in a hot zone. The entire jungle of Vietnam was festered with Viet Cong. The jungles were already soiled with American blood and our brothers not knowing what to do had to become whatever they had to become in order to survive. Unless you have been in a war with bullets flying around you day and night, I am prayerful you can hold on to what I am saying here so you can broaden you understanding. These young men were dropped in the hottest war zone the United States had ever been in with only a few combat skills. It was called kill or be killed of which a split second of thought as to whether the soldier should pull the trigger or not could determine whether he would be coming home again. These men, these Vietnam Veterans had to become the animal they were fighting in order to see their families again. This was the picture being drawn for them and they still did not run off to Canada to hide. These men gave their lives for the betterment of all mankind when they raised their hand to take the oath and stood in the midst of death on the battlefield of "NAM." The oath becomes a transitioning processing not only mentally, but physically as well because it placed all of us in a place of security. Not so much as the have and have nots it just removed us from a place of false hope and placed us in a new environment that would change our lives forever. We raised our hand on our own free will to accept a position in the armed forces, and we were proud to have done so. If the question was asked of me if I would do it again without hesitation or mental reservation my response would be, "Yes! Yes! I would do it all over again as a service to my country." I remember before the oath was rendered to myself and several others in the room, the sergeant who came in the room was telling us that we have come this far and so far everyone had made it to another stage of being accepted in the armed forces and being sworn in. It was a great feeling of acceptance. We were all being given the honor and respect by other soldiers looking on because we had just completed the first step of becoming soldiers. Many of the soldiers in the ceremony room who were looking on had taken the very same oath many years ago. This was a major step in my life, and I wanted to make a change to make a difference and the only way of doing so would be to keep my nose clean. Meaning staying out of trouble and try to make a difference in my life as well as the life of those around me. We were men from all walks of life and for those who could not make the transition their career in the military would be short lived. As for my life I was able to make a decision. I had a choice of going into the military or taking my chances in the civilian part of life. I always felt even as a child there was something special about becoming a soldier. Putting on a uniform that said I represent you, America. There was no racial barrier I was trying to break. My only thoughts was being a part of a brotherhood of men who had the same beliefs and wanted to make a difference in life. The only part of me dealing with my acceptance is not whether I wanted to be a soldier because I joined and was looking forward to whatever came my way. The unfortunate part is the Vietnam Veterans did not have a choice. They were rushed through two-weeks of bootcamp training and taken to Vietnam to fight or die. The biggest question here is how were the soldiers supposed to turn off their now inducted daily killer mode? There wasn't anyone to teach them how to reroute and control the killer instinct they had to incorporate into their daily living while serving in "NAM." How were they going to retrain themselves to recondition their minds? With no military programs to assist the Vietnam Veterans in helping them to readjust back into society. What was going to become of them? How were they supposed to fit in a world where they did not have to worry any longer about surviving? In order to survive in America, since they were no longer in a war zone, who would be there to guide them through the proper channels of them getting the help they obviously needed? There was no sense of urgency concerning their being acclimated back into society and they became the most misunderstood soldiers in America since no one had developed a way to prepare these soldiers to return to a nation of people they had to live and work with. There was nothing set up to prepare the Vietnam Veterans on how they were supposed to function not only in an environment of people who considered them to be murderers, but also a society of people who had never been to war but in an environment where they did not have to kill in order to survive. There was no longer a ranking structure the soldiers had to follow. These Vietnam Veterans had now made it back home to only see the backs of those who should have been there with open arms to assist them. The open "Free World" America of which the Vietnam Veterans who were able to make it home in one piece were now put into a system where they would actually go into what I would call a mental inclusion inverted of personal reconditioning within their own mind. This would truly summarize how each soldier individually would have to function on a daily basis. What you see is not always what you get, in reference to the soldier this was more than just a saying from the "Flip Wilson" show. It was the truth about each of the military soldiers who returned home either damaged or whole. What the world could not see was their internal suffering. It's not a mystery to anyone other than those who try to understand the power of God. What I am getting at here is how can you patch up a wound you cannot see? How can a person who has not served one day in a war zone dignify themselves to let the words I so often hear concerning the service of military soldiers come out of their mouth? I have heard these words so many times, "I don't see anything wrong with you." My response is usually related to the inner pain. Excuse me but can you see inside of me, my brain aches, my back has discs missing, my shoulder are brittle and have arthritis from carrying all of those heavy sea bags, my feet, my hands and legs are worn. My heart is enlarged, my knees need replacing. Yes, all of this is going on inside of the soldiers today and trust me when I say for the Vietnam Veterans it is even worse. This is what myself and my brothers and sisters who have served have to deal with everyday just to be able to function and at least look normal when we are out in society. There is a lot going on with us but what about the Vietnam Veterans? They did not have the opportunities we have today, what about their suffering? I will also tell them this, "It's not that we are not in pain, but every soldier wants to feel like a soldier and be able to move around without moaning and groaning with every step we take. Fortunately for us it is not that we are not in pain, but as soldiers as men and women who have fought in wars in defense of this nation we are trained on how to endure the pain as it relates to each of us on an individual basis." In respect to the men and women of the armed force who have served and are now serving in defense of this great nation, I must say the world of a military soldier is much different in its relations to the Uniform Code of Military Justice. America, the "Free World" is based on a Constitution of which a civilian is born into inalienable rights. The first Amendment clearly expresses the freedom of speech in the military the freedom of speech is based on rank and structure. If you would take a closer look at military structure, there is no grey area to question. A soldier of lesser rank must do what they are told to do within reason of the officer or senior ranking person's request. In the military it is "Yes Sir", or "No Sir", there isn't any maybe. In the civilian profession it is understood that you call this a grey area. Meaning there is no right or wrong involved and the two parties in disagreement will come to some kind of an amicable agreement. There are many issues of concern which involves the soldier's release from active duty. This is where the system fails the soldier after his or her release from active duty. They return home without an understanding of how to proceed in order to get their life back on track after leaving the military. This is what happened to the Vietnam Veterans; there wasn't any training programs available for them to be allowed to blend back in the system socially. I believe the government can do a lot better concerning the releasing of a soldier back into the civilian side of life. The ACAP program can be a little more intensified and give more involvement with the soldier after his or her release other than waiting to see how the soldier is going to adjust on their own. Due to the Vietnam Veterans not having the resources to cope with the Post Traumatic Stress Disorder (PTSD) they were suffering from. They were left to figure it out for themselves and judged by those in society who did not have any idea as to what the Vietnam Veteran had been through or were going through at the time. I do not want to point fingers in this book because it is not going to resolve the suffering of those who are still alive today from the Vietnam War. What we must do is that we should come together to try to alleviate their suffering. I must reiterate that "Agent Orange" a chemical herbicide sprayed in the forest of Vietnam to kill the foliage in the forest is still killing the Vietnam Veterans and their children forty-five years later.

I have not heard a formal apology given to these men who were injured for life. Men who gave their lives for the betterment of all mankind. I know I have said this before, but I want to make sure those of you who will be reading this book receive a clean and concise understanding of what is being said here. Those of you in high ranking positions with all due respect, the President of the United States of America, The Congress and The Senate. I am asking you all to not let this problem of struggle concerning "Agent Orange" and the disrespect the Vietnam Veterans have received continue as it has since their return to the United States. These men are dying without the respect they should have been given years ago. They are dying because of our government lack of acceptance of fault. But let's not point fingers it's been over forty-five years now and still no one wants to accept fault on behalf of what has been denied to the Vietnam Veterans through the years. Can we sit back as a nation of educated men and women and say the Vietnam Veterans are at fault? No, we cannot. They fought in the Vietnam War after they were taken out of bootcamp and forced to fight without any orders or training schools to teach them and were taken straight to Vietnam where they have remained in the shadows of our thoughts. Many of you hoped the tragedy of "NAM" would just go away. Well it's not, Agent Orange is still very much alive in the Vietnam Veterans' children, grandchildren and possibly great grandchildren's DNA.

If you are asking me where does it stop, it stops with our President, Congress and Senate stepping up and putting not the non-governmental but governmental researchers in place to give a better and more concise analysis on the effects Agent Orange has had on the Vietnam Veterans.

CHAPTER XIII

THE SCRIPTURAL VIEWS IN RELATIONS TO WORLD LOGIC

I SAY TO YOU THAT you are not looking at the spiritual connection of understand that because God allows burdens to make us better people. We cannot continue to overlook the suffering of our brothers and the mistakes made in this country after their return from Vietnam. To some of you war may sound senseless, but if you are of the true Christian faith you will find the scripture in the book of Ecclesiastes chapter 3. I am not one to criticize the Holy Bible because it is the word of God. And because as human beings many of us are so quick to point fingers at one another that we forget the ways of human err. There were many speculations made in reference to the Vietnam Veterans and the many social problems they were involved in after they returned to the states. As God fearing nation do we stand back and let the last of these men die off without trying to make it right for them? Do I have to keep reminding you that it was the American tax dollar that sent these men into a war zone of which many fled to Canada to escape the high possibility of them not being able to return home alive. These men, called Vietnam Veterans did not desert their posts in time of need and service to their country, they stood and fought. Whether the outcome of war was good or bad for the country neither has yet to be determined but we sit in awe of the over 58 thousand who died during the Vietnam War. With over 47 thousand of those who died being soldiers of the United States of America and who have been honored with a "Wall of Names" but we have failed to acknowledge those who are still alive and suffering from "Agent Orange" to whom we owe an apology that is long overdue. I am a soldier and blessed to be on the face of this earth having made it back home to America from war. Not the Vietnam War, but my experience of war gave me enough understanding of how these Vietnam Veterans are suffering and waiting on you to say, "Hey we made a mistake and we apologize". I do believe from there this country will begin its healing process and will help the last of the Vietnam Veterans who are alive today to be able to walk the streets of America with their head held high knowing they are loved and accepted as American soldiers who did a job no one else wanted to do. Just remember because mankind should not put himself in the position of judge and jury. It is evident in scripture that we are supposed to be forgiving Christians. Yet the question which still constantly arises is what the Vietnam Veterans are being charged with and other than defending the freedoms of this great nation. We must stop looking at hearsay and propaganda which has not been proven. What remains to be unethical is the cries of these men walking the streets of this country in pain for over 40 years now and no one can find a place in their heart to say these are the real heroes of the Vietnam War. These are the men who fought and did not run. These are the men who fought concerning the controversy of not knowing what the war was about just like the rest of us. To this day the Vietnam War remains a mystery as to why so many soldiers lost their life for a cause that was never clear and for a country who appears to be unforgiving of the efforts of the Vietnam Veterans to complete the missions they were assigned to do. Young boys eighteen years of age were taken to Vietnam to fight a man's war. I cannot reiterate this enough that they were boys not men. Boys who had to become men over night in order to survive. They had to endure more than what we could ever imagine not only to survive in a war that no one understood but also to keep their mind functional if and when they would be able to return to America. We can only try to understand by trying to emphasize how they must have felt. Unless you were in the jungles of Nam fighting the war there is no way you could begin to comprehend the months they spent living in the jungles unaware of what was going to happen next. I can remember my days of training in the pitch-black forest not being able to see my hand in front of my face in the deep black darkness of the night where there is no shadow or silhouette to expose the existence of any life form. In order to understand the soldiers and what was taking place with them mentally you would have had to be there. Going into a dark closet with your eyes closed is still not enough to give you a visual comparison when it comes to comprehending the darkness or the internal suffering of the Vietnam Veterans. They were trying to survive in the jungles of the worst war the United States of America has ever been in. Many of you sit home watching war movies and even then, you can only imagine what you would do if you were in a real war. You see you can always turn off the television or change the channel if the movie got too gross for you to watch. Sadly, the Vietnam Veterans did not have those options. They had to fight next to dead bodies and soldiers' bodies that had been blown to bits with brains and guts splattered all over the place. Yes, the same foxholes the had to remain and trained in. On the battlefield of war, the soldiers were able to adjust to what was taking place in front of them. It was not like they had the time to make an appointment with a psychologist to help them cope with the death of a friend they had just seen get his head blown off or cut in half by enemy fire. Their ability to accept what they saw and to deal with daily was a reality their minds had to be able to digest instantly. This was their reality and they knew they could not turn it off until their tour in "Nam" was over. The most painful thing about war is the soldiers in Vietnam or any war had to become the animal they were fighting in order to survive. What I have found out from being in a war zone is you do not have time to second guess a situation. When I say second guess a situation, I am saying this is a place where death is not a visitor. It's a spirit that lingers in the air and does not discriminate as to whose soul it will take because on the battlefield of death there is life only if you are able to survive for that day. In the state vacations are planned months ahead of time. Business meetings are planned weeks ahead of time but being in a war you plan second by second and pray that you are not one of the sixteen-minute statistics. Death is a permanent guess in the war zone and the joy of taking a like is not a vacancy of thought, but a reality of everyday life captured in the mind of those left to see the lifelessness on the battlefield. Please remember these are eighteen-year-old boys, (Vietnam Veterans) who lived to late become men. When you speak to your eighteen-year-old son at home while you are sitting down having dinner you still advise your son as to what is right or wrong. He still seeks his father's council. No one can honestly say these boys became men with two weeks of military training and were thoroughly trained on how to survive in the jungles of Nam in that short of a period of time. There were mistakes made and these mistakes caused an entire military army of men to remain damaged for life. The Vietnam Veterans need our help in order to move onto their next phase of life. They need to be looked at differently when it comes to looking at what they had to do for a means of survival. They were not cowards when it came to fighting for the freedoms of the citizens of America. They did not run and leave the United States holding the ball. We should be proud of our young men who wore the battle green uniforms. The Vietnam Veterans stayed until the government under which they served said that the war was over. They did not have their own ships, boats or planes. Instead they were taken to their destination and left there to do whatever they had to do in order to make it home. I am more than certain you can figure out who agrees to go into war and how the war is funded. So, you should be 100% sure it was not the young Vietnam Veterans who joined or were drafted, they did not own the boats, ships, and planes that took them to Vietnam. These men were physically, emotionally, economically, socially and mentally damaged. As much as everyone would like to sweep their pain under the rug to this day the Vietnam Veterans suffering has not been recognized as a serious issue. With all of the chemical problems occurring now in everyday society I do believe everyone will began to look at things differently, since these toxic and cancerous chemicals are now affecting the American public, their families and children. I will speak on this a little more in later chapters. This is an issue that will continue to haunt this country if nothing is done to set up federal funding for research to help detect how the Vietnam Veterans can be medically treated for future health problems because of the chemical herbicide Agent Orange. Putting these soldiers in federal prisons when they get into a confrontation is not the answer and denying many of them the claims they have filed and deserve to have is not right. These men who fought in the Vietnam war were never assessed properly for physiological, emotional, or mental issues. This is where the system has failed the Vietnam Veterans and current soldiers of today by putting them in prison when an evaluation and proper medication can resolve the issues. The government refuse to deal with the problem of saying since he is a Vietnam Veteran, we can take an extra step and design a home rehabilitation program where the soldier could attend counseling with a professional in accordance to what the soldier needs. Someone who will be able to help him to learn to cope with the issues at hand. I do not feel that incarcerating these soldiers is the answer unless it is a heinous crime which has been committed. There is a better way to address the soldier's issues and we have the resources to do than to incarcerate a veteran who has served his country honorably. The very same programs that are set up for rehabilitation for those who are on drugs, mentally ill or homeless. These programs can also be set up for the Veterans on them getting acclimated back into society. When we as a nation of people say the United States of America was founded on "In God We Trust." There must be some form of afterthought when we look at what we have done to our own soldiers. We have not come to the end of the road yet because there is so much more that will be done for the benefit of the

Vietnam Veterans who are alive today. There are not many left due to Agent Orange and the toll this toxic chemical herbicide has taken over their lives. When I look at this nation of God-fearing people, I would like to remind you that you have to find forgiveness in your heart. If you have read this far in this book and have not begun to see the mistakes made concerning the Vietnam Veterans and have not found forgiveness in your heart, then I will ask you to please search yourself. At some point in this book I will not have to ask this question of forgiveness again, because I do believe the spirit of love that God has placed in your heart will overwhelm you and bring you to an inner peace. Where you can not only feel as you are reading but be able to visualize the wrong that was done to the Vietnam Veterans.

CHAPTER XIV

THE INNER WOUNDS,
DAMAGE ON THE INSIDE

IF YOU ARE A Christian and believe in God the father of Abraham, Isaac and Jacob. You must realize these men the Vietnam Veterans who defended this country with their life are hurting. They have been in pain for over forty years. Now I want you to go to the question Peter asked Jesus in Matthew 18:21, "Then came Peter to him and said, Lord how oft shall my brother sin against me, and I forgive him? Till seven time." Matthew 18:22, "Jesus saith unto him, I say not unto thee, until seven times; but until seventy times seven." There is a lot to be said when the word of God enters the room. I am not asking anyone to bow their head and run with their tails tucked. I am saying as I have said repeatedly the Vietnam Veterans who served in the Vietnam War and soldiers of current wars will base their life on the battle of war and past examples of previous wars. The cycle of overlooking our soldiers and not setting up the proper facilities needed to assist them on their return to the states and getting them acclimated back into society is going to be an even bigger problem in the future. These soldiers must have programs set up through federal government funding in order to curtail the problems they have faced in past wars such as the Vietnam War. It is not hard to evaluate the soldiers concerning some of the issues they may have and get them started on a positive note instead of looking at the soldier as a problem. There is so much that can be done to prevent certain behavioral outburst some soldiers may exhibit given circumstances they may find to be unfair to them. Even with the return of the Iraqi and Afghanistan soldiers who served in those wars what the United States should already be finding out is if they are going to be needing phycological help as well in relations to postwar stress or maybe even personal problems at home. I will not give out any name but after we had landed and was taken to Kabul, Afghanistan it was probably five minutes after we had arrived and searching for our quarters that a young lieutenant killed himself, one bullet to the head. The reasoning behind it was the girl he loved since high school said she could not wait for him for an entire year. There must be preventive measures set up in matters such as this to let the soldier or officer know that there are other alternatives. It is unfortunate but it happens. We had a Colonel whose situation was almost similar, but he was married, and his wife was leaving him, so he killed himself. Some of these soldiers have completed several tours in these wars of which is going to require more medical assistance than those who have just completed one. Through proper research it should be noted that the amount of tours a soldier should be allowed to sign up for should be limited based on the soldier's mental stability and undiagnosed possibility of the soldier displaying signs of irrational behavior due to the lack of proper medical treatment of which the soldier could possibly display or revert to in the future. This would be based on excessive exposure in what is other than normal conditions due to the lack of medical care and attention that should be given to the soldier prior to their release. A lack of the soldier's knowledge of understanding their need for medical attention as a result of why they are reacting irrationally puts not only the civilian at risk but also the soldier at risk of being incarcerated for a situation that could have been prevented. This is what has taken place with not only the Vietnam Veterans but veterans throughout the United States. What concerns me about this situation is the cycle of soldiers actively serving and veterans are being held accountable for situational problems which are enhanced, and many times leads to the soldier becoming confrontational. This is because the initial help the soldier needed prior to being discharged has not been addressed or medically treated. Soldiers remain to be continuously misunderstood, mistreated and ostracized from those who are not understanding of their need for a full medical evaluation. What I have explained in the above statement is what has taken place with the soldiers of past wars, the Vietnam Veterans and soldiers who served in the current wars in Iraq and Afghanistan. Therefore; I am asking the American citizens, why have you not reached an understanding of forgiveness for the Vietnam Veterans? In their suffering they are having to cope with both a mental, physical, and emotional beating. The mental beating is the anguish they must deal with within themselves each day. This is the illness you cannot see an illness most soldiers try very hard to hide within. Whether it is PTSD, Brain Trauma, etc. their being able to cope daily deals with how they are approached by you the American people. Their physical beating is one that is also hidden from you from the many years of carrying excess weight, marching long distances, the wet clothing from being out in the rain and excessively cold weather, sleeping on the ground etc. Therefore, I am taking the time out to try and explain where these soldiers in the Vietnam War are mentally and emotionally because of your treatment towards them, of which is also going to have an impact on the soldiers of today's wars Iraq and Afghanistan. It has been over forty years now and you the American citizen may not realize the damage you have inadvertently caused the Vietnam Veterans by continuously looking down on them. These men are the brave men who went to war to defend your constitutional rights. Therefore, I question your forgiveness because you have created in the past an environment that would not be considered to be healthy. You made it confrontational by not educating yourself enough to know that your sons, and your husbands, your fathers or boyfriends who returned from past wars, the Vietnam War and today's wars Iraq and Afghanistan are not the same men who left home unscathed. The wounds are there it is unfortunate you cannot see the wounds because of your doubt and disbelief of what the soldiers have been through. I am certain if the soldiers could invite you in so you could see the mental and physical injuries, they suffer from they would be more than happy to oblige you. So, in your mind of doubt things remain questionable which leaves the soldier in an unnecessary amount of pain because so many other stressors have to be exposed. Many times, those stressors are not visual. When I look at the physical ailments and why you doubt, I have to think of it in a biblical sense of which clearly explains your doubt. Please read the book of (John 20: 25-28) "The other disciples therefore said unto him, We have seen the Lord. But he said unto them, except I shall see in his hands the print of the nails and put my finger into the print of the nails, and thrust my hand into his side, I will not believe. (26) And after eight days again his disciples were within, and Thomas with them: then came Jesus, the doors being shut, and stood in the midst, and said, Peace be unto you. (27) Then saith he to Thomas, reach hither thy finger, and behold my hands, and reach hither thy hand, and thrust it into my side; and be not faithless, but believing. (28) And Thomas answered and said unto him, My Lord and my God. (29) Jesus saith unto him, Thomas, because thou hast seen me, thou has believed: blessed as they that have not seen, and yet believe." When you think about Christianity and what is being stated the testimony of Jesus Christ is being given. To the reader I must say your belief in the word of God which protrudes out of your own mouth is in question. It is all about believing as well as forgiving. In the scriptures that follow what you will find is another word of God that gives credence to how we as Christians are not supposed to stand in Judgement. When you remove the sty from your eye, I am certain you will be blind to the faults of others. (I Corinthians 11:31-34), (31) "For if we would judge ourselves, we should not be judged. (32) But when we are judged, we are chastened of the Lord, that we should not be condemned with the world." (33) Wherefore, my brethren, when ye come together to eat tarry one for another. (34) And if any man hunger, let him eat at home; that ye come not together unto condemnation. And the rest will I set in order when I come." These scriptures being given to you are reminders of what thus said the Lord. For those who cannot see any wrong as to what is taking place with not only the Vietnam Veterans but Veterans in prior wars as well as Afghanistan and Iraq. There is a procedure of policy which contradicts human decency and opens up areas of dialogue concerning the humanitarian obligations the United States Congress, Senate and American people should have for those who have served and are now serving in the Armed Forces of America. An Agreement was reached after a vote was taken and the majority in the room voted in favor of sending these young boys (men) off to war. With only two weeks of training the young Vietnam Veterans were dropped into the hottest war zone this country has ever been in. The logic concerning their treatment after they returned home due to a lack of preparation on the part of the United States government leaves many unanswered questions open when it concerns their physical health as it relates to "Agent Orange" of which I will be discussing shortly. The soldier's emotional and mental health as it relates to their functional capabilities after the war and their abilities to be able to adjust to a new way of life after a war no one understood. When it comes down to the red ink on the bottom-line the President, Congress, Senate and the people of the United States of America were not only informed enough but they were totally oblivious to the needs of the Vietnam Veterans and how they were not even aware of how to help. There was not enough research from even past wars on how the soldiers should be helped or what they should be treated for prior to their discharge and being released back on the streets of mainstream America. The sad part of it all is the controversy about the Vietnam Veterans which remains in question over forty years later concerning what did and did not happened over in "Nam." In hindsight when we look at the war, I personally feel every soldier should be held on base for an adequate amount of time and monitored for a stint of time before being released from active duty or coming home from a war zone. There are certain tests involving his cognitive skills, his reasoning and communicative skills before the soldier is returned to his or her place of origin. If you would revisit the scripture John 20: 25-28 when Jesus was confronting his disciple Thomas. Thomas had to feel the holes in his hands and where the spear was threshed into his side. What I am trying to convey to you in this book is that it is impossible for you to be able to see all the soldier's wounds. It is impossible for you to be able to observe each and every soldier's dilemma due to their ability to want to appear as part of the norm in society. As soldiers we leave home whole and return damaged. It is unfortunate the wounds are not all visible, meaning you cannot see the physical, emotional or mental damage that has taken place within the soldier. These are the issues that should have been addressed prior to the Vietnam Veterans being released. These are the same issues needing to be addressed for today's war veterans. The majority of you are not even aware of the trauma soldiers face on a daily basis of just having to deal with wanting to be able to function the way they use to prior to going into the military or even to war. Our training to be the best is continual and we practice for precision. Our struggles are different and can be detrimental to the soldier or inflicted upon someone else if the issues the solider is having are not addressed appropriately. There are not always wounds to feel or see as it was for doubting Thomas. Although the wounds are there it is impossible for you to visually see them. The soldier will hide them so he or she appears to not be in pain. No soldier can totally ward off their inabilities or incapabilities and you generally as a common everyday United States citizen would walk pass the same soldier each day and not know something was wrong. You are not trained to notice dysfunctionalities in the physical body, for instance the bone structure that has been damaged or mangled in the soldier's body, damage to the spine, knees, discs in the soldier's back etc. in relation to their ability to physically function. Damaged knees and bone cartilage that has been worn away due to so much heavy lifting and long marches, cephalgia. Cephalgia is the trauma many soldiers must deal with daily. One of the medical related pains of Cephalgia is consistent severe headaches. Of which is related to the neck and back of the solider due to the soldier having to wear a fifty-five-pound protective vest daily. Because of the heavy weight of the protective vest the blood flow to the neck and brain is slowed down due to the pressure on the upper shoulders. Once again these are pains you cannot see; these are neurological conditions which requires a physician's assistance. Blurred or double vision, dizziness, nausea or faintness are symptoms when the neck is not in certain positions as related to the soldier's war injuries today. Other inner wounds are muscle spasm and restricted reach and motion in the neck as related to the physical inabilities of the soldier you cannot see with your naked eyes. The headaches are of the musculoskeletal origin. I most certainly feel it is important for the physical ailments of the soldiers to be medically diagnosed and treated prior to the soldier being medically released. The process should at least be started in order to help the soldier adjust to limitations that have been acquired through everyday wear and tear of military life. Until people are educated in a sense of knowing when their loved ones return home. Although they may look whole, they are not the same person they were before going off to war. It is important for the American people to grasp the reality of the soldier's change so you can better understand what is taking place within the soldier's body. Hopefully you can get a feel for the soldier's limitations. This did not take place with the Vietnam Veterans as it should have. And this is what caused a crisis in many of the soldiers' homes, social gatherings and why the soldier would isolate himself from society as well as legal issues. On the standpoint of the legal issues as it relates to soldiers being placed in state and federal prisons is where we began to look at the mental issues of the soldier of which in many cases went undiagnosed. This leads to the soldier's incapabilities of functioning normally in society. Mental issues as it relates to soldiers who have not been diagnosed properly is tragic. This is why you find so many Vietnam Veterans, soldiers of past wars and soldiers who served in Afghanistan and Iraq incarcerated in community, state and federal prisons. What you will find after questioning these men and women soldiers who have been incarcerated due to breaking the law is, they were never diagnosed by a military psychologist and haven't a rating in the DSM V of having any mental issues. Therefore, they will not have been assigned a doctor to follow up with once they are released from active duty. These soldiers will not have any prescribed medication from a physician to treat the mental illness which lead to their being incarcerated for a crime which could have been prevented. I personally feel many of the soldiers who are incarcerated today prior to an incident of breaking the law have never been diagnosed by a military psychologist to see if there was some form of mental illness the soldier may have acquired during their tour of service, whether it is in the state or a war zone. For this reason, the number of Veterans collectively need to be reevaluated in relations to the crime committed to see if there is a need for them to be medicated in order to curtail the negative behavior exhibited. In all fairness to the soldier who signed up to defend the United States it is now time to go the extra mile for the soldier. We must question what is taking place concerning the sociological problems of the soldiers concerning their placement in society. It is wrong to continue to incarcerate our soldiers for breaking the law when we are not giving them a fair chance by taking the time to have them properly diagnosed or receive proper medical care. All soldiers need to be properly diagnosed where they can receive the proper medication to help break the cycle of recidivism, of being a repeated offender. It keeps them out of prisons as well as keeps them from becoming repeated criminals. With the help of having the proper medical treatment these soldiers now stand a chance of becoming law abiding citizens. This is the part I have been talking about which involves the invisible shield you cannot see along with the bad press soldiers have had to carry through the years due to their being overlooked or forgotten in the system. This is needed also because soldiers are more apt to be incarcerated than a civilian who never severed. The one issue in question is: have the soldier been diagnosed with a mental illness or any form of ailment prior to his or her arrest? We cannot expect our soldiers to be on their best behavior or anyone else concerned in this matter of incarceration if they have not been evaluated. When we talk about physical, emotional, economical and mentally ill soldiers I say to you this is the pain you cannot see. This is the struggle the soldier is going through on a daily basis to just want to be a part of the normalcy of society once again. The soldier does not want to mislead anyone, the fact of the matter is that he or she may be intentionally hiding a mental illness due to his or her fears of possibly not being accepted. Therefore, I am trying to explain to you about the wounds you cannot see. If you are thinking on a logical and moral level, you will realize no one wants to be considered to be a burden to someone else. So, these soldiers, these warriors of fortune hide their illnesses in order for them to be able to fit in. Please keep in mind many of them have illnesses and do not know. I have personally witnessed veterans telling civilians they have severed in the military and they do not have any vices. For some that maybe true but for the many who suffer because of the lack of medical attention remains hidden and an unknown for most Americans today. There is no time as to when the veteran who has not been diagnosed my snap and do something extremely out of character. This is when family members and friends find out about the hidden wounds which have not been treated but have been harboring for years. When it comes to the needs of the soldiers and understanding policy and procedure, the soldier begins to seek help thorough the Veteran hospital. This soldier should immediately be accepted for examination. When a soldier is standing on the brink of need and does not receive the proper help this is when the soldier may begin to show signs of an irrational behavior or outbursts. This is unfortunate but for future reference the hospital not just the Veteran Hospitals need to set up an emergency staff to always be ready and on standby for matters such as this. Remember just because the problem has not been diagnosed and put on paper does not mean the wound is not there. The soldier's wounds are real, and they exist in many different levels and forms. For justice to be distributed across the board and even more so for the men and women who have served this county something has to be put in place. In order for them to be given a fair chance I ask that the President, Congress, Senate and the American people make it official that every soldier during the Vietnam era who is incarcerated and soldiers returning home from Iraq and Afghanistan who have been detained by the courts be given evaluations to detect whether their PTSD or mental illness was overlooked and not treated by the military as it should have been. Once the testing is confirmed instead of giving the solider that's incarcerated a felony and bringing extra stressors into his life, the soldier can be place in the doctor's care due to the hidden physical, mental or emotional wound the soldier was carrying and went undetected for so long. Remember, unlike doubting Thomas who felt Jesus wounds the soldier will not convey his wounds to the public unless he or she is pushed to expose an irrational behavior.

A Soldier's Wounds, Windows to the Soul

The windows of my soul could not hold my tears, my thoughts;
My heart bled open its hidden wounds of mercy;
My eyes were open like a book being read with no ending;
As I stopped and gasped in dismay, I wondered could they see me;
I was yelling inside of me as I slowly fail
back into an empty dark room;
Trying to open the door everyone was going
through, but I could not enter;
Their plight appeared to be pleasantly calm
only I could not get through;
I began to yell out loud, my inner peace was gone, I became disturbed;
I was reaching and grabbing for things of no significance to hold onto;
What am I missing, what is this on the inside screaming to get out?
This thing hidden on the inside was trying to get out;
Its ugly darkness would not let go; my head pounded in pain;
This was a pain only I was aware of I had to contain my composure;
As I caught myself, I reached for the door once more, it opened;
I was out now but the wound was still bleeding;
The pounding in my head has stopped, the sweating had stopped;
I had been brought out of darkness into his marvelous light;
No one could see the hidden wounds a new day had come;
A soldier's wounds are embedded deeply within his soul;
The new world is a different journey for the soldier to walk;
His dark shades cover the windows to his soul, but he sees your pain;
The ugliness you are not willing to let go of and the wounds you hide;
Your eyes reveal the wounds he sees;
It's really your darkness, your pain trying to release itself;
Hidden desires, as he looks through the windows of your soul.

Written by: Author/Hall of Fame Poet
Raymond C. Christian
Date: 1/11/19
Reason: To question inner peace, hidden wounds of darkness
Place: Home
My reason for writing this prose is to say to those who look down
on military soldiers after they return home from war is to stop looking

at the soldiers as if there is nothing wrong with them. They have been physically, emotionally and mentally damaged, damages you cannot see. I am telling you there is something wrong, which is usually on the inside of them. Curious minds want to know the truth, but they intentionally fail to look at the obvious conditions of the soldier. The human body of which a common person, who is not a medical doctor can detect; those scars can be seen. If you would allow me to share one of my personal experiences as I speak on the (hidden wounds) of a soldier. I was driving my car and a police officer stopped me and told me the tent on my car appeared to be too dark. For this purpose, I always keep a statement from my doctor's office in the car with me which states the severe photophobia I have acquired due to the intense heat of being out in the open sun in Afghanistan. I showed the doctor's note to the police officer who very politely asked me to explain to him what severe photophobia means so he could share it with the rest of the police officers and keep them informed. He told me thank you and of course there was no breach of injustice on his part or mine. He was doing his job and I had the correct paperwork to inform him of my hidden wound, my line of duty injuries. Wounds you as an everyday civilian cannot see. What I have found to be true is the envy many civilians who have not served in the military have against those who have served. There is a consistency of complaints from civilians about what they feel military soldiers do not deserve to have given to them from the government just because they cannot see the injuries. This is one of the reasons why I based my previous chapter on hidden wounds, wounds underneath the skin, inside of the soldiers you cannot see. The majority of soldiers go about their day trying to make it to the next usually minding their own business and hoping for the best. Mainly just wanting to be left alone.

CHAPTER XV

THE JOURNEY THEY TRAVELED

N O ONE REALLY KNOWS the journey the soldiers have traveled. But I say to you until you have sat down and talked to a homeless veteran, until you have reached out to feed a hungry veteran and until you have lived the life of a soldier or have witnessed a soldier finding out his mother, father or loved one has passed and they are not able to make it to the funeral because they distance is too great, then you will understand. It will never amaze you how my brothers and sisters who have served in the military for the benefit of your safety are able to hold up and function in a society they no longer know, but are most certainly being judged in. It is not because they are not wounded but because you pass judgement on the physical wounds not seen by the naked eye. In the meantime, try going out to the parks at night, try going out to the under passes of bridges and visiting some of the street benches at night. This is where they sleep; this is where they eat; this is where they live because of a system that has failed them. A system that says, I don't understand you and some of the things you do or the way you react to the questions I am asking you. Our governmental system is not the ones singly at fault. Yes, we have to look at the families and friends these soldiers returned home to and were rejected thinking they had a place to go to. Many were put out because they did not have any money when they reached home, or their family just did not understand them anymore. Family members were afraid of what the solider may have done while in the war zone. Did the soldier kill someone? This question is continually reoccurring, and no one knows why the soldier is indifferent and why the soldier is acting out irrationally. Believe me when I tell you it is not the soldier who is indifferent, but many times the truth is kept quiet and there is no rational solution for the soldier because the soldier does not want to expose the truth of what his family did to him. These are actual truths that take place in a soldier's life and they are only a few of the hidden wounds a soldier suffers from, rejection. If you would allow me to share with you a true story of what took place with a soldier, I briefly had the opportunity to counsel. This is what happened prior to all soldiers deploying, they are asked to start a direct deposit account so their check will be deposited in their account. Unfortunately, this particular soldier wanted to give his mother and father access to his bank account while overseas. He thought if he was killed or for some other reason, he does not make it back and his parents were not going to be able to have access to his account, so he added them. Now his parents had access to all of his funds he was depositing in his account. What I am sharing with you here is it is not always the government's fault, and no one is pointing fingers. "It's called my family did it to me." During this soldier first tour in Afghanistan his deposits by the military were made, the military met their obligation to the soldier by making sure the soldier was paid on time. It is unfortunate to say the soldier's parents felt they were entitled to the soldier's funds and when he returned home from Afghanistan his parents had exhausted all his savings, by living flamboyantly at the gambling casino. The solider returned home broke. After finding out his parents spent his hard-earned money, he requested to go back to Afghanistan for another tour in Afghanistan trusting his parents would not do the same thing as before. He left his account open for them and returns home a second time from the war zone broke. Not wanting to prosecute his parents the soldier is left with nothing and of course no place to go. The soldier was referred by me through a friend to seek counseling at the VA. This is only one isolated case of many where parents, friends and loved ones feel they are entitled to the soldier's savings even though they have not served one day in the military. Soldiers whose money has been stolen have the right to file a case in court to receive their money back. Unfortunately, many of them do not file a case because, "It's Family." I must ask this question, after you have been done wrong by what means do you use to justify the end? Do you continue to put yourself in the same predicament or do you maneuver to another place and get away? Many soldiers are not referred to counseling and become aggressive due to what was taken from them and chose the other alternative which is usually taking revenge on someone who has wronged them. The soldier wants what was taken from them back. It is only because no one truly knows the whole story of why the soldier does not have any funds or why he begins to drink, smoke or do drugs. I can say this from experience that it is usually because of the hidden wounds no one can see but once again I must tell you, the pain, agony and the frustration is there because the soldier's feelings has been tampered with and the trust the soldier once had in the individual is gone. Be it physical, emotional, economical or mental and you sit and wait for the soldier to react in a negative manner just so you can incarcerate him or her without getting to the facts of the matter. Although the soldier I just spoke of is currently seeking help, there are so many more that are lost to the prison system. When we begin to peel back the many layers of the subconscious mind of the soldier what you will find is a lot of hidden pain that takes years to fix, because of the journey and oath, the soldier decided to take not just for this country's defense but for your defense as well. But this soldier is not repaid properly, and this is one of the reasons why I am writing this book. No one seems to believe the catastrophic suffering taking place in this nation today as it is related to what is needed to make the soldier whole again. This is why the needs of the Vietnam Veterans must be met in order for the healing process to take place. What we as a nation have to keep in mind is, we are still at war with ISIS and we will soon have the same situation if not worse on our hands. The American people and the Veterans Administration are not preparing a way to help the soldiers who have returned, as well as those who are in battle getting ready to return. Soldiers returning home from Afghanistan and Iraq are going to need counseling and guidance to help them through the tragedies they experienced on the battlefield. I strongly advise the government to set up home station counseling that will be federally funded in every state of the United States. This is what home station means, it is the base station from which the soldier enlisted from. Assuming the soldier is going to go back home for a while the soldier should be given a mandatory appointment to go and attend the meeting that fits their medical diagnosis. To be able to assists the soldier in getting the proper help needed in order that there would be help stations set up when the soldier returns home. This did not happen for the soldiers who fought in the Vietnam War and many of them are in prison due to some form of irrational behavior of which could have been avoided if the Vietnam Veterans were not just left on the streets of their home base to fend for themselves. This kind of expertise needs counseling and training to recondition the soldier's mind in preparation to function in a world that is no longer in uniform with a completely different social structure. Therefore, I incessantly say forgiveness is a continual journey of travel of trying to fix something that is embedded in the hearts of those who know what has not been done to come to the aide of the Vietnam Veterans. Is not right and was never right for the Vietnam Veterans and this is why they have suffered for so long and are still suffering. It is all about the journey we take and what you have packed up to prepare yourself on that journey. Whether you took something that was given for you to take or was it something that you may have acquired along the way. Was it instinct, knowledge or was it the experience? Something had to get all of us to a point in life that had some meaningful significance to each of your journey's because no one gets there alone. What remains to be so mystifying as I have mentioned and will continue to do so is how the Vietnam Veterans were left out in the open with nowhere to turn for help. When I think about the hurt in my heart and all that happened in the war itself. The soldiers were dropped off not only in a strange place that was foreign to their thinking but where people they have never encountered wanted to eliminate them. It was just as foreign when they returned home to find out they did not know the people who sent them off to war to fight. The government and citizens of America turned their backs on the Vietnam Veterans and to this day have not given the soldiers an apology for what even the United States did not see coming. As far as America was concerned what was taking place in Vietnam with our soldiers was worse than the atomic bomb being dropped. Only this time it was the American people who should have thought twice before they passed judgement on the Vietnam Veterans, since the United States government and its citizens were just as guilty each and every time a soldier pulled the trigger to kill a Vietnamese. Each time an American soldier cut off the ears of the Vietnamese, for each Vietnamese that was decapitated and for every American soldier who was skinned alive the government and the American people tax dollars, who sent them to war, were just as guilty as the Vietnam Veterans, who completed their mission in the jungles of Vietnam. Many of you will not hesitate to say but you were not there, how can you be guilty. It's called an Accessory to the Fact, meaning because you are attached in some way with the crime you are just as guilty as the person who pulled the trigger. So, while you were putting the Vietnam Veterans on the cross to be crucified remember you were the one who put the rifle, bayonet and grenade in their hands to defend the Constitution of the United States of America. Remember I am not pointing fingers; I am just making a point because it was you America, our government and the citizens therein who actually put these men who had given their lives for you in a field of open fire. Ambushed by the media these men were never given a fair chance due to all that was taking place in Vietnam for them to be able to bounce back from what they experienced in the jungles of "Nam". I am certain not even an animal wants to live like that. Even a mother lion teaches her cubs how to hunt, how to prepare for the game of life in order to survive. The mother eagle teaches her young how to fly and prepares them on how to survive as eagles. Even primates prepare their offspring for survival on how to hunt and how to avoid dangers. This can take up to two years or longer, but what did we do to the Vietnam Veterans? We took eighteen-year-old boys and called them men simply because they had completed two weeks of bootcamp and stuck them in the hottest war zone this country had ever been in. The big question is how far can two weeks of training take a young soldier eighteen years of age who has been dropped in a hot war zone with nothing but death around him to figure out what he needs to do in order to survive? Second guessing is not an option, or a solution and time is of the essence when it comes to making a split decision concerning one's life. The survival skills needed in a war zone in order to fore fill one's expectations about thinking of returning home once the war is considered to be over is something that if you did not know what to do you had to figure it out in a matter of increments of seconds. That's right! We are right back to no time to think about what to do in a war zone. What is your life's expectancy? Of course, no one really knows the time, or the place life is going to end for any of us, but life's expectancy is to live forever. I used to joke with my uncle James about death sometimes and he would make a joke about death. He would first make the statement, "Linger long but die you must." Then I used to ask him how long he thought he was going to live? My uncle James had an acute sense of humor about death and dying. He would say, "I want to live as long as I can and die when I can't help it." It sounds funny but unless you have actually been in a war zone with bombs going off around you all day. You sometimes take life for granted, thinking you are going to live forever. The painful thing about war is that it plays tricks with your mind. It puts you in an illusive place of thought because you are in an unknown place in time never sure if you are going to be the next one to die. Military soldiers really don't have the time to think about death. Our job is to secure the land and to make sure our country is safe. To make sure the assignment given in relations to the mission has been completed without any regards to how many casualties we will take how many wounded or how many lives will be lost. Casualties are of course expected; this is what war is about. Each man has a mission and when time comes for the soldier to go outside the safety wire into the heat of the war zone there aren't any questions asked, everyone knows their mission and the next step is to get it done. We all know we have signed up for a mission. A mission that is going to take us out of the safety zone of friendly's and put us on a journey at any given moment to be ready for combat. All who will be traveling on this journey may not be coming back. This is the mindset of a real soldier, this is what our training is all about, no fear. A soldier is a real man who signed on the dotted line to defend the Constitution of the United States of America, period, no question asked. And by the way you are getting paid to do a job and you do have an employer, the United States government. This is the part where you as a civilian become detached, but please continue reading and I will take you on a mission you cannot see. So, I will be your eyes and try my very best to take you to a place of your subconscious understanding. Remember you are on a journey, a mission with trained soldiers. Let me lead you through the steps; "after watching this trail for several days we are reassured there isn't an IED planted in the road to blow us up because our surveillance team has stated this to be a well-traveled road. We pursued our mission by getting together a convoy to travel this safe route. Our place of contact to set up a Medicine drop, or a Humanitarian Assistance Drop (HA) has already been checked out and established. This area is considered to be safe. While traveling to the site of the HA the soldier's mind begins to wonder has anything been missed, are the roads clear of IED's? The soldier remembers the four soldiers who were blown up by and IED and their bodies were splattered all over the place. This is the mindset of the soldier in today's war in Afghanistan. The Afghan soldiers have a constant adrenalin rush going to the HA site and after getting to the Humanitarian Assistance (HA) site. We are now in the midst of everything that could possibly go wrong. From a suicide bomber in the crowd, a possible missile attack or ambush. So, we have to stay on full alert and watching our perimeters as the Afghans are allowed to come into our safe zone to receive their bundles. This was a long day of which the HA went on for hours. We were going to be at the safe site until we have given away all the bundles of food and clothing, we had loaded in the trucks. This was a big part of Operation Freedom Kabul the Humanitarian Assistance Drops (HA) during my service in Afghanistan. We as soldiers wanting to complete our missions were placed in compromising situations that could have went the other way. Fortunately for myself and others it did not. Just be aware of the soldier's consistent adrenalin rush in the midst of extreme heat and presenting himself as an open target any given day outside the wire. This is what took place in Afghanistan with modern technology in 1998. You see the technology was advanced with better equipment but the one thing that cannot be replaced is the human body, dead is exactly that dead. The men and women who served with me in defense of this great nation were in a journey of which during the time I served 37 soldiers would not be making it home alive. The reception myself and many other soldiers received as we walked through the airport was heard all over the United States "Thank you for your service", "Thank you for serving." This is why I have to ask you the reader to reflect back to what I explained about one of the many missions I went out on and all that it took to remain focused to complete each mission. Well, the Vietnam Veterans had it even worse in relations to the death which lingered around them and the mind set they had to take on in order to endure their tour in battle. They did not have the training we have today. These men lived to survive each day in a jungle filled with underground tunnels of death. Which is where the Vietnamese killed many of our American soldiers coming from underground tunnels. What I am trying to make you aware of is our American soldiers, the Vietnam Veterans, did not stand a chance. This is why there were over forty-seven thousand soldiers killed in the jungles of "Nam" with a total of 58,022 across the board. This is also why they returned home without any governmental interventions set up for them to be treated due to the damages they acquired for fighting in the Vietnam War. It was the journey they were on to resolve a problem they did not create but trained to solve because they were a part the United States Armed Forced. The young (boys) men who returned home to us were not whole and only pretended to be okay. They wanted to be okay when they returned home so they could be accepted as a whole person, a soldier who was not damaged. As a result of the Vietnam War many of these men were not only rejected by friends because their personality had changed. They were also rejected by companies they were employed by because the same people the Vietnam Veterans protected by fighting a war they were forced to fight did not want to work as co-workers anymore. People were saying they were afraid of the Vietnam Veterans because many of the veterans returning home had killed while serving their tour in the war zone of the jungles. What society was not getting was there were no recycling programs set up for the soldiers when they returned so they could vent what they had been through. What Americans were not seeing is the inside wounds that needed healing. When people are suffering or need help normally, they act out of character. There are many physical and mental issues that had taken place with the Vietnam Veterans and it is unfortunate the Vietnam Veterans would not be given the right to claim (Post Traumatic Stress Disorder) until twenty years after the Vietnam War was over. Yes, there was a twenty-year delay by Congress admitting these men were suffering from (PTSD). I must ask this question due to the facts concerning PTSD I just presented to you. With so many Vietnam Veterans incarcerated due to anger and displays of irrational behavior and placed in prison due to fear of what people thought they would do to others, was not the remedy to the problem. The remedy for the Vietnam Veterans would be in the form of a psychological evaluation. This would help a military doctor, or a civilian doctor determine what the soldier needed. Whether it was some form of medical treatment to help contain his behavior or mental assistance. Therefore, to this date there are so many soldiers not just Vietnam Veterans incarcerated but Afghanistan and Iraqi soldiers who have recently returned home from war are having similar issues of outbreaks. What is even worse is the suicide ratio, which is up to 30 suicides a day. I am asking you to review what I am saying here carefully because in today's wars we have men and women to be concerned about. And the issues of soldiers returning home from war is only going to become a bigger problem if these concerns are not addressed. Do you really want a solution to the problems of the high divorce rate in the military? Do you really want to save the soldier from himself or herself? Do you feel the soldier deserves to have the best treatment available? Then there has to be programs set up across the country to gear the soldier towards a better life by setting up free psychological service to help get the soldier back on track. It's a fact that everyone wants the soldier to be the happy go lucky person they use to be before they left home to go to war. In all fairness to the soldier, they did not tuck tail and run. So now due to therapy and the soldier getting better where does the journey take the soldier now? The soldier is no longer looked at as being a loner or anti-social. The soldier now has some help, counseling devises and medication. If you would go back and review the soldiers who are now incarcerated, records will find there isn't any counseling or psychological medication assigned to the soldier to help the soldier to be able to contain any irrational behavior. This is the journey the solider has been on for years and no one else has stepped in to assist in this area because no one has really thought of why soldiers have such a high divorce rate? What remains unquestionably true is that a soldier who has served his country whether in a war zone or peace time is more likely to be convicted and incarcerated than a civilian who has not served. Please keep in mind all wounds are not visible to the naked eye. They are deeply hidden within the body and soul of the soldier and are dealt with by each soldier differently. What I am talking about is the internal inflictions a soldier must deal with. Which also becomes part of the personal mental acceptance of not being able to do basic things he or she use to do prior to going into the military. Basic things like jogging long distances, being able to lift heavy items and carry them a certain distance and being able to focus and read for long periods of time. There are so many more, hearing, seeing and even the simple task of even sitting for long periods of time. Yes, I know it is surprisingly true, but these are ailments the soldiers must be able to cope with and adjust his or her lifestyle in order to function in a society that questions every complaint the soldier makes. The fact is the soldier is not the same person he or she use to be and the pain the soldier is suffering from does exists, only you can't see it. If the conditions I have presented could not be proven there would not be a need for a Veteran's Hospital. And this book would be misinformed and misleading, but as you gather together the facts, I am presenting in this book what you will find is not an overabundance of assistance given to the Vietnam Veterans or veterans as a whole as everyone is proclaiming. What you will find is a need for further research to be done and funding to be given to those who have given their lives and time apart from their families to make this a better America in order to maintain the Free World we live in and love so much. It's a long journey being a veteran of the armed forces. After we have served our tour of duty whether in a war zone or state side the wear and tear of our body is true, the aches and pains don't go away just because we are no longer active. What I want you the reader to know is it is a day by day struggle trying to function like we use to without pain. The pain is persistent. Many of us want to be seen as whole men and women again but we are broken men and women who have left the comfort of our homes to protect yours. We left family and friends. Men have left their wives and children. Men have left their mothers and fathers not knowing if during the time they are serving if they will be able to come home and see their parents alive again. This is a part of the mental damage suffered by soldiers while trying to understand how they were selected by this declared war situation while in the process of becoming a man. Take for instance a civilian who has a choice to celebrate or not celebrate a holiday like Christmas. A civilian may decide not to celebrate because they are at home and do not want to put up a Christmas tree. Now let me take you to another place concerning a soldier's choice. It is a place that is hidden, mentally suppressed by the soldier because he already knows he is in the process of fighting a war and will not be able to make it home for the holidays. He is thousands of miles away from home fighting in a war zone. I know I may sound a bit facetious right now. But bullets don't stop in mid air and bombs do not cease to not blow up because its twelve o'clock midnight. The war does not stop even though it's Christmas all over the world. The battle to sustain one's life on the battlefields of war does not change because people are at home opening gifts. No, it does not work like that. Soldiers are on the perimeters protecting the grounds they have taken and making sure no enemy soldier gets through to interrupt your life back in the United States while you are celebrating Christmas. What about you guys who went to law school or medical school? There is so much the soldier has given up for your benefit. You may think the men and women who served, and signed their lives away freely to become a part of the Armed Forces of America did not have any aspirations in life? That's just not true. Look at it this way they were men and women who decided to come out of their comfort zone to make sure you were comfortable and safe in yours. They put their lives on hold to fight "In this man's army" in honor of being called a soldier in the Armed Forces of the United States of America.

CHAPTER XVI

THEIR JOURNEY TOOK THEM
OVER THE JORDAN

WHEN I THINK ABOUT America and the many battles this country has encountered, I have to think about what has made this country so great. The one thing that enters my mind is its true love for God and its civility for all life. The American way of life is a way of life that has bound this country together in unity through wars where we have had to put aside our differences and fight side by side for the betterment of all humanity, this is how slavery was contained. I will not say slavery was ended but humbled to a significant degree. Many people have already complimented me on my task in writing this book and basing it on the needs of the Vietnam Veterans. Only it is not just the Vietnam Veterans who are suffering but every soldier who has ever fought in a war. I must say each and every one of us suffered great loss. There are so many things we will never be able to regain once we return home to try to find ourselves again. Try to find out who we were before we left to go fight. That is a page in each soldier's life that will never be found again. It is a missing link a blotted-out memory of who we used to be. I don't care how many times we look at our year books or go to high school reunions. It is a big piece of our life that has been removed and replaced with new faces, new brothers and sisters. One that sits by your side in the midst of a firefight and lives out that moment of question of being killed together with you. The moments and memories of the past have all been replaced with the men and women who put on the same uniform, it's a different kind of respect. It's an eternal bond that no one else can break once you hear the word soldier. It's not like the guys you graduated high school with, we were all young and innocent. But during military training we have to remember someone's life is on the line if we screw up on the battlefield. We remember those who stood by our side, hung in there with us and said when the difficult times came, "You Can Do It." When you have someone else's life to think about you must keep in mind that everyone wants to make it back home. Although rank has its privilege no one could ever understand the comradery of being a soldier unless they entered into an area so devoted to brotherhood and sisterhood as the United States Armed Forces. Our training became an unspoken truth a truth of which each soldier who put on the military uniform could openly say yes you are my brother, yes you are my sister that is the loyalty we live for. That is the loyalty we fought for and that is the loyalty my brothers and sisters who put on the uniform each day were all willing to die for. Nothing is taken for granted and there is no closer friendship than the respect a soldier has for his comrades. Although it is an unspoken sense of respect, it's a look of endearment, a look you will never forget for the rest of your life. Just like a soldier walking the streets and a stranger tells him or her, "Thank you for your service", "Thank you for the sacrifice you made." I say to them I appreciate your kindness but please write to your Congressman and Senator and tell them we made it back home. For those of us who made it back please tell your government that we are all wounded soldiers. Hollowed out and empty due to the many vices we struggle with because of the war or wars we have been in. We are soldiers walking around trying to get to the right person in government who will help us get the help we need in order to function in a system that actually rejected the same soldiers they sent to war, the Vietnam Veterans. We are trained by our government and a lot is invested in us to take care of business when we are in a foreign land. You have taught us how to fight and to kill. Now teach us how to live and love again. That is the one emotion that was taken from our hearts and may never be replaced again. Love, this is what was taken out of the Vietnam Veterans. These are men who had to live like animals and in the jungles of Vietnam. They became the same animal that had driven the Vietnamese. When they returned home, this is how you treated them like animals. What you forgot is that you were the ones who sent many of them to war without their confirmation. These young boys(men) had no say whatsoever on whether to go to Vietnam or stay home. Everything was taken from them and nothing was given back not even a simple apology for what you did to them. These men who returned home from Vietnam watched the shores of this nation serving you America in the air, land and sea while you slept in your warm beds at night. And all you can deliver to them for over forty years now is a sob statement of non-acceptance. May I ask where is the God in you? Where was the God in you when you sent them off to war and watched the airplanes return to the United States from Vietnam loaded with nothing but body bags? Please tell me where is your compassion concerning the dead? The "Wall of Names" was a nice gesture for the dead but what about the Vietnam Veterans who are still living. It appears you would much rather praise the dead soldiers for the same job you have cursed those who have made it back alive from "Nam." The blood of the Vietnam Veterans remain in the graveyard of Arlington Cemetery and the streets of this great nation. What is owed to the Vietnam Veterans has not been repaid and please don't get too comfortable because I am not done yet. Their blood remains stained in the Oval Officer of the President, the Veterans Administration, in Congress and the Senate. It remains stained at the doorsteps of homeless shelters that turned them away, restaurants that would not feed them and businesses who would not give them jobs. These were young men (boys) who thought they were doing the right thing in a war you sent them to barely trained. And yes, that is what soldiers do when they go to war they fight and kill if they have to. For those of your who believe in Charles Darwin's theory, "Survival of the Fittest" these men became what they had to become in order to survive. So, after over forty years with only a few Vietnam Veterans left due to Agent Orange, the PTSD, Brain Trauma, the inner wounds we cannot see, the mental, emotional, and physical damage the Vietnam Veterans have suffered what say you. In your prayers at night, pray for the men who gave their lives so we could maintain the America we all know and love. I am going to ask you to do something to help ease the pain of men who did not deserve to be looked down on, the Vietnam Veterans. Please remember this book is not about pointing fingers at what was not done and who did not do their part in bringing our soldiers home safely. This is a book of facts and forgiveness. Just like many of you will not dispute the nature of survival I know you also have a conscious mind for the love of God knowing as Christians we must forgive our brothers. If you will allow me to say the line has been drawn in the sand and if any of you are without sin, please come forth. I know I would be waiting until kingdom comes for someone to step forward because there are none. So, in crossing over to the other side to not be stoned, but in order to save life you must forgive your own sins to be forgiven. Let the word of God come forth, and let it be heard from the souls of the men who lost their lives in order to sustain yours. If you condemn the Vietnam Veterans for accusations of what you think was done and heresies of what was said and heard by others makes you nothing more than hypocrites. But to bring fault against your brothers (the Vietnam Veterans) for a journey they did not partake in concerning the accusations made is wrong. I do not need to mention the heresies that were being reported. It is stated in the Holy Bible that as Christian believers we are to continuously forgive others without condition. The Vietnam War is a perfect example of a war that remains unforgiven and the pains of war concerning what the Vietnam Veterans have had to endure for over forty years remains to be in question with stories being told of which people are not sure of what to believe. I do know for a fact the one thing that remains right and will not change is the word of God. The bible is right, and somebody is wrong. If you are a true believer in God, the father of Abraham, Isaac and Jacob you already know there is history, the eyes of mankind and God who prevails over all. The only Judge who can justify truth. God is sovereign over all for it is he that has made us and not we ourselves. When we look at the suffering of others it is unfortunate that mankind has defined himself as judge. Christians value life and the suffering of others. In order for the Vietnam Veterans to have closure there has to be someone left to tell the story of what took place in a war that has caused pain in two countries, the United States of America and Vietnam.

CHAPTER XVII

———

UNFORGIVEN GUILT A LINGERING MESS

I T IS NOW 2019 and the toxic chemicals in "Agent Orange" a chemical herbicide that was sprayed from the air into the midst of the jungles of Vietnam created a non-ending lifelong disaster of death and hospitalization for the Vietnam Veterans. Agent Orange was not only dropped by American planes from the air and spread over the forest of Vietnam to kill the foliage in the jungles of "Nam." Agent Orange was also sprayed by friendly Air Force planes on our own soldiers American Vietnam Veterans. It is noted that their suffering has been continual since the Vietnam War has ended. The Vietnam War ended in 1973 but the chemical "Agent Orange" is classified as a highly toxic herbicide that now to this day harbors within the DNA of the Vietnam Veterans. The Vietnam Veterans continue to suffer from the chemical herbicide "Agent Orange" today. Before I get into the discussion about Agent Orange of which I will be soon. I first want to finish my discussion concerning forgiveness given to what was done to our soldiers in Vietnam. Of which there needs to be an apology rendered to the Vietnam Veterans that has been long, long overdue. Before I continue, I am a man who believes in writing about the injustices done to others. What has been avoided for over forty years should not go another year without being acknowledged; that is, the apology the United States of America owes the Vietnam Veterans. How these soldiers have been overlooked for so many years is a mystery within itself that still exists; I am speaking about the Vietnam Veterans. I am an ordained Elder, a field grade officer, published author, Grand Marshall etc. Education, my military career and experience in war and life is what helped me to write and publish my 7th book while currently working on my 8th book. Let me get back to the journey of the Vietnam Veterans and where it has taken this country. Unlike the book of Joshua chapter 3 King James Version titled "Joshua at Jordan" put me in a lot of deep thoughts. Even God has mercy on those he chose to have mercy on. At the crossing of the Jordan he could have very easily said no one is going to cross because of their disobedience and the wrong the Children of Israel had done by not following the Commandments Moses had given to them that came from the Lord. As Christians we serve a forgiving God. Our Father in heaven who said in Matthew 11:28-29 "Come unto me, all ye that labor and are heavy laden, and I will give you rest. (29) Take my yoke upon you and learn of me; for I am meek and lowly in heart and ye shall find rest unto your souls." We serve a loving and all-powerful Father in heaven. We serve the one true God as stated in the book of James 2:19 "Thou believest that there is one God; thou doest well; the devils also believe, and tremble." There should be no greater joy than to be able to find forgiveness in others when they have been wronged. During the time of the Vietnam War the country was not prepared for the monster that we going to be released and did not know the Vietnam Veterans would become the victims of unforgiveness and be terrorized for crimes they did not forget. The pictures taken of the soldiers who were returning home from "Nam" should not have been permitted to be taken and should have never been released to the media or shown to the public. We the people of the United States of America were being introduced to a different kind of animal. We were now dealing with a new situation that has continued to haunt this nation and many others to this day. Soldiers, Vietnam Veterans returned home with their battle regalia showing. Wearing necklaces of human ears around their necks and other trinkets of war. The mindset of the Vietnam Veterans was they did to the Vietnamese what they have seen so many Vietnamese do to their friends, their buddies, their comrades when the bodies of dead American soldiers were found mutilated in the jungles of Vietnam. Without a backup plan in place these men (young boys) who were released from active duty did not know of any other way to cope. I will remind you again that you were the ones who sent them on what appeared to be a one-way mission. Everyone knows Vietnam was so hot and filled with death that the expectation of staying alive just one day in Vietnam was close to a miracle. Body bags were brought in by the plane loads. Both young and old, soldiers and officers, African Americans and Caucasians who had fought side by side to make this a better America. This is why I am now giving you the word of God not to burden you with the history that cannot be changed but to make you aware of the needs of finding a better solution when it comes to assisting the Vietnam Veterans and not turning them away. Pretending there is no problem when there is does not make the problem go away or fix itself, the problem will continue to expand and only gets worse. This is what has taken place in reference to the Vietnam Veterans, too many years have passed and the water under the bridge is still rising especially when you look at the casualties and fatalities caused by "Agent Orange." We now have to look at more funding to research "Agent Orange" because there is more research needed from science due to the continual physical ailments soldiers and family members are suffering from. I will get into the details of "Agent Orange" shortly. We as a nation of people also need to prepare for what is to take place with the soldiers who will be returning home from Afghanistan and Iraq. Prisons continue to be broadened with soldiers who have not been treated for PTSD and other mental issues they may be suffering from we can change that America. With the courts feeling the best way to curtail the situation the soldier is having is to incarcerate the soldier. When the solution is for the military/ government to have the soldier treated prior to the soldier being released from the military. The soldier must sit and talk to a counselor after returning home from the war zone. If none is to be lost in the system, we must move quickly in our planning and make arrangements to get veterans off of the streets and fed. What is unfortunate in my findings is that each state relating to Veterans rights and benefits are not the same. There are some states catering more to the needs of veterans than other states. It is interesting to find out all states who are defended by veterans are not conducting business the same when it comes to caring for the soldiers who have served this great nation. The rating chart for each state shows the state of Alaska rating as number one on the chart for states taking care of veterans. The state of Illinois is listed as forty-fourth on the chart for taking care of veterans. This is the type of disarrayed discouragement I am taking about, one state doing more for veterans than another state. When the care for veterans should be the same in every state. It should be across the board care involving the benefits of soldiers who have served in the United States Armed Forces and were honorably discharged. This unbalanced show of support from the VA involving state by state rating is an eye opener for more research and detailed reviews as to why one state would be considered to be more of an advantage for veterans to live in than others. There is so much more to look at and my concerns would be if a Vietnam Veteran is diagnosed with "Agent Orange" in Alaska and is receiving treatment for the ailment and is diagnosed in Chicago, Illinois for the same ailment will the soldier receive the necessary medical care in Illinois knowing that Illinois is rated forty-forth in care for the veterans. If a soldier decides to serve their country does it matter which state, they took the oath in to serve? A soldier's home base should not have effect on the soldier's ability to receive treatment once the soldier is out of the military as long as the DD214 is showing the soldier as having an honorable discharge. When the soldier signed up to defend the United States Constitution the soldier is being given the pretense of a level playing field. Let me give you a scenario as to what soldiers in other states who do not hold the military veterans high on the rating chart appears to be saying. This is why I am saying military care should be balanced equally from state to state but it is not. (Example scenario) ******The soldier is not being told because you live in the state of Illinois you are going to have to wait seven to fourteen years to receive your benefits to help sustain your life. Unlike the soldier who took the oath in Alaska as soon as the soldier gets home and begins to apply for his or her military benefits the waiting period for the soldier in Alaska is only a few months. (I used Alaska because it rates number one on the list for helping veterans) ******. These are unnecessary stressors soldiers who are living in their home state which are not parcel to veterans end up having to wait. This is why it is important for those of you who will be reading this book and passing it along can draw a better picture of military veterans in the future when you find out how your particular state due to its rating is intentionally delaying the soldier's benefits. Simply because they are trying to treat the soldier like a regular civilian when the soldier is not. For those of you who have been in Vietnam and past wars and for those of us who served in Afghanistan and Iraq we already understand the ramifications as to why a soldier cannot be treated like a common civilian mainly because of what the soldier has been through. Which heightens the probability of why the Vietnam Veteran or soldier is going to show some irrationality in his or her behavior because categorically a civilian's files are not going to read the same as a soldier's files. This was the mistake that was made when the Vietnam Veterans returned home. They were released from active duty. For those who did not want to reenlist they were placed back in the population as though they had never been to war. I must bring this issue up because we are in the year 2019 and there still appears to be a lot of dilemma concerning the Vietnam Veterans which will be a reflection on the current soldiers returning home from Afghanistan and Iraq. People are still pointing finger and telling hearsay about what they think happened to the Vietnam Veterans without taking the whole picture of battlefield and war into consideration. Unless you have actually served in the Armed

Forces and slept out in the frigid cold, walked through swamp water or have been exposed to bombs going off on a battlefield, explosions in a war zone and death of your comrades on the battlefield, please tell me you don't understand why soldiers need a lot of care when they return home and I will believe you. This is the purpose for me writing this book since there are lots of people who just don't get the fact of what soldiers go through not just in the military but on a daily basis. Even after they are released from the military the nightmares and flashbacks are real. A soldier's needs are great and should be met without the soldier going through extra added stress to receive his benefits. What happened to the Vietnam Veterans is something that can be helped. Along with the need for more scientific research to be done concerning "Agent Orange". I have talked about hidden wounds not discussed by the soldier. I have talked about a boundless journey of the soldier of which may or may not turn out to be in his favor. It just may depend on which state the soldier decides to call home when he is released from the military. As intelligent as I know you are, I am certain you cannot call the division of treatment for the soldier fair and justify it in accordance to the state the soldier lives in when their benefits should be the same and accessible to the soldier in any state the soldier chooses to reside. It is not fair to the soldier, but this is what is taking place state by state. A man or woman who has fought to preserve the Constitution of the United States is going to receive limited benefits because of the state he or she resides in and this is exactly what is taking place. It is not hard to imagine these states who are now trying to comply with the needs of the soldiers were even less compliant during the earlier wars. Of which really highlights the Vietnam War because there wasn't any plan laid out to take care of the Vietnam Veterans after they returned home. The Vietnam Veterans have been victims of being antagonized for years. You have called them everything but a child of God. Not realizing the blame of what took place in the jungles of Vietnam did not fall on these young soldiers, it fell on those who sent them and more than just an apology is needed. The old saying goes, "If you fail to plan than you plan to fail." I must question your integrity and ask this question, since forgiveness embellishes the Christian faith what happened to "Am I my brothers' keeper?" I can go as far back as biblical times when God was angry with the Children of Israel and told Moses that he was going to destroy them and give him a new people. Even God forgave the Children of Israel. Only due to your own mental inclination you find it is beneficial to you to maintain your prospective position of being innocent and having clean hands than to admit this country failed to prepare and plan for the return of the Vietnam Veterans. You, America did not prepare for the battle injuries, and the toxic herbicide chemical that caused them so much pain because of your lack of knowledge. This is why the Vietnam Veterans are still hurting today. We all must admit that something went terribly wrong, and we must bear the burden of it. I personally feel an open admission would truly be acceptable but that's not going to happen because no one wants to be at fault. My back is up against the wall on this one since I do know for a fact that it took Congress twenty years after the war to admit that our American Vietnam Veterans were suffering from "Agent Orange." Agent Orange was a highly toxic herbicide chemical sprayed over the jungles of Vietnam by the United States Air Force planes. But keep in mind there is no finger pointing in this book. I do not want to lose anyone and finger pointing gets nothing done. So, everyone who is beneficial to the cause of wanting to help the Vietnam Veterans should please stay on board. Let's look at the corrective measures needed, more research and a lesser window of time of closure for the veterans who are serving in today's war concerning their VA claims. More prompt closure for claims eliminates irrational behavior and triggers a positive response to the stimulus being sought and defuses any negativity on behalf of those seeking relief. What the Vietnam Veterans have went through in war and returned home to go through even more scrutiny of which has been over forty years says a lot when it comes to forgiveness. After reading most of the facts I have presented in several aforementioned statements should not leave you with any doubt that the Vietnam Veterans deserve more than a hand up. No one can scream it any louder from the mountaintop, a wrong was done to our own American soldiers and it has not been corrected. We are at a point in time and space where they need to feel vindicated and not scrutinized for doing a job they were sent to do. In the washing out of the old to bring in the new since we are Christian believers, we have to understand that God did not just kill off the Children of Israel he sent them on a journey for forty years to filter out the old. What this nation has done to our own American Vietnam Veterans is put them in the wilderness to roam around unforgiven for life. This is not the Christian way nor is this right for the Vietnam Veterans to have to live like criminals ostracized for doing their job. It is wrong for a nation of Christian believers to not understand the word of God. When he is clearly saying in scripture there is a time to kill, there is a time for war, there is a time to embrace and there is a time to refrain from embracing. This is written in the book of Ecclesiastes Chapter 3. Where has your morality taken this nation and its proclamation to be Christian believers and a forgiving people. In all respect toward human dignity and morals who is forgiving who? The nature of a man of war is to go in and do what he has to do and come back home. The only written document agreed to by America and the Vietnamese that is exhibited concerning the Vietnam War is the Geneva Convention. Although many of you struggle with trying to process logic. What logic is there in war? It is either kill or be killed and according to the statistics in "Nam" the soldier had less than a split second to think before he pulls that trigger. It is not the Vietnam Veterans who failed their position as soldiers, but it is you, the American people who failed the Vietnam Veterans as citizens in a democracy who took the lives of these young men (boys) and left them to fend for themselves. Now it is over forty years later, and the conditions of the Vietnam Veterans are only getting worse. Morally speaking when the Vietnam Veterans returned home, they should have been given a hero's welcome, a parade filled with whistles and graffiti but that did not happen. There were other circumstances brewing in the pot of deception. The soldiers after arriving home put in question the American people beliefs after they were being judged by the citizens they defended. They were taken to a place where joy became tears and the truth became a lie. As I give thought to what is expected when it comes to moral values it would seem improvable that the United States of America and its fine government would want to review what is; Charles Hayes quote on "The Arc of the Moral Universe." Is there an arc in the universe that really bends? This is something I would say remains in question? Given the many false gods and teaching values of today would the suffering of the Vietnam Veterans change the thoughts of many? Of which unjustifiably turned their faces away from the mother scales of justice and gave a blind eye to the truth causing undue pain and disgust in the bending of the arcs elbow towards justice for the Vietnam Veterans. While looking at justice from a moral standpoint it would appear that living in a country which places its trust in God more would have been done to ease the physical, emotional and mental pain the soldiers where dealing with. The moral arc, the conscious mind of the universe is somewhat stagnated in its views of conduct considering what is right and what is morally ethical. Pursuant to one's values in life you can question what is morally right from a legal viewpoint. Which would be relevant to a crime of intent, only in thought although the thought of acting out the crime is found to bring a verdict of guilty. The nature of the crime being only in thought was never committed and should not bring a judgment in the mind of an act that never took place. This is what the people of the United States has done without a judge or jury and very little physical evidence against the Vietnam Veterans. You have condemned an entire era of military soldiers, the Vietnam Veterans for complying with the needs of the people requested by the President of the United States. If these men had failed to meet the orders from the President of the United States during war time what many of you do not know is the soldiers could have been imprisoned. Muhammad Ali was not incarcerated for refusing to be inducted in the Army, but he was later stripped of his title as well as his boxing license for three years. Muhammad Ali was not able to fight due to his being a conscientious objector of the Vietnam War, he was stripped of everything. Of which years later, the United States Supreme Court would overturn the decision of the courts and reinstate Ali's license to box. Watch the 2013 documentary "The Trials of Muhammad Ali" in it you will see Muhammad Ali's resistance to the draft. Years later the government was found to be wrong and millions were awarded to Muhammad Ali. The reason why I am bringing up Muhammad Ali's draft issues is to bring to your attention that you could be wrong about the Vietnam Veterans as well. I am certain you are familiar with the old cliché "Two wrongs does not make a right." These are men, soldiers who fought for this great nation, for you. In order to bring the Vietnam Veterans out of a dilemma of moral pain they have suffered with for over forty years, your moral values is essential in just knowing these men, the Vietnam Veterans trusted in a military system without reservation and did what they were told. No one really knows the horrors they encountered while in the jungles of "Nam". Only while in the states during the war of Vietnam did some form of normalcy exists. No one will ever understand the fear these men had to face during war. They encountered a fear they had to embrace to survive. Through their own eyes, the windows of their soul their fears remain hidden, suppressed intentionally. A fear that hides what they had to become in order to see their family, friends and loved ones again. A fear which remains contained in their subconscious mind everyday of their lives. A fear which stays confined behind a dark closet door not knowing what is going to come out. A fear that will remain barricaded in the Vietnam Veteran and he will never have to venture down or reopen it ever again. Since no one is willing to take responsibility for the lives that have been lost due to war issues in "Nam" called "Agent Orange," I continue to question "In God We Trust" because that is the moral side of justice. It brings out life values and common-sense issues which have an answer. It is now over forty years later, and Vietnam Veterans are still dying from "Agent Orange." I am not asking currently for the President, Congress, the Senate or anyone to admit to being wrong. At some point, we all have to look at the bigger picture and say there is a spoke in the wheel that is broken, and it needs to be fixed. The suffering of the Vietnam Veterans has already damaged many lives. People are still suffering from the hurt of watching their loved ones continue to deteriorate from the inside out due to the chemical herbicide "Agent Orange." We as a nation have always looked up to those in Washington, DC - our government, the President, Congress and the Senate to resolve issues amicably. Yet, the controversy that haunts the Vietnam Veterans is one that has remained open since I was a child wondering why they were being treated so badly. If the Arc of the Moral Universe could lend its views, how would it bend since everything is based on morals? The bend in the curve is not able to question one's ability to endure pain or its mental state of reality if its elbow does not bend towards justice making the moral arc nonexistent. The rejection of the pain and mental anguish the Vietnam Veterans were going through after returning from the war made the soldiers disassociate themselves from the government and civilian population as well as the military. By questioning what is one's expectations of war the Vietnam Veterans remain in the spotlight for many years even until this day May of 2019. I assure you there is no solution going to be reached in a land of immorality. When we as a nation of people look at the arc of morals that not only doesn't bend towards justice but questions the deity of its creation. When we look at the filtering out of the old to bring in the new it is more than likely new ideas, new beliefs and understanding of new ways and changes will begin to take place. With all this being said I say prepare for change. Do not be afraid. What is fear to you? Does fear exists inside of you?

So, You Embrace Fear

In fear I can only assess that you have a lack of love and trust in God;
There is a boundary of bottomlessness. A
limit of where one should tread;
You hinder yourself, there is no need to search
for anything beyond your physical reach;
Your desires, dreams and inhibitions have a set
foundation which you will never cross.

How far should you travel when reaching for a different plateau;
Was your desire to do the will of the Lord, dipped in the cup after him?
You do have a purpose an unwritten obligation,
God has given you a task to complete;
What is your fear, trusting in God is knowing
he did not put fear in you?

But you draw imaginary lines, boundaries
that are setup with limitations;
What's funny is the demon of this world will
have you believe you have limits;
Only believers know there is no such thing as
fear because it stigmatizes itself;
Where is it that a child of God cannot tread
when our foot is on the serpent's neck?

Your contrite thinking discloses your uncertainty,
your fear of moving forward;
Because you have left out your peace and
allowed unruly spirits to enter;
You hide in fear of your own captivity layered in the lust of your mind;
Unable to accept the inheritance of the
kingdom because you embraced fear.

You have made it a part of your daily ritual; therefore, you are limited;
Your physical mind cannot be invigorated
limitlessly, and you are stagnated;

Your spirit cannot grasp what God has put in
you; you are now worse than the fig tree;
There is nothing futile within your empty
scavenged soul, its black and void.

You have forsaken the word of God to embark upon your own defeat;
You claim the defeat instead of the victory,
I mourn for you and your fear;
Unfortunately, I will not dwell in fear with you
nor will I mourn long in your disgust;
Simply because it is not I who fear, it is you,
look at yourself closely in the mirror.

I am a Christian, yes, I am a follower of Christ Jesus;
So, I say take your fear with you wherever
you go and enjoy your travail;
You do understand wherever you go and
whatever you do, your fear rules you;
Even the uncertainty of life should baffle you
so why do you wake up each day?

I see you don't quite get it; you don't understand
that you control nothing;
The vapor of life is only contained for a moment and soon blown away;
Jesus went into the belly of Hell and retrieved
the keys of life and death;
Yet you fear the physical mutilation of your mortal body.

You have forgotten you are subject to both mutilation of body and soul;
Of course, you know that only God can do that, so why do you fear?
What is it that you are so afraid of when even Peter walked on water;
Trusting in God is all we must hold onto in our search for salvation.

Is Lucifer your master, if so than you should
follow your master, embrace your fear;
Not being able to see over the mountain does
not mean there isn't another side;

This is how our Father in heaven would have us,
I am certain, do you remember Thomas;
With that being said I understand why you fear,
now you understand why I am blessed;

For it is written in John 20:29 "Jesus saith unto him, Thomas,
because thou hast seen me, thou hast believed: blessed
are they that have not seen, and yet have believed.

Written by: Author/Hall of Fame Poet
Raymond C. Christian
Date: June 4, 2019
Time: 4:26pm
Place: Backyard Patio
Reason: What is fear?

CHAPTER XVIII

——

A FORTY YEAR JOURNEY

GOD HAS A WAY of unraveling things we will never understand even though there is a reason behind it all. If I may introduce to you the book of Joshua chapter 5:6 how God brings us to a place in the Holy Bible where the Children of Israel appear to be lost. We do not realize God is taking them through a filtering process. Taking out the old and replacing them with a new generation of people. There is a shedding of the old to become new creatures in Christ Jesus. A washing of the souls of what God wanted to get rid of so new life could begin with those he would allow to come out of the wilderness of confusion with clean hands and not those of the past. With this being done the Children of Israel would be able to start anew. Not by destroying them but by giving them a chance to change and serve the father of Abraham, Isaac and Jacob. Please expound on the word of God; Joshua chapter 5:6, "For the children of Israel walked forty years in the wilderness, till all the people that were men of war, which came out of Egypt, were consumed, because they obeyed not the voice of the Lord: unto who the Lord swore that he would not show them the land, which the Lord had sworn unto their fathers that he would give us, a land that floweth with milk and honey." This is where mankind began to realize even more that God is a keeper of his word as he metaphorically uses the terminology of a land flowing with milk and honey is only symbolic of a rich land. A land where we would not have to want for anything. We would not have to suffer because the Lord has already gone before us. I must say God's act of forgiveness by letting the children of Israel come to the land he had promised their fathers show how gracious our Father in heaven is. This reminds me of what is stated in Number 23:19 "God is not a man, that he should lie; neither the son of man, that he should repent; hath he said, and shall he not do it? Or hath he spoken, and shall he not make it good?" What was to take place was the moving of the word of God. There were events destined to happen, with the hardening of pharaoh's heart, the opening of the Red Sea, and finally those who would be able to witness the coming into the promised land. A land God promised their fathers they would be bought to, a land of milk and honey. With forgiveness, being a major factor when we talk about change, it is only God who has the authority to give the burdens. It is our choice this is why free will is so important that we are able to take up the word of God and give light to those who are walking in darkness. As a Christian nation, believers of the word of God, we know it is better to forgive. So, we are not supposed to allow others who feel they are not worthy to walk around in darkness for the rest of their lives. We must show them that through repentance God is the light and we serve a forgiving God. Not a God who wants to see his children downtrodden for the rest of their lives because of mistakes they may have made over forty years ago. What is the probability of anyone making a mistake and seeking forgiveness from God knowing we are all imperfect? We have been designed by our father in heaven and made in a meticulous way that we will always need our father and the forgiveness we seek from him that we might have a chance at salvation. Because our father in heaven loves us so he allows us to call on the name Jesus and for this reason we will suffer persecution. We suffer proudly for the righteous things of God. 1Peter 3:17 "For it is better, if the will of God be so, that ye suffer for well doing, than for evil doing." Although we go through many burdens in life we do not understand as true Christian we stand strong with the Lord thy God knowing he is the one who will bring us out of it if it is his will. II Corinthians 4:8 "We are troubled on every side, yet not distressed; we are perplexed, but not in despair; (9) Persecuted, but not forsaken; cast down, but not destroyed; (10) Always bearing about in the body the dying of the Lord Jesus, that the life also of Jesus might be made manifest in our body." With the scripture I have given you I must once again ask you in reference to the Vietnam Veterans how we as Christians should feel? How are we to embrace them and show them the brotherly love which we as Christians have been taught to do, forgive thy brother and not be his judge or jury for it is not for us to judge. I Corinthians 11:31 For if we would judge ourselves, we should not be judged." Christians do not inflict pain on others but instead seek other ways of remedy to give relief. My reason for giving you Joshua chapter 5:6 is because our creator God Almighty shows the Children of Israel compassion even though he has the ability to destroy them all. The bad blood of disobedience was not to enter into the good land of milk and honey God had promised their fathers. It was through forty years of suffering and watching them wonder in the wilderness as they slowly died off until God was pleased with what the new generation would bring into the new land of their inheritance. As Christian men and women of God we must not look down our nose at our brothers and not forgive. This is not justified in our heart as true believers just as God forgives us, we are to forgive our brothers. The Vietnam Veterans were taken to a war zone and made to fight for their survival. Is there any man without sin let him stand and be recognized? I John 1:8 "If we say that we have no sin, we deceive ourselves, and the truth is not in us." By right we are not perfect, but we are to walk as close to Jesus as we can. I am certain the Lord would not let any of us suffer more than we can bear. If that suffering is of such an abundance of which the bearer of such is seeking a way-out God will make that way by sending the lamb in the bush. The one and only true lamb will and ready for sacrifice. The Children of Israel roamed around in the wilderness for forty years. It is now over forty-five years that you have pointed fingers at the Vietnam Veterans, and have allowed them to carry a burden of unacceptance. If God can forgive the Children of Israel for their disobedience can you forgive the Vietnam Veterans? In all actuality, can you forgive yourself for sending them? The ugliness of war haunts their lives while these Vietnam Veterans are dying off due to "Agent Orange", but their suffering has not been in vain. They fought in belief of what they were sworn in by oath to defend. What this nation has not stood up to is the promise made to these men who served and that is to take care of what was caused by our own friendly aircrafts that sprayed the highly toxic chemical herbicide "Agent Orange" on our own soldiers. It would be an added blessing to the memory of all of the Vietnam Veterans who are still Missing in Action, Prisoners of War, Killed in Action, and those who made it home to talk about the horrifying and disgusting things they saw and had to endure while fulfilling their obligation to the United States of America. There are those who served more than one tour over in Vietnam. These are the things which have been quietly swept under the rug. What we have learned today about past wars and present day wars as we watch closely that the soldiers who are requested to do more than one tour in a war zone should be given at least 15 months of a break before they are allowed to do another tour in the war zone due to the stressors involved. The Vietnam Veterans did not get that kind of break. They did not even get a break from the tour they initially had to serve. When I say a break in the war zone, I am talking about leave from the war zone to get some rest and relaxation of thirty days. If their tour had six months or a year that is what they did. It's sad to say but soldiers' bodies were numbers for a head count that was so badly needed in "Nam". The death toll was so great it was impossible for the Vietnam Veterans to go home on leave. They had to stay and stick it out. These were men of valor, men of dignity, men who showed their dedication to the United States and were given very little in return.

CHAPTER XIX

AUTHORS STATEMENT OF HOPE

B EFORE I GO INTO some of the issues many of the Vietnam Veterans suffer with, keep in mind that it is not just based on their service to the United States and the era they lived in. You must say it was a unique time during the sixties. People were just doing their own thing and trying very hard to get along as well as figuring things out that would make America a better place to live. There were demonstrations taking place throughout the United States of which people were beginning to question our government as to why there was a need for a draft. The Vietnam War was beginning to show its ugly face. It was a face of curiosity which brought along with it many questions like what was our purpose for fighting in this war? I was just little boy at the time, but I can remember so many discussions taking place on television and of course listening to adults talking about the Vietnam War. No one was pleased with all the violence and even more so with the number of body bags being flown back into the states. Whether it was a war on politics or not this question remains one of the deep dark secrets to this day. The Vietnam War brought doubt into the political arena of America and focused on the greed of politicians in Washington, DC. Whatever political secrets of who was getting rich and the dead bodies of these young soldiers returning home in body bags remains well kept to this day. Controversy is what makes people respect what we as Americans stand for, and that is justice. But justice concerning the Vietnam War is what American citizens begin to question. The loyalty and respect the American people had once shown our political leaders that hard working citizens once entrusted their sons lives to was now in question. The effect the Vietnam War had on the United States of America was the beginning of its division of trust. American citizens would never trust their political leaders or their government blindly again. And as much as people would like for our governmental system to go back to the way it was before the Vietnam War, it will never get back to that kind of dedication ever again. The hidden secrets and red tape concerning the Vietnam War will not be spoken of without questionable thought as to why our soldier were there? The problems that begin to capture the hearts of the American citizens, our brothers and sister are the bodies of family members, friends and loved ones that begin to reach insurmountable numbers. The American people wanted answers, they were not so gullible and ready to accept just any response from the political leaders and from those who were serving in an elected office. This war was beginning to touch homes and the truth of why this war came about and how America got involved remains as one of the highest marked red tape cases of this day and its files will never be disclosed to the American people. I can remember as a young boy reading the newspapers that even President Kennedy told Dr. Martin Luther King Jr. to not speak on the Vietnam War. This is just how controversial the Vietnam War had gotten. By the late sixties the Vietnam War became the main topic at everyone's breakfast table asking the American government to open the Vietnam War files to the American people. Well let me put it this way. It's kind of like asking the American government to unlock the files of President John F. Kennedy and why he was assassinated or even unlock the files on Dr. Martin Luther King Jr. as it relates to his assassination/murder. I will not fail to mention Malcom X, another great speaker and leader murdered. Medgar Evers another great leader and of course I cannot be disrespectful to the African nation and leave out Steve Bantu Biko who was murdered fighting against apartheid, or Mahatma Gandhi, a lawyer who later became a humanitarian activists for India, he was murdered. We must not ever forget the first African President of South Africa Nelson Mandela. These are files we will never get a chance to view. The Vietnam War file sits right on the same shelf next to the Watergate Case, what do you think? These are hidden secrets placed in a time capsule of life and will never be opened to the public. With all the great philosophers and speakers etc., we fail to contest what is still taking place today with the Vietnam Veterans, for them it is not over yet. They stand in the presence of the American people daily blending in with the citizens they once defended. They wear their military hats and different little trinkets to let the public know they have been in the Vietnam War. Here is what these men are really saying as they proudly display their trinkets of war, "I have been in a war", or are they really saying, "We the Vietnam Veterans still need your help America". I very briefly spoke on the "The Moral Arc of the Universe" does it bend toward justice? There is a time when you must pick what is the correct time, and the way to say and do things. Many people find it is very easy to say yes to a situation that does not affect them directly. The big question that remains unanswered today is does, "The Moral Arc of the Universe" bend towards justice? If this is true, then why are the Vietnam Veterans still suffering? It is most certainly not from the lack of time but from the lack of assistance needed concerning their bodies being affected by the herbicide "Agent Orange." It appears, as though everyone is waiting for the Vietnam Veterans to just go away. The problem here is that these soldiers cannot just go away because their lives and their future were taken from them by mistakes made by the military. The mistakes made are due to the lack of research prior to the chemical herbicide "Agent Orange" being released. This is where the Moral Arc is supposed to bend toward justice and those who are in charge are supposed to step in and take care of the men who did not desert the United States draft and run to Canada to avoid having to go to Vietnam. The few Vietnam Veterans we have left in the United States today are dying off slowly. After they are dead and gone, we are not going to get rid of the problem of the highly toxic chemical that was once air borne and landed in the jungles of "Nam". What is going to haunt the United States even after the last Vietnam Veteran is dead and buried is the lack of monies needed to be invested in research in relations to the herbicide chemical "Agent Orange". The Moral Arc is not bending toward justice and there is no calibrated scale to balance everything out for the Vietnam Veterans that can ever restore all they have lost. There isn't a virtual reality screen to enhance the bend of the Moral Arc of the soul of mankind to instantly make right the wrongs inflicted on our good soldiers of fortune, the Vietnam Veterans. Now if you want to add insult to injury let me begin by saying although an apology is needed an apology is not the final step in the right direction that no one has attempted to make to correct the problems the Vietnam Veterans are suffering from and have suffered from for over forty-five years now. Covering up a mistake that could have been easily corrected is not the kind of government this great nation was built on. We are a nation of humane people. I would like to believe the country I served honorably in the Armed Forces of the United States is not a country that enforces the suffering of others. Especially not their very own soldiers, the Vietnam Veterans, men who have given their lives for the betterment of this great nation. I am pleading with those who are in government, our President, our Congress and our Senate as well as the citizens of America to open their hearts to a new America. Let's go back to work for the American people in order that the necessary changes that need to be made can be made without blaming a past that cannot be changed. Although we cannot change our past, we can make our future better. So, before I get into the problems caused by "Agent Orange," a herbicide chemical, that was accidentally dropped from the air unto our American soldiers, I will ask for everyone to please take a moment of silence. Stop and think about what is being said here, accidentally dropped means the act itself was not intentional. Which gives everyone the opportunity to rethink what needs to take place today to correct the accident that happened. Since we now know "Agent Orange" still lives as a blood born chemical not only in the Vietnam Veterans' body but in the body of their children and grandchildren.

During the times myself and many other soldiers, who have served the United States in a war, I have never seen such cohesiveness, comradery and will power of the men and women in the United States pull together as a team to help the United States of America show compassion to help other countries in need to maintain their dignity, has always astonished me. What amazes me is this country has helped other countries, given aide and assistance to foreigners entering the United States, but stands divided when it comes to doing what is right for the Veterans who served in the Vietnam War. Our acts of compassion in relations to our own military force must show a greater need of resolving the war issue at hand. A war issue that has lingered for over forty-five years now and the Vietnam War shall remain a blemish since the highly toxic herbicide "Agent Orange" is now in the DNA of the children and grandchildren of the Vietnam Veterans. We no longer have to be a fork in the road when it comes to correcting an accident that happened. The solution to the problem involving the soldiers and "Agent Orange" no longer requires an admission of guilt. What can no longer be overlooked is the continual suffering of those who were participants in the Vietnam War. They had no dog in the fight.

As a nation built on the words "In God We Trust" our government must make the proper changes to assure the Vietnam Veterans and their children's children that scientist will be able to move forward in its research to find the life expectancy of "Agent Orange." If our government does not make it so, we the people of the United States of America must step in to convince our President, Congress and Senate. We are not pointing fingers to condemn anyone of wrong doings, but there is a crisis which continues to haunt this nation. Sooner than later it must be handled, or we will continue to suffer the devastations of the Vietnam War. I say to all please leave the finger pointing out.

The accusing of political leaders, the President, Congress and Senate involved in what took place in "Nam," leave them in a neutral place. Otherwise, the negativity will set in and we will find ourselves back to square one. Nothing will be in favor of helping the Vietnam Veterans get the help they need or anything else that can start the ball rolling in the right direction to correct an over forty-year issue.

The suffering of the Vietnam Veterans which led to the multiple illnesses and later death. Was due to the Vietnam Veterans having to live in the jungles of Vietnam where eleven million gallons of "Agent Orange" were sprayed from the air over them. The eagle being displayed was designed by Edwardo Pott, to symbolically show why they suffered. The eagle holding the can of "Agent Orange" in one claw and death in the other claw represents the suffering of the Vietnam Veterans.

CHAPTER XX

"AGENT ORANGE" THE DAMAGE IT HAS CAUSED

I T HAS BEEN OVER forty years now and I am making my request in this book for our government to stop contemplating on whether it should approve the need of more research and funding needed to understand not only the damages "Agent Orange" has caused but also the life expectancy of the chemical. As I begin to review the causations of the chemical herbicide "Agent Orange" what I am finding out is the specification that soldiers must meet in order to file a health problem they may be having in relations to "Agent Orange." When I think about the men who served in the Vietnam War, I see nothing but heroism. The problem which continues to be persistent is not about the war itself and what was said to have taken place, but a problem which boils down to money and whether "Agent Orange," a toxic chemical herbicide, was what was sprayed right on top of our own soldiers. What remains in question is whether Agent Orange has caused severe health problems in the Vietnam Veterans? Is it still causing health problems in not only their bodies but their children and grandchildren as well? How much longer will we rely on outside research teams hired by the chemical plants who created "Agent Orange"? Chemicals in the body are likened to what is a pathogen, of which many times are not able to be controlled. Chemicals created in a laboratory are known to have extensive, unresolved and inconclusive research involving its findings and it is usually in question by the scientist who created it because of a lack of understanding the chemical created. Many scientists end up asking for more money to assist them with their research. They usually need more time to help to understand the chemicals they created. Whether it is going to benefit the United States in a positive way the findings should be conclusive and not nonconclusive. Damages to the human body when it comes to the advantages and disadvantages involving the longevity of its uses should be a (red flag), warning! If there was a conclusive statement, the scientist who created the chemical "Agent Orange" should have concluded that the findings are not continual and that the chemical which is in its testing stages should not be released. I am not a scientist neither am I a chemical specialist, but rest assured I am one hundred percent certain as it relates to "Agent Orange" that final findings were not reviewed because there aren't any conclusive findings to base what is was needed for a concrete case to close undocumented research on the chemical "Agent Orange." The fact remains that there are Vietnam Veterans still filing claims as their bodies continue to deteriorate from exposure to the herbicide chemical "Agent Orange." If you will allow me, I want you to look closely at what I mentioned earlier to what is called a pathogen. I will use the definition of a (pathogen) to expose the extent of its definition in correlations to the chemical called "Agent Orange."

What is a pathogen? "Disease causing microorganisms, such as bacteria, fungi, and viruses, found commonly in sewage, hospitals waste, run-off water from farms, and in water used for swimming. Most pathogens are parasites (live off the host) and the diseases they cause are an indirect result of their obtaining food from, or shelter in, the host. Larger parasites (such as worms) are not called pathogens."

What we are finding out about "Agent Orange" is that it differs strikingly from a pathogen which opens the need for more research to be done because unlike a pathogen that attacks the host in the body to cause sickness the chemical herbicide "Agent Orange" once in contact with the human body contaminates the blood of its victims. The victims being no other than the Vietnam Veterans. We are not sure whether the contamination comes from breathing in the chemical or just simple contact with the flesh or clothing of the soldiers. I must ask you to please keep in mind the Vietnam Veterans who were walking through the jungles of "Nam" while the chemical "Agent Orange" was being sprayed. They were contaminated with the chemical "Agent Orange". What I am saying here is the clothing the Vietnam Veterans wore, their boots, flak jackets, helmets, socks, t-shirts, pants, belts, shoestrings etc. Everything the soldier had on was contaminated at this point. Unlike a pathogen that can be cured with treatment, once "Agent Orange" was released into the atmosphere everything in its path or that came in contact with it should have been considered to be contaminated. For over forty years now we continue to look at the Vietnam Veterans with health problems caused by the chemical herbicide "Agent Orange" and nothing is being done about it. What we have is over forty years of denial of claims by Vietnam Veterans who are suffering from Agent Orange today. What's unfortunate is there is an Institute of Medicine called the (IOM) from which the Veterans Administration receives their information to get a green light for assistance and funding for the Vietnam Veterans. I will speak on the Institute of Medicine (IOM) in a moment. I first want to remain focused on the Toxic chemical "Agent Orange", its causations and its effects on the Vietnam Veterans in order that there isn't any more doubt as to whether the soldiers you sent to fight in defense of this great nation will not have to suffer any longer. They will not have to endure being either sick or struggle with the chemical "Agent Orange in their bodies or be rejected by the American people because of what they were told by the media while they were at war in Vietnam. How many more stories will have to be told in order for those in the hierarchy of the American government to say these soldiers have waited long enough? It would seem to be a thoughtless effort to come to the aide and assistance of the men who fought in the Vietnam War. This is because they did not ask to be there; many were drafted. These soldiers were never given the chance to pursue their educational dreams or chance to have a normal career or life after being released from the military or should I say the Vietnam War. Many were unable to start a family due to "Agent Orange" affecting their organs of which many soldiers are still in battle with cancer today. These soldiers, these men of loyalty and honor did nothing wrong but to defend what they were told to defend. How is it that they are still being penalized for actions that were not their fault? How does blame falls onto the shoulders of an innocent party, wrongfully accused of doing something they were not a part of? In a way it is like many of the cases of after twenty years or more in prison the person accused has been found innocent of which many states do not have any reparations set up to give them for taking the years of their life when placed behind prison bars. These wasted years could never be replaced. Well if you look closely this is what has taken place with the Vietnam Veterans. They have been imprisoned for over forty years. Not in a physical prison but more of a mental one, not able to hold their heads up and not be judged for something that was only speculated. They have suffered due to harmful propaganda of which mostly went unproven. But they continued to fight for the freedoms desired by the American people. The funny thing is that the Institute of Medicine (IOM) which is now the Health and Medicine Division (HDM) continues to issue their research to the Veterans Administration in relations to their findings in support of their colleagues before them. No one is pointing the finger, but I am certain after over forty years of research and all of these claims being filed by the Vietnam Veterans at least one of those non-governmental researchers of Agent Orange should have found something.

"We the people of the United States of America in order to form a more perfect union, establish justice, ensure domestic tranquility should come together for the greater cause." Yes, "We the people" those first three words says a lot. They tantalize the brain with hopes of unity and with our very own words of love and compassion of which the United States of America has shown the Vietnam Veterans very little. I have found that many people seem to have a loss for words when speaking about the Vietnam Veterans. It's evident neither side wants to talk about how they are coping with untruths. One misguided truth that has lingered for so many years is the denial of the health problems "Agent Orange" has caused. What remains unquestionable is the suffering and death of so many soldiers. Soldiers who never had a chance to do anything with their lives. While in a war zone we always risk the chances of death, of not being able to return home or injured to the degree of having permanent physical damage like missing limbs, an eye, fingers, toes, a foot, an arm. The soldiers are compensated for the physical missing body parts because they are visual and can be accounted for. What is in question here are the inner wounds not visible to the naked eye. How does the claims department access that part of the soldier's life? The internal damage that cannot be repaired and is looked at as being curable though time and counseling, maybe even a little medication. With all of this information being given in this book the one thing that has not been mentioned to give you the reader a little more to look at is the Vietnam Veteran - the individual physical body of each soldier. They were dropped in the hottest landing zone and war zone the United States has ever been in. The black body bags their comrades' bodies were brought home in were real. These were the soldiers killed in action. What is not being said is the Vietnam Veterans are still being killed in action. As it relates to the war with their own country, when it comes to leaving Vietnam only to be scrutinized by the American people. These soldiers can be said to still be at war, still on the battlefield right in the midst of Washington, D.C., where all the answers to why they were sent to Nam and why they have not received the treatment they earned when they returned home. What is being found out is the battle the Vietnam Veterans are fighting is about "Agent Orange", a battle of injustice. A battle that began in the mid 60's. What is not being recognized here is the seriousness of the need for findings of the (IOM). They are to be questioned on other problems of which are currently in existence and are affecting the veteran's children and grandchildren. With what was only thought of being a chemical that was only going to affect the Vietnam Veterans, now is a blood born chemical in the DNA and is now being passed from generation to generation. The research in question of which is needed is to find out the longevity of the toxic herbicide chemical "Agent Orange". Waiting out the Vietnam Veterans for over forty years now has turned out to be a collapsed moral injustice which involves the integrity of this country. Thinking the claims of the Vietnam Veterans would go unheard and unjustified is a humiliating thought of our pression scales of justice. What I am not going to do, once again is to point fingers at anyone, but want you to get an understanding that there is this problem with "Agent Orange and it is not going away anytime soon. Now we are looking at more generation of infections that could be contained and treated if our government contests what they are being told by the (IOM) and begin testing the children and grandchildren of the Vietnam Veterans. The cries of the people must be heard. There are over forty-seven thousand soldiers in the ground. But for those who are alive they will continue to form a band of brotherhood and sisterhood until this ugly and tragic burden which involves "Agent Orange" has been properly put to rest. Unlike the soldiers who were dropped off in a hot (LZ) not knowing their life expectancy if they made if off the helicopter was only sixteen minutes. The bodies of these dead soldiers should not go unrecognized of which I believe is one of the reasons why the truth behind the chemical "Agent Orange" will not be allowed to be covered up so easily. The Vietnam Veterans must be vindicated. The encouragement of more research needed on "Agent Orange" must be heard by our voices. You are hearing mines now! Further down the road we will be looking at the continual suffering of the Vietnam Veterans, and even after their death, more deaths and deformed babies will be born because Congress or the Senate did not vote to do further research into the life expectancy and longevity of the chemical "Agent Orange." YES, this chemical has already caused their children and grandchildren who carry this blood born chemical "Agent Orange" in their DNA, a lot of pain and suffering. The smoking gun is very clear concerning the investigation needed to correct the problem that continues to be passed over to the Institute of Medicine (IOM). Remember the (IOM) is now the (HMD) who changed their name a while back. I informed you of that earlier but just in case you were not paying attention, I am certain you have it now. No one has to look around to see if there's gun smoke coming from behind the grassy knoll. It's obvious as I stated earlier that federal funding is going to be needed and will have to be invested in order for the proper research so as to bring justice to the Vietnam Veterans who have suffered and died from "Agent Orange". For the less fortunate part of the "Moral Arc of the Universe" bending toward justice, we continue to count the deaths and deformities of the children and grandchildren. This nightmare of a chemical called "Agent Orange" is still haunting the Vietnam Veterans while the (IOM)/(HMD) refuses to accept the physical evidence being presented to use in helping to bring an end to their findings by sharing adequate light for closure to the Vietnam Veterans, their children and grandchildren.

CHAPTER XXI

A CHEMICAL "AGENT ORANGE" THAT KILLS

THE MISLEADING PARTS THAT I continue to find out from research involving "Agent Orange" is the denial of not only what the Vietnam Veterans are dying from, but the lack of research needed that has to also be looked upon involving other soldiers and their suffering. What is not being looked at is the contact the Vietnam Veterans had with others. Remember "Agent Orange" was sprayed on the Vietnam Veterans by the United States Air Force, they were assigned missions. I will tell you a little later in the book just how missions were listed to spray other chemicals including "Agent Orange." "Agent Orange" was a toxic herbicide chemical originally designed to kill the foliage/vegetation in Vietnam in order to make the Vietnamese visible to our American soldiers. It would later be found out to be more powerful than expected and once it was released it was considered to be uncontrollable. Or in the case involving the Vietnam Veterans and others who came into contact with the chemical herbicide "Agent Orange" would want to admit. What we are looking at today is a continual backlash of the chemical "Agent Orange" that is now blood born in the soldier's DNA. We now know that "Agent Orange" did not just land on the soldiers clothing. It also landed on their skin, body, eyes, ears, nose, and of course by it being air born the soldiers were also breathing in the chemical; so, let me add their lungs. Please keep in mind "Agent Orange" was a chemical herbicide being sprayed from the air and the soldiers we had on the ground did not have any inkling of an idea as to what was being sprayed over them. Due to the lack of intel and research by the chemical plant who made the chemical "Agent Orange" the intent was not to cause harm to friendly soldiers. After further review of other documents, the chemical companies were said to be aware of the dangers of using "Agent Orange." The original intent was to only kill the foliage/vegetation unfortunately we are still talking about "Agent Orange" in 2019 when the Vietnam War has been over for over forty years now. The facts are here, and you can do the math it has been forty-six years since the Vietnam War, and we are still talking about "Agent Orange" and the wrong that was done to the Vietnam Veterans. Is there any shame at all to be considered? Yes, but I must remind myself, this is not a finger pointing book. The real question here is when will a full admission of fault be given and when will the lies stop? When will the researchers be truthful and say it was "Agent Orange" from the very beginning? The truth of the matter is there is only a few Vietnam Veterans left alive today. The problem is their blood, which is reportedly contaminated with the toxic chemical herbicide "Agent Orange" has been passed on to their children and grandchildren. If you will go to https://veterans.perkinslawtalk.com this is what their study reveals, **"VA presumes many different diseases were caused by Agent Orange exposure. The types of cancer listed above are just some of the many disease that are presumed to have been caused by exposure to Agent Orange in Vietnam."** On August 14, 2017 the Institute of Medicine (IOM) which has now changed its name to the Health Medicine Division says, **"Links between Herbicides (Including Agent Orange) and other Health Effects. Chloracne is an acne-like rash caused by exposure to high levels of chlorine-containing chemicals."** Congress and the Senate listened to the medical reports which involved the research of Agent Orange. What is not inflammable and is no longer disputed is the facts that Agent Orange, a chemical herbicide sprayed from friendly helicopters from the air of Vietnam over the heads of American soldiers. "Agent Orange" is now and has been for over forty years killing our Vietnam Veterans. The denial of claims by the VA from medical reports concerning Agent Orange which caused severe health problems, even death to this day to the Vietnam Veterans continues to remain a mystery only to those who have higher interest of loss to cover up what they do not want to accept. The release of the chemical "Agent Orange" should have never been signed but there is more to this part of its release. As you continue reading you will find out more about its release. Our Vietnam Veterans should have never been exposed to the chemical herbicide which is permanently in the soldier's DNA, their children and grandchildren. The ugliness of the herbicide remains to be uncontrollable and the research needed to be done and the claims needing to be completed and given to the Vietnam Veterans seems to be an endless battle. But the research findings by the **Institute of Medicine (IOM)** who has changed their name to the **Health and Medicine Division (HMD)** continues to change their research findings to show more cause and effect in their research as it relates to "Agent Orange". What appears to be contagious is the new findings of what their science research teams are finding to be factual as it relates to what the Vietnam Veterans have been saying all the time. But the waiting lists continues to get thinner and thinner for a recovery that should have been contributory to the Vietnam Veterans over forty years ago. The problems presented to the VA concerning the illnesses related to "Agent Orange" should have set a precedence for all soldiers who were affected in "Nam" back in the sixties and seventies. What was once not awarded to the Vietnam Veterans is now being reversed with "Agent Orange" being the contributing factor to what is taking place involving the health problems of our American Vietnam Veterans. I cannot say the numbers were too great to take on such a vast number of soldiers who are suffering and dying from something their own country did to them. This question has to be presented to the President of the United States of America, Congress and the Senate: Was the dropping of Agent Orange on our own American soldiers intentional? My belief is, it was not intentional. Could it have been a strategic battle call to assist the Vietnam Veterans on the battlefield since so many soldiers were being killed in action because they could not see the Viet Cong? Yes, that was the intent to kill the foliage but according to other documentation the chemical companies knew otherwise. Due to the lack of research there weren't any relevant findings of the advantages or disadvantages found concerning the dropping of "Agent Orange" since the United States government's intent was to win the war. As a military infantry officer who has served the United States during war time I must say, "it would not be ethically moral for the President, Congress or the Senate to lose a war or the magnitude of lives that were loss intentionally." To be more open with what has taken place it would appear as though "Agent Orange" was being sprayed over Vietnam with intention of helping the soldiers. The United States government hadn't any ulterior motives of wanting to put our American soldiers intentionally in harm's way. I find for the betterment of the military it is only fair to say our government did what they thought was right in order to give the Vietnam Veterans an advantage in the war zone when it came to battlefield movement and maneuver. Although the strategy was sufficient in wanting to help towards the advancement of American troops in the dropping of "Agent Orange", it still does not relinquish the facts of the illnesses, deaths and diseases the Vietnam Veterans are having to live with today because of their exposure to the herbicide chemical. The struggle the Vietnam

Veterans still face today concerning their health leaves the door open for the President, Congress and the Senate to correct the problems which have been persistently related to the lack of research and findings of "Agent Orange". What we need are governmental employees for the research projects not non-governmental employees. That's like asking a man to vote against himself. If the Veterans Administration can accept the fact of not being intentionally at fault and grasp an understanding that there are Vietnam Veterans with health issues as a result of the lack of non-conclusive findings caused by the chemical "Agent Orange" before it was used on the battlefield of "Nam". Then everyone involved must can come to a mutual understanding that a chemical herbicide which is now in the DNA of the Vietnam Veterans, their children and grandchildren caused by "Agent Orange" must be addressed. The findings of what these outside entities so called organizations who have been hired to deliver reports to the VA are obviously not taking into consideration all of the facts. Unless they are being misled to say what the Vietnam Veterans are filing concerning the deterioration of their bodies of which they feel is being caused by "Agent Orange" is not affiliated with the progress of the chemical in their DNA. The kind of action being prompted here cannot facilitate a positive outcome and it has been shown over and over again by the vast number of claims being filed by the Vietnam Veterans which have continually been overlooked. What is not practical is the denial of the Vietnam Veterans claims of which many claims that are being filed bear similarities of Veterans across the United States. On the other end of the spectrum we are looking at outsiders hired to report their findings as to whether "Agent Orange" is the cause of our American soldiers debilitating health problems and internal diseases. What the Institute of Medicine which has now changed its name to the Health and Medicine Division continues to base their research reports on is considered to not be accurate data when it comes to inconsistencies of which their reports refuse to comply with in their lack of findings related to the claims being filed by the Vietnam Veterans to date. You can either agree or disagree that it looks like an intentional lack of findings in not wanting to substantiate what the Vietnam Veterans are filing in their claims. It would be more plausible if there were more research presenting facts equating to the herbicide chemical "Agent Orange" which is genetically in their blood now we have to acknowledge the toxic chemical is now being passed through the DNA of the Vietnam Veterans to their children and grandchildren. Unfortunately, no one anticipated the herbicide chemical "Agent Orange to hibernate in the DNA of the Vietnam Veterans and pass through their genes creating another fifty year or longer problem. You should be able to see where I am going with this, by denying the Vietnam Veterans their claims through the years is what has been substantiated by inconclusive reports and lack of research. If there was concrete evidence that "Agent Orange" was not causing the health problems the Vietnam Veterans are suffering from, then the research teams, consisting of the Institute of Medicine/ Health and Medicine Division would not be changing their findings every few years. We are once again back to inconsistencies. The research teams involving the Institute of Medicine or the Health and Medicine Division are leaving questionable doubt as to why the Vietnam Veterans should not receive the assistance they are requesting. Clearly this opens the flood gates for more research needed due to the herbicide chemical "Agent Orange" now in the DNA of the Vietnam Veterans' children and grandchildren. What this nation is looking at are bodies of soldiers which are deteriorating from the inside. Today further reports are showing deformities which are showing up in the children and grandchildren who are susceptible through the genes of their parents and grandparents who has "Agent Orange" in their system. In order to deny the claims of these men, fathers, sons and veterans there has to be conclusive findings. This is not the case as it relates to "Agent Orange" and the Vietnam Veterans. This matter concerning "Agent Orange" continues to be a nightmare of which the morality of the moral arc has not shown its mercy in the bending of its curve. Since there isn't any conclusive evidence in regard to "Agent Orange" the reality of its hush, hush exposure to the Vietnam Veterans remains non-existent in the eyes of the scientists who created it. It surpasses the realms and boundaries of common sense and has fallen into an empty hole of darkness incubating inside the bodies of its victims, the Vietnam Veterans. The researchers of "Agent Orange", the IOM/HMD team has not shown in its movement to conclude definite facts to refute the claims of the Vietnam Veterans. They will continue to remain inconclusive to the children, grandchildren and possibly great grandchildren who could possibly be found with traces of "Agent Orange" in their system, since the claims the Vietnam Veterans are filing across the United States remain unresolved due to inconclusive evidence. In case you are not fully aware of the what the word "inconclusive" means here is the definition, Inconclusive- "not leading to a firm conclusion; not ending doubt or dispute." What is left open to be reviewed are the soldiers who have been contaminated. There is over forty years of evidence with lists of good men who have given their lives for this great nation buried due to the lack of help and support they needed from the VA in order to sustain their lives. What has become apparent is the fact that even the Veterans Administration (VA) is not operating on its own decision making alone. For the lack of a better understanding of why the Vietnam Veterans have suffered so long is because they also rely on outside entities. Research teams which are considered to be non-governmental were hired to research what the soldiers are complaining about to see whether there is a relationship with the herbicide chemical "Agent Orange". The outside non-governmental researchers bear most of the burden of cause as to why the Vietnam Veterans are not receiving the benefit of doubt. The damage caused to the Vietnam Veterans remain untreated due to reports given to the Veterans Administration (VA) by the Institute of Medicine/ Health and Medicine Division. They will hinder the Veterans Administration in their ability to react. If it be at all possible, setting up programs or treatment centers to aid the Vietnam Veterans to a more comfortable outcome would be of beneficial. Without the backing of the research reports the VA is not able to comply with the needs of the soldiers. The Health and Medicine Division (HMD) formerly known as the Institute of Medicine (IOM) of the National Academy of Sciences, Engineering and Medicine can be located at: National Academy of Sciences, Engineering and Medicine, 500 Fifth Street., North West, Washington, D.C. 20001. This is where the linking of the problems concerning "Agent Orange" appears to be in relations to billions of dollars in claims being denied to the Vietnam Veterans. This research team the HMD, once again is non-governmental which means their affiliation to the Veteran as it relates to their research would also be considered to be bipartisan when it comes to rendering a judgement in favor of the Vietnam Veterans. When it comes to bipartisanship the nature of the beast is to remain inconclusive in their research as it relates to damages and claiming fault. Although bipartisanship are two separate entities with a different format being one is of science and the other is of facts. There is a third entity involved of which very little is mentioned, the Monsanto Company. The Monsanto Company is one of the manufacturers of "Agent Orange" along with Dow Chemical and the other nine companies. These companies were adding different kinds of chemical additives to strengthen the chemical being produced and knowing the damage it would cause not only in the ground but also in the lives of its own American soldiers. If you would like to reach three companies involved in the creation of Agent Orange. Here is their contact information: Monsanto, 800 North Lindbergh Boulevard, Saint Louis, Missouri 63167, next is Dow Chemical Co., 1645 South Kilbourn Avenue, Chicago, Illinois, and Diamond Shamrock Chemical Co. With the admission of their involvement in the making of the chemical "Agent Orange" these three company's Monsanto, Dow Chemical, Diamond Shamrock Chemical Co, would settle out of court to contribute help and to bring some relief to the Vietnam Veterans and the Vietnamese whose health had begun to fail after the Vietnam War. When we start to dig into the company's involved for the creation of "Agent Orange" keep in mind the Monsanto Company creation of "Agent Orange" was more than forty years which puts them at the exact time "Agent Orange" was being prepared to be used in "Nam". When we think about a chemical such as "Agent Orange" we think of a single chemical being used. Unfortunately, this was not the case. "Agent Orange" was one of six different chemical herbicides used by the military to kill the foliage in the deeply vegetated forest of Vietnam. The not so predictable part concerning "Agent Orange" which was produced strictly for military use was the damage it would not only cause to the vegetation but to the lives of our American soldiers, the Vietnam Veterans. The dilemma does not stop with the Vietnam Veterans although some of the damages were partially paid out of court due to the health issues and death that was occurring within the ranks of the Vietnam Veterans. Even though it was over forty years ago "Agent Orange" continues to damage lives due to its continual growth of being passed genetically through the Vietnam Veterans DNA to their children and grandchildren. What was once looked upon as a chemical that was being sprayed to kill foliage in the forests of Vietnam is now eating up the insides of those who once breathed and walked through it. What is unthinkable is the fact that many of the Vietnam Veterans had to sleep in the forest of Vietnam after "Agent Orange" was released as well as drink the water the chemical spray also contaminated. There is so much to be said in reference to the health and the number of lives lost because of "Agent Orange" that even Vietnam Veterans I have questioned to be interviewed about the time they served in "Nam" just did not want to talk about it. There was a few who would tell their story and of course I would just listen. What was really shocking to me as I did my research about the Vietnam War is there were at least six different kinds of chemical herbicides used by the military as a defoliant with all good intentions to help make the fight easier for the American soldiers. As a result of wanting to help the Vietnam Veterans there was a total of six different chemical "Agents" used. **"During the Vietnam War, between 1962 and 1971, the United States military sprayed nearly 20,000,000 U.S. gallons (76,000m3) of various chemicals- the "rainbow herbicides" and defoliants." (https://en.wikipedia.org/wiki/Agent_Orange)**. Because of the six agents being used they were called the "rainbow herbicides" : Agent Blue, Agent Pink, Agent Purple, Agent Green, Agent White and finally the most powerful chemical agent of them all turned out to be "Agent Orange". Mainly because "Agent Orange" contained the chemical dioxin. **Dioxins are, "environmental pollutants. They belong to the so-called "dirty dozen" a group of dangerous chemicals known as persistent organic pollutants (POPs). Dioxins are of concern because of their highly toxic potential… The chemical name for dioxin is 2,3,7,8-tetrachlorodibenzo-para-dioxin (TCDD)." (https://www.who.int World Health Organization, October 4, 2016)** Dioxin can remain in the soil for decades and since there isn't any clear conclusive research done as to how long it will last in the soul, decades could mean an eternity. **"Dioxins are a group of highly toxic chemical compounds that are harmful to health. They can cause problems with reproduction, development, and the immune system. They can also disrupt hormones and lead to cancer. Known as persistent environmental pollutants (POPs), dioxins can remain in the environment for many years." (https://www.medicalnewstoday.com 21 Apr 2017)**. The article you have just read concerning the chemical dioxin which was intentionally put into the herbicide chemical "Agent Orange" to make it stronger should immediately bring to your attention the dangers involved when exposed to such a toxic chemical. I already stated how dioxin will cause reproductive problems, developmental issues will occur and it will also affect the immune system. They can also disrupt hormones and lead to cancer. These are facts mentioned in the Medical News Today article 21 April 2017. This contaminant dioxin is being used in food and can remain dormant in the body anywhere from 7 to 10 years. Most of the food we eat today, depending on the food you eat, contains a certain amount of the chemical dioxin. This is why the non-GMO products are so important to purchase today. Most of the foods with the chemical dioxin in it are the foods that are high in demand. Just think about what I am saying, foods high in demand are usually foods that are cheap or easy to budget. You might want to change your diet. Since my blood type suggest that I do not eat chicken I no longer eat chicken because it is said to cause heart attacks and strokes for my blood type. On that note I have to say you must be aware of even the tiniest increments of "Agent Orange" used in foods today. What is unfortunate for the Vietnam Veterans is the chemical dioxin was not just in the food they ingested. They received a higher dosage of the herbicide chemical of which their bodies were in direct contact with for months. The deadly reaction caused in soldiers who were in direct contact with "Agent Orange" is because of the direct contact of the chemical being sprayed over their heads while they were in the jungles of "Nam". We are going to have to look at the Vietnam Veterans differently in relations to the chemical dioxin which was used in "Agent Orange" in order that the Vietnam Veterans that are alive still will be able to receive some immediate relief after over forty years of suffering. We are a humane people and a God-fearing nation who are fully aware of the problems that can occur whenever there is some form of contact with any foreign chemical that's either ingested or comes into contact with the skin. Even if we are at home doing certain things around the house, we are told if certain products touch the skin to wash it immediately and if there is an irritation or noted unusual puffiness to seek some medical attention. The reason why I am referring to the warning signs on the store products we purchase each day is because we are told to go to our doctors for a rash or irritation if we had too much exposure to the product. What remains unresolved is the exposure the Vietnam Veterans had to the many different herbicides used in Vietnam of which the facts were stated in this article written April 27, 2017 (Agent Orange: Background on Monsanto's Involvement (https://monsanto.com/company/media/statements/agent-orange-background/) This is what is being stated: "**More than 40 years ago, Agent Orange was one of 15 herbicides used by the U.S. military as a defoliant in the Vietnam War to protect and save the lives of U.S. and allied soldiers.**" If you would follow me to the third paragraph using the same article this is what is being stated: "**From 1965 to 1969, the former Monsanto Company was one of nine wartime government contractors who manufactured agent orange. The government set the specifications for making Agent Orange and determined when, where and how it was used. Agent Orange was only produced for, and used by, the government.**" This statement does not free those responsible of their obligations to monetarily take care of the Vietnam Veterans who were exposed to the fifteen different herbicides sprayed over 39,000 square miles of forest area of which our American soldiers were not told it was unsafe to travel through. The soldiers were encouraged to carry on with the mission not knowing they were walking right into the heart of their own demise, "Agent Orange." The first batch of herbicides being unloaded was at the Tan Son Nhut Air Base in South Vietnam, on January 2, 1962. What is rarely mentioned are the missions the Air Force had flown to spray the forests of "Nam". What I have found to be recorded by the U.S. Air Force is that at least 6,542 spraying missions took place over the course of Operation Ranch Hand. These missions flown by the Air Force C-123 loaded with the chemical herbicides were being sprayed over the land of Vietnam. In some areas, the (TCDD) the chemical name for Dioxin, considered to be an uncontrollable chemical which can cause many different types of ailments including cancer was being released directly on top of our Vietnam Veterans. There were areas which (TCDD) concentrations in the soil and water were hundreds of times greater than the levels considered to be safe by the U.S. Environmental Protection Agency. What I want everyone to remain focused on is our Vietnam Veterans soldiers were wrongfully exposed to Agent Orange and were refused treatment of their war injuries for almost twenty years knowing of their exposure to "Agent Orange" and the other fifteen herbicides being experimented with. As a nation, what has been done? Yes, you have left the American soldiers' souls and spirits out on the battlefield of Vietnam without a chance for recovery. What is being done to the Vietnam Veterans is similar to a suicide mission. When I say suicide mission, it may not appear to you that you have not turned your backs on our Vietnam Veterans. Only after sending them into a war zone they did not have any control of, but they went anyway. They did not run to Canada like so many others did to keep from having to go to Vietnam. It is very important for everyone involved to take a closer look at what is being done to our Vietnam Veterans. From a standpoint of a soldier who has been in a war zone it looks very bad for the United States of America when we have soldiers left on the battlefield especially when the soldiers are your own. Which is another reason why we should never stop looking for the POW's that were left behind. In the military we have what is called, morning formation. This is where a head count is made and if there is a soldier missing, we go to the squad leader first to see if he has heard anything and then we make the proper phone calls to see if the soldier can be found. We have a saying in the military and that is, "We will not have any soldier left behind." That saying does not just go for the wound on the battlefield or the dead, but it also applies to the spirit of the soldier.

What was remained in the soldier's mind, who is leaving that battlefield knowing other soldiers are still out there stays with that soldier for an eternity. You will always hear him talking to someone about how he never saw his friend again. If the proper corrections have not been made to restore the soldier, he will always be reliving those moments. Making an extra effort of going that extra mile with the soldier to see if the soldier can grasp onto what he left behind before he went to war would give the soldier a strong possibility of helping him find himself again. For the Vietnam Veterans, the tunnel rats and those who suffered along with the soldiers like their families, who were also devastated and damaged in many ways it's hard to phantom their child returning home from war damaged for life. It's even harder to find out your child's body was left on the battlefield or could possibly be a POW and will never be back home again. It is even more painful to find out that the government who sent him to war does not want to admit to making the mistake. I may ask what is he afraid of? Afraid of what it would cost the country in damages such as counseling, medical and psychological assistance for the soldiers' suffering. Afraid that it would turn out to be an even bigger burden on the country.

By not acknowledging the soldier needs help does not make the problem go away. What happens is the soldier's problems began to perpetuate more and more until his family, friends and loved ones no longer know what to do. This is what has taken place with the Vietnam Veterans and this is why they appear to be so nonchalant when they are questioned about the Vietnam War and for many other reasons why they do not want to talk about the war. The Vietnam Veterans have for over forty years watched many of their buddies pass from wounds on the battlefield. Many have even watched their comrades die from the lack of being able to be treated for what they acquired on the battlefield of Vietnam and that would be because of "Agent Orange." Unless you have served in the military you really do not know what it is like to have to be left behind and forgotten. This is one of the reasons why I am writing this book to help give you a visual picture of what is taking place in the soldier's minds. If you have ever been through an ordeal in your life that brought you to great feats of thought, this is what I am trying to share with you concerning the Vietnam Veterans. Their minds never left the battlefield because the United States President, Congress, Senate and the American citizens would not allow them to leave. Once they returned home their battles continued as it has for over forty years now and it has not changed. These men who fought to protect your rights as citizens left their soul, and mind on the battlefield of Vietnam. They are still looking and waiting for you America to give them back what they gave you, their lives! To be able to return home from war is a blessing. Even more so to be able to return home from war and be greeted with honor by hearing those words "THANK YOU FOR YOUR SERVICE" sometimes makes it all worth the sacrifice. When you think about the sacrifices the Vietnam Veterans made you are going to have to say to yourself at some point "America, we have not done enough!" The chemicals that were continually sprayed over the heads of our own soldiers is a burden this entire country is going to have to bear. Until we are able to get that last Vietnam Veteran's mind and soul off of the battlefield and give him the ability of being able to know what it is like to smile again, then and only then we know we have started the process of healing. There were mistakes made on and off the battlefield. What took place behind the meeting doors of the oval office was something that we will never know. But the order was given to use the chemical herbicides and our soldiers are still paying for it. The only thing about President Kennedy giving the order to use the herbicides he was never made aware of what the chemical companies were conjuring up called "Agent Orange." I will discuss that a little later in this book. The President and Congress and Senate never knew about the newly added ingredients the chemical companies were adding to the mixture of chemical to create "Agent Orange." I am certain many of you try to overlook the pain these men are in by not asking questions. As the author of a book covering issues brought about by the Vietnam War I have had to listen to many stories. Some of these Vietnam Veterans are not even able to function as men. Some are being eaten up from the inside, some have watched their comrades die a slow death. Many have lost organs etc. as this herbicide chemical slowly eats away their life and you want to say the soldier is over exaggerating or his suffering is not that great where he should be given certain benefits. With all of this being said the Vietnam Veterans feel like America has left them to die on the battlefield of Vietnam by not coming to their rescue here in America and by not allowing them to put the war behind them. This is being done by letting the claims the Vietnam Veterans have filed linger on the desks of the Veterans Administration for so long knowing they are dying from being contaminated with "Agent Orange." In 1962 The Air Force flew their C-123's 6,542 recorded missions and they dropped herbicide chemicals over 39,000 square feet of "Nam". As a military officer who is very familiar with going to war I can adamantly say the process of forgiveness should come from within the higher ranks of government. The healing process of these men is stained with what is considered to be hidden secrets of what went wrong, but no one wants to accept fault. We all know the order came from President John F. Kennedy. "In November 1961, President John F. Kennedy authorized the start of Operation Ranch Hand, the codename for the U. S. Air Force herbicide program in Vietnam." (https://en.wikipeidia.org/wiki/Agent_Orange). I do believe President John Kennedy issued the order without being informed by the chemical companies of the full criterion of the chemical herbicides used. What many people are not aware of is that "Agent Orange" was the last chemical created and it was created by the chemical companies that began to use TCDD (dioxin), a chemical that is highly toxic and deemed uncontrollable. President Kennedy never received any information from the chemical companies explaining the dangerous use of the chemical TCDD which was added to make "Agent Orange." In my eyes President JFK was a compassionate man who showed love to all of the citizens he served. I do not believe the President was given the full impact of what a chemical such as "Agent Orange" would do to his soldiers who went to war in defense of the United States of America. I must also say President Kennedy would have never authorized the use of such a chemical herbicide knowing it was highly toxic and hadn't any limitations concerning its destruction to human life. What is even more important to know is President Kennedy nor any other president of the United States of America would have a reason to destroy their own armies. It just doesn't make sense!!! My belief is that the chemical companies expressed their concerns in wanting to help and how they could help, but intentionally held back the dangers of what the chemicals would do to the soldiers in the future, keep in mind "Agent Orange" was the last chemical herbicide produced. There is a gap in communication at this point because 20,000,000 gallons of various chemicals would not suffice President Kennedy's purpose of winning the war on "Nam" if he would have known it was going to kill his own soldiers. There is no other way to look at this situation logically, a President, a king, a leader of any nation cannot win a battle destroying his own military. It is recorded there were millions of tons of various chemicals being used in Vietnam. And with the President and other government officials agreeing to spray the original chemicals had nothing to do with the release of "Agent Orange". This tells me that our President and government were misinformed. They were not given the truth concerning the horrific nightmares this country would face once "Agent Orange" was released in Vietnam while our American soldiers were there. Ask yourself this question. I have already given you the basic information about "Agent Orange", its disadvantages which causes kidney and liver cancer, prostate cancer, heart disease and other ailments in the human body of which there isn't a cure to this day. It would be highly improbable that President John F. Kennedy, Congress, the Senate and other high-ranking government officials would have given the okay to use "Agent Orange" knowing the health problems it was going to cause. The issue that remains open is the research extracted from the conclusive findings of "Agent Orange" have never been released because there aren't any conclusive findings, for the lack of a better word called research. To say that "Agent Orange" which attacks the DNA of humans is not responsible for the health problems the Vietnam Veterans have been complaining about for over forty years now is notorious. The chemicals involved in the herbicides with TCDD (dioxin) being the detrimental additive once added to the chemical herbicides makes it one hundred times more dangerous to not only use but to also to cause problems with human organs and other parts of the human body. Who's at fault? Is it the United States government or the chemical companies involved in the creation of "Agent Orange?" That is the question! The next question we must address is; what chemical company releases a chemical out to be sprayed over thousands of miles of vegetation without knowing its conclusive findings or the capabilities of the chemical? If the chemical is touched or walked on, what is it capable of eating through? What will it do to the human body if it is in contact with open sores? How will it affect the eyes which are unprotected? The final question is, what is the life expectancy of the chemical once it is inside of the human body? Is there an inoculation to get the chemical out of the system of the Vietnam Veterans, their children and grandchildren? The answer is NO. Remember the Health and Medicine Division is still conducting ongoing research. To this date 2019 there isn't any cure, while "Agent Orange" continues to do damage in the system of the Vietnam Veterans' DNA, their children's DNA and their grandchildren's DNA. I might have to add the great grandchildren for as slow as the research is going by the time the researchers find an answer the great grandchildren will probably be born with deformities as well. While you all sit and ponder on who's at fault, I must ask you to stop pondering and do something right for a change. The situation concerning the Vietnam Veterans is no longer a questionable doubt. It is within reason that we must confirm the importance of getting the proper research on the herbicide chemical "Agent Orange" so we can bring the suffering of not only our American Vietnam Veterans to an end, but also their children and great grandchildren. We might just be able to contain the movement of the chemical herbicide "Agent Orange" and bring it to an end so it does not continue to spread in the DNA of future generations. At this time the damage being reported by the Vietnam Veterans is that "Agent Orange" is causing birth defects or deformities in the children and grandchildren. I will discuss this a little later in the chapters to come on what recent studies have found. For the meantime it is important for our government as well as the manufacturing companies of the chemical "Agent Orange to accept fault. Those who collected a paycheck from the United States government for the production of "Agent Orange" should recognize their position at this time of which I am definitively speaking would be considered to be guilty as charged once charges are presented in the proper courts. Accepting fault now will be a small gesture of kindness for what is long overdue to the Vietnam Veterans. You have not only destroyed these soldier's life's and livelihood, but you have also destroyed their future - over forty years of it. Denial from what I have been able to address in my research has only been a practical standpoint of falsehood without acceptance or facts. Which the burden of proof should without doubt fall upon the creative manufacturing of a chemical agent. The chemical was yelling out contamination at the site of its creation, that is, prior to getting it to the United States Air Force before it was dispersed in the jungles of Vietnam. It already bore an invisible warning tag on the barrels of which should have openly been tagged "Danger!" "Danger!" "Danger!" avoid human contact at all cost. This chemical "Agent Orange" is extremely toxic and contagious, stay away, do not touch!!! It should not be breathed, consumed, or have contact with anything. Monsanto and the other nine contractors involved in manufacturing "Agent Orange" have distributed a chemical product without conclusive findings of what the side effects were or what the pros and cons would be if the product was used in an uncontrolled environment especially around the Vietnam Veterans. They did nothing more than expose the United States Veterans and areas of Vietnam sprayed with the herbicide chemical "Agent Orange" to nothing more than a chaotic lifetime crisis. If I may review from where I have guided you to this point it has been expressed since the Vietnam War that our Vietnam Veterans were dying from being exposed to the herbicide chemical "Agent Orange". When we look at confirmed research of the damage dioxin triggers when used with other chemicals, we see it is capable of destruction. Its limits are insurmountable and nonconclusive. It is not understandable of what other evidence is needed since we are aware of its use in the herbicide chemical "Agent Orange". I can only infer that Monsanto and the other ten chemical companies would be considered guilty without an admission of guilt or even a trial. It is without reservation the damages which have been acquired through contact with "Agent Orange" making the chemical, as to what it is mixed with and the causes, one the most deadly chemical produced in the history of the United States of America and used by the United States government during the Vietnam War. It is listed feasible enough to know without a doubt that "Agent Orange" causes cancer, liver and kidney failure, high blood pressure and heart problems. It is ridiculous to assume otherwise that these soldiers who were openly exposed to the chemical herbicide "Agent Orange" intentionally for some unknown reason used themselves as guinea pigs. Do you think they actually told the United States government to dump chemicals on them so they could be used for scientific studies, and be poked and probed for over forty years? Which still makes my point of a lack of research and no conclusive findings as a result of the chemicals advantages and disadvantages. Any virus, foreign pathogen or chemical exposure that comes into contact with the skin or breathed in will affect the body in some form or the other, even though many of us who have strong immune systems and are able to fight off viruses and other infectious diseases. What would seem to be unable to fight out would be a blood born chemical infection of which an individual would be infected with something like TCDD (dioxin), a very powerful chemical used in "Agent Orange". Due to dioxin being used during the Vietnam War and the lack of researched evidence not revealed to the United States government the chemical dioxin being used to enhance the potency of other herbicide chemicals being used by combining it with TCDD is how it became "Agent Orange." It was not just destined to kill the foliage in "Nam" its potency had not been researched enough to know exactly all it would be capable of damaging once it was released. The United States government was not, I repeat, was not involved in any under handedness or ever a part of the creation of "Agent Orange." The chemical companies are the only ones who took part in its creation, a creation that it has not only devastated this country but has turned out to be quite disastrous. I am putting it mildly. The spreading of the herbicide chemical "Agent Orange" is not just affecting the Vietnam Veterans. As a nation we are going to have to go back to the drawing board of morality once more. We are going to have to claim the dignity this great nation was once respected for. We must bear down on the loyalty, dedication and fairness to other nations we once proclaimed while we maintain being a peaceful nation. Simply because we are all Americans and we operate under the premise of Mother Liberty. A nation that has extended the torch of "Mother Liberty" by taking it upon itself to maintain the integrity of all Americans by its many "Peace Keeping Missions" and serving as the Ambassador of Peace at the round table of the United Nations. The integrity of the United States is not just in question concerning the herbicide chemical "Agent Orange" with our own American Vietnam Veterans. We are in conflict as a nation of endless means concerning areas of contamination of drinking water, innocent Vietnamese villages within and in the outskirts where "Agent Orange" was sprayed. I will discuss this a little later in the book. I just want to let you know that it is not just our Vietnam Veterans who were suffering with "Agent Orange". Just remember the Vietnamese had to live with the chemicals on their land long after the war was over.

As we continue to look at how the Vietnam Veterans' DNA has been contaminated with the chemical herbicide "Agent Orange" it is very difficult for me to understand why the acceptance of the problems caused by this herbicide chemical with dioxin in it has not been easier to validate. I explained it in chapter 19 that the chemical is not something that's just on the skin or feet. It is literally in the blood of our American soldiers who fought in the Vietnam War. Therefore, I am not able to understand how the many claims filed due to health problems by the Vietnam Veterans continue to be denied. What remains to be a given fact is that everything in the bloodline filters through the liver, kidneys, heart, lungs etc. Remember it is in the blood of these men who have served this country honorably. Many of whom I have spoken to their bodies are slowly being decomposed from the inside out. We once again cannot sit back and watch for another forty years without claiming the need for proper research to be done. We need to request that this research be done by our own government employees since it is the non-government employees who have been continuously finding nothing for over forty years. I am certain it must be by coincidence that they keep missing the new findings. We must come to some form of conclusion of which I feel in all fairness it would be justified in saying damages caused to the Vietnam Veterans body is concurrent all over the United States in every states where there is a Vietnam Veteran living. The fact is that the chemical herbicide "Agent Orange" has now been found to be in the DNA of the Vietnam Veterans, their children and their grandchildren. What I want to stipulate here is the word DNA. There is not much more that can be said about a foreign chemical which has not been given a life expectancy range of extinction to say the problems being caused in the bodies of these soldiers is now and has been a problem due to the inhabitance of the highly toxic chemical herbicide "Agent Orange".

CHAPTER XXII

WAS THE COURTS FINDINGS FINAL

WHEN WE LOOK AT the chaos that has been caused in this country due to "Agent Orange." We are no longer looking at the war in Vietnam. We are looking at the aftereffects of "Agent Orange." It no longer lies dormant in the bodies of our American soldiers. The chemical herbicide continues to call the names of the Vietnam Veterans and it has followed them until it has begun to cry out from their grave. There are an estimated 800,000 veterans left at a rate of approximately 1560 dying a month. The Vietnam Veterans will soon be non-existent therefore it is so important that a book like this is published so all those concerned will know the truth. I am certain that waiting on the Vietnam Veterans demise is not something our government would have ever been a part of or involved in. If you think about it on another level it is very important to understand that in order to have planned something this diabolical, every state and government official in the United Sates would have had to be involved. In my heart I believe that this is something that just did not happen. In other words what I am saying here is because of the pride I have had in the service I have given to my country, I refuse to believe that the U. S. government is simply waiting for the Vietnam Veterans to die off so everyone can stop talking about "Agent Orange" and the government does not have to pay off the claims that have been filed. The problems the herbicide chemical "Agent Orange" has caused our Vietnam Veterans for their entire life is not just going to go away. I see we are right back to the morality of life once more. I must say on behalf of the Vietnam Veterans there appears to be some form of uncertainty involved whenever the Vietnam Veterans are mentioned. This is the well-kept secret in America but just like the "Moral Arc of the Universe is Long" so is the "Long Arm of Justice" **"I must say the weight of its gavel will bear the morality of the inner soul of the one who has been blessed to grasp its handle in order to render judgement."(Raymond C. Christian)** Only because hope appears to be an esteemed truth towards all men and women based on the validity of facts and not moral ethics.

How do we get to the truth about the Vietnam War? That is something that may never be told: the truth, on why and how our American government got involved in Vietnam. How do we go back in history and correct all the life-threatening devices that should have not been used or created? Did mankind and his selfless greed corrupt his moralistic views and distort his normalcy of righteous thinking? And make him turn away for the incorrupt man to the corrupt man in order to position himself and proclaim himself as being sovereign over all? Where does our value system as humans take us today? We are still talking about a war, the Vietnam War to be exact over forty years later and people are still running away from the truth. This book is not being written to open a can of worms. You know the old saying when people start to dig in the past, "When you start digging in the past what you do is open a can of worms and everything involved gets to wiggling around." Well the truth of this matter as it relates to the Vietnam War is that the wiggling has been continual since the war began, and it has not stopped. As I stated earlier in this book, it is in close resemblance to the Dr. Martin Luther King Jr. assassination and President John F. Kennedy assassination which is a truth this world will never be privileged to read about. Unfortunately, the Vietnam War did not just affect the American Vietnam Veterans. From researched documents of what has been written about the Vietnam War we all are going to have to pray on where the forgiveness will start in order to have some form of recovery for the two nations, who have done irreparable damage to one another and will be able to shake hands at the meeting table and call themselves allies? There isn't a darker hour then than of seeing the last rays of sunlight. Although what is finite is that even though we know the sun never ceases to shine we must keep in our hearts the remarkable power in keeping hope alive. The men whose lives were lost on the battlefield cannot be replaced. The civilians who lost their lives also cannot be replaced. It's time to stop pointing fingers at one another and understand that due to the ugliness of war it is not just the American families who have suffered but the Vietnamese as well. War is war and there is nothing anyone can do about it once it starts. Lives are lost and people are caught up in a frenzy because someone they love will never return home again. The answer here is not to hate but to love those who persecute you, to love thy enemy this is the walk of a true Christian. Matthew 5:44-45, **"But I say unto you, Love your enemies, bless them that curse you, do good to them that hate you, and pray for them which despitefully use you, and persecute you.(45) That ye may be the children**

of your Father which is in heaven: for he maketh his sun to rise on the evil and on the good, and sendeth rain on the just and on the unjust." In our service to our Father in heaven he continues to give us the perfect example as to how we as believers are to live our life. And in making it realistic what is also stated in scripture in John 8:32, **"And ye shall know the truth, and the truth shall make you free."** Can we change the past? The answer is we cannot. So we are going to have to move forward in a positive way. Moving forward does not mean forgetting the past but giving some form of rendition to a new and bright future. "Agent Orange" changed the lives of millions of people and they were not all Vietnam Veterans. Before I present documented numbers of American soldiers and civilians, as well as Vietnamese soldiers and civilians lost I want you to read this prose I have written because it talks about the abusers in the world today. They are people who only care about their own self-worth and will do whatever they can to get what they want or are trying to achieve without any concerns whatsoever. The abusers are people walking the face of this earth without a conscience deliberately hurting others because of what may or may not have happened in their life. They feel no remorse, they haven't any remorse and will only justify their actions as being correct. The prose about the abusers was written in order that others may take a closer look at themselves and see the wrong before it is done. When I think about the Vietnam War, I can only say it was another place and time. An unforgotten era of secrets that lay buried in the depths of red tape sealed in files in Washington, DC. Concealed files that will not be released. Files of a war that took place in Vietnam and its over forty years of tears, pain and suffering. Its long roots of pain stem under a veil of hurt which has not been lifted. A veil that bears the lives of so many soldiers who fought in a war that took their young lives. What remains real is the abuse the few Vietnam Veterans which are alive today have to deal with on a daily basis. There is a lot we can do for change and progress concerning the Vietnam Veterans and the military. Although some progress is slowly being made, it's just not being made fast enough. When we think about how we as a nation have abused our own soldiers for doing what they were taught and trained to do, it is an embarrassing thought of negligence on the part of the American people who forgot they were the ones who sent these young boys to war. I do feel you have been fed a lot of untruths to protect another cause that quietly began to spread throughout the United States. And this well-hidden cause has been kept submerged beneath the surface of truth and has remained a nightmare for so many of our Vietnam Veterans. The well- kept name of this hidden cause is a nightmare called "Agent Orange." Due to rumors and heightened negative media propaganda that turned the American people heads and made them look the other way by reporting in such a negative way something that had only partially been proven. I say partially proven because there is two sides to every story. Due to a lot of propaganda, the media and news reporters reported what they were told. These reports revealed nothing more than a lack of disrespect for the Vietnam Veterans and the Vietnam War. What should have been asked then is why was our boys in Vietnam when the United States "had no dog in the fight" and nothing to gain? Many questions were asked, and many protested by marching with signs saying, "Bring our soldiers home." American citizens came out by the thousands to openly demonstrate their feelings about the Vietnam War. While the sixties and seventies hippies displayed their memorable peace signs and made their voices heard. Let's not forget about the musical artists who expressed their feelings by letting their voices be heard through music they created. Remembering many of our all-time favorites when music was music. There was Marvin Gaye who gave us, "Mercy, Mercy Me" (1968) and "What's Going On" (1971) songs that were influenced by Marvin Gaye's brother Frankie Gaye who served as a combat soldier during the Vietnam War. These where songs of which the lyrics had touched many peoples heart from around the world and their artistry keep right on coming. Edwin Star wrote "War" (1970), The Animals "House of the Rising Sun" (1964), and celebrities like the Beetles, "Revolution" (1968). The list continues with Bob Dylan & Jimi Hendrix "All Along the Watchtower" (1965), Bob Dylan "Blowin in the Wind" (1963), the Rolling Stones "Gimme Shelter" (1969), Phil Ochs "What are you fighting for" (1963). There was also Bill Withers who had the entire world singing "Lean On Me" (1972). There were so many more songs and entertainers who expressed themselves emotionally through the music they had written in protest of the Vietnam War. American soldiers were being brought home in body bags by airplane loads. The United States citizens, celebrities, actors and musicians made their voices heard by taking it as far as Washington, DC on the grounds of the Washington Memorial protesting for the President, Congress and the Senate to bring our "boys" home. On November 15, 1969 the largest demonstration against the war in Vietnam lead by the Vietnam Moratorium took place and as many as half a million people attended to demonstrate peacefully showing their disagreement concerning the Vietnam War. There's two more artists I must put in this book because their songs also had a meaningful impact during the Vietnam War: Otis Redding "Sitting on the dock of the bay" (1968), and finally Neil Diamond's song "He Ain't Heavy He's My Brother" (1970). This song by Neil Diamond had a major impact because he was writing about what the American citizens had already forgotten about which was to take care of our wounded, our battered and bruised soldiers. It was a song stating the burdens the United States, during that time, was not willing to carry due to the impact the media and newspapers had already put out there. As a nation who have put together a military and sent them out to do battle our position when they returned was to make them whole again. Although the United States government was not at fault in the creation of "Agent Orange." They did not want to admit mistakes were made by them for not monitoring the creation of "Agent Orange." Our government officials in Washington did drop the ball somewhat as to having the chemical companies monitored and fully researched as to how each chemical being used in Vietnam was produced. It later became a known fact with those in Washington that "Agent Orange" should have never been released. The bigger question here is was our government officials in Washington, DC intentionally misled for the chemical company's monetary gain? Was the United States of America government under the impression that Monsanto Chemical Company and the other ten chemical companies involved were being clear and concise with our leaders in Washington at that time about the use of "Agent Orange?" Was "Agent Orange" being presented as just another practical "Agent" without any heightened dangers involved? Keeping in mind there were five other agents being used at that time to kill the foliage in Vietnam. Out of the six herbicide chemicals being used in Vietnam nothing would become detrimental until the chemical TCDD (dioxin) was added to "Agent Orange." The 64-million-dollar question here is, were the eleven chemical plants up front with our government officials about the chemicals being used and the dangers of each one being used? On the other hand, was information being withheld by the companies in order to pad their own pockets? I am going to create a hypothetical question right now and say, could Monsanto, Diamond Shamrock Chemical Company, Dow Chemical Company and the eight other companies with their knowledge and understanding of what the chemicals were going to be used for have said, "since the stuff is going overseas and will not be used in the states, so let's do whatever it is going to take to get the government contract"? Let's not tell the government all of the problems that could occur through the use of certain chemicals otherwise we will not get the contract. Do you think this conversation could have taken place? A very strong possibility, you think? I am just brainstorming right now throwing up hypothetical situations. Pay me no mind I am just a person writing a book. You know just putting my thoughts on paper. The only thing I can say to that is what if the conversations with the chemical companies did take place and what I am stating really happened? I would never believe what as the chemical companies tried to state that our President and government officials Congress and the Senate had something to do with the creation of "Agent Orange." There isn't a President the United States of America ever had in office that would intentionally jeopardize the safety and wellbeing of his troops. That is not the way you win a war and I can rest assured through my own personal experience of being a military officer, it will never happen that way!!! We will always have eyes out for the betterment and concerns of this nation. The responsibility of course would have to fall on each of the chemical companies because they would have to have known the use of dioxin mixed with other chemicals would make the chemical sporadically uncontrollable and its mixture would turn out to be disastrous. There would not be any recovery from contact with the chemical due to its attack on the human body, the DNA and its TCDD classification. Negligence is a word that is putting it too mildly when you think about a word to use when it involves a situation that has caused death in thousands of our Vietnam Veterans for over forty years. Who was the culprit(s) behind the drive that influenced the chemical companies to add TCDD dioxin to the herbicide chemical? In our search for the truth the chemical companies must be held accountable on both counts. The first being, distributing a toxic substance without full research and with only inconclusive studies for the damage it could cause when mixed with other chemicals. The second, distributing a toxic chemical substance knowing it could cause an unlimited and uncontrollable range of contamination and their failure to stop the distribution of this chemical herbicide. This is abuse at the highest level concerning the responsibility the chemical companies may or may not have had knowing that dioxin is as a TCDD which is classified as a human carcinogen by the United States Environmental Protection Agency. Who would produce such a powerful chemical? Who would knowingly sale such a powerful chemical (dioxin) to the United States government without first informing the government of the damages the chemical can do if used outside of an uncontrolled environment? When we think about abuse this is exactly what it is. Whether "Agent Orange" was sold for greed or for military purposes, this nation continues to suffer forty years later behind a chemical that should not have been made. What were these chemical companies thinking about? These are trained men in the chemical field who have shown very little remorse through the years towards our Vietnam Veterans, their families and loved ones. There have been human lives lost due to negligence and a lack of research. Although the question of fault remains to be established it has not been brought to the forefront on a legal standpoint as to who owes what. What is not in question is the long list of diseases, medical issues and deaths the United States of America Vietnam Veterans has suffered due to "Agent Orange." So, who is abusing the system when we retrace our tracks? Does it lead to the White House? That would mean John F. Kennedy would be at fault. Does it lead to the Congress or the Senate? That would mean "Agent Orange" would have been the biggest government conspiracy in the history of the United States. The order was given to drop Agent Orange in the war zone of Vietnam. But it was only done out of intent of saving our soldiers. This is what President John F. Kennedy ordered. He did not order the use of Agent Orange to be dropped on the Vietnam Veterans so they could return home and be used as guinea pigs after the war. The last resort, which is probably the most likely is that the chemical companies withheld the information about dioxin (TCDD) from the President and added it in with the rest of the chemicals without giving the Presidents, Congress and Senate knowledge of what they wanted to experiment with. Whatever took place within the ranks of the chemical companies involved has left the United States of America and Vietnam in disarray. There isn't a President, Congress or Senate that would have intentionally released "Agent Orange" with all of the facts before them. Our government would not have ordered the use of "Agent Orange" while the troops were in harm's way. And given the damages in Vietnam to this day, if the knowledge about dioxin would have been disseminated with proper research and documentation President John F. Kennedy, the Congress and the Senate would have agreed unanimously to not use the chemical herbicide and the United States would not be subject to scrutiny as it is today. I am also certain President Kennedy and other government officials would have had to acknowledge the civilian Vietnamese towns, churches and schools in the areas where they were fighting in Vietnam. The United States Commander and Chief would have had to have a recon report either from air or land stating their crops and food supply in the villages of civilians would also be in danger of being contaminated. No one would be allowed to eat from those natural resources because of "Agent Orange." The United States would have known all of what was taking place in the area due to intelligence reports and of course our recon missions. "Agent Orange" would have been what we call in the military a, "No Go". I want to leave you in deep thought before I go to the next chapter with this: What were our soldiers, who did not have "a dog in this fight" to do? The one thing you will find to be true about the military is that soldiers were not allowed to make certain decisions. Soldiers only followed orders and you have blamed them for being good honorable soldiers, sent to Vietnam to complete a mission. Have you ever felt bullied, or left out of something you wanted to be in? Well, this is how the Vietnam Veterans feel. They were the abused victims during their stint in the jungles of Nam and after their return home to the states. The Vietnam Veterans returned home with a lot of unknown problems and were not told until twenty years later that they were suffering because of the devastating effect of the herbicide chemical that was now in their DNA. So, who are the abusers? Please read the prose below and you just might get an idea of what it is like to be a victim of abuse. The Vietnam Veterans did not deserve any of the suffering they were going through and are still going through in 2019. Nothing is going to be done until someone admits to being at fault. Oh, but this book is not about fault right, or pointing fingers. I guess we are going to have to wait to see how the future generations, you know the Vietnam Veterans' children and grandchildren. It's an even stronger probability that the great grandchildren are going to genetically have "Agent Orange" in their system. Did I say future generations? Well I guess I forgot to tell you that you do not have to wait for the future generations to find out if Agent Orange is also in their DNA. The children and grandchildren are already being born with deformities because of Agent Orange.

The Abusers Who are They"

In the shadows of my mind hidden secrets lie there;
A cross that stands over an empty grave of fear;
I see how you look at me in your ugly way of disgust;
It was me; I know I am sorry for laughing too
loud, I know that is why you beat me.

When you passed by me did you smell the soiled odor on my clothes?
You see, I haven't any water at home to wash with, please forgive me;
Once you get to know me you will see I am really a good person;
I will make sure I stay my distance so you will like me, okay?

I must stand to stay awake; I had a long and sleepless night;
I was up listening to the little girl down the hall, being beaten all night;
I thought for sure I would be next, so I was afraid to close my eyes;
I wondered, if I would have closed them, when
I opened them who would be there?

No one knows the abusers; their faces and gender are hidden;
They are empty souls with a damaged past,
hidden in a reality we don't understand;
These abusers are normal people, quote, the always nice guy;
They are regular people, yes, people you and I know.

Can you see the inside scars, they are trying to heal;
The prayer that is needed for the victim is shared;
With the abuser who was once the victim and scared;
Not knowing how to let go of being the victim of a victimized past.

Dreams and visions of a neglected life, disbelief in a fore thought;
Still able to hold up my head and look in the mirror;
Telling the world, I am a winner with God;
I dream to seek; I ask in order to be able to receive;
Not from you but God he is the only one who knows my fate;

I deal with my accusers every day, not just Satan but you as well;
The demons which are around me cannot penetrate the positive forces;
Forces that are channeling my life, the strongholds are pulled down;
My God, my God, what a blessing it is to know;

You are my final destination my suffering is not in vain;
My abuser will be brought to justice, yes, justice it must prevail;
Even though I have been abused;
I am still saved, sanctified and Jesus Christ is my redeemer.

My innocence was just taken away, although I pray;
I continue to get up to regain my strength, my composure;
The abuser will be dealt with; I know the word of God,
Will not come back void remember the double-edged sword?
I know the Holy Bible speaks of Gods little ones, "Abusers beware";
It is better for you to get into a boat and go to the deepest part of the lake,
Tie a milestone about your neck and jump in
then to me with one of Gods little ones;
This is the word of God; this is where I stand;

Please do not worry about the tears forming in my eyes;
May I ask you this question, without insulting you?
Tell me why are the children suffering, what have they done?

I heard a voice out of nowhere saying forgive the sinners who abused you;
I answered back and said father I forgive them
for they know not what they do;
You are the abuser, my father which art in heaven said he still loves you;
Yes, I love you too, I forgive you of the sins
you have committed against me,
I ask that God's mercy be with you always;

Now, you, the sinner has to ask forgiveness for the sins
of abuse no one else knows about but you, you know
the sins you repeatedly had gotten away with.

Say a prayer of repentance on your knees, I am
sorry little boy, I am sorry little girl;
I am sorry wife, I am sorry for verbally, for
physically mistreating a child of God,
I am sorry, I am sorry, I am sorry, I am sorry, I am sorry, God bless you.

Written by: Author/Hall of Fame Poet
Raymond C. Christian

CHAPTER XXIII

PREPARING FOR WAR

MANY SOLDIERS ARE ABANDONED due to a lack of understanding of what they went through while serving their country stateside and upon returning home from a war. The lack of understanding is perpetuated by what is called change. Their family, friends and loved ones have to adopt to a totally different person. I can remember when I first returned home for a visit as a Marine. I remember waiting by MEPS and calling my mother to come and pick me up. My mother drove right past me and I had to wave her down to tell her it was me. My physical appearance had changed so much. I remember her asking me what had the military been feeding me, because I had gotten so muscular. But I was not just changed physically I was also changed mentally and emotionally. And trust me when I say emotions are something that would be considered lacking in the Marine Corps, because we are taught not to feel but to complete the mission. I recall after getting home how I was told by family and friends how I had changed. What most people don't get unless you have served in the military is you really begin to think differently and the silly things that you used to laugh at have no bearing anymore. So many times, the soldier's family may not understand the change the soldier struggles from within themselves in trying to find the person they were before they left to go through military training. They will never see the same personality simply because the soldier has been broken down and mentally reshaped. The person that left home to become a man is no longer the little boy they once knew but he is now a man with priorities. For many others and I, who signed up for the Marines we only had a taste of what being in battle is like. Only for us it was not a battle of being in a war zone but a battle of wanting to be a part of "this man's army". The objective for us as young recruits was to not let go of our dreams of becoming Marines but to hold on so we could graduate with the rest of the class and be able to hold that title of becoming a Marine. That was our battle and the first change of my life as an enlisted soldier. I would later push myself a little harder and join the ROTC Program at the University of Central Oklahoma where I was challenged even more before becoming a military officer. After ROTC there was another six months of training. I would later accept my commission from the President of the United States to become an (Infantry) Officer. I then would continue my training at Fort Benning, Georgia to become a part of the military's most elite force, graduating from the Infantry Officers Basic Course (IOBC). I am giving you all of these training situations I had to go through as a young enlisted soldier and officer to help you see how important training is and that it is a big part of preparation for any soldier or officer. Simply because you do not want to go to war unprepared. Marine Corps bootcamp was three months, ROTC was four years of continued training in preparation to becoming an officer, and there was still (ROTC) Leadership Academy to graduate from. The final training in IOBC was six months of the most rigorous and mind challenging, schools and forest marches, weapons and tactical training, hand to hand combat training anyone could take and not everyone who starts graduates. Many who wanted to be officers were sent home for failure to pass mandatory tests, failure to train or injuries. I am bringing up all this training to get you to a point of understanding just how important being trained for combat is in the life of a soldier. Training is vital to the survival of any soldier in a war zone. Therefore, I have continuously told you throughout this book that you owe the Vietnam Veterans an apology. These were young boys who wanted to be men but were never given a chance. After two weeks of training they were dropped in the hottest LZ this country has ever been in. I repeat myself, and please listen carefully. **After two weeks of training these teenage boys were dropped in a war zone and told they had to stay there and fight or die.** There was no other choice for them to make. Not only did they stay in Vietnam and fight the Vietnamese, but they also had to fight the rain that was coming down on top of them. I am not talking about the rain from the sky. I am talking about our military Air Force c-123 planes pouring out "Agent Orange" a chemical herbicide that was on top of their heads in the midst of the jungle. Of which there was a very toxic herbicide chemical being used to kill the foliage in the forest so our American troops could see. Only years later "Agent Orange" has turned out to be one of the worst kept secret killers of the Vietnam Veterans. It is now understood that today we are looking at three generations of contaminated DNA caused by companies who are not willing to accept fault in the production of "Agent Orange". The Veterans Administration continues to receive the blame alone and they should not. There is the Institute of Medicine which is now the Health & Medicine Division (HMD) who relays their findings of "Agent Orange" in a report of what it could possibly cause. Once the (HMD) which is an outside organization and nongovernmental accepts their findings as being contributory in a negative way towards the veterans' health problem then the Vietnam Veterans claims can be added to health care coverage. Depending on how long the Veterans Administration is going to react in making the necessary changes is solely up to the Veterans Administration. When it becomes permissible for the Vietnam Veterans to be treated and cared for is based on stipulations stated in the (HMD) reports. Funding must be made available in order for the VA to be able to assist the Veteran with his or her claim.

CHAPTER XXIV

SETTLEMENTS & COURTS RULINGS ON "AGENT ORANGE"

WE HAVE A CLEAR understanding now that the Vietnam Veteran has been victimized due to neglect and poor research. It is transparent on how a lot more needs to be done to help the Vietnam Veterans live out the rest of their lives comfortably and to not be turned away or denied. There should be an obligation on the governments part to have in place whatever assistance is needed to treat the Vietnam Veterans for what he is being diagnosed with, free of cost to the Vietnam Veterans. It is important that those who are in leadership, the President, Congress and Senate and those involved in the research process take a closer look at their findings. Review the findings and give the Vietnam Veterans who has filed his claim the advantage of receiving treatment for the ailment(s) he is complaining about. Which is more than likely caused by the herbicide chemical Agent Orange. Although the Health and Medicine Division (HMD) which are the current researchers and the past Institute of Medicine (IOM) has been hired to research Agent Orange the researchers which are non-government workers continue to find no co-relations to what the ailments that are being reported by the Vietnam Veterans relate to Agent Orange, this is why certain claims and treatments have been denied. The Health and Medical Division who are not military researchers, they are non-governmental researcher hired by who? But they continue to rein havoc and bear the burden over why the billions of dollars in claims the Vietnam Veterans have filed has not been given to our American War hero's, the Vietnam Veterans. The sad thing about this is "Agent Orange" is a toxic herbicide chemical another battle called of which no one wants to be liable for the billions of dollars in damages already owed out in claims to the Vietnam Veterans. In order for due diligence to take place concerning a situation like this it would have to bring up one's moral values and an urgency to want to do the right thing even though the damages of the Vietnam Veterans diseased bodies are evident of what Agent Orange has done to them.

Now we are looking at the children, grandchildren and possibly the great grandchildren of the Vietnam Veterans will suffer the same deformities, health problems, ailments and illnesses and painful death as the Vietnam Veterans. In 2009 courts got involved and ruled with the lower court's findings that the manufacturers of "Agent Orange" were not responsible for the implications of military use of "Agent Orange." Because the war materials were supplied at the direction of the United States government. The companies in their creation of "Agent Orange" are responsible for being negligent and irresponsible in their failure to properly research and give conclusive findings before the release and use of a chemical solution to the public or private buyer. In this case the buyer is the United States Armed Forces. Of which the military was not given any conclusive findings or any contamination possibilities or warnings not to use the toxic chemical herbicide due to the lack of finding its conclusive limitations. To this day there isn't any conclusive evidence to be found on "Agent Orange." Not even on the life expectancy of how long it will remain active and be genetically transferred in the DNA of those who are already affected like the grandchildren of the Vietnam Veterans for many more years to come. Were there warning labels posted on the gallon cans with orange stripes that stated avoid human contact, (highly contagious)? The answer to that would be no because the barrels would have never been loaded on the planes to be flown to Vietnam and secondly, they would have never made it on the military base. Was there anything labeled that showed could cause cancer, heart problems, liver disease, etc., where were the labels. They never made it to the barrels of "Agent Orange". Our President, Congress and Senate were misled, which led to the Vietnam Veterans being abused since no one was told about TCDD being a highly toxic chemical contaminant or that the chemical once combined with other chemicals would not only be sporadic and unpredictable but should have been contained and used in a closed and sealed environment. They were not told about the TCDD which is classified as a human carcinogen. This means this chemical being used has been classified by the United States Environmental Protection Agency as dangerous, deadly and contagious, cancerous. Due to the damages "Agent Orange" has continued to cause over the past forty years. The TCDD dioxin which makes the chemical so deadly and toxic should have only been used in a contained and enclosed environment. The companies involved in the distribution of "Agent Orange" to the government settled with a very small settlement which would not be enough to cover the damages "Agent

Orange" would be capable of doing in the years to come. The children and grandchildren were not included in the settlement because what had not been discovered about Agent Orange is that it would be genetically transferred to the grandchildren and great grandchildren DNA and that it was uncontainable. The eleven chemical companies involved have done nothing more than to subject our American soldiers, the Vietnam Veterans their children, grandchildren and possibly great grandchildren to a life full of pain, hospital visits, physical health issues, and death. Our soldiers did not stand a chance in Vietnam because of the dioxin that was later mixed with other herbicide chemicals to create "Agent Orange." Not only did dioxin kill the foliage in Vietnam without question and without prejudice this chemical herbicide did not discriminate as it began to take the lives of our Vietnam Veterans as well. The chemical herbicide "Agent Orange" was not able to be contained and should have never been released in an open environment until the limitations of its growth causes and affects had been discovered and findings were conclusive. "Agent Orange" still lingers in the soil, the water and vegetation of the areas it was sprayed over forty years ago in Vietnam.

With dioxin being such a powerful and uncontrollable chemical, I am adamant in saying that our President, Congress and the Senate during the time John F. Kennedy was serving as president or Lyndon B. Johnson who became president after the assassination of JFK were not aware and did not know anything about the highly toxic chemical dioxin which was now being used in the herbicide chemical "Agent Orange". I believe this to be true and this is why I am going to repeat this again our Commander and Chief John F. Kennedy would not have ordered the release and use of such a highly toxic chemical as "Agent Orange" on his own soldiers. In service to my country the United States of America and the practice of what we as officers and senior ranking non-commissioned officers have been taught it is always safety first. It would be impractical and highly improbable for President John F. Kennedy as much as he loved the United States of America. And President Lyndon B. Johnson as much as he loved the United States of America to have knowingly given the order to release "Agent Orange" on his own men in Vietnam in order to annihilate his own military force that is ludicrous. What would appear to be more practical is the advantage the chemical companies had over government in not letting the President or government officials know what kinds of selective chemicals were being used in the barrels to kill the foliage in the jungles of Vietnam. What is also highly improbable is the use of such a chemical being dropped in what would be considered as non-combative areas of Vietnam where there were small villages, who harvested vegetation used for feeding villages close by. Streams, rivers and lakes being used as their water supply for villages nearby. The entire situation involving Vietnam is tragic. The herbicide chemical "Agent Orange" should have been only used in isolated areas where people were not bathing, washing their cloths and using their streams to swim in and drink. Did the communication ball get dropped at some point for this matter concerning "Agent Orange" to have gotten this far? With all the other herbicide agents being used there was none more powerful than the barrel rapped in an orange ban which was later called "Agent Orange". Where did the lines of communication fail or did the chemical companies intentionally withhold information in order to test a new product? I have to ask this question, due to a very potent chemical dioxin which is also considered to be sporadic. Which means not even the chemical workers were aware of the limits of its control. The chemical dioxin was mixed in the barrel with other chemicals and used in the barrel with the orange band later called "Agent Orange." Since the life expectancy of the chemical "Agent Orange" has not been established the limits to its contamination remains open and vital to all who come into contact with "Agent Orange" to date. We can honestly look at the damages the herbicide chemical "Agent Orange" continues to cause. And see that it remains to be consistent in the health and medical problems it has caused with the Vietnam Veterans concerning the claims they have filed. We must also look at the billions of dollars in claims that remain open on the desk of many Veteran Administrative offices due to new diseases popping up in relation to the claims on Agent Orange. Soldiers are still fighting for their life due to a lack of research on Agent Orange and more adequate findings. On August 10, 2018 an article reads... "Jury Awards Terminally Ill Man $289 million In Lawsuit Against Monsanto." **"The ruling in San Francisco was that Monsanto intentionally concealed the health risks of its popular Roundup products."** This statement alone would make it feasible for the United States Armed Forces to want to go back to the grinding board of legalities for our Vietnam Veterans. It gives us reasonable cause to say if Monsanto would withhold pertinent information as it did in the creation of its Roundup products. The chemical company would also withhold information from President John F. Kennedy and Lyndon B. Johnson during their time in office. It is obvious now that the chemical companies were only interested in taking care of their own personal needs. The creators of "Agent Orange" did not show any remorse for human life that was being taken away not only in America but also for the Vietnamese. The affects Agent Orange has had on everyone is sad all the way around. The Vietnam War is over but the suffering of so many still prolong the agony of this deadly and highly contagious chemical Agent Orange. Which still shows the ugliness of what it left behind in the jungles of Vietnam, in the Vietnam Veterans and in the villages of the Vietnamese. With that being said Agent Orange has been responsible for a vast amount of deaths across the United States and abroad. I know we are concerned about our Vietnam Veterans but please keep in mind that due to our civility we must not forget the Vietnamese whose people and the areas in which they live are still contaminated today. There has not been one chemical company that has stepped forward to accept fault and if you are waiting for an apology keep this in mind that due to possibility of being held liable for all of the deaths that may have occurred from Agent Orange the chemical companies will never admit fault. Due to their large corporations and lawyers to back them for a very long time an admission of guilt from the chemical companies is something we will never see. Once again that would be like opening JFK and MLK files for the public to read, it just not going to happen. Of course, the problems Agent Orange has perpetuated cut much deeper than what is being revealed. Which is another reason why the non-governmental researchers are so consistent in finding nothing so nothing can be updated or contributed to the deadly chemical Agent Orange.

You see as a nation of people we were limited to certain information during the Vietnam War. This is a testament to what has been taking place all along there were those who were concealing the truth concerning the lack of research that involves TCDD dioxin which is highly contagious and there isn't any expiration date concerning the longevity of the chemical. Since I have the utmost respect for President John F. Kennedy and Lyndon B Johnson of which they both served as our nations President, our Commander and Chief in the United States during the Vietnam War. Of which both Presidents are of course considered to be intelligent, moral and humane President John F. Kennedy nor President Lyndon B. Johnson, would not have given the order to have a chemical as toxic and contagious as "Agent Orange" released on their own military force. Let me take you just a little deeper as I stated the chemical "Agent Orange" was not just released on American soldiers but also the Vietnamese soldiers. Its purpose was to kill the foliage in Vietnam so the American soldiers could see their enemy. Unfortunately, the chemical dioxin does not discriminate, and it remains highly toxic and contagious today. Proof being if the company Monsanto failed to disclose detrimental information to the courts during the hearings of "Agent Orange". It is by preponderance of evidence the chemical companies involved would be found guilty of failing to reveal the toxicity problems with warning labels and information to President Kennedy, Congress and the Senate. Whereby Monsanto and the other ten companies involved in contracts with the United States government would be found guilty of releasing a highly toxic chemical and endangering the Armed Forces of the United States of America. Of course, it goes much deeper and it's not a pretty sight all the way around. What is also being kept very quiet is the exposure the Vietnamese children have had to "Agent Orange. Unlike our American children whom we as Americans take so much pride in protecting and making sure they have the best of everything. The Vietnamese children have had to live close to areas the chemical herbicide "Agent Orange" was sprayed. Some lived by rivers, ponds, streams, rice fields and vegetation which were all contaminate. Therefore, we suffer as a nation because we have not lived up to what was done to innocent Vietnamese, their children and unborn. We cannot plan to move ahead as a great nation while trying to cover up what has not been cleaned up in the past. It is unfortunate to say that through my research what I have found out is although the targeted mission of spraying "Agent Orange" was to kill the foliage to give the American soldiers site and alinement on their targets. What was not calculated was the exposure the towns and villages of Vietnam that would fall subject to "Agent Orange." I must reiterate what has been stated that President John F. Kennedy neither did President Lyndon B. Johnson have knowledge of Agent Orange being a human carcinogen (cancerous). No American Commander and Chief would do this to his own military force. The chemical herbicide was created to kill foliage in the jungles of "Nam". The "Agents" were later given one of the most toxic and sporadic chemical additives known to its developers. The additive is called TCDD dioxin and it has been like a parasite feeding off of the land of Vietnam for over fifty years and nothing is growing to this day. **"Toxic byproducts of "Agent Orange" are polluting the environment in Vietnam, including its food supply, 50 years later."** We know war is war. I begin this book I believe in chapter I with the Geneva Convention. Meaning there are rules and regulation all countries involved in the war who have agreed to the rules of war provided by the Geneva Convention has to follow. What remains to be a continued problem is an admission of the problems "Agent Orange" has caused. What remains to be an issue are the basic facts of what we have seen in the Vietnam Veterans children and grandchildren. There are problems attributed to their health situations caused by "Agent Orange" of which I will list soon in this chapter. But let me first began to tell you about the issue of "Agent Orange" the United States is a civil and a God-fearing nation of people that has been kept in the dark about Agent Orange and the destruction it continues to cause for the past fifty years. We have not been kept abreast about how "Agent Orange" has polluted the Vietnamese ability to grow healthy vegetable, fruit and fish due to the toxicity levels of "Agent Orange" which still contaminates the farmlands of Vietnam. Let me continue by saying TCDD dioxin was a sporadic chemical used in "Agent Orange" meaning this chemical is capable of causing unknown, unresearched problems and is hindering the normal reproductive growth of the Vietnamese children today. We all know whatever the mother consumes the fetus, the babe also consumes. By "Agent Orange" being spread over 39,000 square miles in Vietnam logically speaking that would be 39,000 square miles of contamination that continues to grow, it is growing and has been growing for fifty years now. This means since "Agent Orange" is more so like a parasite it will continue to spread without any retention. This is why nothing has grown in those areas of Vietnam where "Agent Orange" was sprayed for over fifty years. You should be able to grasp what I am saying here quickly, and it does not take a rocket scientist to figure it out. There is most certainly a lot of inconsistencies and discrepancies concerning the herbicide chemical "Agent Orange" and the testimony being given by the chemical companies concerning the settlement of the Vietnam Veterans and "Agent Orange." It is understood that the water sources of Vietnam due to the 6542-mission flow by the United States Air Force was contaminate. This would also include the fish in the water as well. Which would also mean that since Agent Orange is being spread to the children and grandchildren of the Vietnam Veterans genetically through sexual intercourse. Then the fish and animals in Vietnam would who also reproduce are also passing Agent Orange in their DNA. The U.S. Air Force used the c-123 planes to release the toxic chemical "Agent Orange." The amounts of Agent Orange that was sprayed over the jungles of Vietnam were highly contagious and the amount that was sprayed is realistically not normal for not just the plants, animal and fish but also unsafe for mankind. "Agent Orange" is a highly toxic chemical of which is considered to be uncontrollable (sporadic) in reference to the unsafe amounts of the toxifying chemical dioxin that was used in an open field environment and its spray that was carried for miles in the air. Which made its airborne travel possibly even further than what is documented of the 39,000 square miles we show on record. Due to its airborne travel over rivers, lakes, ponds, streams, animals and vegetation. I would be truly warranted in saying Monsanto's one of the chemical plants the lawsuit was brought against would be responsible for using the chemical dioxin as part of their mixture of chemicals to create the highly toxic chemical "Agent Orange." And remember there were ten other chemical companies involved. I do not feel I would be overreaching when I talk about the problems the Vietnamese would be having with their children today due to the toxic amounts of "Agent Orange" dropped in the vicinity of their villages. I am also certain that some of the chemical herbicide which was airborne could more than likely have been blown into the area which had nothing to do with the war zone. This toxic and contagious chemical dioxin used in "Agent Orange poisoned the Vietnamese waters and areas of vegetation and made their farmland and food supplies not safe to eat or drink due to the spreading of "Agent Orange" and its travel through the air. This would make the chemical companies which are the creators responsible for all the babies being born with deformities. As well as early miscarriages for the Vietnamese women who suffered from the effects of "Agent Orange" which lead to them having premature hysterectomies and babies born with deformities of which is also taking place in the United States today. Fault would not go to the distributors because life threatening information concerning the use of the herbicide chemical dioxin which was later added to the mixture to make "Agent Orange" was not presented to President John F. Kennedy or President Lyndon B. Johnson to our government officials or Armed Military Forces. I do not believe any of the formulas used to create the chemicals agents, or the chemical Agent Orange to be used in the Vietnam War was ever discussed with President John F. Kennedy, President Lyndon B. Johnson the United States government or the Armed Forces of the United States. The different chemical agents where created to protect the American soldiers who were in the jungles of Vietnam fighting for the United States. What is unfortunate is chemical companies did not disclose pertinent and detrimental information to President John F. Kennedy, Lyndon B. Johnson our government officials or Armed Forces of the United

States prior to or after the release of said chemicals. The chemicals agents 20,000,000 gallons were released in the midst of 39,000 square miles of forest turning those areas that were sprayed to desolate areas to this day. The President, Secretary of Defense, Congress and the Senate could not have known about the highly contaminate chemical TCDD dioxin being added to the chemical herbicides being sprayed over United States troops. I am certain you would like to know who is liable for the damages done to the Vietnam Veterans and the Vietnamese people who lived in villages near the war zone of Vietnam? Although it has escaped the United States government and the courts for years. A recent article stated the intentional concealing of health risks by Monsanto was their way of defending their popular product Roundup. The jurors gave out an award of 289 million dollars against the chemical company Monsanto's. Please note that the liability does not fall on the United States government. The one who is liable of which will never be admitted to will receive a judgement against the chemical companies Monsanto's and others who were in a contractual agreement to make the chemical herbicide to only kill the foliage in the jungles of Vietnam so the soldiers could find the enemy. Monsanto's chemical company has been caught concealing detrimental evidence concerning human health problems that lead to (Cancer) caused through the use of Roundup. It's been fifty years later with similarities of the case concerning "Agent Orange" of which Monsanto's was also involved in a contract with the United States government defense department. During such time Monsanto's said they were not responsible for the health problems being caused by the "Agent Orange" that the soldiers were complaining about. Due to the most recent 2018 judgement which states there was "intentional concealment" of information on the part of Monsanto's. What would be appropriate at this time is for the VA who still has billions of dollars in claims sitting on their desks backlogged and waiting for approval. The Veterans Administrative office is going to have to go back and review the records of what took place during the hearings of Agent Orange. That would give one man in California in 2018, 278-million-dollar judgement then turn around and only award the Vietnam Veterans who had health problems in 1984 to date only 180 million? The 180 million was for claims of a class action suit that was to take care of Vietnam Veterans who filed claims which I believe the number was 8300. They had to split the settlement agreement and according to research many Vietnam Veterans did not get a penny. What needs to be considered is nothing more than a case of concealed information on the part of Monsanto's and the other chemical companies involved. Who is all for opening new cases the soldiers have filed referencing "Agent Orange" as their reason for having cancer and other health problems? If one company, Monsanto an agricultural giant has been found to have intentionally concealed health risks which could result to humans being plagued with the big (C) Cancer and they still marketed Roundup. We now must look back and question the same company Monsanto who said they were not responsible for the outbreaks of health problems the Vietnam Veterans were having while they were returning home from "Nam." What was taking place with the soldiers coming out of Vietnam was unspeakable as to how our country received them. If I am mistaken could they have "intentionally concealed" information concerning the Vietnam Veterans? I know it sounds a bit harsh, but can we trust a company who intentionally misled the courts and jurors? No! We must be vigilant in our pursuit to ensure the safety of our children and our children's children. This is something the Vietnam Veterans are not privileges to do because of the lack of research and denial of the companies that used "Agent Orange" without revealing the health risks involved. One of the most disturbing things I found in reading about the recent case with Mr. Johnson and the courts rendering a verdict in his favor. **"Monsanto has consistently denied that glyphosate-based herbicides cause cancer."** I am not understanding of such a denial when the concealment itself raises the burden of discontentment and doubt of Monsanto agricultural company being able to be trusted now. Could they every tell the truth? Not only about Roundup but also about "Agent Orange?" Could the long wait be over? Do we have an admission of fault? Could we finally be getting to the truth when it comes to the lack of research and denial of any intentional wrong Monsanto and the other ten chemical companies had in relations to "Agent Orange" and the health problems it continues to cause today? Not just in with our Vietnam Veterans but also in the villages of innocent Vietnamese families, and their children who lived near the war zone.

What's really heart wrenching is what Monsanto agricultural company and the other then chemical companies involved in their manufacturing and distributing "Agent Orange" would like for the people of the United States to believe that our own government conspired against its own troops and ordered the destruction of its troops. Once again this would not be acceptable because John F. Kennedy who was the President of the United

States, our Commander & Chief would have not given such an order for the United States Air Force to spray "Agent Orange" intentionally to commit such a horrendous act of neglect on his own military force. Secondly the American people would never believe the order to spray the herbicide chemicals on the Vietnam Veterans was given with the President of the United States or any other government officials have knowledge of it being cancerous and highly contagious. They were not aware of all the hazardous information the chemical companies did not disclose to them. And they would not have put Operation Ranch Hand in effect knowing the dangers of the highly toxic chemical Agent Orange. Fortunately, although it is fifty years later, and we are finding the testimony given by the chemical companies in the 70's as it relates to the settlement agreement could possibly show signs of perjury. Which was stated concerning "Agent Orange" that Monsanto and other chemical companies involved said "Agent Orange" could not have caused the health problems the Vietnam Veterans were claiming. Monsanto and other chemical companies involved statement of not knowing their chemicals were the cause of the Vietnam Veterans suffering due to the case in relations to what has been discovered concerning the product Roundup should now be in question? Because of what has taken place with the claims of veterans and the health risks of "Agent Orange" and how the two products came from the same company. The chemical companies cannot be trusted, due to their failure to admit that they knew that "Agent Orange" could have created the problems they are having with their health today. Monsanto was recently found in a court of law to have "intentionally concealed" health risking information from the courts. Information that states Roundup contained a human carcinogenic chemical. Robert F. Kennedy Jr. was one of the attorneys who represented the plaintiff in the case of Roundup stated at the hearing against Monsanto that they had no value for human life, **"The jury found Monsanto acted with malice and oppression because they knew what they were doing was wrong and doing it with reckless disregard for human life."** In order for the chemical companies to say our government new every inch of research and the problems the use of the chemical dioxin would cause would be saying to the American people, the chemicals sprayed on the Vietnam Veterans was done intentionally. Monsanto could not present any evidence of such. Due to the recent findings of Monsanto "intentionally concealing" life threatening information reasonable doubt has been set to possibly reopen claims against a testimony which has now been proven to be fraudulent and non-creditable over thirty years ago. We as a nation of people who believe in justice and the American way of life cannot just standby and allow companies such as Monsanto and other chemical companies to not be held responsible for what was done to the Vietnam Veterans. They did not care about the dangers the chemicals they have released causing problems with the value of everyday life. They stood to make a profit off the government for the manufacturing and distribution of "Agent Orange" without remorse. The chemical companies are trying to say they did not know by mixing TCDD dioxin with the chemical herbicides it would cause cancer and severe health problems. Due to the lack of research and due to the sporadic nature of TCDD dioxin when mixed with other chemicals the damages it may cause could be insurmountable and this is what took place during the Vietnam War. This was a chemical that would be considered to have an undetermined and uncontrollable reaction to it hosts. And an undeterminable life expectancy due to the fact that the research had not been conclusive in its findings. The United States of America is not a nation that believes in killing innocent men, women or children. We are not a nation of people that would intentionally set out to bring undesired attention to ourselves since the United States has always been the lead nation of which the majority of countries follow. We have sacrificed our own soldiers and their safety for the safety of other nations. It is our battleships that set on the waterfront of our nation on the waterfronts of our allies to assure they are protected from a sudden invasion. There are United States soldiers who sacrificing their life in today's wars. I can proudly say American soldiers both men and women swore their oath of protection to the United States of America. United we stand in our battle against terrorism. Terrorists is something we are not. Terrorism is not something the United States President, the Secretary of Defense our Congress or Senate will tolerate. The United States government officials have already given so much, and we continue to give and neglect our own in a quest for world peace. I can say in our giving we have shared the bountiful blessings of this great nation in abundance. I can say this truthfully because in our mission of peace we have put our soldiers in harm's way as a way of showing our act of compassion for other nations. While I was serving in the Afghanistan War as part of "Operation Enduring Freedom," I was on what is called a special assignment, it made me realize many things. The giving of our nation's best of food, clothing, shelter and medicine to the Afghan people to let them know the United States of

America was there to assist them in getting back on their feet. The Human Assistance drops, and the Medical Assistance drops were two of many missions I was able to go on outside the safety wire. The threat of our lives being taken was always present, we were sitting targets sacrificed to protect another nation. There was so much open land and we were open targets and we knew it, but our daily missions had to be completed. I can recall many of the provinces in Afghanistan needing drinking wells. They had wells dug but could not figure out why their water remained so polluted. In our mission of peace, we went to the village to observe the wells only to find out they had no linings in them to keep out bacteria and any other ill-gotten diseases that might transpire because of their customs. With all kind of debris going into the wells their water was not safe to drink for anyone. One more thing to add to their wells was the Afghans did not believe in embalming their dead. They would bring their dead in the house wash them and bury them next to their homes. This meant that as the dead bodies began to decay parts of the body corps would wash down the hill into their drinking water. Therefore, we were told as soldiers not to drink their water or eat their fruit and vegetables. The bacteria from their drinking water was the same water used to water the plants and other vegetation. Due to the United States showing compassion we were able to fix some of the wells by putting linings inside of them that the United States not only furnished but also used our soldier's manpower to do the work to put the linings correctly in place. So, when we talk about compassion this government that I served faithfully must have the biggest heart ever. Which is why I will not standby and allow the Monsanto and other chemical companies who had a vested interest, which was nothing more than making as much money as they could off our government did not expose the chemical TCDD dioxin as it should have been to all parties involved. What is so sad about the dioxin is the Health and Medical Division are still researching "Agent Orange" or should I say TCDD dioxin today. No one knows the extent of its capabilities and the damages it can cause. As a military officer who served as a Commandant it would be impossible for me to believe that President John F. Kennedy or President Lyndon B. Johnson or our government representatives were made aware of the damage's TCDD dioxin would cause and would still give the order for its release, I will never believe that. The United States of America is a humane nation. Our government would not have allowed the release of such a toxic and contagious chemical on the open fields of war. Knowing because it was airborne and there were woman and children in the vicinity that could possibly have been endangered of being contaminated for life along with our own American, Vietnam Veterans. This is what the chemical companies along with Monsanto are asking the citizens of the United States to believe. The United States of America is a peace keeping nation run by a democracy of people. We would not have a President who would be considered to be a dictator. This is why we have the Congress and Senate in places along with the Supreme Court to help correct the wrongs as much as possible and to prevent any if not all violation of the law. What the chemical/agricultural companies did not prepare for and I am going to try to give them a slight edge here and say they did not know the effects of "Agent Orange" would have on our Vietnam Veterans, and the foliage in the forest of Vietnam which has not grown back in over fifty years. Now we are looking at the people and children being born with shocking birth defects due to the use of TCDD dioxin in the area of Vietnam. That would be 39,000 square miles of which included farmland, rice fields, vegetation and last but not least water. For the companies who are hiding and have not come forth we are fully aware that Monsanto is not the only company involved. A death trap was created in the jungles of Vietnam where Agent Orange was sprayed over 39,000 square miles in the jungles of Vietnam. The survival ratio was never ever considered. Was it all about money? If your son, or daughter were born deformed due to a war they had nothing to do with, Please!!! Tell me what would you do? Now we not only have children and grandchildren of the Vietnam Veterans being born with deformities caused by "Agent Orange" it is a systemic problem that continues to grow. The Vietnamese children are also being born with severe deformities. They need medical assistance as well. After reviewing the case of Mr. Johnson who won the $289 million-dollar lawsuit against Monsanto the agricultural giant. Monsanto remains in denial of any wrong doings of their product Roundup causing cancer. This is what the Vice President Scott Partridge had to say in a statement following the verdict. **"We are sympathetic to Mr. Johnson and his family." "Today's decision does not change the fact that more than 800 scientific studies and reviews…support the fact that glyphosate does not cause cancer and did not cause Mr. Johnson's cancer."** Mr. Scott Partridge Vice President of Monsanto went on to say the company will appeal the decision while defending the product. After looking at who's at fault and who's in denial we must now begin to take a closer look at

Monsanto's and ten other companies' involvement in the manufacturing and distribution of "Agent Orange."

In 1970 nine years later Former President Richard Nixon ordered the United States military to stop the spraying of "Agent Orange" in Vietnam. The worst dioxin contaminated site in Vietnam is Bien Hoa Airbase which is thirty miles from North of Ho Chi Minh City. From what my research is telling me is TCDD dioxin is in the trees and shrubs and the chemical has been absorbed. It destroyed the foliage and has dropped into the soil and continues to grow and spread. Is there an end to the life expectancy of the chemical dioxin? How long will it be able to survive and how many hosts will it attach itself to since there is no research showing a life expectancy date? When it begins to rain will the chemical wash off the soil into the water around it? Since it has lived like a parasite inside the bodies of the Vietnam Veterans for over forty years now the question that needs to be asked is will it live as long as it has a host? Running from the truth is a cowardly and horrendous lack of empathy when it comes to accepting fault as it relates to dioxin. But we now know from the Vice President of Monsanto's agricultural company statement that they feel their product has nothing to do with cancer. After they have been convicted in a court of law the spokesman from Monsanto's the VP still refuses to accept fault and thrives on their intent to file an appeal. Knowing this Mr. Johnson has a family and according to what the doctors are saying not much time left to enjoy with his family. The trial in America carries a lot of precedence being set forth for so many who has suffered behind these chemical company's mishap. Arbitrarily speaking, would it be okay to say something like, hey we made a mistake by releasing this chemical out in the open. We are going to do everything we possibly can to make sure those who have suffered are going to be taken care of. This is not going to bring back the Vietnam Veterans who suffered and died doing battle with the toxic herbicide chemical in their body or those who have spent a lifetime running back and forth to the hospital. This is not going to mend the broken hearts of the soldier's family members who had to watch their sons and their son's children go through the pain of not knowing what happened to their father, their husband, their child. But it's a start in the healing process of taking responsibility from where we have come. There should not be any more disputes about what a chemical herbicide being released which is toxic as well as contagious the damages that could be done. How do you quarantine 39,000 square miles of Vietnam regarding the areas "Agent Orange" was released in and contaminated? Even with an incineration team of experts going to Vietnam to try to contain the chemical from a runoff there are many things we must look into. There will be a runoff of the toxic chemical herbicide "Agent Orange" into the Vietnamese local lakes, ponds, rivers and sea it's been over fifty years now. Procrastination is a delay in time of which we now have fifty years of, and nothing has been done to change Vietnam for the better. How does one contain a product that not even our researchers know how to contain or control its toxicity? Even if incinerating the land were to take place, we would now have to look at time wasted without knowing the seepage of the chemical or where it may be lying dormant. Is there a chemical reaction of growth to the highly toxic herbicide? Is it able to spread? Where did it runoff or attach itself too? What's the life expectancy? Will the herbicide continue its life by living off hosts it comes into contact with? What I am trying to point out to you is if you look at the life of many of the Vietnam Veterans what you will find out is the chemical herbicide named "Agent Orange" is now in the DNA of the veterans. So, it would appear as though this chemical has the ability to pray on other host as it continues to move about in the body attacking vital parts of the body until it eventually causes death to its host? The next question I am going to present is has any research been attributed to TCDD dioxin and how to contain the chemical or how to destroy it? It is understandable that the chemical herbicide notably described as "Agent Orange" which contains a highly toxic chemical known to be a carcinogen. Its name is TCDD (dioxin). Dioxin is TCDD and classified as a human carcinogen by the Environmental Protection Agency. Although the EPA has stated the dangers of dioxin (TCDD) it has been continuously denied by Monsanto as being cancerous. This is where the problems with the Vietnam Veterans and their claims against "Agent Orange" being filed with the Veterans Administration comes into play. This is also where the decision of the (IOM) Institute of Medicine whose name has been changed to the (HMD) Health & Medicine Division shows a division in their findings which is considered by them to be inconclusive with the soldier's health problems in comparison to "Agent Orange" which contains the chemical TCDD (dioxin). The Health & Medicine Division of the National Academy of Sciences every two years scientifically reviews on long-term health effects of Agent Orange and other herbicides the Vietnam Veterans were exposed to. Keep in mind the HMD does not work for the VA it is non-governmental. The Health & Medicine Division (HMD) is independent and non-governmental organization. It's an outside organization, a team of experts with supposedly nationally renowned subject matter when it comes to researching "Agent Orange". The HMD are supposed to gather all the scientific material to assist them in rendering a justified decision as to whether the Veterans claims are a result of what their scientific findings stipulate. What many of you do not know is the Veterans Administration does not operate on its on fruition. The Veterans Administration (VA) has to rely on the information being relayed to them by the Health & Medicine Division before movement can begin in making the soldier whole again. This means the Health & Medicine Division looks thoroughly through their scientific studies as it relates to "Agent Orange" and other chemicals they are studying. They also do what is called a peer-review which would be of other prior colleagues or associates and apply their comparisons to see if anything may have been overlooked. The HDM base their findings on the highest determining factors of what the study shows. The Health & Medicine Division makes its determination and surrenders its findings in a report. From this report given to the VA the HDM also includes its final review and also gives its recommendations to the Veterans Administrations, Congress and the public. I find this to be repulsive because constituents very seldom go against what their co-workers or associates adamantly say what they have found. There would have to be a different venue of facts and both inside and outside professionals involved in such a serious analytical break down of facts involving the Vietnam Veterans and "Agent Orange" in order to make an investigative team conclude in an agreement that all facts are conclusive, and they are not. How does the chemical dioxin get into the Vietnam Veterans DNA? I also want to explain something else before I continue. It's simply a matter of defining "Agent Orange." "Agent Orange" got its name from the orange ban on the barrel it was placed in. "Agent Orange" is not the chemical it was the name given to the barrel that contained the chemical TCDD a dioxin with a orange band later called "Agent Orange." Remember there was at least six different chemicals being dumped over 39,000 square miles of Vietnam. They are listed as follows, **Agent Blue, Agent Green, Agent White, Agent Pink, Agent Purple and finally "Agent Orange"** which was the most potent because it was the only agent that contained TCDD. These different agents were initially being used to destroy the enemy by contaminating their food supply. It was called "Operation Ranch Hand." The problem both sides continue to clash at is where the chemical companies do not want to accept fault and they remain in denial after the suffering and death of so many of our Vietnam Veterans. There is going to have to be some form of agreement met in order for not just the Vietnam Veterans but their children and grandchildren to have funding set up for their future medical treatment and living expenses concerning their health. This is not acceptable on the part of the Vietnam Veterans who fought a war unfortunately where (it is said) that during the Vietnam War the life expectancy of a soldier serving in Vietnam was sixteen minutes. The Vietnam Veterans returned home to a country already in chaos. A divided country and their position of division was based on whether the Vietnam Veterans violated the Geneva Convention. This also caused a rift amid the Vietnam Veterans heroic efforts to make sure the United States of America remained safe. With "Agent Orange" still being researched by non-governmental organizations it is over forty years later and there has not been any conclusive findings of what is actually non-conclusive as it relates to the research being done every two years as the reports says on "Agent Orange" and other Agent herbicides used. Which sounds to be a bit unbelievable because the Vietnam Veterans are still dying, and claims are still be filed claiming "Agent Orange" as the cause of illnesses the Vietnam Veterans continue to suffer with. The companies responsible continue to deny the chemical TCDD (dioxin) is carcinogenic, while the EPA (Environmental Protection Agency) says it is a human carcinogen. What is not unbelievable is the chemical company's denial. We can go as far back as the true story of Erin Brokovich where the companies involved with poisoning and entire community of innocent people with their chemical waste never admitted they were the cause. That is the problem with settling out of court and giving the companies the right to file appeals. There is no admission on record of the chemical companies admitting to the mixture of chemicals they were using to have caused cancer. It was settled out of court, but Erin Brokovich won the largest lawsuit against a chemical plant in the history of America. The chemical companies named in the lawsuit with Erin Brokovich were Pacific Gas and Electric Company (PG&E). What is not normal is the air pollution caused by these plants and the damage done to so many families with most of these companies being left with the thought of feeling they have the money to pay for another person's loved one's life. How does someone believe wholeheartedly that they can replace somebody's loved one with money? They feel they can come up with a settlement and buy the individual out before going to court. Cancer is not something to take lightly and rest assured these chemical companies who are not following the EPA rules and doing what they want knowing the chemicals they are releasing have a high probability of killing someone's father, mother, son, daughter etc. and all they can say is "the chemical we created is non-carcinogenic". Well then please explain why these soldiers who returned home from Vietnam just out of the blue started coming down with cancer and other health issues? Why is there a continual team of research experts from the Health and Medicine Division put together every two years from different parts of the world to review records on "Agent Orange" if they were certain the chemicals, they are using are not carcinogenic? There are 390 Vietnam Veterans dying each day. Out of the 2,709,918 Americans who served in Vietnam. Less than 850, 000 are estimated to be alive today. The age range of the Vietnam Veterans today would have to be close to 72 to 76 years old. According to the Sobering Statistics concerning the Vietnam Veterans there are at least 390 Vietnam Veterans dying a day. Statistically speaking there are 2,730 dying a week, 10,920 dying a month, 131,040 a year can this get any worse. So, if this Sobering Statistics Report concerning the Vietnam Veterans is close to being even minutely accurate there are approximately 850,000 Vietnam Veterans left. Which means at the rate they are dying it is sad to say but we are looking at maybe another 6.4 years before the Vietnam Veterans will have all died off. When we look at the claims being filed by the Vietnam Veterans the estimated claim being processed takes about seven years in order for the soldier to receive the benefits from the claim filed. Seven years is not considered to be in the life expectancy of the Vietnam Veteran since there is an estimated 131,040 dying a year. What are the odds of the Vietnam Veterans getting a chance to see the benefits from any of the claims he or she has filed? I would say slim to none in accordance to the stats given by Sobering Statistics as of April 2016. When we look at the chemical companies and their place of business being so close to neighborhoods, schools, parks, lakes, oceans and seas. We all need to stop and find out what is taking place within our own communities and find out how these chemical plants will affect us as a whole. Therefore, the true story of Erin Brokovich is so important, this is why I am referencing it in this book. Just maybe some attorney will get the hint and follow suite. I will continue to point out the chemical companies based on the true story of Erin Brokovich case. Even with a settlement agreement made they never admitted to any fault of their chemicals causing cancer and health problems with over 400 people within the community the chemical company Pacific

Gas & Electric Company (PG & E) operated. Young girls having a hysterectomy, some of the women had breast cancer and had to have their breast removed. Others had pancreatic cancer, liver cancer and some died before the case was resolved with cancer, some never got a chance to enjoy any of the monies they had won. This is all due to chemical plants hiding their poisonous chemicals in our communities and our children end up suffering behind their negligence. Right here in Chicago we are looking at a chemical company called Sterigenics their headquarters is in Oak Brook, Illinois. In the areas I am about to mention there are people fighting for their life and trying to get this company out of their neighborhood, Willowbrook, IL and Waukegan, IL. ABC news has covered stories of what has taken place near these chemical companies that continually deny that facts that their chemical (Ethylene Oxide) is not the cause of their sudden cancer outbreaks in the area. Although Sterigenics is sticking to their word and saying (Ethylene Oxide) is not giving people in the area cancer. The (EPA) Environmental Protection Agency singled out Willowbrook as one of a few dozen communities across the nation facing alarmingly high cancer risks from toxic air pollution. While Sterigenics remains in denial the plants forgot to say they put out an estimated 169,000 pounds of cancer-causing ethylene oxide into the air every year. There are families literally dying in Willowbrook, Illinois and Waukegan, Illinois from exposure to a toxic chemical used by Sterigenics called (Ethylene Oxide) classified by the Environmental Protection Agency as being cancerous. This is why it is so important for everyone to stop and take another look at what our Vietnam Veterans are saying about "Agent Orange" the toxicity levels their bodies had to absorb with the chemical TCDD (dioxin) sprayed directly on them in Vietnam is highly toxic and deteriorating the soldiers body from the inside to this day. Right now, we should all be thinking about what we should be doing to protect our communities and our value of life of which it appears as though the chemical companies who are making these cancerous chemicals haven't any value of human life. I am certain the chemical companies' children and grandchildren are in safe areas where they will not be affected by the chemicals being released. What is not understood is the EPA has declared TCDD (dioxin) cancerous, the EPA has declared (ethylene oxide) cancerous, the EPA has declared (chromium 6) cancerous. The reason I continue to mention the Environmental Protection Agency (EPA) is because they were established in December of 1970 by an executive order of the Former President of the United States, Richard

Nixon. The EPA is an agency of the United States federal government whose mission is to protect human and environmental health. My understanding to this job description is once the EPA has established something to be a health problem and dangerous to people that the company should be made to stop using the chemical or either closed once there is a contaminant detected as serious as a carcinogen. If it is a problem concerning the environment, then the company should be given ample time to clean up the environment, in order to make the people safe and whole again. There appears to be very little enforcement taking place and people are suffering. Just like the Vietnam Veterans have been suffering for over forty years and very little has been done for them When we look at the Vietnam Veterans and their suffering for over forty years now, I find it to be irreparable as to what they are owed and will more than likely never receive, not at their death rate. The people in Willowbrook, Illinois are talking about their having to be in the area of a chemical plants and want Sterigenics moved. The Vietnam Veterans had to live, sleep, eat and drink in an area that was literally spayed with the cancerous and highly toxic TCDD chemicals used in "Agent Orange." Remember these chemicals were not diluted while they were being sprayed over the fields and forests of Vietnam. They were considered to be contagious the second they hit the air and literally sprayed on top of our Vietnam Veterans. There isn't any other way to describe the suffering the Vietnam Veterans have had to live with for a lifetime. And it is not over yet. The battle with "Agent Orange" continues. The Health & Medicine Division and their researched findings through the years does not reflect what the Vietnam Veterans are saying what is taking place within their bodies. The Vietnam Veterans have reported the toxicity levels of "Agent Orange" is so powerful it is now been discovered that it is in their DNA. Once again, we are looking at the life expectancy of their children because it appears the toxic chemical herbicide has used the contaminated blood and body of the Vietnam Veterans as its host. Of which its genealogy of DNA has transferred from one body to the other where the chemical herbicide has now been transferred from the Vietnam Veterans DNA, genetically to their children and grandchildren. But the studies and research by the Health & Medicine Division, if I might add which is a non-governmental organization continues to be ongoing and non-related. No findings, no new discoveries to relate "Agent Orange" to the health problems the Vietnam Veterans have had for over forty years now, Oh! My God you have got to be kidding me? The facts that cannot be disputed are the bodies of the Vietnam Veterans where being used as a host to be fed off of by the TCDD until the Veterans body became like the trees and shrubs in Vietnam drained of all life. There is no other way to get you to see the horrifying tragedy that has been allowed to go on for over forty years now. As I stated earlier in this chapter it has been fifty years now since the spraying of "Agent Orange" and nothing is growing in the areas that were sprayed with "Agent Orange" in Vietnam. "Agent Orange" continues to sap the life out of everything and anything it comes into contact with. Claims from the Vietnam Veterans continue to be filed with the Veterans Administration. The chemical plants seem to think they have dodged a bullet in anticipation of the Vietnam Veterans soon demise. Thinking the Vietnam Veterans are going to be a non-existent part of history they no longer have to be ashamed of. From what I have researched it is not the Vietnam Veterans who should find a need to hide their faces from society. It is the chemical companies and their contribution to a much larger problem. They are the ones who should have their heads bowed for causing the Vietnam Veterans so much grief in their life and their families and loved ones who had to watch them suffer and die through the years. That battle after they returned home became a battle within itself of the Vietnam Veterans not knowing what they were dealing with in relations to "Agent Orange" because they were not told. These soldiers had to deal with family, friends and loved ones in the process of them not understanding the change their bodies had to go through and their and minds would have to cope with. Due to the toxic chemical herbicide "Agent Orange" which was in Vietnam Veterans system they were not aware of the molecular changes taking place from within their bodies, they were slowly deteriorating Being eaten up by cancer from the inside but the Institute of Medicine said in their research findings that Agent Orange was not the cause. They were going through mental issues, heart issues, liver and kidney issues. These were health issues they did not have prior to joining the military. I can say this because the military would not have let them enlist with an already noted heart problem. During that time a lot of men were not able to join the military if they were flat footed, color blind, could not see (red), or if they had asthma. These were some of the basic problems men who wanted to join faced and the military rejected them. Now let me take you a little further. The soldiers who returned home from Vietnam began to all of a sudden having heart, liver, kidney, prostrate problems and of course pancreas problems. Since every human beings' body is made the same internally, we are all aware that the blood in our body is filtered through the liver. Since "Agent Orange" has now been discovered to be in the Vietnam Veterans (DNA). As the contaminated blood flows throughout the soldier's body each soldier is affected in a different way. I feel it is because of various reasons but one reason would be because of the body make of the soldier, whether he is short, tall, skinny or fat, a drinker or smoker etc. The herbicide chemical being TCDD (dioxin) in his body will cause a problem at some point in time during its attack inside the soldier's body. Given the fact that our blood does flow up to our brain. I find it feasible to say the soldier's brain would also be affected in some way, the soldier's logic, mental alertness, memory, PTSD heightened due to the foreign chemical TCDD (Agent Orange) which was also now being circulated in the brain. Cancer formed in the brain and body of the soldiers due to their exposure to the chemical herbicide "Agent Orange" TCDD (dioxin) as it became genetically bloodborne. This is another reason why it would be relevant to say due to the direct exposure the Vietnam Veterans had with "Agent Orange" and how the TCDD (dioxin) has attacked their system psychological help should have also been given to these soldiers once they returned in order to assist them with what they would eventually have to be prepared for in the future. Counseling, counseling and more counseling would be needed for the Vietnam Veterans to be able to cope with such a powerful toxic herbicide chemical that was now a part of their DNA. They would have to cope with the breaking down of the normal functions of their body. The suffering of these soldiers cannot be and should not be hidden any longer. Their entire life was not only put on hold due to their exposure to the highly toxic chemical herbicide "Agent Orange." What has taken place with the Vietnam Veterans will never be justified. Their lives were taken from them and their normal functioning days as proud men would be no more. With Parkinson's Disease being one of the health conditions of Agent Orange, www.publichealth.va.gov **Parkinson's Disease** is considered to be an progressive disorder of the nervous system that affects muscle movement. What I am going to do here for you is not just list the disease linked with "Agent Orange" because all you are going to do is read them and say, WOW! I did not know that. What I want to do is to briefly give you an analysis of what the disease causes in the soldier. I just gave you Parkinson's, and how it affects muscle movement. Meaning the soldier could have been totally immobile, wheelchair restricted, unable to run, throw a ball or play with his children or even make love to his wife. Please feel free to count these health problems of which the Vietnam Veterans are suffering with and remember the majority of the Vietnam Veterans have more than just one health risk which is contributory to "Agent Orange" which is a highly toxic herbicide chemical. Another link to Agent Orange is called, **AL Amyloidosis,** is the growth of abnormal cells that produce amyloid. Amyloids are aggregates of proteins that become folded into a shape that allows many copies of that protein to stick together, forming fibrils. Amyloids have been linked to the development of various diseases. It is also noted as a skin condition that occurs soon after exposure to chemicals and looks like common forms of acne seen in teenagers. www.publichealth.va.gov Chronic B-cell Leukemia, "A type of cancer that affects white blood cells. Chloracne (or similar acne form)." Chloracne is an acne-like eruption of blackheads, cysts, and pustules associated with over-exposure to certain halogenated aromatic compounds, such as chlorinated dioxins and dibenzofurans." Next **Diabetes Mellitus Type 2,** www.drugs.com "Type 2 diabetes is a chronic disease. It is characterized by high levels of sugar in the blood. Type 2 diabetes is much more common than type 1 diabetes and is really a different disease. But it shares with type 1 diabetes high blood sugar levels, and the complications of high blood sugar." www.publichealth.va.gov **Hodgkin's Disease,** "is one of two common cancers of the lymphatic system, which is part of the immune system. The other, more common cancer of the lymphatic system is called non-Hodgkin's lymphoma. Signs may include fever, fatigue, night sweats, itching, loss of appetite, and weight loss. Painless swelling in the lymph nodes in neck, armpits, and groin also may occur." www.publichealth. va.gov **Ischemic Heart Disease,** "a disease characterized by a reduced supply of blood to the heart, that leads to chest pain Multiple Myeloma A cancer." www.publichealth.va.gov **Multiple Myeloma,** "A cancer of plasma cells, a type of white blood cell in bone." www.publichealth.va.gov **Non-Hodgkin's Lymphoma,** "A group of cancers that affect the lymph glands and other lymphatic tissue." www.publichealth.va.gov **Peripheral Neuropathy, Early-Onset,** "A nervous system condition that causes numbness, tingling, and motor weakness. Under VA's rating regulations, it must be at least 10 percent disabling within one year of herbicide exposure." www.publichealth.va.gov **Porphyria Cutanea Tarda,** "A disorder characterized by liver dysfunction and by thinning and blistering of the skin in sun exposed areas. Under VA's rating regulations, it must be at least 10 percent disabling within one year of exposure to herbicides." www.publichealth.va.gov **Prostate Cancer,** "Cancer of the prostate; one of the most common cancers among men." www.publichealth.va.gov **Respiratory Cancers**, "Cancers of the lung, larynx, trachea, and bronchus." www.publichealth.va.gov **Soft Tissue Sarcomas** (other than osteosarcoma, chondrosarcoma, Kaposi's, sarc0ka, or mesothelioma), A group of different types of cancers in body tissues such as muscle, fat, blood and lymph vessels, and connective tissues." This list which is linked to the Veterans Administration has listed only some of the health problems "Agent Orange" has caused in the Vietnam Veterans body. Since the research concerning the disadvantaged health risk for those who have been in direct contact with TCDD = (dioxin) = "Agent Orange" please note the research continues to be ongoing and has been ongoing for fifty years now. With that being said the Vietnam Veterans are still filing claims. Doctors reports are stating the problems with their health since having been in contact with TCDD which is the real name of the herbicide chemical in "Agent Orange" and classified as a human carcinogen by the Environmental Protection Agency. I cannot make it any plainer than that since the EPA was established by the President of the United States of which their job duties are to protect human life and environmental dangers. What appears once again to be a problem with these selected non-governmental researchers of science is their colleague affiliation. It's just like being a doctor, or a judge or someone in law enforcement, a lawyer. It is rare for anyone who has trained under the same code of ethics to go against their own constituents. Because going against what your constituents already voted on or agreed to is like telling yourself that you are right and they are wrong, and it starts to bring bad blood within its ranks. Organization, companies, political people, judges, lawyers, police officers, congressmen and senators, doctors etc. all want to feel that everyone is on the same page in their group. This is an expected unspoken agreement that they thrive on in order to become a part of the group, this is why you were hired, "to go along." As the old saying goes, "You scratch my back and I will scratch yours." Although this is unfortunate and many go along with other people expectations but not everyone does, for this reason we have what is called the whistle blowers. Whistle blowers are usually people who have gotten tired of seeing good honest hard-working everyday people messed over or fired because their beliefs are different, and they want to do the right thing. Whistle blowers will talk to sources outside the organization to get the wrong that is being done corrected and they give up valuable information in doing so. Well! I am not asking anyone for an admission of guilt. What I am asking those of you who are in charge of these chemical plants and to your own denial or admission to stand up and say we want to help correct a problem that (may) have been caused by our company's. An admission of helping someone to heal is not saying you are guilty. The Vietnam Veterans never had a life after the war was over. Their life was literally stolen from them while protecting you, America. And if things are not corrected soon what we are looking at in the near future is going to be even more chaotic. Reason being is because of the list I just posted above about the cause and effects of "Agent Orange." They are only a few of the problems the soldiers in "Nam" are categorized in as health issues and that is only what has been discovered so far. Even with that being said the Vietnam Veterans are only going to receive assistance (if) and only if they meet the VA's doctor's diagnosis. Remember the research is ongoing and there are a lot of listings for cancer of which is first detected in the blood work. I gave you the U.S. Department of Veterans Affairs website to find the listings of the symptoms related to "Agent Orange" here it is again www.publichealth.com you must type in the search box whatever aliment concerning the Vietnam Veteran you are looking for.

I also want you to understand the problem does not stop with the Vietnam Veterans. The next thing I am going to list is the Vietnam Veterans grandchildren diagnosed symptoms for "Agent Orange." Now this is a dilemma of which shouldn't leave any questionable doubt about what is taking place with the children and grandchildren of the Vietnam Veterans. What remains constant with the chemical companies is their denial of any wrong of being a part of the health problems some communities are coming down with what is basically cancer. I don't have the time to say it any other way other than to ask the question what is wrong with people today? We have not banned together as we should to stop the wrongs taking place in the world today. And cancer is not something we as a people in America are going to be able to overlook when it comes to human life. The people in Willowbrook, Illinois and Waukegan, Illinois have a battle on their hands concerning Sterigneics new name as of November 7, 2017 (Sotera Health LLC) and the cancer pollutant (ethylene oxide) being release in the air in their communities. Since the discovery of the cancerous toxic being released in the air on March 8, 2019. What Sterigneics who has a new name (Sotera Health LLC) is noted by the new Governor of Illinois J.B. Pritzker's administration due to air monitors in the area as recording the highest levels of ethylene oxide in close proximity of homes, where families live, where people walk their dogs, children play in the park, outside in the community, and homeowners give barbeques for their friends to come over and enjoy good company. Who wants to be doing any of those things while having to breathe in the cancerous chemical (ethylene oxide)? But Sterigenics who has now changed their name to Sotera Health LLC continues to function. They are not only poisoning the air they are damaging the lives of people while spreading their (ethylene oxide) throughout the community. We do not have to wonder what these people are breathing because that has already been determined (ethylene oxide) of which federal inspectors has already began testing. It makes you wonder just how much ethylene oxide has been sucked up in the air of their homes and how it has affected, or should I say infected their children through the years. Will it have an effect on their children pursuing a higher degree of learning in the future? This is what the civilian's side of the fence is protesting about as it relates to endangerment of their health. From what I have reviewed in relation to their complaints is that many people in the community have already become sickly with breast cancer, prostate cancer and other forms of cancer. The EPA has already classified ethylene oxide as a human carcinogen. That should be enough to close the plant down but now since Sterigenics has changed its name to Sotera Health LLC who knows how long that will take. You know how it goes, new name new function but the whole sham for the chemical company remains the same. Toxic chemicals are in the air and the community and other officials are fighting back. I am not mentioning Sotera Health LLC chemical company just to say it is wrong but violations of their means of testing for (ethylene oxide) should also be in question. From my understanding of research if the testers they use are placed a certain way like in the opposite way the wind is blowing than there is going to be a low-level reading of the (ethylene oxide). On the other hand, if the testers are placed with the chemical blowing directly toward them like they should then the toxicity level in the area is going to usually read high. This is something that needs to be closely monitored in order to have a safer environment for all.

CHAPTER XXV

BITTER HUMOR- NO SUGAR FOR "AGENT ORANGE"

I F I MAY, LET me ask of you to allow me to sound a bit facetious at this point? I am quite sure if you have read this far already you will definitely know I am just kidding around trying to make you really think in this chapter. I personally feel any form of cancer would be considered to be a serious matter. But I guess to those chemical companies that enjoy contaminating the air with cancer causing chemical pollutants have an inside joke that says there is nothing wrong with a little cancer!!! Remember I am trying to be a little facetious here, so let me ask you just what kind of cancer would you like sir, or madam? It's all free and you can have it according to how many cigarettes you smoke, how much contaminated air you breathe, how much of the wrong foods you eat etc. Would you like to inherit a little cancer of the kidney or cancer of the liver? You know you only have one liver. How about cancer of the brain? There is no need for you to want to be able to think for yourself. Can we get you to try a little cancer of the ear, eyes, or foot? Oh, I know you are one of those people who just happen to want all the cancer you can get. Right? So, we are going to give you stage four cancer of the pancreas that way you don't have to worry about missing out on anything. You see, stage 4 pancreatic cancer is the one that spreads through your entire body. It gets into the brain, the bone and the bone marrow and just eats away until there is nothing left. It cannot be contained, and you are guaranteed to be dead in a very short period of time. I am so sorry I almost forgot to ask; did you tell your wife you love her enough? Did you get a chance to kiss your children goodbye before you left to go to the hospital? What about your grandchildren, did you get a chance to see them grow up? I was just wondering out of all of the things you wanted to do while you are alive on the face of this earth, did you have the opportunity to do them? And by the way since our chemical companies are passing out cancer choices just which one would you like? And please let me explain our cancer products are a little different. I am sure you are going to ask in what way are they different? The cancer we have here in the states is not like the kind our Vietnam Veterans acquired. You know that "Agent Orange" stuff. Those soldiers never stood a chance. At least you civilians have the backing of the governor J.B. Pritzer, Senator Dick Durbin and those who are on their communities who are watching the chemical companies closely. It wasn't monitored like that for the Vietnam Veterans. I guess because it was used for war, "Agent Orange" did not have any restraints, it was just sprayed on the soldiers and forgotten about. Who was there for the Vietnam Veterans when the herbicide chemical TCDD (dioxin) = "Agent Orange" was being sprayed right on top of our soldier's heads? They had to breath, eat, sleep and live in that toxic chemical substance for their entire tour of duty in Vietnam. The cancer the Vietnam Veterans acquired is infused in their DNA, it's now genetic. Meaning because it is now in their blood, they have passed it on to their children and from their children to their grandchildren and possibly great grandchildren.

The cancerous chemical herbicide TCDD (dioxin) = "Agent Orange" is much worse than you could ever imagine. It is uncontrollable, sporadic and without limitations. The chemical TCDD which is the scientific name now has a host and believe it when I tell you the host is the soldier's body. Just about every Vietnam Veteran I have spoken with tells me their friends are being ate up from by the toxic chemical herbicide "Agent Orange" from the inside. Once the TCDD got into the Vietnam Veterans body it became infused and began to travel genetically into their bloodstream to where it is now a part of the soldier's DNA. In the process of the TCDD (dioxin) being now bloodborne, it has now been passed to their children and their grandchildren genetically.

I thought you may have wanted to laugh just a little because it is so weird that all of a sudden people in different states in America have been complaining about chemical plants causing cancer in their communities. The Vietnam Veterans have been telling America how they were literally sprayed with cancerous chemicals for almost fifty years now. So, I must ask another question, why have the Vietnam Veterans been overlooked for over forty years? They were the ones who went to war to defend your rights and they did not leave you stranded and hide from the enemy so why did you leave the Vietnam Veterans in the cold. I am certain with all of the claims they have been filed with the Veterans Administration Office throughout the United States it should have left no one in doubt that "Agent Orange" has caused an insurmountable amount of grief in the lives of the Vietnam Veterans as well as their family's life. Watching the Vietnam Veterans going back and forth to the hospital for over forty years now should have been enough signals for the VA or the (HMD) non-governmental researchers of "Agent Orange" to recheck their findings and come up with a solution to helping the Vietnam Veterans and their families.

CHAPTER XXVI

———

THE UNEXPECTED RETURN HOME

WHEN YOU TALK ABOUT wiping out a community with controlled cancerous chemicals in the air. I have to wonder is it the same as having cancerous chemicals sprayed on top of your body and the outcome becomes impossible for you to recover, to heal, to survive? What I am telling you is the Vietnam Veterans cannot get rid of TCDD (dioxin) named "Agent Orange" because it became genetically a part of their DNA infused in their blood. They were overly exposed to the chemical while they were in the war zone without any protective clothing or antibiotics to fight off the chemical. Our soldiers were being infused with a carcinogenic product produces by the chemical company's in American. The soldiers did not stand a chance. And what is taking place with the Vietnam Veterans is similar to my sixth book title, **"The Cocoa Plantations America's Chocolate Secret, Forced Child Labor, Rape, Sodomy, Abuse of Children, Child Sex Trafficking, Children Organ Trafficking, Child Sex Slaves." And also what is** taking place with the seven-year-old Hispanic children working on the tobacco plantations in Texas and Florida. The seven-year-old children are coming down with terminal cancer from bacteria slug that gets into their skin and their young bodies cannot fight it off. So, these children are dying at a young age of seven with cancer and no one is doing anything to correct that situation either. Just like the young children on the tobacco plantations did not have a clue about the bacteria on the tobacco leaf giving them cancer. The Vietnam Veterans did not have a clue as to what kind of cancer-causing chemicals were being sprayed over their heads in the jungles of Vietnam. What appears to be a very true statement to make here is, "no one cares about the have nots." The Vietnam Veterans did not have a clue as to what was being sprayed on them from 1961 until 1970. Remember Former President Richard Nixon gave the order to stop the use of "Agent Orange" in 1970.

I am certain many of you should be able to remember the Vietnam War. Which is also another reason why it was important for me to write this book. So, the Vietnam War as well as the Vietnam Veterans will never be forgotten, they were honorable men of valor. The Vietnam Veterans were sent to Vietnam to fight for you, the American citizens to defend our President, our nation. For their reward they were given a life that consisted of a continued battle with cancer and other health problems. A life that would bring them back to America appearing to be whole but all the while TCDD (dioxin) = "Agent Orange" the highly toxic cancerous herbicide was eating their bodies up and it was being kept very quiet. Through denial and inconclusive research by non-governmental organizations the chemical herbicide had become a separate issue from the wrong that was done in both countries during the war. How do we, being Americans condemn our own military soldiers for a lifetime? Then captivate the minds of the American people through propaganda and say the soldiers did some horrible things to the Vietnamese, well the Vietnamese also did some horrible things to our Vietnam Veterans? Keep in mind it was a war in Vietnam it was not a movie where you can turn on and off what soldiers on both sides might have been doing to one another. We can go back and forth with the finger pointing but it is not going to heal either nation. We no longer need to be sidetracked with blaming one another. Simply because both countries have been infected with the highly toxic herbicide chemical "Agent Orange." Even more so the land in Vietnam where nothing has grown for fifty years now. And the seepage of the toxic chemical continues to contaminate the villagers close to the war zone. The Vietnamese men, women and children including their vegetation, crops, rice fields, ponds, lakes and rivers. It's so sad to say this but in a few more years from now the Vietnam Veterans will be almost extinct. Their life expectancy has already been figured out with 390 Vietnam Veterans dying a day. Their cause and their suffering will never be forgotten because they have become immortalized through their children and grandchildren who are now being born with TCDD (dioxin) = "Agent Orange" in their body. Therefore, I am asking everyone to continue to look toward the chemical plants. I keep asking the owners of the chemical plants to find a place of peace within their heart and conscious mind to come up with better research techniques. The Vietnam Veterans have been talking about their suffering and filing claims all over the United States not just to get a reaction from the government but to let America know they are still suffering. They are filing claims because it's true, they are filing claims because they know the changes "Agent Orange" has caused within their body. More money is needed to fund further research in order that the Health and Medicine

Division (HDM) who are researching "Agent Orange" can better assess the health issues the Vietnam Veterans have been speaking out on for over forty years. Remember as I continue to reiterate the Health and Medicine Division (HMD) are non-governmental researchers. I do not expect them to find what the Vietnam Veterans are saying to be true. Who is hiring them to research Agent Orange? Could it be that the chemical companies decided to step in and foot that bill to avoid paying the bigger one. The VA can only step in and make the necessary adjustments needed toward the Vietnam Veterans claims once the HMD reports their findings to be in relation to the Vietnam Veterans medical complaints. More monies are going to be needed because we are now looking at an over forty-year crisis that has not rendered any movement of change to enlighten the health issues being addressed by the Vietnam Veterans. Not only health issues the Vietnam Veterans have but their children and their children's children are now suffering from the same toxic chemical in their DNA. Yes! Believe it when I tell you that "Agent Orange" has catapulted into a much larger venue. One that now leads to the Vietnam Veterans grandchildren being born with deformities. As I stated earlier in the book, I am certain it was unimaginable by those who created "Agent Orange" to ever phantom it being able to be found in the DNA of the Vietnam Veterans grandchildren. Their children and grandchildren had nothing to do with the war. They had no dog in the fight. I wonder do the American citizens blame them too. Please keep in mind these children were not born yet so what is the delay on proper funding needed to help contain this toxic chemical "Agent Orange." Their children and grandchildren were not a part of the war and never once did anything to violate the Geneva Convention. So, now who does the American people channel their hatred towards? Are the researchers going to remain consistent by continually not finding the associated effects of "Agent Orange" and the health problems it is capable of causing. Both externally and internally as it relates to the chemical TCDD (dioxin)= "Agent Orange" as these non-governmental researchers refuse to submit what is needed to show that since TCDD (dioxin) is what's inside "Agent Orange." That this chemical TCDD (dioxin) which = "Agent Orange" is wiping out the last of 850,000 Vietnam Veterans. Soldiers who served the United States of America's military honorably and to this date they have not received their proper diagnosed admission from the IOM or the HDM for over forty years. That their ailments are related and caused by Agent Orange. What appeared to be the intended plan to let the Vietnam Veterans die off over the next few years along with the claims filed with the Veterans Administration on "Agent Orange." It was a hopeful thought for those who just wanted to be rid of hearing about "Agent Orange" and pray that it would just go away with the death of the Vietnam Veterans has turned out to not be the case. The problem has gotten even bigger, it has grown into a toxic nightmare. The unexpected happened and its unexpected findings has left science and its researchers baffled. The herbicide chemical that once hibernated in the bodies of the Vietnam Veterans has been found in the DNA of their children and grandchildren. TCDD (dioxin) = "Agent Orange" has been transferred genetically into their children's DNA and now we are finding the grandchildren are also being born with deformities due to the TCDD (dioxin) = "Agent Orange" in their blood and bodies. With the Vietnam Veterans dying away in vast numbers through the years, you must understand their bodies have been infected with the cancerous chemical that has been eating them up from the inside for over forty years now. Unfortunately, the chemical herbicide dioxin has been transferred over to the grandchildren and it is affecting their birth because the TCDD (dioxin) that is in the blood of the Vietnam Veterans DNA is causing their children and grandchildren to be born genetically deficient. Some people would consider "Agent Orange" to be a curse well it is a curse just like the toxic chemical (chromium 6). Chromium 6 was another highly toxic chemical. It was the main cancerous chemical focused on in a true story of which the chemical chromium 6 was giving people cancer. Little girls and boys, families were being ate up with the chemical (chromium 6) which caused cancer in a legal case and true story titled (Erin Brokovich). Chromium 6 was wiping out an entire town of at least 400 residents. I repeated this just in case some brilliant attorney would like to look into the situation of "Agent Orange" for the Vietnam Veterans, their children and grandchildren and reopen the case. I am certain a judge would not have a problem hearing a new case of chemical plants causing cancer because (Erin Brokovich) has already set precedence for it to be heard. TCDD = Dioxin = "Agent Orange" is a case that need to be brought before the Supreme Court and presented in such fashion that TCDD which is more so an uncontrollable toxic chemical was sold to the United States government without any value for not only human life but for the soldiers who fought to protect this United States of America, the Vietnam Veterans. Without conclusive research released to the United States government for the chemical "Agent Orange" to be used in the war zone of Vietnam or how to use it. "Agent Orange" was sprayed in the air and over the heads of our American soldiers subjecting them to become infected due to the extremely high levels of chemicals that were being sprayed. In the areas of which our Vietnam Veterans had to eat, sleep, live, breathe and drink waters of which the highly toxic contaminant TCDD (dioxin) was being used. This is not omitting the fact that there were also Vietnamese villages of which there were inhabitants of innocent men, women and children in the local area who ended up suffering from "Agent Orange" and they were not a part of the Vietnam War. This part concerning the Vietnam War must be included as a part of the healing process we are seeking as an unintentional incident that continues to haunt the United States of America and its respect for all nationalities, ethnicities, religion, race, creed and color. As well as its respect for human life whereby I as a military officer and Commandant can say without reservation. The men who have fought in battle in the wars before me and the wars I have served in I can proudly say the United States of America has stood its ground graciously while defending the rights of other nations. I can also say our Commander and Chief who stood watch during the time of the Vietnam War which was President John F. Kennedy, President Lyndon B. Johnson and Former President Richard Nixon as well as the House of Congress and the Senate were not aware of TCDD (dioxin). TCDD is noted by the Environmental Protection Agency (EPA) as being classified as a human carcinogen was being used as a vital part of the chemical herbicide mixture to create the highly toxic cancerous carcinogenic herbicide chemical called "Agent Orange." President John F. Kennedy nor any other President of The United States of America having knowledge of what TCDD was going to do to the Vietnam Veterans would (**NOT**) have knowingly ordered the slaughter of their own troops and released this chemical to be used in open combat. And neither was our President or government involved in the creation of "Agent Orange" this is what the chemical companies who were involved in the lawsuits were trying to insinuate, and of course it could not be proven and has never proven that President John F. Kennedy had any knowledge of Agent Orange. What is unfortunate is that the chemical companies go without blame or fault pretending that all of the six Agents, which consisted of 1. Agent Blue, 2. Agent Green, 3. Agent Purple, 4. Agent Pink, 5. Agent White and 6. Agent Orange the most potent of all the agents used were made the same. It is obvious that the chemicals used in Vietnam were not the same and the one that caused the most damage was Agent Orange of which 11,000,000 gallons was used in the jungles of Vietnam. Our government was under the impression believing that all the agents used in Vietnam were basically all the same. To no avail the herbicide "Agent Orange" is still running ramped and nothing has grown in those areas in Vietnam fifty years later. The seepage of "Agent Orange" which is unnoted and has not been researched concerning its survivability or its ability to be contained. It is polluting farmland, rivers, lakes, ponds and streams. The local Vietnamese have to use this water to wash, bathe in, and drink from. "Agent Orange" has affected the life expectancy of the men, women and children of Vietnam. Like the way it has affected the Vietnam Veterans here in America. The children being born in Vietnam are being born today in 2019 with severe deformities, much worse than the children and grandchildren of the Vietnam Veterans in America. Therefore, the nightmare continues as it relates to the Vietnam Veterans and how they are dying off because of "Agent Orange." I really do not like repeating myself, but nothing is being done about it. It is estimated that in six years and six months there will not be any more Vietnam Veterans alive. When we look at the bigger picture as a civilized nation of people we are going to have to go back and take another look at our American history. We are going to have to accept what we have done to another nation of people the Vietnamese, their homeland and their children. Although it was done accidentally by the United States government which was unknowingly aware of the horrendous damages and insurmountable health problems created and understand we are unintentionally at fault. Why! Simply because it happened. It is not just the Vietnam Veterans who indeed need to be vindicated we also must look at what we have done as a nation to innocent men, women and children in Vietnam. We are going to have to ask ourselves are we willing to continue to allow the chemical companies involved to deny their position of fault in the creation of "Agent Orange?" Another question is why they released Agent Orange without thoroughly testing and researching it's contagious and dangerously toxic nature. When other chemicals are mixed with TCDD (dioxin) its abilities to do damage hasn't any limitations. This was already known by the chemical companies before "Agent Orange" was released to be sprayed over our soldiers in the jungles of Vietnam. Are we going to sit back another fifty years and wait for the children and grandchildren of the Vietnam Veterans to begin to die off? To suffer knowing they had no dog in the fight. Like we have waited for the Vietnam Veterans which are still dying and fighting for their benefits while facing their death bed. They are waiting for their claims to be approved from what "Agent Orange" has done to them for over forty years. And the Vietnam Veterans have also had to watch their friends and relatives die without receiving their benefits from "Agent Orange." Once again, we have to look at the Institute of Medicine (IOM) whose name has been changed to the Health & Medicine Division (HMD) to see if they will give the proper researched reports that will differ from their colleagues in order for the Veterans Administration (VA) to be able to approve the claims filed by the Vietnam Veterans. We also need to look at hiring government research teams instead of non-governmental organizations to step in and help with the research of "Agent Orange." My question once again is who is hiring the non-governmental researchers of "Agent Orange." There seems to be a problem with the corroboration of information being researched as it relates to the soldier's health problems and the unrelated findings the HMD and other non-governmental organizations are coming up with that may or may not be intentional to what the claims the Vietnam Veterans are filing. Will we now wait to see if the Vietnam Veterans children who are being born with deformities will continue the process of filing claims for medical and financial assistance to help with their battle against "Agent Orange". This is where we are headed as a nation. Will we stand by and watch the innocent children of our American soldiers start to die off or suffer because we have not pushed to expose this inexcusable problem as it relates to the Vietnam Veterans and "Agent Orange?" How long will it take before we start to look at the great grandchildren of the Vietnam Veterans to see if they are being born with the same genetic problems as their parents. Will the great grandchildren inherited "Agent Orange" in their DNA as an unexpected gift for their parents as the chemical was genetically transferred into their DNA? Which is an inheritance that a sane person would not want. It is and will be much easier to assist them with what they need in order that we as a nation will be able and prepared to better understand what is taking place with the children and grandchildren of the Vietnam Veterans. The medical issues the Vietnam Veterans grandchildren are coming down with are quite disturbing this is why it is important to make this a priority to get this issue straight by literally investing more federal funding to research "Agent Orange." It is better for everyone to get this taken care of now then to let it linger as it has for the past fifty years. As I stated earlier the Vietnam Veterans are dying by the thousands. It is estimated that at least 390 will be dying a week, which mean we will be losing at least 2730 a month. There is estimated to be about 850,000 Vietnam Veterans alive. If my math is correct, 131,040 will be dying each year. Even if we look at an estimated six years and six months for the 850,000 that are left there will not be any more Vietnam Veterans because of "Agent Orange". Now let me throw in the age factor. The average age of Vietnam Veteran who joined at the age of eighteen years old should be at least seventy-six years old. This means most certainly that age will also be a determining factor in their future as far as collecting any claims are concerned. Realistically they might see another six years given all the medical problems, their age and health issues involved. Another six years and six months would really be pushing their life expectancy.

What remains to be unresolved and I have to ask, is how is it that these life and death statistics can be given in relations to the Vietnam Veterans life expectancy without at least some coincidental findings from the research that has been done? What remains evident is that TCDD (dioxin) = "Agent Orange" which is supposedly not the common denominator in this issue which has given so much credence to the life expectancy of the soldiers if it's not considered to be a part of the equation of research which has already been discovered? They have to base their facts on their findings in order to say 390 Vietnam Veterans are estimated to die a day. When in fact "Agent Orange" is and has always been the main factor in the equation as it relates to the medical and health issues of the Vietnam Veterans and their life expectancy. What is not speculative is the diagnosis of the Vietnam Veterans children and grandchildren. Agent Orange has passed into their DNA genetically and is now in their blood. The one unexpected thing that happened concerning "Agent Orange" is that it was the TCDD that became genetically transferred into the Vietnam Veterans children's DNA. Of which I am certain was not a part of the plan when "Agent Orange" was being sprayed on our American soldiers in Vietnam. I will not excuse the prior statement because although it was an accident which happened on our governments watch. You still have to understand that it did happen. We have the Vietnam Veterans who have been dying off for the past forty years behind this mistake. Now because of the lack of research we have the children, grandchildren and possibly great grandchildren in the future who could also possibly be dying because of "Agent Orange in their DNA." There is no stopping unless proper research is done by those who are hired to do the research and not cover up the truth. All of this is factual information concerning Agent Orange and the chemical companies who created it knew exactly what the outcome would be. And the importance of human life was not taken into consideration. What we don't know is how many children of the Vietnam Veterans have had children who were born contaminated? How many girlfriends of soldiers who returned home from Vietnam were infected? What we do know is because TCDD (dioxin) the highly toxic chemical herbicide was genetically transferred to the grandchildren they are now being born with deformities in 2019. Of which are listed in the website http://www.healthfreedoms.org/agent-orange-is-causing-horrific-birth-defects

If you are brave enough to have read this far then you most certainly are bold enough to understand the importance of knowing why the Health & Medicine Division (HMD) a non-governmental organization that researches "Agent Orange" does not want to admit to new findings on "Agent Orange" their findings will remain inconclusive. Due to the facts of the same reasons found in the true story in Erin Brokovich case that the chemical companies involved do not want to admit fault. So, they hide behind the settlement agreements whereby the charges brought up against them would be considered by law to have somewhat never existed, once you settle. But now we are looking at a new venue of health problems of which involves the grandchildren diagnosis of what "Agent Orange" is doing to them. The grandchildren of the Vietnam Veterans are suffering from genetically transmitted "Agent Orange" which has passed from their parents into their DNA. Remember these are innocent children that were not a part of the war. Grandchildren of the Vietnam Veterans and they, "had no dog in the fight." Will we in hindsight watch these children die as we have watched our Vietnam Veterans die? If nothing is done and we sit back and watch for another fifty years we can expect the same results. Eventually the grandchildren are going to suffer and die from the highly toxic herbicide chemical TCDD (dioxin) that is now in their DNA. No matter how we turn the dial and try to look for a positive outcome research remains to be the only key to their future of hope.

One story that was up close and personal for me was when I told an older lady that I was writing a book on the Vietnam Veterans she said, "thank you, they need all of the support they can get." She did not want her name exposed but she went on to tell me what had happened in her life. She said her husband was a Vietnam Veterans and had just passed away. The other shocking news that came from out of her mouth came within seconds when she told me her daughter who was only 36 had just had a major heart attack and died just weeks after her father. Because of failed research by these non-governmental people be prepared to hear more stories like this as time goes on about young children passing. The Health & Medicine Division (HMD) which is a non-governmental organization continues to say they have the best world picked researchers who are also non-government employees that refuse to link the highly toxic TCDD (dioxin) with the herbicide chemical in "Agent Orange" and say it was the reason for the health problems the Vietnam Veterans have had for over forty years. Since the grandchildren now have TCDD which is the scientific name in their DNA it is going to be an amazing story on how the non-governmental top researchers in the world who may possibly be protecting the chemical companies are going to explain this one away? What this discovery has led to is that our American Vietnam Veterans stated what they were going through due to "Agent Orange" over forty years ago and no one wanted to listen to them. Now that their children and grandchildren who were not in Vietnam but were born after the soldiers returned home from Vietnam have acquire the toxic chemical TCDD (dioxin) in their DNA. I do want to state for the record "Agent Orange" is not a myth or a hoax, it's a real killer and our Vietnam Veterans have been dying for years behind it. "Agent Orange" is the most toxic of the six chemical agents used during the Vietnam War. Unfortunately, it has left lots of residue behind and no one wants to take responsibility for what they have created. When we talk about killing babies in the womb that is what's literally taking place today. The grandchildren of the Vietnam Veterans are being born with other health issues not only cancer. These innocent children are being born with inflammatory bowel diseases, spinal problems, malformed limbs, speech difficulties, heart disease, cleft lip palate, webbed toes, fibromyalgia, arthritis, crooked fingers and autism. They are also being born with birth defects that consist of but are not limited to missing limbs, and extra limbs. These are just some of the physical discrepancies that can be listed. Simply because many of their wounds are visual to the human eye. What we cannot see is the mental deformities before the baby is born. Will there be any form of mental illness involved in this child's life in the future? Will the grandchildren be able to have a normal childhood knowing this toxic chemical is in their body eating away? We already know TCDD a named carcinogen did in fact affect the Vietnam Veterans entire life after the war and continues to this day 2019 going into 2020. Will TCDD affect the children learning capabilities? Their analytical and coping abilities? How will "Agent Orange" affect parts of their body, will it affect their vital organs, will their motion and movement be affected? These are questions which will have to be answered through more research and funding needed for "Agent Orange." There is so much to look at of which nothing has been resolved concerning the Vietnam Veterans dying from their unprotected contact with the highly toxic chemical "Agent Orange." Now we have found that their children and grandchildren have it in their DNA. Who in their right mind wants to see a newborn baby go through all of this? I must say this to the chemical companies what programs or monies has been put aside or have been set up to support these children if they are blessed to be able to grow up to become adults. We already know TCDD is a carcinogen which means it is cancerous. So, there are even greater odds of these children being diagnosed with cancer in the future. One of the most painful parts of this entire book is the Vietnam Veterans have received very little for so many years of suffering for something they did not cause. Their bodies have literally been taken apart piece by piece and there remains to date a lack of admission of fault no apology no nothing. What is not being acknowledged here is no one had asked them to go to war to fight, but they fought for you and it did not matter whether you were a democrat or republican, they fought for America. No one asked them to deny themselves, but they did. No one has stood up and said, well how is it that your non-government organizations said you could not find any medical or health related problems that "Agent Orange" has caused the Vietnam Veterans. So, please tell me if the evidence does not speak for itself, how in the world did their children and grandchildren get the chemical in their blood? Their grandchildren birth defects are because of defective genes transmitted from the Vietnam Veteran to his wife or girlfriend and from inside of his wife or girlfriend a baby grew from the contaminated and toxic sperm which carries blood inside of the mother's uterus. Now we have given the United States of America another issue of "Agent Orange" which is more than likely not going away any time soon. The children and grandchildren are being born with the noted health problems I have listed above. This is the reason why once again more research is going to have to be done to help to control what has gotten out of hand and bring some normalcy to the table. This is something our Vietnam Veterans, their children nor their grandchildren asked for. What medical funding is going to be set up for the future treatment of their medical and health needs? Once the TCDD (dioxin) begins to make them the host as it did the Vietnam Veterans and begin to feed off their organs and damage the organs in their body? That is the one thing you can rest assured of that medical programs and funding for such programs will be needed for the children and grandchildren of the Vietnam Veterans. It appears that the nightmare of "Agent Orange" is not going away by itself anytime soon. More intense research is needed. And must be funded in order to understand this uncontrollable chemical TCDD that was released directly on our Vietnam Veterans over forty years ago. It continues to haunt the Vietnam Veterans, the government and citizens of the United States of America. With the chemical companies going with the settlement agreements in the past. One would think there would not be any recourse should anything else pop up in the future involving "Agent Orange". That is most certainly not the case since the chemical company's did leave out a few niches to cover themselves. No one was aware of what was going to take place in the future. And who would have thought it would be almost forty years down the road as far as time was concerned that "Agent Orange" would raise its ugly face once again. Only this time it is not in the Vietnam Veterans or the Vietnam Veteran's children. I am certain what I am about to say will astound you. What is being found out now is the grandchildren of the Vietnam Veterans has the TCDD genetically transferred and infused in their DNA. These beautiful American babies are being born with deformities. For the good of all humanity do not think for one second it has only affected our American children genetically. You must be made aware that over the 39,000 square miles the highly toxic carcinogenic chemical herbicide "Agent Orange" was spread over in Vietnam is causing even more serious birth defects and deformities in the Vietnamese born and unborn babies today. There were so many things that were not considered as it relates to settlements and future programs being set up for those who had been diagnosed with cancer as a result of being in contact with "Agent Orange." What is even more horrifying is the land, rivers, water, lakes and vegetation over in Vietnam that the Vietnamese and their children have had to live with for fifty years now. Let's stop for a second and take a closer look at the problems caused by the highly toxic carcinogenic chemical herbicide TCDD (dioxin) = "Agent Orange". We have talked about the Vietnam Veterans, their children and grandchildren who are affected. We have talked a little about the Vietnamese men, women and children who are affected. What we have not discussed is how the highly toxic carcinogenic chemical herbicide has affected the animals in the area. Since they have been breeding did, they pass the toxic chemical genetically into their offspring? What affects has it had on the animals in Vietnam? Some of the animals that have been contaminated by "Agent Orange" are being hunted for game and some for food. It's not just the four-legged animals you also have to look at the fish and birds. In the villages of Vietnam that encircles the areas in which

"Agent Orange" was sprayed the wildlife must have also been affected. Which would mean that every animal that is breeding and some who cross breed has infected one another. I know I am asking you a lot of questions in this book, but I have to in order to get you to think. My next question is how badly has the animals been affected since their body mass is smaller, and what has been the extent of their suffering? If the Vietnamese are hunting these animals for food, then they are eating contaminated meat? "Agent Orange" was sprayed over 39,000 square feet of Vietnam. There was 20,000,000 U.S. gallons of different agents sprayed over the jungles of Vietnam. 11,000,000 was "Agent Orange. And those areas that were sprayed were considered to be way above the normal rate and toxic level that should have been used in one area. The drinking water in parts of Northern Vietnam is contaminated with arsenic levels 50 times higher than Vietnamese standards (read the July 1 issue of Environmental Science & Technology dated July 6, 2001). "Agent Orange" has contaminated the lakes, ponds, streams and rivers of Vietnam. This would also mean the fish the Vietnamese catch to feed their families are also contaminated with "Agent Orange." Further research and studies should reveal not only is the Vietnamese drinking water, streams, rivers, ponds and lakes are polluted. We also have to look at the existence of the chemical TCDD and its survival needs. How does it live? What is its needs and means of survival? Does it need a host to survive or is it possible for it to survive on its own? Since we are now aware the water is 50 times its arsenic standard level, we must also realize the fish in the waters in Vietnam, Laos and Cambodia are not safe to eat. Just like the animals that at one time fed off the trees, leaves and vegetation would be contaminated from eating from its fruit trees, leaves, vegetation and contaminated animals eating one another. Fish that eat other fish pass on the contamination as they continue to feed. Mating would be something similar to what the Vietnam Veterans did to pass their DNA genetically to the genes of their children. The same applies to the fish in mating they will transfer TCDD (dioxin) to their offspring. As you can see there are major problems that needs to be corrected for everyone to be able to move on and heal.

Denial! Denial! Denial! Monsanto is being sued once again; this is the second case they have been found guilty in. March 20, 2019, after another customer develops cancer from using Monsanto's product Roundup weed killer. Another jury finds them guilty for failure to warn customers of the potential cancer risks which is glyphosate considered to be in the weed killer Roundup. Monsanto's continues to deny that it's their product that is the cause of the cancer the people are claiming to have. It must be something else? Humm, well please inform us as to what exactly you think it might be. Right now, as far as the giant agricultural company, Monsanto, is concerned they are getting hit with verdicts of guilty, guilty, guilty. All the ducks are quacking, and they are all quacking about the same thing, your product Roundup, the cancer it is causing and Monsanto's failure to inform the public. I guess if you look at it realistically if Monsanto agricultural company did put on their warning label that their product is classified to be a human carcinogen then who would buy it. So, Monsanto agricultural company remains in denial just like they remain in denial when spoken to about "Agent Orange" and the health problems it has caused through the years in relation to cancer. The only thing that is consistent with their products is that they have a cancer trail of victims no one has taken responsibility for. One of its major victims are the Vietnam Veterans and how they have suffered with cancer for over forty years now due to Monsanto and a few other companies making "Agent Orange." Now we have farmers and everyday people, people who love doing their gardening and taking care of their lawn are coming down with cancer. For a better word called the lack of (RESEARCH). There is no doubt that what was once being held back from the public has now altered the lives of so many people. Yes!!! It's "Agent Orange" and the culprits behind the making of "Agent Orange" has altered the lives of so many people who have fallen victim to cancer. Jurors are now saying Monsanto intentionally withheld information from the public about Roundup having a chemical (glyphosate) which is classified by the EPA as being a human carcinogen and the product does cause cancer in people. Here is the science of dioxin, **"Dioxins are a family of compounds that share distinct chemical structures and characteristics. Numerous dioxin-like compounds have been identified that are considered to have significant toxicity and can cause disease. The singular term dioxin refers to the most toxic compound, TCDD."** What many of you do not know is that Monsanto and several other companies settled out of court when it came down to admitting that "Agent Orange" was cancerous and that it was the cause of all of the health problems the Vietnam Veterans have today. No that is not the case what transpires when there is a settlement no one accepts fault. There is no finalization of fault and no judgement against anyone due to the other party accepting the settlement offer. This means that the companies who are brought to court are still able to function and continue with "busy as usual the very next day." When we take for instance the contributory factors of why the Vietnam Veterans have suffered for so long. Do we really need to ask whose fault is it? In hindsight many people who are in position to protect their friends normally do. Some people would say that is the American way of life. I am saying this because from the looks of it all and with all of the so-called top professionals involved with the research of "Agent Orange" from what I have discovered that is exactly what the researchers have presented to not only the Veterans Administration, but also to the Vietnam Veterans, the President, Congress and the Senate. That they do not have any intent on ever finding anything wrongfully connected with "Agent Orange." As far as it being carcinogenic because their colleagues before them did not find anything connected and those are the notes they are going to follow. It would be against the researcher's better judgment to go against a comrade, another researcher who deals with the agency and those they sit and sup with. What gives a little light to the inadequacies in the non-governmental researchers hired is that every two years they are given time to research for new findings to find new developments in the herbicide chemical "Agent Orange" and submit a new report to the Veterans Administration showing those findings. This must be done in order for the Veterans Administration to move forward in getting old claims the Vietnam Veterans had filed taken care of. If there are companies who have settled out of court and have set up funding for medical attention needs and health care needs for the Vietnam Veterans who have been exposed to "Agent Orange" please note the need is much greater today. Because of what we are finding out concerning everyone "Agent Orange" has affected. There are no relations to cancer is what the chemical companies are saying, but the EPA is saying different. The EPA is saying that "Agent Orange" is carcinogenic and causing cancer in those who were exposed to "Agent Orange" during the Vietnam War. These companies continue to say that TCDD is not carcinogenic and it has very little significance to the Vietnam Veterans medical and health problems, but the soldiers continue to visit their doctors and hospitals for surgery until they are dead. These companies moved to settle out of court and their settlements have been worth far less than what the Vietnam Veterans, their children and their children's children could ever be repaid. The one thing money cannot buy is life. And this is exactly what was taken from the Vietnam Veterans, their life. There isn't any amount of money that could ever restore, remake or replace a person's life.

CHAPTER XXVII

LAW SUITES AND SETTLEMENTS ON AGENT ORANGE

IT APPEARS AS THOUGH we have forgotten the Vietnam Veterans were Americans. They served their country by fighting in a war that appears to have been one of the most senseless wars America has fought in. Yet, one of the most devastating wars involving America due to so many Vietnam Veterans killed defending it. The question I and many Americans ask is, "who won the war" and exactly what were we in Vietnam fighting for? Can either America or Vietnam claim the victory? These are questions no one to this day are able to answer. The lives lost were senseless and unnecessary and money was paid to American citizens for their sons who gave their life. I must say this is the one thing that was done in behalf of the soldiers who lost their life. Their families received money from the government as a show of compassion, empathy and appreciation for a great loss. Even with all of the monies given out to the families the memory of their son leaving and not returning home alive will always be on their mind. The memory of their son returning home in a body bag will be the last memory they will have of him. The gift of God is eternal life. Every last one of the Vietnam Veterans who served and did not run exemplified courage, tenacity and a willingness to stand and fight for a cause they believed in and a country called the United States of America and every citizen in it. It did not make a difference whether you were Black, White, Jewish, Greek, Hebrew, Spanish, Italian, Latin, Muslim, or any other ethnicity. They went to war to protect everyone in the great "Melting Pot." The Vietnam Veterans laid down their life with love and it was for love which became their God given drive for the greater love and freedoms of all Americans, foreign and domestic that they fought. Whether you are a Democrat or Republican they went to war for everyone in America and willingly gave their life for their friends, for a much greater love. As a nation we remained non-responsive over the past forty-five years to the cries of the Vietnam Veterans. Their cries that said look at what "Agent Orange" is doing to us. It has been over forty years now and the Vietnam Veterans are still crying out for your help. We have continued a journey where change as far as findings are concerned in favor of the Vietnam Veterans is a word that is lost in time. Yet their wounds from "Agent Orange" continue to worsen but the research findings remain inconclusive. Unless you have been paying close attention, time is not something they have a lot left of as far as life is concerned. At the rate of 131,040 dying a year who is going to be there to pick up the pieces. I have not met one Vietnam Veterans yet who has not told me he was having to go to the hospital or into surgery the following week for some health issue relating to "Agent Orange." It sad that I have to say it this way but America this is one check concerning the Vietnam Veterans and how they have suffered. That your pockets will never be deep enough to write or to cash, the damage you have allowed to be done to these men is pernicious. This is where you have failed our soldiers and I say this because from the looks of what is taking place even in the courts today with the chemical companies. They are never going to admit to their product being at fault of causing cancer in people even though the Environmental Protection Agency says that TCDD (dioxin) is a human carcinogen. Therefore, we are where we are today with not just the Vietnam Veterans, but civilians are also coming down with cancer from chemical companies operating in their communities. Whether it is TCDD (dioxin), Chromium 6, Glyphosate, or Ethylene Oxide, cancer does not discriminate and the companies that are making it are only trying to create a product that can be sold to the public so they can make money. Look at how many years it has taken before Monsanto agricultural company has now been questioned in a court of law and found guilty of lying in court with an intent of intentionally misleading the public with its product, Roundup. Monsanto still defends their product by saying it is not carcinogenic (cancer causing). As I stated earlier in the book Monsanto was one of the companies involved in Vietnam that made the chemical herbicide called "Agent Orange". Due to not wanting to lose their right to manufacture chemical products and trying to avoid being sued by multiple people. Monsanto agricultural company and other chemical companies refused to reveal the facts about their products possibly being contributory to cancer being found in human beings. Despite what the EPA has stated in their reports many of these companies would rather deny the faults discovered in their products and issue out a check for settlement than to admit their products are at fault and not be able to practice anymore. Giving no regards to human life only money. Due to so many deaths involved concerning "Agent Orange" and the billions of dollars involved in back payment owed to the Vietnam Veterans companies are more than likely to go bankrupt. And from looking at their situation prophetically as far as the opposition is concerned. It is easier for them to deny their products being at fault in causing cancer than to accept fault. What remains to be kept very quiet also is the suffering of the Vietnamese. The damages done to their villages that have been contaminated. The birth defects of their children and how the 39,000 square miles of which 20,000,000 gallons of different chemicals were sprayed with 11 million being "Agent Orange" was sprayed over the jungles of Vietnam. Which reached 50 times the standard level of toxicity in the areas in which they lived. Therefore, I am revealing to you some of the settlement agreements in this chapter of which some of the lawsuits were settled in the millions. I would like to save the total stats of all lives lost during the Vietnam War close to the end of the book which will help to understand why a lawsuit was needed to be brought against the chemical companies, so many lives wasted due to pertinent information that went undistributed. Just like I am discussing the problems of what appears to be taking place with the chemical companies and their denial of any wrong doings at this point in the book. Mainly because [knock, knock, knock] I do not want you to forget the importance of what has been taken for granted for so many years. It is important to remember the suffering of those who died for you in order that you can live in a "Free World". Okay, let's take a look at some of the settlement agreements made. Please pay close attention to this chapter because you are going to find out just how the chemical companies involved with the making of "Agent Orange" concealed the information for monetary gain during the Vietnam War. The same concealment takes place with Monsanto who did not reveal information as it relates to the product Roundup. You will also learn a lot about the settlements that took place and if there is a possibility for an attorney to go back and sue again due to information that was intentionally overlooked or just not heard. You can also look at new findings in relations to "Agent Orange" where the grandchildren and great grandchildren have been coming down with deformities some at birth and it has recently been discovered that the children's DNA also carries some of the herbicide chemical "Agent Orange." Hopefully since there is so much going on with the chemical companies right now especially, Monsanto agricultural company and their product (Roundup) we just might be able to come up with a legal remedy. And since the jurors stated Monsanto agricultural company has not been truthful with the public and has jeopardized the health of innocent human beings due to information they intentionally withheld. There just might be some attorneys out there who are willing to step in and represent the better interest of the Vietnam Veterans. And help them to get what they truly deserved when they first returned home in the seventies because of what the chemical companies did not report in their findings of which are still not conclusive. American citizens have their conclusive findings of "Agent Orange" and of course this book speaks for the random Vietnam Veterans and people I was blessed with the opportunity to randomly meet. Some I spoke briefly with in the mall, restaurants, hobby stories etc. These were soldiers who were hurt by the government and the citizens of America which has failed to render them an apology. For the wrong that was done to the Vietnam Veterans prior to them leaving Vietnam that "Agent Orange" is the cause of their failing health, medical problems as well as the cause of the many forms of cancer they suffer from. Why should the American citizens have to wait another forty years and watch the children and grandchildren of the Vietnam Veterans suffer the way the Vietnam Veterans suffered and are still suffering. This is why we need to hire governmental researchers and not nongovernmental people to research the different effects "Agent Orange" has had on the Vietnam Veterans. The eleven companies who were originally named in the lawsuit are listed as follows:

The list of the chemical companies involved were published 2017-04-10 in an article titled:

"In re Agent Orange Product Liability Litigation (1979-1984)"

1. **Dow Chemical Company**
2. **Thompson-Hayward**
3. **Diamond Shamrock**
4. **Monsanto Agricultural Company**
5. **Hercules Inc.**
6. **Ansul Company**
7. **Riverdale Chemical Company**
8. **Uniroyal**
9. **Occidental Petroleum Company**
10. **N.A. Phillips**
11. **Hooker Chemical Company**

What continues to be quite intriguing to me is that evidence continually conveyed to the judge was not heard and the military was for a lack of choice words ushered into a settlement agreement they did not want. Which caused the lawyers who were fighting the class Action lawsuit to have to settle for 180 million dollars. Of which I personally feel was not acceptable for the soldier's attorneys who were given no other choice but to settle if the judge is not going to allow damaging evidence to be presented in court. The settlement agreement of 180 million dollars would not carry enough funding neither was it a large enough settlement for the problems "Agent Orange" was going to cause in the future for some of the soldiers. They were already having mental, physical and emotional problems the Vietnam Veterans lives were literally just torn apart. That settlement most certainly was not going to take care of the Vietnam Veterans children or their unborn grandchildren. Looking even further down the road what has turned out to be at stake here is what was also not considered in the lawsuit and that is the grandchildren and great-grandchildren of the Vietnam Veterans. They are now being born with deformities from the impact of "Agent Orange" an herbicide chemical which contained TCDD and noted by the EPA to be a highly toxic human carcinogen. Which means it was a chemical that will cause cancer in humans. Unfortunately, as time continues to move another important factor that was not revealed to the government before using the chemical "Agent Orange" was that the chemical TCDD (dioxin) which is the most deadliest of all chemicals when mixed. It would not only cause cancer in the Vietnam Veterans, but it would also be passed genetically transferred into the DNA of their unborn children and grandchildren. These are very critical and crucial facts that either were not revealed to the judge or just went undiscovered because there weren't any new findings to look at. Either way it would seem that the chemical companies having the responsibility of what would be considered, thoroughly researching their products before allowing them to be released to the public. Even more so to be used in military jungle warfare where the friendly soldiers would be just as susceptible to any diseases or future medical problems as the enemy they were combating. Some of the areas that were sprayed contaminated both soil and water of which the concentration levels were fifty times greater. Of course, beyond the level which were considered to be safe by the United States Environmental Protection Agency as well as the protection agency for the Vietnamese. Our Vietnam Veterans were in just as much danger of being contaminated as the enemy they were fighting. Please keep in mind our American soldiers were eating, sleeping, bathing, washing and drinking the same air, water and everything else the Vietnamese were. They were actually living in a contaminated environment. Of which we are finding out fifty years later that the soil, trees and shrubs have not been able to reproduce. Nothing can grow. Which only shows us this chemical TCDD was and is highly toxic and the magnitude of the research that should have been implemented before it was released never happened. Our Vietnam Veterans, children and grandchildren are suffering. The Vietnamese who lived in the jungles of Vietnam families also suffer even greater lost years later. From what research is showing it has been fifty years and nothing is growing in the areas "Agent Orange" was used or sprayed over. The Vietnamese land, water, vegetation, irrigation and farmland, food supply and fish remain contaminated from the 11,000,000 gallons of highly toxic TCDD (dioxin) "Agent Orange" that was sprayed over Vietnam. Those numbers of 11,000,000 U. S. gallons are recorded. This is also what was used MC-1 Hourglass, pump systems and 1,000 U. S. gallons (3,800L) chemical tanks. On the ground there were spray missions that took place from trucks, boats, and backpacks of the soldiers. It is clear to say the chemical companies had a contract with the government to produce the herbicide chemicals needed to help the United States to win the war. We all understand the missions had to be completed and the chemical companies had to complete their obligation in accordance to the contract drawn up or forfeit the monies paid. But on the other hand, the chemical companies were also under an obligation to the United States government, its citizens and soldiers. To convey the dangers of the use of the product purchased under any circumstance, in this case it would be "Agent Orange" the most deadliest and most toxic chemical used to kill the foliage in Vietnam. The chemical companies did not reveal the problems "Agent Orange" would cause because they never completed their research. There aren't any conclusive findings to reveal how "Agent Orange should and should have not been used. And if they would have completed the much-needed research instead of looking for a big government contract and payoff. From what I have read about "Agent Orange" it should have never been released in an open and uncontrolled environment. Judge George C. Pratt made it very clear to the chemical companies that if they were going to try to use the government contract defense and be dismissed from the case, they would have to prove the following:

(1) The companies must first show that the government gave them the specifications for orders of Agent Orange.
(2) The company met those specifications in the Agent Orange they supplied to the government.
(3) The government had more information about the risks of Agent Orange than did the companies.

These three questions presented to the chemical companies are what brought Judge George C. Pratt to the determination that only a full trial could determine whether any of these requirements were met. The three questions presented to the chemical companies are all damaging and could not be answered with any form of evidence from the chemical companies. This was due to the chemical company's negligence in their own behalf knowing it would have been impossible for them to have told the government of the dangers involved with "Agent Orange" because they would have lost their contract with the government. If they would have told the United States President, at the time was John F. Kennedy, the Congress and the Senate they were using TCDD (dioxin) in "Agent Orange" and it was going to cause chaos in the United States for more than fifty years. And the Vietnam Veterans would be returning home with the insides of their bodies contaminated with the toxic chemical herbicide inside of them. Nevertheless, I am certain the President and both Houses would have said there is no way you are going to use this kind of highly toxic chemical with our soldiers in the area and there is no validated research to present to our government its limitations. Getting back to the documented information concerning the court case on why the ruling of 180 million was the settlement agreed is because another judge took over in 1983 Judge Jack B. Weinstein. Due to Judge Pratt not filing a formal dismissal of the United States government from the case. Judge Weinstein reopened the issue of the government role in: In re Agent Orange, holding the government liable for the birth defects of the children of the Vietnam Veterans. Due to this case being reopened the men and women claims of injury against the US government were barred under federal law. But were not barred where the Vietnam Veterans children, grandchildren and possibly great grandchildren who were genetically affected. It was not their fault their parents fought in the Vietnam War to defend the Constitution of the United States of America and was exposed to excessive amounts of Agent Orange. The government was liable for their injuries because the children did not acquire their birth defects as men or women of the armed forces due to the course of military service. This ruling would set off a great impact in future medical aide and support of the children of the Vietnam Veterans. It established a new venue for a different case study, a new lawsuit that Vietnam Veteran's children may sue the government for developmental damages. We must give a big Whoa! To Judge Weinstein and the foresight he presented in preparation of taking care of the unborn children of the Vietnam Veterans. But if by chance there was going to be damages which needed to be filed by the children of the Vietnam Veterans the door was open for such. Due to other negotiation that needed to be met it would be unconstitutional when given the high cost of today's standard of living based on the right now attitude and the extreme cost of proper medical treatment or even hospitalization. This would be consistent with what the Vietnam Veterans needed in relations to health care and medical needs. The other thing that would have had to have been considered was a lifetime of medical care, surgery and hospital visits or stays which would have been an unpredictable amount to have settled out of court. Cancer treatment can be quite costly as well as birth deformities that developed on their newly born babies. Because these surgeries would cost the families lots of money to correct the deformities more monies would be needed to be put aside for the unborn children. In May of 2019 a couple was just awarded two billion dollars against Monsanto because of their cancer-causing product Roundup. What was left unquestioned by Judge Weinstein is what the chemical companies knew about the chemical in question. The chemical companies were fully aware of what they had created which means they knew the mixture of the chemical TCDD (dioxin) would create problems with the Vietnam Veterans health and that the damages would not be able to be controlled. The attorney's fighting the case in behalf of the Vietnam Veterans would not have settled for a mere 180 million. Documentation was presented and was not heard, or should I say it was presented and ignored. Unfortunately, you cannot ignore cancer. The judge was repeatedly told they have physical evidence to prove the chemical companies knew all the time what mixing TCDD was going to do in their creation of "Agent Orange" and they continued to produce it. The Vietnam Veterans health and medical issues were just as real then as they are today. Real life-threatening illnesses then which have grown even worse today due to continual neglect and denial of the dangers involving the use of the highly toxic herbicide chemical "Agent Orange". The very same chemical TCDD that contaminate the bodies of

Vietnam Veterans when it was mixed with other chemicals and called "Agent Orange" is the same human carcinogen that has lived inside of the bodies of our Vietnam Veterans today. During past years we have trusted companies who were brought to court to tell the truth. There was a time when a man's word was his bond. It is unfortunate it has taken over forty years to find the testimony given to the courts by the chemical companies could possibly be in question. It is with grave concern that we go back and take a closer look at what was not heard or admitted as evidence in court verses the facts of why our Vietnam Veterans have died off so quickly. I will give you the yearly expected deaths of the Vietnam Veterans for one year, estimated to die 131,040. Why so many illnesses? Why so many medical operations? Why so many hospital visits? Why so many heart, kidney, liver, and pancreas problems for the Vietnam Veterans? Why? Why? Why? These are questions we are looking at today that must be answered. In the process of answering these questions the Vietnam Veterans must be given the opportunity to be vindicated for what the chemical companies have been allowed to hide, and that is the truth. The chemical companies knew what was going to take place all the time. Although evidence presented in the case of "In re Agent Orange Product Liability Litigation (1979-1984) new evidence must be presented. Which should start with probable fraud that was committed and the chemical company's intent to mislead Judge Weinstein. The chemical companies withheld damaging evidence which involved warning information on the highly toxic TCDD (dioxin) was at that time. It is still considered to be the most dangerous of chemicals used today. It was most certainly the most toxic deadly chemical used during the Vietnam War and it was sprayed on our Vietnam Veterans. But chemical companies like Monsanto remained subtle as though there wasn't any real danger. Even though the EPA found TCDD to be a human carcinogen the companies remain steadfast in their product. They are going against the Environmental Protection Agency (EPA) warning and saying that TCDD is not a human carcinogen. The fact of the matter is the companies were fully aware of the dangers and did not convey their concerns to the President of the United States of America. They did not convey their concerns to the Armed Forces of the United States of America. They did not have a commitment, a vow or moral values to protect human life. If they would have given honest testimony it would have given the chemical companies some credibility of trying to be truthful as was as sympathetic to what was taking place with the soldiers. By presenting the facts of what they had already known about the highly toxic chemical herbicide. What the chemical companies' findings should have said is that "Agent Orange" was dangerous and should not be used in an open and free environment, it must be contained. But instead the chemical companies reframed from committing to the truth and withheld pertinent information concerning what they knew about the chemical herbicide they created. This information was not allowed to be heard in court; it was continuously suppressed. When looking at hindsight can you see the lives that could have been saved. The suffering that could have been avoided. The soldiers, our American brothers, the Vietnam Veterans would have never had to go through all the pain they have carried for over forty years if the chemical companies would have used better judgement and tried to find a solution forty years ago. The Vietnam Veterans have continually through the years been going back and forth to Washington, DC. They are going there to present their case to Congress and the Senate as to the health problems "Agent Orange" had caused them. The chemical companies did not show any concerns for the soldiers who had died or their families. These soldiers are literally being eaten up by the TCDD and the chemical companies still would not admit fault. Not then and not today as these chemical companies are continually being brought to court for not following proper procedures to protect the citizens of America and all human life. We must also be concerned with animal life as well since a lot of chemical companies bury their waste in the ground or in the sea. The companies aren't giving any credence to the truth. Not during the Vietnam War and definitely not today's society after watching what's taking place in small cities in Illinois like Willowbrook, Illinois and Waukegan, Illinois. People are coming down with different kinds of cancers both male and female due to (Ethylene Oxide). They said its being released in the air by a chemical company near their community called Sterigenics. Monsanto Agricultural Company has been named in a lawsuit for their product (Roundup) causing cancer in people. The hideous thing about all the chemical companies involved in lawsuits is they have in common one specific testimony. No matter how the evidence points to them being guilty, "**They are convinced it is not their product or their company that is causing cancer**" in people or anyone else. Once again this is after the Environmental Protection Agency has stepped in to investigate the companies that are being reported. Through further research the test cannot be substantiated in some chemical companies because the wind might be bellowing in the opposite direction their readers are set up.

Therefore, giving a false reading or an unvalidated reading due to the wind blowing away from the testers. One day the reading may be high due to the wind blowing directly into the instruments reading the toxic levels. On other days the toxicity levels will be low due to the wind blowing in another direction that is not directed to the testers reading the toxicity levels. This can be a problem especially if an investigation is being done and instruments are set up and the wind is blowing the opposite direction. In the matter concerning the Vietnam Veterans the issues of "Agent Orange" remain unresolved because the chemical agents are still being researched, at least "Agent Orange" specifically is being researched by non-governmental individuals who are supposed to be the best in their field. If that is truly the case, I am certain it would not take over forty years to come to some kind of understanding of the product their own companies created. It is obviously damaging information that has been withheld intentionally concerning the problems the herbicide chemical "Agent Orange" has caused as well as the lives it has wreaked havoc in for over forty years. What we are finding out today in relations to the problems TCDD, Ethylene Oxide, Chromium 6, and Glyphosate are the four chemicals listed that I am aware of which are noted as being carcinogenic, meaning they cause cancer in humans. I don't know how many more there are that cause cancer in humans, but these are the four I am aware of? TCDD is equated with "Agent Orange", Ethylene Oxide is equated with Sterigenics Chemical Company, Chromium 6 is equated with the true story of Erin Brokovich and Glyphosate is equated with Monsanto Company (Roundup). But the monumental result high point which all the companies who have been either brought to court or charged with causing cancer due to the use of their products are all saying their product is not the cause. Although confession is good for the soul, I don't believe any of the chemical companies will ever admit to knowing the chemicals they put in some of their products are cancerous. Because once they admit to knowing their product causes cancer in humans, they will become liable. Even with the Environmental Protection Agency saying the product classified as a human carcinogen. Now take a look at the case of "In Re Agent Orange Product Liability Litigation (1979-1984) there are many things left in question? First question being since the case and its issues of "Agent Orange" was being base on the illnesses, medical problems and death of military soldiers. Did the people hearing the case not realize the importance of the soldiers, the Vietnam Veterans who gave their life for the betterment of this great nation should have been able to have the same judge who heard the case in the beginning but he was changed after four years of the initial hearing of the case? Secondly, is there any evidence that the United States government requested in any contract with the chemical companies to specifically use TCDD (dioxin) to create the most toxic chemical herbicide "Agent Orange?" Thirdly did the chemical companies release to the United States government any warning of not to use the chemical TCDD? What amazes me is the chemical companies already had knowledge of the damages TCDD would cause due to its uncontrollable nature? I don't feel that any of the three questions presented could have been answered in the affirmative because the most damaging evidence was not permitted during litigation prior to the settlement. Since physical evidence was not allowed to be presented in court that should raise an eyebrow or two knowing that due to the lack of damaging information not being admissible Vietnam Veterans were not able to file a massive rain of claims against the chemical companies. Due to this evidence not being heard left the doors open for the chemical companies to return back to work like they were never charged or contested in the affirmative to them being at fault for their product causing cancer in the Vietnam Veterans. One term of the settlement that was allowed in favor of the chemical companies was that the chemical companies renounced all liability for injuries in return they would establish a settlement trust. What remains to be un-soothingly disturbing is why the most devasting evidence the soldiers and the lawyers for the Vietnam Veterans tried to have heard was not given the freedom of being able to be presented: The companies were allowed to renounce liability. What should be disputed in future hearings is that despite the fact that over the duration of the case, the veterans and their attorneys had found messages sent by the chemical companies which validated facts for the defense team, that the chemical companies did in fact know about the toxic effects of Agent Orange. Hold onto your set for the finale this piece I am about to present is bigger than life. This evidence if it had been permitted would have changed the course of the suffering of so many of the Vietnam Veterans who watched their body being taken apart piece by piece until there was nothing left. If the evidence presented would have been heard it would have also put a stop to having to wait so long for their claims to be approved and some Vietnam Veterans are still being denied their claim today. The opening to prove what the Vietnam Veterans was saying all the time was true. Only the lawyers were not able to get it heard. It would have questioned the settlement of 180 million dollars which was nothing for eleven chemical companies to come up with. The Vietnam Veterans were on their way to being vindicated for all they had given to the United States of America but there was one glitch in the way. This evidence was not allowed to be heard as the Vietnam Veterans and their attorneys tried to let the judge see this was a case that would not have had to go to a settlement agreement. Simply because the defense had damaging evidence in their possession. **They had messages that were sent by the chemical companies saying the chemical companies new about the toxic effects of Agent Orange before** manufacturing it and had manufactured it anyway. If this new discovery was heard it would have made the chemical companies liable for the medical problems, hospitalization, operations etc. for the Vietnam Veterans and their children. And the cost would have been far more than 180-million-dollar to settle. As damaging as this evidence would have been it was not heard. Could it be heard in today's courts in representation of the fraud that is being committed today involving some of the same chemical companies? According to the evidence that was not allowed to be heard by the court if it were heard it would have easily convicted the chemical companies. **The evidence not heard was evidence of their own admission that they did in fact not tell the truth of them knowingly producing a chemical that would have such a massive negative effect in the homes, families and life of the Vietnam Veterans.** Don't forget those who watched their friends' bodies literally decomposing because of exposure to "Agent Orange." Should they give it another go in the court system today? Since Monsanto one of the eleven chemical companies involved in the "Agent Orange" case was found guilty by a jury that their product (Roundup) was causing cancer in people. The jury after carefully reviewing the evidence presented in court based their decision on the fact that Monsanto Agricultural Company was intentionally lying to the court to protect themselves and the product they created? What remains to be unfair as far as the Vietnam Veterans are concerned is that Monsanto and the other ten chemical companies were able to get away with paying a very small settlement amount to the Vietnam Veterans, only 180 million. And how was this supposed to take care of a class-action lawsuit of at least 8000 soldiers. The courts were misled during the Vietnam Veterans era and are still being misled today. How does anyone keep a straight face when they have egregiously misled the courts and the people of the United States of America? Monsanto an Agricultural giant has continuously refused to admit their product (Roundup) is causing cancer in everyday people who are only interested in beautifying their home and garden. The courts are being intentionally mislead and taxpayer's dollars are being wasted because Monsanto continues to refute the fact that their product Roundup is cancerous, and it is noted by the EPA to be a human carcinogen. We must also look at the fact that Monsanto was also a part of the Agent Orange case in the 80's. I am trying to tie Monsanto in with the present cases on why the Vietnam Veterans deserve so much more because there is a very high probability Monsanto was withholding pertinent information in the 80's to protect itself. If we are basing the discovery on trust than information found that could have change the judge's decision should have been heard and not suppressed. Since a person's testimony in court is based on a trust issue because they have sworn to tell the truth. Then there is a strong possibility that Monsanto committed perjured to the courts and the government by selling a product that was knowingly cancerous and not telling the government contractors or the United States Air Force about it. With the most damaging evidence coming from years and years of suffering and death of the Vietnam Veterans. They have had to endure over forty years of not being able to go after the companies which caused the cancer due to what is stated in the settlement. The attorneys who represented the Vietnam Veterans were limited in how they could pursue the chemical companies due to damaging evidence they possessed that was not allowed as part of the testimony. Which is the same testimony being given today by Monsanto that the chemical they use in Roundup which is glyphosate is not a human carcinogen and this comes after the EPA said it is a human carcinogen. Monsanto is saying their product does not cause cancer. But even the jurors in today's cases stated that Monsanto's has intentionally misled the court and the people by keep out warning information that could be detrimental to human life of which they (Monsanto) appear to have no value of. If you need to review the case history of the eleven chemical companies named in the lawsuit, they are listed in this chapter XXVI attached to the settlement agreement of which the testimony given in the 1979-1984 litigation should be in question today or has the statutory limitations expired.

CHAPTER XXVIII

"AGENT ORANGE" SETTLEMENTS IN QUESTION

I T WOULD APPEAR TO me given the legalities involved concerning so many deaths of our Vietnam Veterans that the testimony given was not forthcoming by Monsanto. And lives have been damaged, good men who have served this country during the Vietnam War never had the opportunity to do anything with their life because they were infected with the highly toxic herbicide chemical "Agent Orange." The Vietnam Veterans were being maligned with untruths of false claims because the chemical companies already knew that the chemical "Agent Orange" would be unpredictable when it was exposed to any environment. The did not want to take responsibility for a lifelong battle of supporting the Vietnam Veterans with their medical needs and continual health issues so they intentionally withheld information. Our American soldiers, the Vietnam Veterans have suffered for over forty years and they continue to suffer due to their over exposure to "Agent Orange." Due to this new information coming out in 2019 with the jurors stating that Monsanto intentionally mislead the court concerning their product (Roundup). Because of the lives that have been lost, the agony, humiliation and torment our military soldiers the Vietnam Veterans have had to endure for over forty years. If possible, it would be only right when given consideration to the calibration of our scales of justice when it comes to fairness and making people whole again. That the United States Supreme Court would reopen this matter for further review as it relates to the eleven chemical companies involved by allowing pertinent information of what was not allowed in the first case to be heard in the new case. 18 U.S. Code 1621 **Perjury, giving the legal definition is as stated: Whoever having taken an oath before a competent tribunal, officer, or person, in any case in which a law of the United States authorizes an oath to be administered, that he will testify, declare, depose, or certify truly, or that any written testimony, declaration, deposition, or certificate by him subscribed is try, willfully and contrary to such oath states or**

subscribes any material matter which he does not believe to be true." What is insightful is the incredulous thinking of the chemical companies that they have done nothing wrong and there is nothing wrong with the products created in the past namely "Agent Orange." Monsanto also believes (Roundup) is not cancerous. These chemical companies remain to be extremely scrupulous in their way of thinking that the products they have helped to create is not causing cancer now in the lives of good hardworking American citizens. And has not caused cancer in the past as it relates to "Agent Orange" and the cancer that has been found eating up the insides of the Vietnam Veterans body due to exposure of the highly toxic herbicide chemical, "Agent Orange." This has turned out not to just be a problem for the United States involving the Vietnam Veterans consistency of claims concerning their health and medical needs. It is also a problem that remains unresolved in Vietnam where it is noted that out of the 20,000,000 million gallons of "Agents" sprayed in the jungles of Vietnam 11,000,000 gallons were "Agent Orange." The Agents were sprayed in the air over 39,000,000 square miles of jungle and right on top of the Vietnam Veterans and the Vietnamese land. The intent of spraying the toxic herbicides was to contaminate our own American soldiers. The intent the United States Government had was to kill the foliage in order to clear paths of sight for the American soldiers so they could see. Therefore, it is so important to rehear the case and new evidence that was not permitted in the 80's to be presented and heard today. Same company, same cancer just different products created by the same company that causes cancer in people. Much of what took place inside of the jungles of Vietnam during the Vietnam War was all in concern for assisting our American troops into finding the enemy and destroying them. At the order of President John F. Kennedy in 1961 to begin spraying the herbicide into the jungles of Vietnam. Our President was not made aware of what the mixtures inside of the chemicals being used were. President John F. Kennedy was not made aware of the toxicity levels of that involved later contaminate problems that would come from the use of "Agent Orange." President John F. Kennedy was never made aware of TCDD. He was never advised that the use of the human carcinogen TCDD (dioxin) would cause the physical, emotional and mental damage to the Vietnam Veterans and they would suffer for a lifetime if they returned home due to Agent Orange being cancerous. The Vietnam Veterans were young soldiers who believed in our Constitution and defended the name of this great nation in battle. One of the question

Judge George C. Pratt presented to the chemical companies was for them to present to the court documentation showing that the United States government gave the specification for orders of "Agent Orange." There was never any evidence presented by the chemical companies to show proof of such a specific ingredient. The chemical companies to this day remain steadfast on their belief that TCDD did not cause cancer in our soldiers. They also will not claim the damages done by the 11,000,000 gallons of "Agent Orange" sprayed over 39,000,000 square miles of Vietnam. You can question exactly what were the chemical companies thinking when TCDD was added to another chemical to create "Agent Orange?" The other thing that was done wrong is they released it in an open environment without knowing the boundaries of its potent toxicity levels but all the time knowing it was a chemical that was sporadic, uncontrollable, cancerous and deadly? It is stated in the litigation notes the chemical companies were fully aware of the dangers of the chemical "Agent Orange" before manufacturing it. "The chemical companies did not care that it was cancerous they manufactured it anyway" knowing the consequences involved. The mission was called "Operation Ranch Hand" that sprayed a total of 20,000,000 U.S. gallons of herbicide over Vietnam, Cambodia and Laos from 1961 to 1971. Out of the 20 million gallons sprayed 11 million was "Agent Orange." Of which, the toxicity levels reached 50 times it standard levels of acceptance for the areas it was sprayed over. Although "Agent Orange" was designed to destroy the foliage originally it is only due a lack of concern for human life and greed that the chemical companies did not set any boundaries concerning its usage. Today we suffer as a nation alongside our Vietnam Veterans as we watch them to continue to deplete in life and draw nearer to death. What went wrong? That is a question that may or may not ever get answered. Did the chemical companies every think the Vietnam Veterans would make it back to the United States of America contaminated with "Agent Orange?" Or did the chemical companies mix the most potent chemical herbicide of all time thinking it was going to stay over in Vietnam and its history of being carcinogenic would never be told in America? This was the blinding side of war they could not see, the repercussions behind what I would call mad scientist who appeared to be out to annihilate a nation of people would do. This is why the lawsuit and its disallowed evidence against the chemical companies is important to be heard today so the Vietnam Veterans can be justly redeemed and compensated according to the claims they have filed. It must be allowed to be brought back up on the testimony of what is taking place with the reasons behind why the attorneys for the Vietnam Veterans also did not want to settle for only 180 million dollars they knew it should have been so much more. This information is vital to what needs to take place today as far as a new trial with new evidence that will be heard. We are also looking at Monsanto's representative's integrity as they were sworn in to give testimony concerning the relationship to Agent Orange being a human carcinogen. It (should) be hard for any chemical company to want to coverup any kind of scandal related to the loss of life. Unless the chemical was intentionally released without any moral value of human life, then they would want to keep that a secret. Especially something as serious as other human beings' lives are concerned and the value of how precious life is. This matter relates without question to our American soldiers the Vietnam Veterans being hoodwinked by fraudulent testimony, given by the chemical companies. They proclaimed to not know what "Agent Orange" was going to do to the soldiers but Agent Orange (TCDD) is stated as being uncontrollable. I often find myself wondering just how much longer were these chemical companies going to sit back and act like two-year-old children who got caught with their hands in the cookie jar and say, **"We didn't do it and we haven't any idea as to who ate the cookies."** Who caused the problems? Were the problems created for the Vietnam Veterans to suffer? As the truth slowly begins to come to life, we are now discovering the true nature of the beast. Which is what appears to be that the chemical companies are not to accept fault under any circumstance. This is not for the betterment of humanity but for the betterment of their chemical companies being able to remain in existence. It is understood they do not have a lot of respect for human life which reflects from the 80's and currently today when you look at the cases concerning Roundup. This is why having a good name is so important and this is also why testifying under oath establishes what your words mean to you morally. In hindsight we have to look at the pleads of the Vietnam Veterans and their cry out for help for so many years. Claims were being filed with the Veterans Administration Office. The Vietnam Veterans who were able to make it back home from Vietnam had already begin to feel the effects of the chemical TCDD (Agent Orange) in their body. In the case of Monsanto agricultural company and the other chemical companies involved with "Agent Orange" it is very important to make note of how they have represented themselves in the past (!984) and how they are currently representing themselves now in 2019 going into 2020 with cases pending against them. The owners and staff, even the attorneys that represent the companies can ask themselves is morality and dignity a part of their constitution? It was in 1984 when the chemical companies continued to stand up for themselves and say they are not the cause, but they ended up settling out of court. The case is they were not truthful with the courts back in 1979 which is a reflection of the chemical companies' testimony today of which they have been found guilty of intentionally withholding critical information from the public. The chemical companies have continued to conceal vital information. They do not feel their chemical company and the products they make are causing cancer in humans. But the Environmental Protection Agency (EPA) says it a little different. The EPA says they are responsible, and their products are cancerous. Monsanto swore in court again and their testimony was found to be untruthful and once again made the statement their product is the best and it is not cancerous. But the jurors are saying their testimony cannot be substantiated because they are intentionally not being truthful. This statement of Monsanto and other chemical companies not being truthful makes them venerable for the Vietnam Veterans their children and their grandchildren to request a new hearing and maybe just maybe this time they will not settle out of court. Erin Brokovich the true story and movie that was played by Julia Roberts is a rendition of what needs to take place with the chemical companies today. People are dying from breast cancer, liver cancer, and pancreatic cancer right in the midst of Willowbrook, Illinois and Waukegan, Illinois due to (Ethylene Oxide) being used by Sterigenics a chemical company that sterilizes operating equipment for hospitals. There are so many deaths on both sides both civilian and military with the greater deaths being of course because of "Agent Orange." The Vietnam Veterans are being estimated to have another maybe six years before they die off. We are losing 131,040 a year. If we are not getting the information straight, of which we should all be getting it by now. These chemical companies are not going to stop their practicing of using certain chemicals and could care less about the value of human life. Since it is not their life or a family members being shortened due to an over exposure of carcinogenic chemicals. The chemical companies could not come up with any evidence saying our President at the time John F. Kennedy or the United States government had anything to do with the creation of Agent Orange or knew what was in "Agent Orange." Nor did President John F. Kennedy or the United States government give them any written specification on what to mix to make

Agent Orange. That was really overreaching for the chemical companies to come up with such a suggestion and of course there wasn't any evidence ever submitted by the chemical company's because it simply did not happen. In today's news we are finding (Roundup, Roundup, Roundup) products produced by Monsanto Agricultural Company is and has caused cancer in individuals but Monsanto denies that (Roundup) is cancerous. This is the type of response we have to look forward to concerning the chemical companies. They will remain forever consistent with their statement of denial because they do not want to be held liable in a court of law. The chemical companies clearly show a lack of respect for human life and the families it has destroyed.

Should I bring up Charles Darwin and his theory of "Survival of the fittest." Since this is where we seem to be headed, does life set its practical goals of others existence based on common factors of, what they can afford? What they are able to purchase? Where they are able live? And what they are able to afford to eat? Given this denominator of Charles Darwin's theory it would all be based on where do you stand in the social ladder of life? How high are you really able to reach when you are challenged with certain obstacles? Will you be able to overcome those barriers? I must say it is unfortunate that we have, the have and have nots throughout the world. But we have a governing system here in America enforced by a democracy of those who are able to reach the elite at the top. Although the system is somewhat limited to a certain few there is a greater compassion that some of those at the top of the social ladder will show mercy on those who fought to bring about positive change, for the good of all humanity. This is where America stands today when we look at the suffering of the Vietnam Veterans and how they have and continue to struggle with "Agent Orange" since their return from Vietnam. It should really leave the majority of those of you who do not understand an inkling of ideological thought the importance of being able to give something. This is what our Vietnam Veterans did for the United States of America they gave something back to a country they believed in and carved it in their hearts with their own blood, their own life. I am very proud to say that serving my country, the United States of America gave me a feeling of pride, honor, respect, dignity and loyalty to my country. To be able to do something constructive and not destructive, being able to build up and not to tear down. This is what I felt as a Marine Corps enlisted soldier, and an Army military field grade officer who served in one of the highest ranking positions in the military as Commandant. I must say this is what the majority of all the soldiers and officers feel and talk about when we served this great nation as one. Finally, this is also what the Vietnam Veterans felt when they were called to serve, "One God, One Nation, and One Family with Liberty and Justice for All." When we raised our right hand to swear in as soldiers as officers, we stood alone as soldiers and officers united. As men and in today's armed forces women taking our oath of allegiance to serve and protect the United States of America even if it cost us our life. We did not run or hide we fought. When we talk about "Survival of the fittest" I would like for everyone reading this book to take a long look at what I have been saying throughout the pages of this book. I have talked about the sacrifices of what the Vietnam Veterans did for this country, and it is you who have let them down. "Agent Orange" which dispersed the highly toxic chemical TCDD (dioxin) is a human carcinogenic which means it is cancerous. This was known before the chemical companies manufactured it, it is stated in a few documents I have researched. The other critical factor that remains is that the chemical companies did not reveal this to the President Kennedy or U.S. government officials that they were going to put TCDD as a mixture with other chemicals. www.history.com/topics/vietnam-war/agent-orange-1 "**Studies done on laboratory animals have proven that dioxin is highly toxic even in minute doses. It is universally known to be a carcinogen (a cancer-causing agent).**"

www.history.com/topic/vietnam-war/agent-orange-1 "**The TCDD found in Agent Orange is the most dangerous of all dioxins.**" It is not beyond human understanding that the President of the United States of America which was John F. Kennedy and the two Houses that represent our great nation, they would not have been involved in the killing of our own American soldiers or the killing of innocent women and children in Vietnam. This is what "Agent Orange" did to America and Vietnam but Vietnam got the worst of the chemical of which is a reflection in their country to date 2019 going into 2020 over fifty years of suffering. The Vietnamese people are suffering in abundance. It is imperative that we as a people that govern this great nation, the United States of America with our moral values and judgement has not indulged in any kind of a conspiracy to commit genocide on an entire nation of people. These facts remain to be true that our Commander and Chief, President John F. Kennedy, the United States Congress and the United States Senate nor working government officials who were involved in trying to get our soldiers home from Vietnam had nothing to do with Agent Orange. They had nothing to do with the chemical mixture and specifications of any of the created agent herbicides including that which involves the use of TCDD during the Vietnam War. The United States government only intent was to use a chemical herbicides to get rid of the foliage in order to give better pictorial sight alignment to the American soldiers in Vietnam and kill the foliage in the jungles so maneuver of the troops would be a little easier. The Presidents intent was to help the soldiers. The chemical companies took it upon themselves to use TCDD which is classified as the most dangerous of all dioxins. TCDD originally was not used when they began making the different kinds of "Agents." I mentioned earlier in the chapters remember there were five other "herbicide Agents" created before "Agent Orange". And of course, with "Agent Orange" being the most toxic chemical herbicide of the six created. It was "Agent Orange" that contained TCDD. I have to repeat what I have stated concerning fault which does not fall on the President or the United States government since they remained in the dark on any kind of collusion involving TCDD or any other mixture to wipeout the entire nation of Vietnamese people. This is something the Vietnamese cannot fault the United States of America's government in. The fault lies with the chemical companies of which was stated in the court documents that the chemical companies knew of the dangerous toxic nature of TCDD (dioxins) before it was manufactured and continued to manufacture it without any regards to human life. It is unfortunate how war creates enemies of countries. But what determines the fate of one's survival? Do you feel that Charles Darwin's theory "Survival of the Fittest" is correct in saying that every man, woman and child dependent on the nature of the individual in question is responsible for their own fate? If that is the case and you feel Charles Darwin's theory to be correct, then please tell me that given the innate abilities of mankind to be able to survive beyond the impossible at times. Is it simply natural survival instinct or is it because they were given a chance in life, right place, right time? What remains in question is the inability of a fetus to fight back. For those of you who believe in "Survival of the fittest" how does that relate to a stillborn baby verses one that lived. There is no book a mother can read that will guarantee the life of an unborn child. What the mother takes in is what the unborn fetus is subjected to. But suppose the mother hasn't any warning signs signaling her that something is wrong. This is what has taken place with the grandchildren and possible even the future great-grandchildren of the Vietnam Veterans.

The damage done to the fetus is not something the mother ingested. We now know that "Agent Orange" is in the DNA of the Vietnam Veterans, it is being genetically transferred. Meaning that since it is in the DNA and the sperm of the Vietnam Veterans has its blood in it before it attaches to the mother's eggs. Then the probability of the children being born deformed or with some form of deficiency would be expected. This is what is taking place with the children, the grandchildren and possibly down the road the great-grandchildren because TCDD will be in their DNA. So, we are still looking at years and years of research needed to be done so we can better understand a chemical such as TCDD which at the present time appears to not have any limitations. Once it has crossed over into the genetic lines of human DNA will it remain there forever eating away the insides of its host or causing further damage to the makeup of the human body as it passes from host to host? What did these chemical companies create and who do we blame for their creation? Should the chemical companies be held accountable for the health damages as well as the medical and emotional damages they have caused in so many peoples lives? That is a trillion-dollar question, but the final result is quite obvious today, it's the chemical companies who caused it? Therefore, "Survival of the Fittest" would be proven to be an inconclusive theory which cannot justify the life of a fetus in the womb of its mother. A fetus that hasn't any ability to fight for its life by rejecting TCDD to protect itself from being born with deformities. While we look at what is called the fittest in being able to survive this theory does not justify weakness or strength since a fetus in its developing stages is not able to fight off an infectious chemical as toxic as TCDD. Or even what is called the abortion pill. Babies are being born with TCDD (Agent Orange) already in their DNA as it begins to feed on the inside of the mother while developing a new deformed life. So, where does it take us today when we look at not just the Vietnam Veterans and their children, we now must look at the grandchildren and possibly the great-grandchildren who will be affected with "Agent Orange." Will they be able to survive with this toxic chemical in the DNA since we do not know the limitations of the TCDD what kind of deformities will these infected children being born are we going to have to face in the future? What will the defects be, and to what extreme? When we begin looking at their medical conditions will these children who are being born with birth defects which is contributory to "Agent Orange" have to be treated in order to function on a daily basis as they grow into adulthood? This is why I am asking for more research on Agent Orange to be done and this time I would like to see government employees doing the research not some outside team, it just doesn't make sense. This is what we the people of the United States of America are going to have to look at as a nation.

Who are the weak? Would you say just because the Vietnam Veterans who were just common soldiers, just everyday people don't deserve to be told the truth or have the proper medical treatment available to them? Or maybe they don't deserve the proper treatment because they would be considered the, "weak." And how will you explain this to the Vietnam Veterans children they never entered a war zone, but their DNA is contaminated? How about the grandchildren, they never entered a war zone and their DNA is contaminated? And guess what! I have not heard anything being mentioned about the great-grandchildren of the Vietnam Veterans. This is only going to get worse until these chemical companies are held accountable for the irreversible damage they have caused in the life of good people. **There's documented evidence found by the litigating attorneys from the chemical companies stating the chemical companies knew about the dangers of "Agent Orange" before they manufactured it and produced it anyway.** What I am trying to get you to see is in Charles Darwin's theory of "survival of the fittest" everyone loses since eventually everyone will be consumed. If you are looking at survival of the fittest at a wholistic viewpoint survival of the fittest really means last man standing and if this is the case, there would not be any room for reproduction since the strongest have consumed the weakest down to the last one. If we look at it with evidence presented with facts about the chemical companies producing "Agent Orange" then the guilty party has to stand. Just because the military soldiers don't have the finances to fight against legal teams who have unlimited monies does not mean we as a nation of people just stand by and watch. Wrong is wrong and these chemical companies must be made to pay for the lives they have interrupted and for the families they have destroyed. We are still looking at the Vietnam Veterans, their children and their grandchildren. There hasn't been anything mentioned about the great-grandchildren which is a strong possibility that their DNA will be tainted with (Agent Orange) as well. That's another lawsuit that needs to be looked at a little closer for the grandchildren and the great-grandchildren. That's a start then we have to look at what the United States of America stands for. Those of you who are in the decision-making positions who can grasp what I am about to say must bear witness to the truth. The United

States of America is a nation built on "In God We Trust." We are not a nation of intellectuals trying to hide from the truth. Because we stand for what we believe in justice for all. Throughout my service to my country I have found there are more of us who care about what happens to others than those who don't. Since the 20,000,000 gallons of chemical herbicides was sprayed throughout Vietnam, Cambodia and Laos of which 11,000,000 gallons were "Agent Orange" the most toxic and deadliest of all chemical herbicides. We now have to look at a cleanup process for the Vietnamese even though it is fifty years later. What the Vietnamese need to understand is the United States did not specify at any time what chemicals were to be used or how they were to make the chemical herbicides used to kill the foliage in the jungles of Vietnam. What needs to be looked at is the fraudulent information being given today by the chemical companies and whether it is possible to question this legally in a court of law. Due to the chemical company's refusal to admit fault and accept responsibility for damages leaves everyone on the side of the law in a dismal state of mind. With the greater understanding being winning a lawsuit where everyone knows justice has been served.

Or do we begin compromising with no fault being directed towards anyone and no one can actually point the finger. Settlement defers blame when certain finite evidence has been requested by either side to be restrained as part of the settlement agreement. Which is usually the defendant's requests to withhold damaging evidence. There isn't a guilty party, and everyone comes out of the courtroom as though the case itself never existed, as far as the defendants are concerned. When I look at how the chemical companies have come out smelling like a rose with very little damages done to its name. It's horrific to know it would be just a matter of time before the chemical companies will begin to produce the same toxic chemicals all over again. Or either change its name or go back to "business as usual. What is even more horrendous is the value these chemical companies have for human life, none. There are families who are suffering today behind chemicals being released in the air in our communities. And if the chemical companies can get away with not paying any compensatory retribution for what they have done they will not. There are some people who have money to through around and really don't care about the internal suffering of others. They have very little value of others life and their personal goal is to give away money thinking a little money will help take away the pain. In accordance with the word of God, Ecclesiastes 10:19 says,

"A feast is made for laughter, and wine maketh merry: but money answereth all things." Let the will and word of God Almighty move forward and may the hearts of those who are suffering receive their just due in accordance to what they need in order to be made whole. A life cannot be replaced once the breath of God is taken out of it. Because the dead haven't any life left in them, the Holy Bible tells us the dead don't even know they are dead. These companies must be made accountable for their actions and they must be made to see the pain and hurt they have inflicted in so many homes. The joy that have has been intrusively taken from the lives of our American Vietnam Veterans and the non-combative citizens of Vietnam. This is what has been taking place in the past with the chemical companies being able to get away with just paying out a little money. Never admitting to anything and because the case was settled out of court the chemical companies turn right back around and run the same operation as before. Although it is not a criminal case the legal terminology I am going to try to explain (nolo contendere) is a given example as to why these chemical companies are still able to function. They settled out of court (nolo contendere). In a criminal proceeding, a defendant may enter a plea of nolo-contendere, in which the defendant does not accept or deny responsibility for the charges but agrees to accept punishment. The plea differs from a guilty plea because a "no contest" plea cannot be used against the defendant in another cause of action. In our attempts to correct the wrong doings of the chemical company's we cannot standby and just take the money in order to make the people whole. There must be some form of punishment or penalty concerning perjury that the chemical companies should be enforced to uphold. Although they want to remain in busy to make money with no regards for human life, they must be made accountable for the pain and suffering they or their products have inflicted upon innocent lives. This is the only way to make sure the same similar cases referencing the chemical companies will not continue to be repeated. Certain provisions can be introduced by the plaintiff(s) where stipulated specifications can be mandated for the chemical companies to follow. A precedence must be set whereby the chemical companies will fear to do what they in the past had gotten away with so many times. This is what the chemical companies have been doing by making sure it is put into law they have a statement placed inside the settlement agreement of which **they claim no admission of their product causing cancer by freeing themselves of all fault and liabilities so their company can continue to produce human carcinogenic products.**

I did not want to say it this way but I will make it plain and this is how I feel, the chemical companies do not care how many citizens of America die. They do not care about the soldiers who fought in the Vietnam War and are dying from the chemical Agent Orange. They do not care about soldiers or citizens who are still dying as long as they are allowed to put that clause in the settlement, **"that they claim no fault and they believe their product is not cancerous"** this statement will continue to allow the chemical companies to manufacture products that cause cancer. Please keep in mind that the Environmental Protection Agency already stated the product due to the use of glyphosate which is cancerous does cause cancer in human beings. We must admit the courts have been intentionally misled as stated, and they are being misled intentionally by the chemical companies. This is a reflection of the companies past and its ability to be trusted today? What should be questioned today since these same companies' testimony in similar cases are being found to be not truthful, we must question did they intentionally commit perjury during the case with "Agent Orange?" The chemical company Monsanto is found to not be truthful in today's court in 2019 based on the testimony of their product not causing cancer, but the jurors are saying it is causing cancer and so is the EPA. The settlement for the Vietnam Veterans was a measly 180 million dollars which involved 105,000 cases filed by veterans and their families which left only 52,000 claims that received a monetary amount of compensation which turned out to be on the average of 3,800 dollars per claim. This is where the problem of chemical contamination continues to repeat itself the chemical companies paid out the 180 million but one of the stipulated terms requested was that **"the chemical manufactures would be allowed to renounce liability for injuries in return for establishing a settlement trust."** During the time claims were able to be filed in behalf of veterans, and their children. The veterans felt it was an unreasonable settlement and their attorneys agreed it was too low and voiced their opinions to the deciding judge Weinstein who ruled it was fair. The settlement paid between 1988 and 1994. Due to the vast number of veterans and family's members filing in behalf of veterans. Cases were accepted for settlement until 1994 until the 180 million in settlement funds expired in 1994. Today there could possibly be new hope for reopening the case concerning "Agent Orange" due to the continual pain and suffering it has caused in the grandchildren and possibly great grandchildren. Of which, **the children as I have stated did not serve in Vietnam so they would not have to ask permission from**

the government to sue. Of course, I also feel monies as well as future research should be put aside for the grandchildren and great grandchildren since no one has found out the life limitations of the highly toxic "Agent Orange." If at all possible since hearings were heard, and the 180-million-dollar settlement was reached for the veterans and the veterans' children. I would say the one thing that was forgotten was the settlement of 180 million dollars did not established an expiration time for the future of the veteran's children who were still being born after the settlement funds were expired in 1994. The settlement proposed was to establish a trust. If there was a trust set up for the veterans' children, then how did the 180 million in settlement funds run out in six years? There is nothing there for the grandchildren who are now being born with deformities and it has already been discovered they have "Agent Orange" in their DNA. Where is the funding? What happened to (the Settlement Trust)? It was supposedly set up for their medical and health problems that will most certainly come in the very near future? We must also look out for the great-grandchildren who will be in the making in the next few years. Will their DNA also be contaminated with the highly toxic chemical TCDD (dioxin) that will be passed genetically to them from their parents who are already contaminated? The same chemical TCDD that ate up the insides of their parents and great-grandparents is what we are looking at today. It is in their DNA everyone therefore I am asking for further research to be done by our personally employed government research teams. Simply because the non-governmental teams that were hired in the past have not been cited many changes as it relates to "Agent Orange." And they had to battle with cancer throughout their body, going in and out of the hospital for over forty years now. Are we going to continue to allow these chemical companies to get away with just a slap on the wrist and not take responsibility for the sickness and diseased deaths they have not only caused in thousands of the Vietnam Veterans but also women, and children? Now the very same problem lurks right in the communities of normal everyday American citizens. The settlements that have been paid out to the Vietnam Veterans was not enough to take care of the suffering and illnesses they have had to deal with daily for over forty years. That settlement was not enough to pacify a newborn baby. And please keep in mind it was not just the soldiers who suffered. You have forgotten about the wives, sons, daughters, family members and friends who are still suffering today because of the way their family member who served the United States of America was allowed to suffer and die. If nothing is done to change how things are going to be done as far as the chemical company's settling out of court with no stipulations added to their settlement. Then we will be looking at this matter in another forty years from now with the grandchildren and great-grandchildren of the Vietnam Veterans. There is nothing left to be said concerning this matter other than the monies that should have been put in the (Settlement Trust) for future medical or health problems for the Vietnam Veterans children is not there. I may be wrong to ask but can a settlement trust that is to be put up for future needs expire with the rest of the monies? If there was ever such a settlement trust put up? It is mentioned in the settlement about the (Settlement Trust). If there was not a settlement trust put up for the Vietnam Veterans children, then there should have been? That 180 million dollars awarded in a (settlement trust) in 1984 should have never been exhausted. By all means monies should have been put up and set aside where if there were future problems that would be occurring with the children of the Vietnam Veterans, they would be able to draw what is needed from the settlement trust. Which would have been used for the medical treatment needed and any reoccurring health problems. This is unfortunate because neither the judge in charge of the case nor the legal team working in behalf of the Vietnam Veterans had any idea "Agent Orange" would be genetically transferred from the infected Vietnam Veterans into their children. This is why further research is needed by government employees and funding for health and medical bills need to be put up for the grandchildren and great grandchildren of the Vietnam Veterans. It is questionable whether the chemical companies knew the DNA of the veterans would be genetically infected due to the sporadic and uncontrollable spontaneity of the chemical TCDD (dioxin).

At this point I am probably overreaching when I ask the chemical companies to show their compassion. Wow! Did I say the word compassion? I did not say admit fault but show your compassion for the unborn grandchildren and great-grandchildren of the Vietnam Veterans. **It is very easy to have a meeting of the minds where a conference can be called, and monies can be setup in a place of need as well as health care and provisions needed for the children of the Vietnam Veterans. The funding must be unlimited since no one knows the extent of the life expectancy on how long TCDD (Agent Orange) is going to stay in the DNA of the children.** No one should be left behind and made to suffer for something they haven't any idea as to the reason of why they are being left to suffer, animals are even taken out of their misery, but we are leaving human beings to suffer. Why? This is what's taking place with the grandchildren and possibly great-grandchildren of the Vietnam Veterans. The grandchildren who are not named in the settlement because they were not born yet. I did not see where future problems concerning health and medical was being looked at in this case settlement. I do not believe that Judge Weinstein or the attorneys for the Vietnam Veterans had any idea that Agent Orange was going to be transferred to their grandchildren and possibly great grandchildren DNA. There isn't any mentioning of it in the settlement it was missed, it was not documented to cover the future of the grandchildren who are now infected and great grandchildren in the future will stand a chance of being infected by the chemical herbicide "Agent Orange." Please keep in mind I am only mentioning Judge Weinstein because he helped prepare the settlement and he was the hearing judge in the case. Since the grandchildren were not mentioned or the contemplation of great-grandchildren not being born yet there is a strong possibility that no one was looking that far ahead. Or maybe they just thought "Agent Orange" was going to end with the Vietnam Veterans. I am certain Judge Weinstein and the attorneys had honestly missed it because no one knew that "Agent Orange" was going to be transferred genetically. So, where does this leave the grandchildren and great grandchildren? It would appear as though the only people who were minutely taken care of was the Vietnam Veterans. Some of them received a whopping check for $3800.00 dollars for a lifetime of medical problems. Is this some kind of a joke? I say minutely taken care of because the 180 million dollars presented was probably enough to cover maybe five soldiers if you are looking at a lifetime settlement. Out of 105,000 cases filed only 52,000 were compensated with $3,800.00 and the 180 million were depleted in approximately 6 years. Now the grandchildren are being left subjected to the TCDD that has been transferred to their blood. My question at this point is do you feel that the grandchildren and future great-grandchildren should be compensated? The next question as you can see, I have lots of those please bear with me?

It is presented with the understanding that "Agent Orange" is still in the research process as far as the Veterans Administration and the Health & Medicine Division (HMD) is concerned? If the Health & Medicine Division a non-governmental entity has not completed their research of which has been ongoing concerning what "Agent Orange" either has caused or is not capable of causing in the Vietnam Veterans has been ongoing forever.

Leaves a lot of doors open for questions of uncertainty as to what "Agent Orange" has done to the Vietnam Veterans since it has been discovered to be in their DNA. We must begin looking at what affects will it have on their children, their grandchildren and possibly great-grandchildren if this monstrosity of a problem is continuously pushed aside and not corrected? Therefore, let's look at it this way since everyone is trying to avoid accepting fault for the medical and health problems the Vietnam Veterans have had to suffer with for over forty years. Let's try as God fearing human beings to mend a whole everyone has been dancing around. And from the looks of everything I have reviewed the litigation case in 1979-1984 which only covered issues concerning the Vietnam Veterans. In relations to the lawsuits filed I have not come across one that covered the grandchildren or the great-grandchildren to be able to attain medical treatment if in fact they began to have problems with the effects of "Agent Orange" which is already in their DNA. No one knows the problems that are going to occur in the future because non-governmental research are still searching for more cause & effects of which is still being done after fifty years now. The nongovernmental organizations who are being hired to research "Agent Orange" have not given a conclusive check list of what the herbicide chemical will or will not do to the Vietnam Veterans or to their children, grandchildren and great grandchildren. In order to protect the grandchildren and great-grandchildren in the future we as a nation must be prepared to cover any issues of future problems caused by "Agent Orange". The Vietnam Veterans deserve to have their loved ones protected by having monies put up for future research and for possible hospitalization or medical treatment their grandchildren and great-grandchildren that are being born with deficiencies and deformities due to "Agent Orange" are going to need at some point in the near future. It is unfortunate due to testimony given by the chemical companies that may or may not have been fraudulent in the past to protect the chemical companies. Although it should have been requested that monies also be made to be put up by the chemical companies for future children and childbearing. It is unfortunate that the plaintiffs' attorneys were not knowledgeable in the realms of science and what a toxic chemical like TCDD was capable of doing to the human body but that is understood, attorneys are not chemical specialist. A separate settlement involving the payment of hospitalization any surgery and medical treatment should have been also part of the settlement agreement to avoid having to go back to court. But since the original agreement has been paid out in full to its exhaustion. That since the grandchildren and great-grandchildren have the same highly toxic chemical, TCDD "Agent Orange" in their DNA. Could it be possible to go back to court to set up more research and funding for TCDD research. And to setup a reserve funding in order that families do not continue to suffer. Whereby hospitals and medical treatment across the United States of America will be ready when the Vietnam Veterans grandchildren and great-grandchildren health begins to fail them. We as a nation must be prepared for this in the future. This is a big pill to swallow but for safety of all human life that accountability does not have to be done by an acceptance of fault and an agreement to discontinue the use of such chemicals that are cancerous. Or if you want me to get more technical in the description of such mentioned chemical TCDD. Chemicals that are said to be toxic to humans in relations to what the legal terminology would state a human carcinogen. These are only a few of the chemicals noted for causing cancer by the Environmental Protection Agency (EPA), **Glyphosate, Ethylene Oxide, TCDD (dioxin)= Agent Orange, Chromium 6**. Therefore, it is important to make sure we are safe in the products we use and the foods we eat. This is why the chemical companies should by all means make it right for those who are less fortunate. Those of you who hold the positions of president, executive officer etc. of the chemical companies should make a humanitarian effort to resolve the damages that TCDD is going to cause in the lives of children who were never given a fair chance at life. I feel it is ethically important that we don't have to always look at the grounds of legality based on the case. There are many things that could be done morally. I will ask at this time that you go back through the pages of this book and read my prose titled, "The Dim Light of Justice." There is a reason why we must make sure others are okay without over stretching our cable tow. These families who are damaged realize everyone makes mistakes. The problem comes in on the cleanup and how you choose to do it? I am certain your children who have finished college and are now starting their families and enjoying their career jobs? But the fact of the matter is the Vietnam War is still taking place inside of the minds of our soldiers. Because the chemical herbicide sprayed on the Vietnam Veterans by our own Air Force planes placed our soldiers on the ground in the jungles of Vietnam into what I call a living death hole. Somewhat similar to the "Art of War." When I define a living death is what our Vietnam Veterans had to go through because no one wanted to tell the truth or should I say admit fault, take the blame, write the book as to what really happened to them. **They never really had a chance to live their life and that is the God given truth of this matter the gospel as you might have it.** A living death is what is equated to someone who has life in their body but no purpose. All the living the Vietnam Veterans wanted to do and all the exploring and fun they wanted to have with their families the same way you enjoy your families today. Is something that did not happen for the Vietnam Veterans, to be able to enjoy their families and watch their children grow. A living death is someone who is walking upon the earth but only on the verge of existence. This is what was done to the Vietnam Veterans they gave you their all. And when they returned home you gave them nothing to grasp onto, that is unless you want to claim the heartaches and insults you put them through. In the years to come they are still waiting for a thank you from this nation. These valiant men, young boys eighteen years of age "had no dog in the fight." Yet they were treated like they were the ones who started the war when they returned home. The fact of the matter is that our Vietnam Veterans who went to war in defense of the United States of America deserve much more than this country could ever repay them. I would ask you as an officer and a gentleman to stop looking at the small mistakes that were made during war time. And look at what God Almighty has continued to bless the United States of America with. It is unfortunate that we cannot redo the past. If you allow me to go to scripture briefly, I will say this is why we cannot look back, as soldiers for the Lord we continue to drive on with the mission. Looking back can become detrimental in many ways. Only in hindsight are we able to make corrections to assure the mistakes made in the past do not happen again.

The Eye of the Needle

"As we go through our difficulties in life. We begin to realize our journeys are not the same. There are emotional feelings and personal attachments some of which we feel we are not able to let go of because they are nurtured within our very spirit. Our soul is burdened with excess weight of trying to juggle our inner self by seeking our strength from a divine power that dwells within. Then there comes a moment of separation, a fork in the road. One that will change your journey, your direction for the rest of your life, only everyone will not be able to make it through. You have made it to that point in your journey. You are now at the Needles Eye and you must relinquish something.

You have to let go of excess weight, things that trouble your mind, your spirit, your oneness with God. You must relax your grasp and let go of whatever is restricting your movement. You find the Eye of the Needle to be too narrow to take all of the excess baggage you would like to take through with you. And if you want to continue this journey without letting something go you will find you will not be able to make it. You now have to make an instant decision. You must define the necessary items, things which are going to be left behind. The key is being careful because once you take them off, they cannot be put back on. What stays behind will be permanent there will be no opportunity to come back and get them. Now you realize the decision of making it through to the other side is based on the load you are carrying and what you have decided to remove. This is also how everyday life is determined, making sometimes quick and crucial decisions. The shedding of the old that could possibly determine your success in life. When does one let go of the excess? Knowing the natural nature of a human being is of a nurturing instinct, of sharing and wanting to help others to get to their pinnacle in life. The question you must ask yourself is why do you keep holding onto so many unnecessary things? Things of no importance and people who say they love you but haven't any self-worth for themselves. They are not ready to let go of their own downfall. It's unfortunate that some people and even things can become toxic. So, will your decision be to make it through the Eye of the Needle or will you stagnate yourself with unnecessary luggage and be left behind with the others? Or will you let go in a spiritual sense of getting in tone with Gods divine power, knowing you do not have the authority to save anyone not even yourself. The only way you can complete your search for God is to go through the Needles Eye. You want to see the face of God, so you start your search by letting go of all the dead weight because in all actuality you truly do not have control over anything. God is the overseer of it all. Keep in mind that once the day is gone it is gone, you can't go back and redo it over. Holding onto your own insecurities hampers our position to grow. But indulging in other's demons hinders them not you and only prolongs their recovery. You see if you really think about it you are not curing them because you don't have the authority. You are only pacifying yourself. Let go and take your journey through the Eye of the Needle. You will shout with joy when you go through the other side. Whatever you do, don't look back. There is nothing you can change; it has already happened. Remember it is easier for a poor man to go through the Eye of a Needle than for a rich man to enter into the gates of heaven. It is easier for the poor because they never had anything to lose but the rich attained a piece of the world and does not want to let go of anything. What decisions are you burdened with? Are you able to let go and trust in the Lord, thy God? He said he will never leave or forsake you. Trust in God he already knows the way. He already knows your blessings and dispositions in life. Follow the Lord because he is the only one who knows the heart."

If in fact the eleven chemical companies named in the lawsuit concerning "Agent Orange" are without reservation trying to do what is right. Now! Is the time to do it. The way it is looking right now is as if they are trying to say they are not at fault because they have never admitted fault. And that a plea of nolo contendere releases them of all responsibility concerning that matter. Unfortunately for the chemical companies all the parties involved in the (settlement trust) were not named. Due to the fact the Vietnam Veterans grandchildren and the great grandchildren were not born yet which should open the door for further discussion which involves the lives of their grandchildren and great-grandchildren. I was doing my best to not name these chemical companies again that were involved in the Litigation case of 1979-1984 they are listed as follows:

1. **Dow Chemical Company**
2. **Thompson-Hayward**
3. **Diamond Shamrock**
4. **Monsanto Agricultural Company**
5. **Hercules Inc.**
6. **Ansul Company**
7. **Riverdale Chemical Company**
8. **Uniroyal**
9. **Occidental Petroleum Company**
10. **N.A. Phillips**
11. **Hooker Chemical Company**

This case started with Yannacone and his associated representing 8,300 clients which ended up with a settlement trust of 180 million dollars. Of which is evident that 180 million was not enough because those funds in the (settlement trust) expired by 1994, those funds only lasted about six. What I am trying to get your attention and help you to understand is just because the funds had expired does not mean the health or medical problems the Vietnam Veterans had acquired magically went away. You should be asking yourselves, what happened to the (settlement trust) if the monies are all depleted? There was nothing put aside or created for the future generations who might need special medical attention. Since we are now aware of the highly toxic chemical herbicide TCDD (dioxin) and it being a human carcinogen we must make intelligent and accurate decisions now in order to protect as well as limit the damages that could possibly happen to the grandchildren and great-grandchildren of the Vietnam Veterans. Once again, they were not mentioned or even thought of from what I have researched in the lawsuit. The Vietnam Veterans children and grandchildren are being born abnormal and with deformities due to the TCDD in their DNA. Now with the Health & Medicine Division which again are non-governmental researchers moving forward with their investigative studies on "Agent Orange" there still has not been enough medical health claims filed by the Vietnam Veterans completed and paid out. If possible, just how long do you figure it is going to take the grandchildren and great-grandchildren of the Vietnam Veterans to need a special needs program concerning their health. Or are we going to sit back and allow these children to suffer like we sit back and watched these chemical companies for years deny, deny, deny, and deny of having any knowledge that "Agent Orange" was a human carcinogen as it continued to eat up the Vietnam Veterans. Will we watch our children suffer as these chemical companies continually remain in denial? What makes these settlements that the companies are coming up with so simplistically contrary to their knowledge or TCDD is they continue to stipulate in record their ability to renounce all liability. What is taking place right before the world right now is several cases involving several chemical companies. One chemical company Monsanto Agricultural Company is being sued for the weed kill (Roundup) which is said to be using (Glyphosate) of which is classified by the EPA as a (human carcinogen). Then there is Sterigenics which is said to be using (Ethylene Oxide) which is also classified by the EPA as (a human carcinogen) another chemical company which stands a very high probability of causing cancer (of which people in their community) are getting sick with breast, liver, pancreas and kidney cancer where the company is located. Yes, I am certain you are shaking your head right now saying, which is what I said, (Wow, this is an Erin Brokovich) movie. I am certain we all will eventually get to the truth of the matter. I have even seen the most respected Senator in Illinois who everyone holds in the highest honor, Senator Dick Durbin on television speaking out on Sterigenics. Senator Dick Durbin has done a lot for the state of Illinois in his speaking out for Veteran rights and other issues involving humanity. He has also spoken out on the rights of the citizens of Illinois to not have to be made to live in unsafe areas that are producing such a high level of toxic poison in the air such as (Ethylene Oxide). The EPA classified (Ethylene Oxide) as being a human carcinogen and the hard-working citizens of Illinois should not have to live under those conditions especially in their community. It is not like leaving a war zone where the Vietnam Veterans left everything behind, they thought. But the citizens of America have the EPA to take care of situations such as what is taking place in Willowbrook, IL and Waukegan, IL and look at the affect the chemical companies are having on this community. There has already been one young man who has died trying to tell the news media and everyone else how the cancerous (Ethylene Oxide) in the air in his community was taking his life. I must add this young man who had a wife and son did end up dying.

What seems to be hands down as far as moral ethics concerning the chemical companies that has brought so much attention to themselves in recent years would be to close them down. That would be the moral side of it but there is also a purpose of need in relations to the contributory factors involved. That would be supply and demand. In the process of looking at human life and the value of such as a nation of working people we look at the insured verses the uninsured. Those who have insurance in America receive prompt treatment and those who are not insured must wait their turn. This is how the chemical companies have been treated by our courts at least up to now. Because they are able to pay millions as it relates to damages and without admitting fault the settlement goes to a (nolo contendere). I already explained what this legal term means, and this is why we are finding these chemical companies able to continue to function under their own auspice. From a legal standpoint they have continued to refuse to accept fault even though the EPA say their product is cancerous, the chemical companies are wrong. It would seem like after catching Monsanto the creator of (Roundup) intentionally misleading the courts and the jurors that the judge would have found them as being untruth and intentionally withholding pertinent evidence from the court as well as the public who buys their product. They are also putting innocent lives in danger by continuing to manufacture and sell cancerous products. Here is a piece of information all chemical companies including Monsanto just might want to take. It is called simple logic which also involves telling the truth. If you look at the situation this way the chemical companies should first, ask themselves this question. Is there a need for such a product and if so, can the product be modified to receive a passing (okay) from the Environmental Protection Agency to continue to function? The same will be looked at for the betterment of the people and the Monsanto Agricultural Company as well as Sterigenics when it comes to judges making decisions on certain products that consumers may need. As far as "Agent Orange" is concerned the matter is just a little more complex. "Agent Orange" has almost wiped out the Vietnam Veterans who had boots on the ground in the jungles of Vietnam. Former President Richard Nixon gave the order in 1970 to stop spraying "Agent Orange." The eleven chemical companies involved did not admit fault, they only settled with a financial agreement, there was never an admission of any one accepting fault. Weighing the odds gets technical and personal when it comes to loved ones who are either dead or dying from "Agent Orange." The monetary value is nothing more than a slap on the wrist a formality paid out by insurance companies or wealthy investors only because they got caught. Should they be held liable? I would say yes to the full extent of the law. But the courts will look at it from another standpoint. They will look at it from a legal standpoint and take into consideration the good the companies are doing. It sad to say but life to some people are no different than the chess pieces on the chessboard. The little pieces are sacrificed first and the wall of protection is built around those who are in power. Those with money are closely guarded. It most certainly seems unfair to those who do not understand the normalcy of loss and gain, love and war. What will we benefit out of closing down chemical companies that we need permanently? Maybe we should penalize them by closing them down for five to ten years like we do drug dealers, murderers, etc. put them out of commission for a while. As infectious as they may be to the communities around us. The question which remains is will the chemical companies if given a chance to balance out the potency by using less dangerous methods for product distribution and inform the public be able to function? For the reason I just stated here (for the betterment of the chemical companies). Leaves a very bitter taste in my mouth but remember this is what was done to the Vietnam Veterans for years and now it is touching home, right in the cities and towns of America. It should have never gotten to this point. What I am saying here is if the evidence presented by Yannacone the attorney who represented the Vietnam Veterans was allowed to be heard we probably would not be reading this book or requesting further research to be done on "Agent Orange." What is unfortunate is everyone wants to play ostrich and hide their heads in the sand when everything else is sticking out. What is taking place today in 2019 going into 2020 is that it's just not the Vietnam Veterans who need the help with research programs and medical care, but American citizens are crying out for help as well. In trying to overlook one problem that was created forty years ago in Vietnam with "Agent Orange." Everyone let that problem escalate and paid the Vietnam Veterans no attention at all as they died off. Now the problem is sitting right in the living room of American citizens as they watch their loved one's struggle with cancer in their body that was created by nearby chemical companies in their neighborhood. They are losing their family members and loved ones because of their exposure to toxic chemicals which cause cancer the same as the Vietnam Veterans struggled after returning home with "Agent Orange" in their system, you see cancer is exactly what it is cancer it does not discriminate. And believe me when I say no one and I do mean no one deserves to be wrongfully exposed to toxic chemicals or have a chemical as toxic as "Agent Orange" sprayed directly on them and everyone just sits back and says well they were soldiers, what did they expect. No, they were men, Vietnam Veterans who left home to protect the country they loved and the citizens in it. Everyone deserves a fighting chance and those of you who are living in Willowbrook, Illinois and Waukegan, Illinois deserve to be able to come home to your family after a hard day's work and enjoy being around family and friends. Have cookouts in your backyard, swim in the pool, go walking, jogging, running etc. No one should be fearful of living in their community in the United States of America of breathing in air that could possibly be cancerous. This is what I wanted you to get to see for yourself as it relates to the Vietnam Veterans. You see the soldiers wanted the same things you wanted but instead they sacrificed their lives for a later to make sure everything was secure. To see their families when they returned home from war. To be able to watch their children grow, to have cookouts in their back yards. To be treated with respect and honored as American War hero's but "Agent Orange" took the normalcy of life away for them, the Vietnam Veterans never had a chance. This is why I am asking the United States of America to give the Vietnam Veterans the apology they are really due. No one deserves to be treated or overlooked the way they have been treated and overlooked. But the citizens of America stood back and watched the Vietnam Veterans mistreated thinking it would never happen here in your own backyard. Now that it is happening, now that that chemical companies are sitting at your front step you can see the pain and fill the anguish the Vietnam Veterans have had for over forty years. I am not saying this in a good way but being the God-fearing man that I am I must say God has a way of bringing everything full circle. Karma is exactly that karma, it has no mercy on the merciless. We all are going to have to stand back and take another look at how the Vietnam Veterans have suffered for so many years and no one said a word. You can mark my words on this when I say the men, I am speaking of who gave their life for you will not hesitate to give it again if they had to. We combined our forces to become stronger not weaker. To understand the intent of humiliation only there is no humiliation if we are all humiliated together. This is what has been taught for to every soldier humiliation and how to handle being intentionally overlooked. We were taught how to crawl in the mud together, how to starve together, how to cry together and how to die together. This is the meaning of what being a soldier, an officer, a leader of men means when we put on our uniforms and say, what is the mission for today? Now the citizens of America are going to have to do the same. We have to look at the politicians in Washington along with the soldiers we will be there beside you. Look at the politicians and tell them we want better control of these chemical companies they are killing our children, our babies do not have a chance. Let them know we are their help now not forty years later like they did the Vietnam Veterans.

As I stated earlier this is not a finger pointing book. I am prayerful that it will not be perceived in that manner. I wanted to be articulate enough to put into words something that both the American citizens could understand as well as my Brothers the Vietnam Veterans who have paved the way for those who followed behind them in combat and future wars. This book was written to bring forth issues of change and to help the American people understand as well as bring honor to the Vietnam Veterans. An honor they more than anyone else deserve due to the way they have been disrespected for over forty years. Even the recent celebrations for the Vietnam Veterans given in 2019 was very low keyed a few Vietnam Veterans told me the celebrations were just weak. Open discussions need to take place where the Vietnam Veterans can speak. Whether there is an admission of fault by the chemical companies or not something still needs to be done to come up with some kind of future assistance planning for the grandchildren and great-grandchildren of the Vietnam Veterans, and that funding needs to come from the chemical companies and some from the United States government. The 180-million-dollar (settlement trust) by the eleven chemical companies involved with producing "Agent Orange" was considered to not be enough. And only caused the Vietnam Veterans to suffer even more humiliation through the years. That 180 million was used up in about 6 years. There was no mentioning of medical care, health treatment or life funding set up for future ailments that would come from Agent Orange. I am not overreaching in requesting this because future problem in their health is definitely going to happen. There was a very small monetary award that was awarded in 1988 and by 1994 the monies were already depleted. I am asking again where is the (Settlement Trust), if there ever was any setup for the Vietnam Veterans children etc.? We now have to look at "Agent Orange" which is being found in the DNA of the grandchildren. There was never anything mentioned about the genetic problems that would occur in the future with the grandchildren and great-grandchildren, where is the (Settlement Trust) today? As these grandchildren grow their bodies body will be under attack with the chemical herbicide TCDD in their DNA. We are looking at children who will have to endure the same suffering, pain and slow death the Vietnam Veterans did because the toxic chemical TCDD is now in their DNA. This also means the probability of it being transferred to their great-grandchildren is a strong possibility. This book is an open effort to help everyone understand the need to not be complacent any longer. To not point fingers at the eleven chemical companies because of the civil and criminal charges that could be brought forth. But to work together to come to an amicable agreement and a better solution to help the Vietnam Veterans and American citizens. I will explain the criminal aspect of this issue concerning "Agent Orange" a little later but for right now please keep reading. There is a need for the chemical companies to be more compassionate and forthcoming in their showing of financial support in respect to matters of contaminated DNA being transferred to innocent people in the future. We are talking about babies, unborn babies who "had no dog in the fight" innocent babies who do not deserve to suffer. For this reason and many more it should be evident to you the reader that more funding should be set up for researching "Agent Orange." More funding and research for the medical and health problems their grandchildren and great-grandchildren will someday have to face. We have listened to the chemical companies through the years state they knew nothing about the highly toxic chemical herbicide TCDD (dioxin) = "Agent Orange" being a human carcinogen, cancerous. Or a chemical they created had anything to do with the suffering or deaths of the Vietnam Veterans. Due to the facts of the case possibly going from civil to criminal which would then make them not only liable but punishable as well. Which would lead to time in prison for the death caused by the creation of such a chemical and knowingly releasing this to be used would also be putting the public or those who were in contact with the chemical in eminent danger. It is with a greater understanding of the law with all due respect to life and humanity that the chemical companies would continue to plead not guilty and contest any such knowledge or understanding of what TCDD can do. The legal standpoint says, (It is for the betterment of society) and the need of such companies to exist and remain within a functioning capacity for the good that they do. Then to be closed bankrupted and done away with then to be able to function in their actual purpose which is to assist mankind with similar products needed in the future. It's my understanding after doing some legal research and assistance with some legal understanding of a case in reference which would be the true story about Erin Brokovich. The companies did not confess to any wrong doings they settled out of court. Settlement is usually the remedy recommended if at all possible, in most cases. In a court of law there is what is called (Business that Affects Public Interest). Meaning because the chemical companies are what is called a necessary benefit to the public it is not going to be bankrupt by the courts out of existence. Due to lives that have been lost or the suffering caused by the chemicals some companies put in their products unknowingly caused them to suffer? This is what we are looking at when we look at the courts verses the value of a persons loved one who has passed away from using the wrong product. When we look at right and wrong fingers begin to point and there isn't any solace involved. Everyone is wrong when people are planning their loved one's funeral and rationality goes out of the window. When someone is preparing to go to surgery to see their loved one's arm, leg, or foot amputated due to cancer that was created inside of their body because of the chemicals some company used inside their product. The situation stands unquantified but legally justified when it comes to (Business that Affects Public Interest). Merely because it is a fact there will never be enough money that can be paid for a loved one to say, "thanks, although my child is dead you have paid me enough." That will never happen because the one thing money cannot buy back is life. And our time with our loved ones is more precious than any amount of money that can be given. As human beings we learn to value life, it is so precious. James 4:14 "**Whereas ye know not what shall be on the morrow. For what is your life? It is even a vapor, that appeareth for a little time, and then vanisheth away.**" What took place in Vietnam was horrifying even as I speak of it today. But everyone needs a sense of relief everyone need to have an understanding as to why the chemical companies are not going to be shut down as we look at it in a way of saying, for the betterment of humanity. It's just not going to happen. There will never admit to being wrong. If the chemical companies were to say, "Yes we created a chemical product that we knew was going to cause cancer in the Vietnam Veterans and we created it any way." They can be found liable for intentionally causing the deaths of so many Vietnam Veterans and also those who live in Vietnam. We would then also have to look at the number of Vietnamese who are still dying today because of "Agent Orange." They will also have to be compensated for the medical and health problems in Vietnam caused by "Agent Orange" a chemical that has contaminated their forest lands, lakes, rivers, streams, fish, crops and vegetation. This is not something a nation of civilized people can continue to overlook. To hold one another accountable for a war that changed the lives of so many families, both American and Vietnamese. The compensation involved is beyond my being able to set a monetary value on. I believe we can work with the chemical companies to bring change. Is it important for fault to be admitted in order to bring change the answer to that question is, NO! But support, assistance and rebuilding is part of change which is also a unified effort on everyone's part. The chemical companies can help, and this would be a way of doing so without the finger pointing. Everyone lost something during the Vietnam War.

There is still so much that's involved with the Vietnam War. Have you forgotten about the POW's or the MIA's? As American citizens we must look at the strong probability that there are American soldiers who are still alive, and their families would love to see them brought home. Avoidance of the truth means a longer term of captivity and torture for them they have suffered long enough. As I stated earlier in the book due to the toxic chemical "Agent Orange" nothing has grown in the areas it was sprayed in for the past fifty years. If you want to look at this statistically then here are the numbers, you can do the math and then review the entire book again. Just keep in mind an admission of guilt means the chemical companies will also be tried as being liable for the deaths that has taken place due to "Agent Orange." Who do you think in their right mind is going to confess to that, nobody? But working together and trying to come up with a better solution for the future generations would carry more weight towards a positive future for all. Soldier are still suffering from the aftereffects of "Agent Orange" and they need help now!

Although it is unfair it would seem to be even more relevant for the chemical companies involved to set up a continual settlement trust that maintains an account balance of billions of dollars where the people meaning the Vietnam Veterans, their children, grandchildren and now great-grandchildren can seek the medical assistance they need because of the continual funding from the companies set up for them will be there waiting. We need research programs to find out the life expectancy of "Agent Orange" and how it can be properly researched and not just tossed to the side because no one really wants to deal with it. We have to make an honest effort to connect with the Vietnamese government. We need to give assistance and funding where it is needed to help with the damages done to their children who are being born with deformities as well as trying to do something to rebuild their country. I AM ASKING THAT YOU PLEASE DO NOT POINT FINGERS AT THE CHEMICAL COMPANIES OR OUR GOVERNMENT. LET GOD BE THEIR JUDGE BUT WHILE THEY ARE HERE ON THIS EARTH LET THEM BE A PART AND JOIN TOGETHER IN CORRECTING THE WRONGS THAT HAVE BEEN DONE. **PEACE BE STILL.**

As we look for something positive to hold onto as a nation of people still trying to understand why this Vietnam War happened. What did we actually learn from this war that we could have done differently? We must also understand there are approximately 1700 American Vietnam Veterans still (MISSING IN ACTION). Our American soldiers would love to come home, and I believe they are still alive in the concentration camps of Vietnam. As a military officer and war veteran it is not hard to imagine what the enemy would do to not just torture the body of a captured soldier but to also torture the mind of the POW. But in order for this to change there is going to have to be major changes on part of Americans and on part of the Vietnamese. I did not say an admission of guilt but of understanding. The Vietnamese wants assistance from America for the 20,000,000 gallons of herbicides sprayed over 39,000 square miles of their country, 11,000,000 gallons were "Agent Orange." The United States citizens want the 1700 Vietnam Veterans who are still (Missing In Action) home. The Vietnam Veterans need assistance with the claims they have filed in relations to "Agent Orange" and claims that have not been paid. The grandchildren and great-grandchildren of the Vietnam Veterans need future medical and hospitalization programs setup for them. Our stats show the Vietnam Conflict Extract Data File of the Defense Casualty Analysis System (DCAS) Extract Files contains records of the United States military fatal causalities of the Vietnam War. These records were transferred to the custody of the National Archives and Records Administration in 2008, Jan 11, 2018

As of 1995, the United States military has estimated that between 200,000 and 250,000 South Vietnamese soldiers died in the war.

There in Vietnam

Dropped in a field so far away with only two weeks of training;
No MOS for a special field of study, straight from bootcamp to "Nam";
It was the hottest war zone American has ever
been we were being tagged and bagged;
The choppers were flying live soldiers in and dead soldiers out;
Life in Vietnam was worse than being underwater trying to breath.

The story was told, you really had to bold and
love America with all your soul;
Everyday all day and every night all night we
dance around in the pale moonlight;
Bushes were moving and clusters burst overhead to give us a little sight;
Charlie was cleaver and elusive and moved
better than the shadows at night.

Before the choppers hit the ground, we were locked and loaded;
Bullets were hitting everywhere there was no time to despair;
You see life in "Nam" was a short-lived visit
If you were not careful being there in it, our life
expectancy was only sixteen minutes;

I was eighteen at the time, given the basic
needs of life what it took to survive;
A machete and machine gun were laid by my
side and I could feel the cold steel
Unaware of the cost of my innocence, when I
pull the trigger with no hesitance.

I did three tours in Vietnam to fight the Viet
Cong, they came from out of nowhere
It was like a dream they came out of walls of
grass and holes tunneled in the ground;
Bullets were flying all over the place with missiles
and bombs blowing up all around;
No such thing as safety in "Nam" you were in it
the second you had "Boots on the Ground

The Viet Cong used wounded soldiers as a
hoax to scream and moan at night.
We could not go out because Charlie was good,
cutting off our heads to warn us;
In the morning this is how we found our dead
covered in fesses in a puddle of blood;
The woods were green and so were they,
blending in like a chameleon, I'd say;

They killed my brothers in some hideous ways,
stripped, gutted and heads on display;
We needed help and they sent it from the sky, it was
called "Agent Orange" now I know why;
The jungles after the sprayed were no longer green,
it became a cancerous, death scene;
As I saw Agent Orange fall from the sky, I had no idea I was going to die;
I returned home 250 solid pounds, now all I am is just skin and bones.

My Brothers in "Nam" did not deserve this
deal "Agent Orange," is oh so real;
The herbicide chemical, was truly no joke, it
ate us alive from the inside out;
It was twenty years later when they agreed
the Vietnam Veterans had PTSD;
But it was "Agent Orange that did us in not the Viet Cong we call Charlie;
The doctors said "Agent Orange" had spread
as they cut every inch of my body.

I remembered how it all begun, it was I who decided to go to Vietnam;
I was a young man, I said "I raised my own
right no one held my hand up."
I took the oath to defend my country with pride and dignity;
It would not have even made a difference if I had lost my life you see.

Some say the Vietnam War wasn't a win; so many lives were lost;
When I hear those conversation, I look at them and say;
If you don't mind me asking, where you in "Nam" back in the day;
58,220 lost their life for you to secure your future in so many ways.

Now let me stop speaking for a second so I could say it with pride;
Please, let me take a deep breath and wipe the tears from my eyes;
For my brothers who gave their life, I want to say it and be calm;
So, I smiled and said Yes! Yes! I was there, my brothers and I were,
"There in Vietnam"

Written by Author/Hall of Fame
Raymond C. Christian
Date: April 10, 2019
Reason: For all Vietnam Veterans know they are not FORGOTTEN

In Loving Memory of the Vietnam Veterans

Remember

"All Gave Some and Some Gave All."

What is so disgustingly true is that our country did not give enough
to the Vietnam Veterans. I commend and salute the Vietnam Veterans
and our men and women who put on the battle uniform daily. Thank
you for your service and for giving your life to a call for duty.

EPILOGUE

For the Vietnam Veterans who paved the way for the soldiers who trudged in behind them in later wars and military service. Just know the soldiers who came up behind you could not have survived without the letters and documentation you all were sending to Washington, DC in bringing up matters of change as it related to war. It was you who helped the Armed Forces of the United States Military to see what soldiers in the war zones needed. You have survived over forty years of being mocked. When the praise we received after coming home from Beirut, Dessert Storm, Iraq and Afghanistan, really belong to you, the true warriors, the Vietnam Veterans. You are the true brothers in war. You went back into the battlefields of "Nam" to pick up the wounded and dead, no soldier left behind. To this day you continue to fight for the 1700 soldiers that have not been found. Our Prisoners of War (POW's) who could still be alive in Vietnamese concentration camps. You taught us how to continue the fight until every soldier is accounted for, this is how we do it while in search for those who are still Missing in Action (MIA's). What you have done for the United States Armed Forces and your service to the United States of America will always be remembered and will never be forgotten.

I will fly my Vietnam Veterans Flag on Memorial Day, and Veterans Day in honor of the men who gave their life in defense of the United States of America. You came to the United States of America's defense by fighting in a brutal war. You showed your country fellow men and women the citizens of America that we stand with unity indivisible and we stand for justice for all. We will always protect the shores of this great nation from all foreign and domestic enemies. Although some of us are retired, for every man or woman who have put on the uniform at least once in their lifetime we know you will always be ready for battle.

You gave the only life you had down to your last drop of blood, until there was nothing left to give. People stopped listening and "Agent Orange" was slowly being swept under the rug. But there are consequences in life in making the choice of doing what is right. There is a scripture that says, Galatians 1:10 "For do I now persuade men, or God? Or do I seek to please men? For if I yet pleased men, I should not be the servant of Christ." This is how the United States of America should see our war hero's, the Vietnam Veterans. They did a service for the United States that not many were willing to do. They gave their families, their wives, their children. The joy of seeing their parents, their brothers and sisters, their friends most of all they gave something that can never be given back. They gave their LIFE.

Please keep in mind this is not a finger pointing book. Because you know and I know there is nothing that can be settled with putting the blame finger on someone. I am asking you all graciously with the love of God in my heart to put aside the blame difference and take care of the Vietnam Veterans the way they fought for you not just the defense of this great nation. They fought for your freedoms to not be tampered with and please note this. Every Vietnam Veteran I spoke with said without hesitation they would do it all over again. God Bless you all and God Bless America!!!

Printed in the United States
By Bookmasters